Foundations of
CANADIAN
Physical Education, Recreation, and Sports Studies

Foundations of
CANADIAN
Physical Education, Recreation, and Sports Studies

David Anderson
University of Winnipeg

Eric F. Broom
University of British Columbia

John C. Pooley
Dalhousie University

Edward C. Rhodes
University of British Columbia

D. Gordon E. Robertson
University of Ottawa

Barbara Schrodt
University of British Columbia

wcb
Wm. C. Brown Publishers
Dubuque, Iowa

Consulting Editor *Aileene Lockhart*

Cover design by Jeanne Regan

The credits section for this book begins on page 365, and is considered an extension of the copyright page.

Library of Congress Catalog Card Number: 88–071227

ISBN 0–697–00191–1

Printed in the United States of America by Wm. C. Brown Publishers 2460 Kerper Boulevard, Dubuque, IA 52001

10 9 8 7 6 5 4 3 2 1

Contents

Foreword   xi

Preface   xiii

**PART ONE: INTRODUCTION TO CANADIAN PHYSICAL
EDUCATION, RECREATION, AND SPORT STUDIES**   1

1 The Discipline and the Profession   3

   Historical Problems in PERS Studies   3
   A Definition: The Discipline and the Profession 5
   The Title Question   7
   One Model: Sport Studies   9
   Summary   11

**2 Basic Terminology in Physical Education, Recreation,
and Sport Studies**   13

   Leisure   14
   Play   20
   Recreation   24
   Physical Education   25
   Sport   26
   Athletics (Elite Sport)   29
   The Continuum Theory of Physical Activity   31
   Summary   34
   Suggested Readings   34

3 Careers   37

The Interdisciplinary Approach   37

Additional Studies   38

The Coaching Profession in Canada   42

Summary   44

Suggested Reading   44

PART TWO: PHILOSOPHICAL AND HISTORICAL FOUNDATIONS   45

4 Selected Philosophical Concepts of PERS Studies   47

Developing a Framework   48

Reasons for Philosophical Study in PERS   48

Methods of Philosophical Inquiry in PERS Studies   52

General Philosophical Concepts in PERS   56

Summary   62

5 Canada's Sport Heritage   65

An Overview   65

Outstanding Achievements by Canadians in Sport   66

The Nineteenth Century   66

The Early Twentieth Century to World War I   72

The Golden Age of Canadian Sport   75

Toward Another Golden Age: Post–World War II   80

Highlights in the History of Sport in Canada   84

6 The Canadian Amateur Sport and Recreation Delivery System   97

Defining the Sport and Recreation Delivery System   97

The Education Sport Delivery System   101

Universities   112

Community Colleges   114

The Amateur Sport Delivery System   115

The Recreation Delivery System   125

Private Agencies   128

Commercially Operated Recreation Centres   128

Employee Recreation Programs   128

Recreation Associations   129

Summary of the Recreation Delivery System   129

Summary   129

7 Government in Sport and Recreation   131

Early Government Involvement   131
Federal Government: Sport and Recreation
    since 1969   137
Provincial Governments: Sport and Recreation
    since 1969   153
Summary   157

**PART THREE: ANATOMICAL, PHYSIOLOGICAL, AND
BIOMECHANICAL FOUNDATIONS**   159

8 Human Anatomy   161

Anatomical Terminology   162
Movement Nomenclature for Applied Anatomy   166
Levers of the Musculoskeletal System   177

9 Physiological Basis for Exercise: The Motor Team   187

The Skeletal and Articular Systems   188
The Muscular System   195
Neural Involvement of the Motor Team   203

10 Support Systems to the Motor Team   209

The Respiratory System   209
The Cardiovascular System   215
Nutrition and Human Performance   219

11 Selected Principles of Biomechanics   235

The Mechanics of Rigid Bodies   235
Fundamental Concepts of Newtonian Mechanics   237
International System of Units   237
Linear Kinematics   240
Angular Kinematics   246
Kinetics   248

Excellent

PART FOUR: SOCIOCULTURAL AND PSYCHOLOGICAL FOUNDATIONS   265

12 Sociocultural Context and Values in Sport   267

Sociocultural Studies: Their Genesis and Development   269

Sociology of Sport   270

Sociocultural Studies in Canada   271

Definitions of Major Concepts   271

Goals and Methods   273

Social Theories   276

Sport Reflecting Societal Values   277

Applying Social Theories to Sport in Canada   280

Comparison with Other Societies and Cultures   282

Summary   284

13 Socialization Into, Via, and Out of Physical Activity and Sport   287

The Process of Socialization: Its Relation to Sport and Physical Activity   288

Socialization Into Physical Activity and Sport   290

Socialization Via Physical Activity and Sport   293

A Highly Competitive Model for Youth Sport   295

Alternatives to the Highly Competitive Model   296

Lessons to Be Learned from Those Continuing to Practice Sport   297

The Capacity of Sport to Mirror Positive or Negative Values in Society   299

Violence and Cheating   300

Socialization Out of Physical Activity and Sport   303

Summary   305

14 Psychological Concepts of Physical Activity and Sport: An Overview   311

Areas of Study   311

Growth and Development   313

Motor Learning and Development   314

Sport Psychology   319

Personality Development in Sport   324

Social-Psychological Concepts 326
Psychology of Leisure and Recreation 328
Summary 330

**PART FIVE: SOME CONTEMPORARY TRENDS WITHIN
PERS IN CANADA** 333

15 The Present and the Future 335

Physical Education Trends 335
Leisure Society and the Recreation Imperative 337
Legal Liability in PERS 338
Individual and National Fitness 340
Postsecondary Education in PERS Studies:
   Under Review 341
Women in Canadian Sport 343
The Environment: Its Uses 344

**Appendix A Outstanding Sports Achievements by
Canadians** 347

Canadian Medal Winners at the Olympic Games 347
Canadian Gold Medallists at the Commonwealth Games 352
Canadian Gold Medallists at the Pan American Games 357
Canadian Gold Medallists at the World University Games 360

Appendix B International System of Units (SI) 361

Credits 365

Index 367

FOREWORD

There are few human pursuits that excite the emotions or bring as much pleasure to the involved as does sport. The enormous demand by Canadians for access to opportunities for participation in a sport of their choosing continues to escalate across the country as, indeed, does the desire of millions to learn the necessary skills to meaningfully engage in such pursuits.

The allied domains of sport, physical education and recreation together comprise an important industry in every modern industrial and post-industrial society. The economic dimensions of this industry have long been overlooked and, because the overall dimensions of the industry are difficult to define, they are also poorly understood. Nonetheless, the economic impact of these domains is being increasingly recognized to be a significant factor in national economies. Apart from its significance for economic purposes, this is an industry that should also be recognized for its positive contributions to a society because it is focused almost exclusively on benefiting human lives. Further, political awareness among governments for the importance of promoting active lifestyles through participation in sport and exercise programs has also become an increasingly important platform for advancing national health goals. Hence, there is an obvious need for Universities to educate and train graduates to pursue a multiplicity of careers in this industry to serve the public interest.

The variety of career choices in sport science, physical education and recreation has created some problems within the physical education curriculum structure. Different university faculties of physical education have responded in a variety of ways to maximize their own potential for servicing the changing market place. Without a well ordered and rationalized knowledge structure, a plethora of titles, courses and programs have recently emerged across the nation, giving further the appearance of a field lacking in focus.

In an attempt to respond to this apparent diversification in programs of professional preparation, several of the Deans and Directors of Physical Education across Canada have, in recent years, debated the need for a common introductory knowledge core to the various subdisciplinary components subsuming the study of physical education as a discipline. For some of us, this has been an important issue. A widely accepted common core of knowledge, virtually standardized among the Universities or at least several of them, would be an important step toward gaining broader recognition for disciplinary status. Achieving agreement as to what such a common core might look like is, unfortunately, another matter.

The appearance of this volume is therefore very timely for it can serve as a first step in the direction of defining a basic core in subject matter. This book provides the first year physical education, recreation or sport studies student with both an introduction to study in the field along with some exposure to the overall complexity of the issues and problems facing it.

In only a few short years, perhaps twenty at the most, the knowledge base underlying the study of sport and exercise, along with the applied knowledge required for professional practice, has expanded at an unprecedented rate. Only twenty or so years ago, physical education professionals relied almost exclusively on borrowed knowledge from allied parent disciplines. Today, much of our knowledge, by contrast, is generated within the field. Physical education and sport science scholars seek not only to solve the unique problems associated with the phenomena of physical activity but also to better understand these phenomena as distinct entities in society. Gradually, also, the sub-fields that exist under the umbrella of physical education and physical activity are developing specific vocabularies appropriate to their knowledge domains, and the day is not far off when the field as a whole will stand on its own feet without having to coin terms, titles and descriptors borrowed from other disciplines.

While not all will agree on the approach taken by Dave Anderson in presenting an introductory knowledge core for the field, he and his contributors have nonetheless made an important contribution toward consolidating an introductory core of knowledge basic to physical education and sport. Having taken the initiative, the authors of the chapters in this volume may well have focused future discussion on what the appropriate core of knowledge might more ideally be.

W. Robert Morford
University of British Columbia

PREFACE

This text presents a selected overview of the discipline and its professions which are a part of physical education, recreation, physical activity, and sport in Canada. It is developed so that prospective students might acquire an understanding of the vast dimensions of the various fields of knowledge which are the foundations of study and research in the area.

Although there still exists a lack of scholarly agreement as to what this discipline's descriptive title should be (e.g., kinesiology, human kinetics and leisure, physical education and recreation, etc.), what created and unites it was and is the need and desire of man to better understand the art and science of the why and how of human movement and physical performance. The body of knowledge, procedures, and processes of dissemination stem from many of the more established disciplines such as history, philosophy, psychology, sociology, biological sciences, and physics. This interdisciplinary approach, explained in the text, is also applicable to the descriptions of the careers and professions which are the product of the study of the discipline. The structure of the text follows these diverse sources of knowledge and ultimately applies them to physical activity—the core of physical education, recreation, and sport. A further stated purpose of the authors is to present original content pertaining to a Canadian thrust in the study of physical activity.

The reader will find that segments of the text such as the biological, psychological, philosophical, and definitional areas are for the most part universal in content, presentation, and scope. However, even these areas are based, where appropriate, upon Canadian research data and cultural identity. In fulfillment of the aim of the authors to present a point of view based upon Canadian cultural adaptations and developments in physical education, recreation, and sport, this publication becomes a much-needed introductory text for professional preparation. Due to the need to be selective in a text of this nature, omissions inevitably occur. Instructors should supplement this work with selected readings, information, theories, or concepts which would be personally, locally, or regionally appropriate. In addition, it may be necessary for an instructor to use only selected sections of the book because of course length, course description, or institutional curriculum needs, thus utilizing the text as a basis for a series of courses within a program of professional development. This use of the text is especially evident in Part III (the bioscience chapters) which can be significantly modified by the deletion or expansion of many of the mathematical formulas expressing the theories of physics relative to the mechanics of motion.

A brief explanation should be given with regard to some of the choices in content and emphasis that have been made by the authors. First, in the introductory unit (Part I) one will find that such concepts as leisure and play receive a more thorough examination of source, meaning, and application of the term than do, for example, recreation and sport. The concepts of leisure and play are broad terms in both nature and application and they are the antecedents to the understanding of the more exact concepts of recreation, sports, and/or athletics. Therefore, it was determined that they required a more extensive description.

Second, in Part II, *Philosophical and Historical Foundations,* two points should be realized. (1) The chapter dealing with sports heritage does not identify recent internationally recognized athletes (e.g., Wayne Gretzky and Ben Johnson). As indicated by the authors, one of the criteria used in determining who should be recognized in the chapter was that their performance careers in sport would be, for the most part, finished. (2) Within this same unit, in the chapter on philosophical concepts, there is a section on method of inquiry of philosophical ideas in physical activity and sport. This section is meant to introduce students to some of the ways by which they will proceed in further study of this area. Hence, it may not be appropriate to all introductory courses in undergraduate curricula.

Additionally, upon a closer examination of the chapter structure one will be aware of the significant Canadian content and presentation within some of these: *Canada's Sport Heritage; The Canadian Amateur Sport and Recreation Delivery System; Government in Sport and Recreation; Sociocultural Context and Values in Sport; Socialization Into, Via, and Out of Physical Activity and Sport;* and the contemporary issues chapter—*The Present and the Future.* The attention of the reader should also be directed to two other factors which may not be considered as dramatic as those mentioned above but which are, nevertheless, noteworthy. First is the *concepts by principles* approach to the understanding of the beginning principles of biomechanics and exercise physiology in Part III, which has been used most successfully in the publications of the National Coaching Certification Program in Canada. Second, the commitment to metric scales throughout Part III, while not original, is a relatively new practice in North America.

Finally, those using the text should be aware of the two basic methods used by the authors in presenting the material. Some chapters use the technique of *sampling* by developing selected study areas within a foundation topic (for example, Part IV, chapters 12 and 13 on sociological concepts in physical activity and sport) while other chapters present an *overview* of the foundation subject (for example, Part IV, chapter 14 on psychological concepts).

Although much of the content and approach identify the book as a Canadian text, its contribution to the discipline is not limited to national confines. On the contrary, as one of the first in its field, it should be a useful addition for many instructors, students, and researchers who work in the area of comparative studies in physical education, recreation, leisure, and sport. It is the opinion of the authors that *The Foundations of Canadian Physical Education, Recreation, and Sport Studies* will demonstrate both unique and typical aspects of physical activity in other societies as well as our own.

A special note of appreciation is extended to Professors Arnold Lowenberger (Brock University), Glynn Leyshon (University of Western Ontario) and Ross Macnab (University of Alberta) for their very helpful reviews of the manuscript.

PART ONE

Introduction to Canadian Physical Education, Recreation, and Sport Studies

CHAPTER 1

The Discipline and the Profession

David Anderson

For decades it has been a common practice for authors in introductory texts such as this to attempt to identify and clarify for prospective students of an academic and professional discipline precisely what the discipline is, exactly what it offers for study, and how it differs from other disciplinary subject areas and their related professions.

HISTORICAL PROBLEMS IN PERS STUDIES

In the case of physical education, recreation, and sport (PERS) studies, this is no easy matter. To begin with, the discipline referred to in this text as PERS has yet to gain a universal academic identification or title such as those its sister disciplines are known by (e.g., biology, sociology, psychology, philosophy, history). Further, we are confronted with the fact that most students entering a postsecondary institution for advanced study in PERS have participated in programs of physical education, recreation, or sports but have studied little of the meaning, purpose, or content of the subject area in a formal way, as they would have done in their school curricula in the traditional disciplines. They have *participated* in the subject area, not *studied* it.

Our difficulty is reflected in the compound nature of the title of this text which for many, and rightly so, would not be considered all-inclusive in its description of the discipline. However, some semblance of reason must prevail with regard to length of a textbook title. Additional discussion concerning the question of title of the academic discipline will occur later in this

chapter. At this point let us simply realize that problems of definition and title have always beset developing disciplines such as ours.

Another difficulty one faces when asking the above questions of the what, why, and how of this area of study is the significant complexity and the variety of knowledge which comprise PERS studies in either a pure disciplinary approach or in its corresponding professions. However, this complexity can perhaps best be understood by realizing that much of what one must learn and know involves the same knowledge and skills as those demanded by humanities and the social sciences. This is often referred to as the **art of PERS.** In this context, the authors are not merely indicating the classical art forms of sculpture, painting, dance, or rhythmics as they pertain to human movement, but to a broader meaning of art as exemplified by those areas of knowledge and skill which are an integral part of the humanities and social sciences and which may be applied to physical activity. Some examples are the many sociological theories and concepts that are a part of PERS studies; the unique skills needed in its methods of instruction and communication; the understanding of the characteristics of human behaviour, personality, and intellectual development; the learning and growth of physical skills; the development of philosophical precepts and historical framework; and a host of other cognitive and psychomotor knowledge.

On the other hand, the **science of PERS** is no less formidable in its scope and content than the continuing explosion of man's knowledge and understanding in the biology, physiology, and mechanics of the human body in movement and stress which is the foundation of much of our study of man and physical activity. Therefore, one must recognize that to be a good teacher, coach, scientist, recreationalist, fitness instructor, therapist, or any other kind of practitioner in the many and varied professions related to PERS, there is a blending of the art and science of PERS which must take place—both qualitatively and quantitatively. In other words, if a student in PERS chooses to be a recreationalist, then the content of his professional preparation will be significantly different than if he chooses to be a secondary school physical education teacher or a sport scientist. Students entering the field of PERS should be concerned with an emphasis in study which will satisfy their personal needs and professional aspirations. Counselling in curriculum development is necessary as students become aware of the variety and complexity of choice and direction that confront them.

Finally, there exists a constantly changing body of knowledge within the subject area of PERS. It is therefore hoped by the authors that this chapter and chapter 3 on careers will assist in the process of decision making as the student tackles the problem of personal choice and direction within PERS. These choices will become clearer as the student becomes more familiar with what the discipline and its many subject fields and related professions achieve, and why and how one reaches those levels of achievement.

A DEFINITION: THE DISCIPLINE AND THE PROFESSION

The discipline of PERS cannot be considered as a traditional one such as mathematics, philosophy, English, biology, or history, but is of the family of new **compound disciplines** whose examples would include sociology, psychology, ecnomomics, and political science. This latter group of disciplines has been developed from the specific knowledges of other disciplines (traditional or compound) and, when combined and directed to a new and original focus or purpose, forms a specific area of study which is unique and different from its initial parts. It establishes its own identity. Such is the discipline of PERS, which selects knowledge and skills from biological sciences, psychology, sociology, history, physics, philosophy, and others and then focuses the information upon human movement, physical activity, recreation, and sport.

As implied earlier in the chapter, one of the difficulties which has historically hindered identification of the discipline (and which also occurs in other recently developed bodies of knowledge) is that the professions related to PERS were recognized and functioning as a part of our cultural institutions before the development and perception of the discipline. As an example, the *profession* of physical education was established within the educational system by the early part of the twentieth century, yet the development and recognition of the *discipline* only began to focus some fifty years later. Franklin Henry (1964) argued for a "scholarly field of knowledge basic to physical education" and this served as the banner by which many prominent scholars of physical education set about identifying the knowledge unique to human movement:

> [It is] an organized body of knowledge collectively embraced in a formal course of learning. The acquisition of such knowledge is assumed to be an adequate and worthy objective as such, without any demonstration or requirement of practical application. The content is theoretical and scholarly as distinguished from technical and professional.[1]

A discipline and a profession have different goals. Richard Rivens states in his *Foundations of Physical Education:*

> A discipline describes, explains and predicts phenomena related to a subject matter; it develops a body of knowledge. A profession, on the other hand, tries to improve the conditions of society through some kind of a service. A discipline seeks to understand a subject matter; a profession to implement change.[2]

Robert N. Singer submits that an academic discipline has a focus, structure, a body of knowledge, and distinctive modes of inquiry. Engineering is a profession based upon the disciplines of physics and chemistry; medicine is a profession based upon the biological sciences; and physical education is one of the professions based on a yet universally unnamed discipline which the authors are currently calling physical education, recreation, and sport (PERS) studies. Likewise such descriptive terms as sport scientist, coach, athletic therapist, recreationalist, and many others are labels for professions related to and stemming from PERS. It should, therefore, be easily perceived that the term physical education cannot serve as both the title of the discipline and as a branch of the education profession concerned with physical activity. Figure 1.1 may help to relate the concepts expressed to this point.

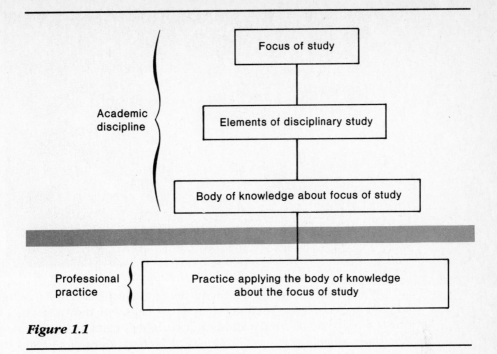

Figure 1.1

As Singer indicates, when people are involved above the heavy line in figure 1.1 they ask the question, What is it? Curiosity is a prime concern. As one functions below the heavy line, one asks the question, What does it do? Thus all professions are intimately linked and developed from academic disciplines.

We move now to the next problem in definition that confronts observers and beginning students in the field of PERS: What is, or should be, the title of this unique academic discipline?

THE TITLE QUESTION

There are those scholars and professionals who say that, until something better comes along, "physical education" will suffice as a title. Others move to the next step of clarification by at least compounding the title, as have the authors of this text, to include a number of descriptive subdivisions of the discipline. This is still the practice of the national service organization, the Canadian Association for Health, Physical Education, and Recreation (CAHPER). This association title sits uneasily with the pure and applied sports scholars, practitioners, and scientists whose knowledge and skills in their specific areas have exploded both in quality and in quantity in the last few decades through aggressive pure and applied research. This rapid advance has been aided by the vast public recognition of the importance of their work to Canadian society. Prominent academics such as Gerald Kenyon, Harold J. Vanderzwaag, John W. Loy, Jr., Clark Whited, T. J. Sheehan, Earle Zeigler, and many others maintain that the descriptive title should be "sport science" or "sport studies."

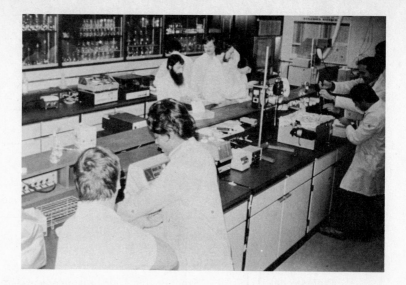

Without entering into the derivation or the justification of the following additional examples, a student entering the field will find these disciplinary titles or department identifications: human kinetics and leisure (University of Waterloo), kinanthropology (University of Ottawa), kinesiology (Simon Fraser University), recreation and athletic studies (University of Winnipeg), physical education and sport studies, as well as recreation and leisure studies (University of Alberta), and others. It is maintained by the authors that there should be a concerted effort within the next decade to find a resolution to this problem of title, and national and international symposia and conferences should be formulated and directed toward this goal. Some points seem relatively clear from the deliberations of the last several decades. (1) The term physical education is no longer applicable because of its limited connotation to school curricula and the teaching profession. (2) The future universal title may have to exclude (or at least limit) its concern for some selective areas of study now included such as the more passive elements of leisure. However, such limitation would certainly not exclude the main content and purpose of recreation studies and in particular those areas of study within "physical recreation." Passive activities may seem more appropriate in a purely sociopsychological context, not a physical one. It has been suggested that a new focus of study ("leisure studies") should be, and is being, formulated independent of the study of human movement. Perhaps this is a more logical and scholarly development. (3) The Canadian disciplinary and professional preparation structure will likely demonstrate a difference from that of other more universal models of study. This is due to the uniqueness of having an indigenous **mixed or integrated sport and recreation delivery system** which now seems historically and culturally a permanent reality. It should be realized that although all cultures have had to blend to some degree the educational and club delivery systems both at the public and private levels, the Canadian solution has been a much more complex and differential blending of these systems.

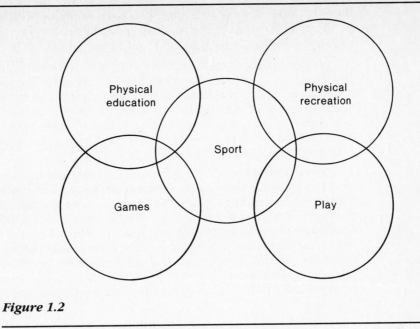

Figure 1.2

ONE MODEL: SPORT STUDIES

To conclude this chapter the authors wish to present one construct with which they feel comfortable—that is, the formal **study of sport** as the basis and focus for an undergraduate disciplinary/professional-oriented program of studies. It can be entitled sport science or sport studies; the general relationships of physical activities can be seen in figure 1.2. Much of the organization and analysis of this model of sport studies is an adapted or abbreviated version of that presented by Robert N. Singer in his text *Physical Education: Foundations.* The authors are most indebted to him for his concise description which would be difficult to improve upon for undergraduate students in PERS.

Further discussion as to the significance of the model may best be left to the following selective statements by physical activity and sport studies scholars who have so clearly presented the rationale for the position of sport studies to supplant traditional physical education postsecondary programs. First is the following statement from Gerald S. Kenyon.

> Regardless of the nomenclature that meets the greatest favor, there is no logical reason why the study of all the various manifestations of sport, exercise, and dance cannot be put under a single umbrella, one that could include the traditional approaches, whether they be scientific or humanistic. It is conceivable that certain subfields would emerge, based primarily on different approaches to truth, and perhaps to some extent, on interest in particular forms of physical activity. Thus, one major classification may be the *sport sciences,* which in turn could be subdivided into the physical science of sport, the biological science of sport, and the social science of sport.[3]

The Discipline and the Profession

9

Harold J. Vanderzwaag and John W. Loy, Jr., continue with similar reasoning by putting forward the concept that sport studies and exercise science are the focus of physical education and human movement study.

> . . . physical education should not and will not be replaced by the concept of human movement. There has been a tendency to contrast the profession of physical education with the discipline of human movement. The net result is a comparison of one abstract entity with another. Both have risen from the search for appropriate umbrellas. In this search, concrete components have been overlooked. These components are *sport and exercise* [emphasis added].[4]

> . . . several leading physical educators have suggested that human movement provides a particular focus of attention for physical education; and they have indicated that the study of human movement using different modes of inquiry can result in the establishment of a unique body of knowledge. One may legitimately ask, however, whether human movement is the only viable focal point for a discipline-oriented physical educator. We contend that sport provides an equally viable focal point and strongly suggest that the study of sport is more likely to result in a body of knowledge related to physical education than is the study of human movement.[5]

Figure 1.3 vividly illustrates the disciplinary/professional-oriented model of sport studies. One can perceive the interdependence of this model on the historical concept of human movement and physical education by identifying the characteristics of a discipline-profession form with those of sport studies. This categorization is as follows:

> For example, the functional elements of sport consist of rules, boundaries, and tasks indigenous to all existing forms. Further, i) sport has a history; ii) groups interact in sport (sociology of sport); iii) individuals are motivated to enter and leave sport and something happens to them as they engage in this activity (psychology of sport); iv) in order to participate actively, people must possess a certain degree of motor skills (sport skill acquisition and/or motor learning, sport biomechanics); v) individuals are affected organically (sport physiology); and vi) sport has meaning (sport philosophy). Investigating these characteristics will yield a body of knowledge that, in turn, will make possible questions of interrelationships . . . questions the sport scientist asks as an academic disciplinarian are limited to how, when, where and with whom sport functions. Whether sport is beneficial or nonbeneficial to a particular group, or whether it should be an environment for personal involvement are questions related to the function of the professional.[6]

The purpose of this section was to present one view or construct of a disciplinary-professional undergraduate or graduate precept for study and research. It is by no means the only model, but it is one which clearly depicts the parameters of examination without losing the necessary association with human movement and/or physical activity. It must also be understood that a clear but broad definition of sport would be a precondition to the sport studies model. This definition would include those activities often developed and included within physical and outdoor recreation.

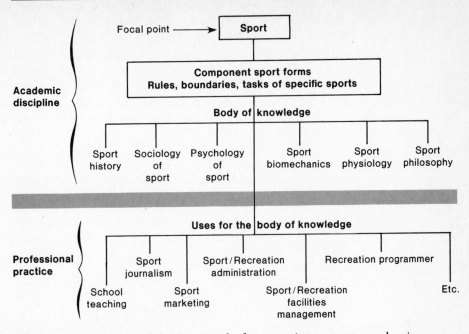

Figure 1.3 Structure of the potential of sport science as an academic discipline and as a profession

SUMMARY

In this initial chapter the authors clarify and define that body of knowledge which is the essence of the study of the discipline referred to in this text by the compound terminology of physical education, recreation, and sport (PERS) studies. Part of the chapter is spent on the descriptive title question which has plagued all emerging disciplines including PERS studies. As a possible choice, one model of many is presented to the student concerning the content and title of the discipline: sport studies and/or science. The relationship of the discipline to its professions is examined as well as how this relationship has historically caused problems of identification and growth of what it is we should know, what it is we should do, how we should do it, and in what sequence undergraduates in the field of PERS studies should follow their curricula.

NOTES

1. Franklin M. Henry, "Physical Education: An Academic Discipline," *Journal of Physical Education and Recreation* (September 1964): 32.

2. Richard S. Rivens, *Foundations of Physical Education* (Boston: Houghton Mifflin Co., 1978), 8.

3. Gerald S. Kenyon, "A Sociology of Sport: On Becoming a Sub-Discipline," in *New Perspectives of Man in Action,* ed. R. C. Brown and B. J. Crathy (Englewood Cliffs, NJ: Prentice-Hall, 1969), 165.

4. Harold J. Vanderzwaag, "Historical Relationships Between Concepts of Sport and Physical Education," in *Proceedings of the National College Physical Education Association for Men* (Minneapolis: The Association, December 1969), 88.

5. John W. Loy, Jr., "Sport Science: The Academic Dimension of Physical Education," in *Physical Education: An Interdisciplinary Approach,* R. N. Singer et al. (New York: The Macmillan Co., 1972), 173.

6. Robert N. Singer et al., *Physical Education: Foundations* (New York: Holt, Rinehart and Winston, 1976), 37–38.

CHAPTER 2

Basic Terminology in Physical Education, Recreation, and Sport Studies

David Anderson

One of the necessary tools for individuals who wish to comprehend the scope of physical education, recreation, and sport (PERS) studies and its varied programming possibilities, either in whole or in part, is a full understanding of the evolving terminology and concepts of the discipline as well as the interrelationship of one to the other. It is therefore hoped that this clarification will assist a student to a greater insight into his or her chosen area of study and its professions. The terms and concepts described or defined are leisure, play, recreation, physical education, sport, and athletics (elite sport).

Too often many of these terms and/or concepts have been used in an interchangeable or a synonymous fashion which has led to considerable confusion and misunderstanding by beginning practitioners and concerned observers alike. It must be realized that interrelatedness does not necessarily mean "the same as."

Scholarly works of the past within PERS studies, as well as within such sister disciplines as philosophy, sociology, psychology, and anthropology, have helped to clarify the meanings of these frequently used terms and concepts.

Further, theoretical understanding of nomenclature by a practitioner must precede practical application of the ideas contained within each term. The interrelatedness of these terms is equally significant to the leisurist, recreationalist, physical educator, or instructor/coach, as comprehension will give direction in career choices, program planning, development and content, and possible methods of instruction. Finally, with the assistance of the extensive past and present research of others, the concept of an activity continuum theory will be developed which may serve to clarify the previously mentioned interrelatedness of terms as they apply to the vast spectrum of physical activity.

LEISURE

Leisure can be considered one of the more abstract terms that will be discussed in this text. When it is placed within the context of universal usage and understanding, there exist several meaningful descriptions of what leisure is or can be. Yet to an individual who is deeply involved in leisure pursuits its meaning could be, to that person, very specific and concrete in nature. This indicates the individualism of interpretation and of application that the term leisure has. Simply, **leisure** can mean different or the same things to different people and is based upon the individual's own perception of the usage of the term regarding an activity or situation. In addition, the word leisure by derivation (from the Latin *licere*) means "to be permitted" or "to be free," therefore implying a second basic concept—the pursuit of leisure activities is of **free choice** with the absence of compulsion. Implicit in the idea of individual free choice is the premise that sufficient spare time is available to a person after he has completed all that must be done for sustenance and survival.

From a conceptual point of view one may categorize leisure in at least three basic contexts: "time, activities, or a state of mind."[1] One could add two additional categories: (1) leisure as a symbol of the social class, which stems from the work of Thorstein Veblen, a leading American sociologist and (2) leisure as viewed holistically. Veblen traced through history how the ruling class identified itself with the possession and use of leisure. Also, leisure can be perceived in a holistic sense, which involves the incorporation of the first three previous orientations of leisure as time, as an activity, or as a state of being.

Leisure Defined as Time

The most common approach to leisure is to regard it as unobligated or discretionary time. It is contended by Brighthill and others that leisure in its relationship to time "is a block of unoccupied time, spare time or free time when we are free to rest or do what we choose."[2] To express this leisure/time association in yet another way, it might be said that leisure "is the time surplus remaining after the practical necessities of life have been attended to."[3] In developing this relationship of time to leisure, one must consider separating time into segments: **existence**—the biological things we must do to stay alive (eating, personal health care, sleeping, etc.); **subsistence**—the things we must do to make a living (work) or prepare to make a living (school); and **discretionary** or **unobligated** time—the time which one uses as he or she pleases. It is obvious that for the most part, leisure pursuits will occur during this last segment of time.

However, it would not be difficult to realize that there are many vague areas within the relationship of these segments of time, for in our society it is particularly difficult to determine the exact parameters of what is true free time and what is not. For example, is all our eating or sleeping needed for existence? Do not some people freely and voluntarily choose to do certain things for which they are remunerated in some way? Is the time taken for this subsistence or discretionary? Can not discretionary time be forced upon us, such as the time of illness, of dismissal from work, and of forced retirement? Furthermore, we may feel compelled to do things during unobligated time such as to attend church, participate in social events, or lose weight through exercise. Does this not put compulsion upon this time, a compulsion which by definition should not be there? These situations and others are not normally considered true leisure time, and they tend to complicate the categorizing of time into definite segments; in fact, they may be referred to as situations which demand *enforced leisure time.*

It is also quite possible for both subsistence and existence time to be enjoyable, creative, productive, and worthwhile, therefore complicating the notion that these qualities or others are the values and ideals reserved solely for discretionary leisure time. In this complex society each segment of the leisure/time relationship should be flexible within individual circumstance. Generally, the thesis holds that leisure pursuits and activities occur during unobligated time and this relationship is consistent.

Basic Terminology in Physical Education, Recreation, and Sport Studies   15

Leisure Defined as Activity

There is, at times, in common practice a tendency to describe leisure in terms of the kinds of activity in which one participates. An exercise frequently assigned in graduate studies in leisure and recreation is the creation of a taxonomy of leisure activities for a particular cultural or social grouping. "When leisure is defined as activities or occupations, it quickly becomes apparent that, while no activity can always be said to serve as leisure for the participant, many activities are typically undertaken in the role of (name of) leisure."[4] Games of a passive nature or those of limited structure, organization, or quality of physical skill are often cited as leisure activities. Characterizing leisure activity in this manner is for the most part an inaccurate procedure and the exceptions are as numerous as the number of games and sports in any culture. Any given sport, or a variation of it, could be pursued as a leisure activity. However, there is a persistent generalization that leisure activities are normally less physical and structured than a similar activity in a physical recreation setting or than a like sport.

Another way of substantiating the public perception that leisure is activity is to ask the question: What do you do in your leisure time, or more precisely, what are your leisure activities? There will always be an answer and invariably it will be an activity. Therefore, one cannot deny that at the level of public consciousness there is a strong linkage between an activity, whether it be a passive or active pursuit, and the concept of leisure. Furthermore, statistical data is frequently presented to the public as a comparison between leisure or recreation activities and the number of participants involved or the amount of monies or time spent. For example, Statistics Canada reports that in 1960 approximately 1.5 billion dollars was spent by Canadians in their pursuit of recreational leisure, cultural activities, and personal growth. By 1977, the total amount had increased to approximately 13 billion dollars. These figures, when compared to other spending indices within the family, indicate that the above category grew at a faster rate than did any other indices over the same period of time.[5]

A similar type of sample would be obtained by viewing the participation growth rates among amateur sports bodies in Canada or within its provinces. This can be illustrated by the participation numbers from Manitoba. In 1975–76, approximately 170,000 persons were registered members of some fifty-two amateur sports associations within the province. By 1985–86, this number had increased to approximately 191,000 persons in seventy-five amateur sports associations—an increase of some 11.8 percent.[6] These figures show not only increased involvement by the citizens of Manitoba but also that the variety of activities to choose from expanded. Similar growth statistics are evident in all provinces of the nation.

The vast majority of these monies and participants listed above are involved on the basis of the individual's choice in search of a leisure or recreation activity. A frequently cited leisure theorist, Joffre Dumazedier, supports the concept that leisure is activity in which people engage during their free time. He defines leisure in these terms:

> Leisure is activity—apart from the obligation of work, family and society—to which the individual turns at will, for either relaxation diversion, or broadening his knowledge and his spontaneous social participation, the free exercise of his creative capacity.[7]

It is not difficult to realize that if theorists can describe leisure as an activity, then the public will do likewise, even though this association is tenuous at best.

Leisure as a State of Mind or State of Existence

Historically, the concept of leisure as a state of mind or a state of existence (being) receives its foundation in Greek philosophy. Although certain premises of Athenian leisure may have little application to contemporary western civilization (e.g., that leisure was the prerogative of the upper class, or that work, when prioritized in the light of man's needs and attainments, was basically a "monotonous, boring and ignoble necessity"[8]), other philosophical concepts or views of leisure of this period have transcended time and are as applicable to individuals in the twentieth century as they were in Aristotle's time.

One such concept was the consideration of leisure as a state of existence (being) in which activity is performed for its own sake and which occupies a period of time in which an individual can experience significant positive spiritual or emotional feeling. In addition, it is a period of time when one can experience intellectual, cultural, or artistic growth and creativity, and a time when different and experiential learning can take place. Presently, many people in the mechanistic and technological twentieth century can readily identify with leisure as a state of mind or existence. What outdoor sportsman, outdoor recreationalist, or naturalist has not had the experience and exhilaration of "oneness" with nature and come back for more? The golfer who plays on a lazy day in the colours of autumn or for that matter a lazy day in any season; the climber who has reached the top of his hill or mountain to view the world below; the skier in the early morning powder; the sailor in his boat in a brisk breeze—the enjoyment of all these leisure experiences conveys the thought to the individual: "At this moment this is the only place for me to be, this moment is not easily duplicated, this moment is mine. There is a feeling of wholeness, a oneness with the experience that borders on a spiritual occurrence."

Many readers who respond to the activities described above may easily identify with the phrase that leisure can be a "state of existence"—without denying that it is also a "state of mind"—for the sole reason that feelings and emotions are as much a part of this kind of leisure experience as is the intellect in the planning and seeking of it.

De Grazia indicates that free time is not necessarily leisure. Most individuals have free time, but few have leisure experiences. Leisure is "an ideal, a state of being, a condition of man, which few desire and fewer achieve."[9] Hopefully in future time, the "few" can become "many."

Leisure as a Symbol of Social Class

As previously mentioned in this chapter, leisure can be associated with a social class. In his major work, *The Theory of the Leisure Class,* Thorstein Veblen demonstrates that during the feudal and Renaissance periods and finally during the industrial age, leisure was a consistent social element of the upper class or, as he described them, the "idle rich." He saw leisure as a way of life for the privileged class who lived on the toil of others. However, to place this concept of leisure as a symbol of a social class in the perspective of contemporary times, note the following brief analysis by Richard Kraus:

> . . . chiefly through Veblen's influence, the concept of the leisure class came into being. His analysis is not as applicable to contemporary life as it was to the time it was written (19th century), since the working classes today tend to have far *more* free time than industrial managers, business executives and professionals. Veblen's contempt for leisure as belonging only to the "idle rich" no longer applies with full force, both because of this greater working class leisure and because of the involvement of the present generation of our most wealthy families in finance, public life, etc. Thus with the exception of a small group of "jet setters" the class he criticized no longer exists.[10]

It is relatively true that this unproductive leisure so vividly described by Veblen has given way to the democratization of leisure. Nevertheless, there is a lingering belief that leisure cannot only be unproductive but that it springs from the privileged class and is normally used in ways that have little value to society. Some leisure theorists maintain that because of technological advancement, the redistribution of work time, extensive retirement plans, and other socioeconomic adjustments, some western cultures are now entering the first stages of the **leisure society**—a society in which leisure time is the largest single block of time to be managed by individuals. Historically, attempts to manage a leisure society, even one for a selected ruling class such as in the Roman or Greek cultural examples, have failed abysmally (note chapter 15 for further discussion on this theory). Hence, the ability to use leisure time intelligently, as Bertrand Russell observed, is the final test of a civilization.[11] Since it is also contended that democratization of leisure is continuously growing, it now becomes imperative for all people to learn how to manage their leisure time meaningfully and constructively as well as with pleasure.

Holistic Concept of Leisure

As the term implies, the **holistic** view of leisure (i.e., leisure as time, as activity, and as a state of existence) involves the incorporation of the previous orientations. As Kaplan suggests, whether leisure is to be considered as an end in itself (a state of existence), as a means to an end (leisure as time apart from obligatory work), or as a list of recreational activities seems of limited significance as they all may be fused together in a holistic concept of leisure where leisure must be considered the central element in a culture.[12]

Murphy, another theorist, indicates that leisure

. . . as a construct (comprises) a full range of possible forms of self-expression which may occur during work or leisure . . . this perspective eliminates the dichotomy drawn between work and leisure, which has been a formidable barrier in the path to enjoyment of leisure opportunities for many people. According to the holistic concept . . . the meanings of work and leisure are inextricably related to each other.[13]

Leisure Defined

It is somewhat presumptuous to think one definition could incorporate the various views of leisure that have been expressed without sacrificing some elements of one of them. However, some commonality is present in all. The strongest of these commonalities is that there is individual freedom of choice of what one would wish to do in his leisure time. Godbey has provided a useful definition and explanation of leisure in his book *Leisure in Your Life* and it seems most appropriate to present the term within certain social conditions as he does. However, a more traditional and long-accepted definition of the concept of leisure is that which is expressed by the eminent recreationalist and leisurist Richard Kraus:

> *Leisure* is that portion of an individual's time which is not devoted to work or work-connected responsibilities or to other forms of maintenance activity and which therefore may be regarded as discretionary or unobligated time. Leisure implies freedom of choice, and must be seen as available to all, whether they work or not. Leisure is customarily used in a variety of ways, either to meet one's personal needs for self-enrichment, relaxation, or pleasure or to contribute to society's well-being.[14]

PLAY

The concept of **play** is now generally recognized as a cornerstone of human development and well-being. As man attains more knowledge through the scholarly activities of a variety of disciplinary studies and research into human social and psychological behaviour, we begin to realize that the quality and quantity of childhood play experience has a continued and lasting effect upon the nature of the adult person. This is not to deny that play can be a most sought after experience or even a need in adulthood. As Vanderzwaag has indicated, this is especially true when the play of adulthood is contrasted with work, although not too sharply, but more as opposite sides of a continuum:

play ⟵————————————————⟶ work

In this way, through ". . . the understanding that the vast majority of situations lie somewhere between [play and work] . . . allowances are made for individual differences among people and situations."[15] As will be discovered later in this chapter, there are numerous theories as to why people play. Some of these relate most directly to adult play and include the following: (1) the **relaxation theory** which states that play relieves the stresses and strains of the individual, providing release from work, compulsion, and struggle to live; (2) the **compensation theory** which states that play is used by individuals to satisfy psychic needs not satisfied by their work; (3) the **recreation theory** which indicates that play, rather than serving to "burn up" excess energy, provides for conserving or restoring it, thus recharging one's energy for renewed work; and (4) the **balance theory** which suggests that recreational play experiences tend to satisfy a need in individuals who are engaged in intellectual work by providing the physical activity necessary for a balanced existence. In these four theories and others there is little relationship between the meaning of play assumed and child's play; however, they do demonstrate that "to play" may not be the sole prerogative of children. Further, adult play seems best to be characterized as a more formal, stylized, intense, and even serious presentation of some aspect of life rather than a light, informal, make-believe action such as the play of children.[16] In support of this is the view held by Vanderzwaag, among others, that although adult play may be described in the manner suggested,

Adults have found that plans and preparation for play do not necessarily enhance their realizing the potential of playing or increase the values which they derived from the play. One can much more easily plan the time for play than he can the play. It may be said that true play is unpredictable both in terms of its form and its results.[17]

It would then be reasonable to consider that much activity considered as adult play would be better identified as recreational or sport participation in one's leisure time.

Even though play is a voluntary activity for child or adult, its necessity for human well-being is clearly demonstrated by the following assertion of von Schiller: "For to speak out once and for all, man only plays when in the full meaning of the word he is a man, and he is a man only when he plays."[18] Although recreation and play have often been used interchangeably, this textbook, like most, will distinguish between the two terms. Both may be described as free-choice, spontaneous, physical activity. However, recreation is considered to be recreative, more organized, and yet relaxing activity, while for the most part, play has little or no measurable outcome such as revitalization and is engaged in for its own sake and for the fun, satisfaction, and self-expression that is derived from it. It would seem that recreation is dependent upon work for its meaning and function while play can be in contrast to work only in the sense of adult play and not really within the meaning of child's play. The latter is often carried on in a spirit of exploration, fun, make-believe, and elementary competition.

Theories of Play

The following are just a few selective theories of why people play. Some have a lengthy historical foundation and others are of a more contemporary nature. There is much need for a thorough empirical examination into the legion of play theories and for a discarding of those which are inadequate or of no use and an acceptance of those which are appropriate. With this end in view, the selection of play theories here will attempt to recognize the commentary and analysis of scholars. However, it should be realized that a single, universal theory of play is not yet possible, considering the degree of understanding we have of the why and how of play. Many theories are only partial explanations and many do not interrelate to each other. Since four theories have been previously mentioned in explaining why adults may play, the following brief descriptions of theories will tend to be concerned with child's play for the most part, as this seems to be by far the more significant concept in reaching for the meaning of play.

It would seem appropriate before listing play theories to bring to the attention of future practitioners in programs of physical activity, recreation, or sports a comprehension of what theories are. Stemming from his examination of play theories, M. J. Ellis states: "Theories are important because they are simplifying explanations of previous experiences and data that seem to have the capacity to predict what will come about. A theory has no worth beyond its value to promote insights into and predictions of outcomes."[19]

Let us now consider some of the early classical theories of play. Herbert Spencer's view of play was primarily motivated by the need for one to burn up **excess** or **surplus energy.** Since human energy has limited storability and energy greater than that needed for survival must be expended, Spencer believed that surplus energy was transferred into play even as it is in survival activities by animals and humans alike. Also, he maintained that this play represented the dramatization of adult activities which involved predatory instincts, such as chasing, wrestling, and taking one another prisoner.[20]

Often linked with the above view of play is the **catharsis theory** which is based on the idea that play can be a harmless way of expressing or releasing bottled-up emotions such as anger, frustration, or aggression. Play is therefore viewed as a socially accepted safety valve for their release. There may be limited validity to this theory as it implies activity and therefore cannot encompass passive play, which is often a characteristic of children playing. Nevertheless, when we consider the necessity of active play to assist children with excess energy and pent-up emotions, we can understand the desire that this kind of motivated child's play should be directed through socially accepted activity.

One of the most widely discussed theories of play has been Karl Groos's **instinct theory.** In searching for a biological justification of human conduct and play he studied and compared animal and human behaviour. The conclusion to his observations was that all animals, including man, play because of natural instincts and that this instinctive play was the preparation of the child for adulthood. A suggested weakness in this theory is that it does little to explain the motivation of adult play. The latter assumes that one accepts the view that adults do play, and although this position seems to have traditional acceptance, it can be maintained that these adult "play-like" activities are better categorized or explained by involvement in recreational and sporting activities in leisure time. When true child's play is engaged in by adults, it is owing to an individual or situational desire to regress to the fun and enjoyment of childhood and is usually in conjunction with children.

Closely related to Groos's theory is the concept of G. S. Hall's **recapitulation theory.** This theory is also based on the premise that the reason for play is that it is an inherent characteristic from previous generations, and therefore hunting or survival games are a natural activity.

Some of the more contemporary play theories will now be reviewed. The **developmentalism theory** finds its roots within the examination of play as a psychological and emotional experience. Weiskopf states: "Play is caused by the way in which a child's mind develops. Thus play is caused by the growth of the child's intellect and is conditioned by it. As a result of play, the intellect increases in complexity."[21] Jerome Bruner, psychologist and educator, one of the foremost authorities on cognitive growth and the educational process, agrees that even the most casual play expressions contribute in a significant way to childhood development and learning. In referring to the observations of the Swiss psychologist Piaget, Bruner states:

> . . . play helps the child assimilate experiences to his personal schema of the world . . . play is serious business, indeed, the principal business of childhood. It is the vehicle of improvisation and combination, the first carrier of rule systems through which a world of cultural restraint replaces the operation of childish impulse.[22]

A further concept of play which has been widely accepted by early twentieth century recreationalists and educators is the **self-expression theory.** Two leading physical educators, Elmer Mitchell and Bernard Mason, perceived that man was ". . . an active, dynamic creature, with a need to find outlets for his energies, to use his ability, and to express his personality."[23] The specific play activities in which an individual is involved are influenced by one's physiological and anatomical structure, one's physical fitness level, one's environment, and one's family and social background. Additionally, *universal* wishes of man are influential in shaping play attitudes and habits: the wish for new experiences, participation in a group enterprise, security, response and recognition from others, and a wish for aesthetic appreciation.[24]

M. J. Ellis's work "Play and Its Theories Re-examined," which is considered an outstanding analysis of play theories, focuses one's attention on two additional closely related current concepts of why one plays. The first theory is submitted by social psychologist D. E. Berlyne who believed that "play is caused by the need to find some optimum level of arousal for the individual. Finding this optimum level causes the individual to interact with the environment of self to increase his/her level of interest or stimulation."[25] This **arousal-seeking theory** of play suggests that the purpose of play is frequently to stimulate individuals, rather than to be used to create a calm, relaxed state or to reduce tensions. It also suggests that a motivation for play is the fulfillment of an individual's requirement for physical challenge, risk, excitement, or novelty.[26] The second of these contemporary theories of play identified by Ellis is the **competence motivation theory** which is based on the observation that a great deal of play consists of exploration and that the purpose of such play is to demonstrate competence and to master the environment. Many play theorists consider this view of play a subclassification of the arousal-seeking theory.

In conclusion, we are not about to define play as a term but are merely trying to suggest some characteristics of play. Hopefully, clarity will come as scholars continue to search for a fuller understanding of why and how individuals play. Certainly the definition of play stated by Pooley in chapter 12 is most appropriate.

The importance of play theories cannot be ignored as the effect of the quality and quantity of play experiences upon the child has a direct relationship to mature human development and therefore to the sociocultural structure of any society. Also, one would be remiss in not recognizing the significant contributions to the comprehension of play by the French sociologist Roger Caillois, who has examined the play experience itself by classifying the characteristics of games of various cultures and identifying their apparent functions and values. In addition, the work of the Dutch social historian Johan Huizinga must be noted. He defined characteristics of play in his work *Homo Ludens* as follows:

1. it is voluntary behaviour;
2. it steps outside of ordinary life;
3. it is usually secluded and limited in time and space;
4. it is not serious but absorbs the player intensely;
5. it is bounded by rules; and
6. it promotes formation of social groups which surround themselves with secrecy.[27]

With these ideas and thoughts in mind, let us now consider some common play characteristics by way of summary: (1) it is an activity which is voluntarily pursued for the purpose of pleasure and self-expression; (2) it is self-motivated, universal behaviour, found in humans and animals; (3) it is carried out in a spirit of exploration, fantasy, and/or competition; (4) it is done for its own sake and is not likely to withstand rational analysis; (5) it intensely absorbs participants but they know it is not real life and therefore consequences are limited; (6) it is often a culturally induced activity; (7) it contains elements of learning and therefore affects the development of social, physical, and cognitive growth in the participant; (8) it can be a casual or structured activity; and (9) through increased arousal it perpetuates its own development toward more complex play.

RECREATION

The term **recreation** comes from the Latin *recreatio,* meaning that which refreshes and restores. Further, in a traditional sense, Max Kaplan wrote: "Recreation has been viewed as a period of light and restful activity voluntarily chosen, which restores one for heavy, obligatory activity or work."[28] Recreation in this sense is dependent upon work for its meaning and function, and in addition it creates limits upon itself by indicating light and restful activity. In recent years, with the combined realization by all levels of the socioeconomic strata of a greater personal commitment is total individual fitness, coupled with the imminent approach of a leisure society within certain western cultures, recreation has become popularly associated with a more vigorous approach to activity as opposed to the earlier discussions of the term leisure. Therefore, much of the recreation presently participated in by individuals has emphasis on physical activity, and the term physical recreation has found common usage. The connotation by Kaplan of "light and restful activity" seems to have limited meaning in today's western societies and this reference seems more appropriate in the sphere of leisure activity.

Recreation is also referred to, and justly so, as a state of being—an emotional or aesthetic experience that reinforces a positive self-image and therefore has little to do with activity and could be any sort of personal enterprise.[29] This description tends to place some aspects of recreational activity in a close association with many leisure activities. Although this infers a "muddying of the waters" when one views leisure and recreation as a certain kind of activity, it does strengthen the proposition, to be examined later in the chapter, that an activity continuum has some basis in theory. A further insight into recreation is given by John Hutchinson when he suggests that recreation should be "a worthwhile, socially accepted leisure experience that provides immediate and inherent satisfaction to the individual who voluntarily participates in an activity."[30] With these concepts of recreation in mind and with the general agreement that recreation is an activity or an experience, the following definition by Martin and Esther Neumeyer seems appropriate:

> (*Recreation is*) . . . any [physical] activity pursued during leisure, whether individual or collective, that is free and pleasureful, having its own immediate appeal, not impelled by a delayed reward beyond itself or by any immediate necessity.[31]

PHYSICAL EDUCATION

There is a certain lingering view by some scholars within the fields of study of physical education, recreation, and sport (PERS) studies that the term physical education is the descriptive title for the academic discipline. In chapter 1, "The Discipline and the Profession," a fuller discussion of this issue is conducted. Suffice it to say that though there presently seems little to support the use of physical education as a term for the discipline of PERS studies, there seems to be significant support and justification for the term as one that describes an educational profession. It is in this context—a professional function—that the term physical education will be used in this text. Although for some this seems a limiting characterization of what physical education is, let us realize that the public educational systems are the largest structured social institutions within Canada—whether it be by compulsion (physical education curricular requirements) or by voluntary choice (intra- and extramural teams and clubs)—that are committed to the teaching of and participation in a vast variety of physical activities.

A well-developed core curriculum in physical education, with appropriate class time, can without doubt be just as vigorous in content, methodology, instruction, and evaluation as any other subject area within school curricula. The qualification of *period time* for physical education is still one of the greatest barriers to curriculum vigour within the Canadian school systems. If, as is the case in many United States and European school systems, daily periods of physical education (of approximately 55 minutes duration) throughout all elementary and secondary levels of education were mandatory, curriculum content would be of the quality that educational scholars and theorists have long sought. In brief, content should involve areas of body

awareness and function through movement education and exploration, physical fitness, physical activity and sports motor skills, recreational and leisure skills, games and sports knowledge and strategies, bioscientific knowledge of the human body's physiological and mechanical functions, and positive social and personality characteristics which are so necessary in child and adolescent development. This list of areas of study is not necessarily complete in itself, nor is it meant to be prioritized regarding objectives, as this can be accomplished only through an individual's comprehension of basic educational philosophy. However, an exciting, meaningful curriculum in physical education is a practical possibility if professionalism and time are present within a school system.

In conclusion, **physical education** is the educational profession which is responsible for the instruction in physical activities involving sports and games, motor skills and knowledge, physical fitness, and other rhythmic and movement forms.

SPORT

It is the view of the authors of this text, as it is of many other scholars in the field of physical education, recreation, and sport (PERS) studies, that sport studies is the main academic and activity focus of physical education, physical recreation, athletics (elite sport), and to some degree leisure and play. It is probably the most central concept to be understood within this chapter on terminology because it is the term most frequently applied to a large body of activities.[32] There seems little doubt that sport has one of the broadest interpretations and applications when one takes into account that even certain forms of play can be sportlike in nature, as play is often considered the antecedent to sport. Yet all play is not sport, though much sport can be playful.

Also, much of the physical activity which we observe as recreational in nature, participated in during our leisure time, has strong characteristics of what constitutes sport. The position of sport within an activity continuum is therefore self-evident and is discussed later in this chapter.

The generally agreed upon characteristics of sport seem to be fourfold. **Sport** is a physical activity which (1) must contain elements of physical prowess and skills, and is vigorous; (2) must include an element of competition or challenge whether that be abstract or concrete in form; (3) is institutionalized, in that it has predeveloped rules, regulations, and strategies of play; and (4) is involved in a socialization process.

Further, it should be realized that although an activity, to be called sport, contains these four elements, it is likely to do so in varying degrees thus allowing, as previously indicated, an extremely broad application of the term. These criteria will not necessarily create a clear distinction between recreational activities and sports but will assist in grouping activities which have similar objectives, meaning, and structure. For example, a street game of "shinny" is not a sport but a recreational/leisure pastime as it does not follow the accepted conditions of ice hockey with regard to such items as playing surface, equipment, playing area, and rules. A skier moving down a hill or mountain at his own leisure would not be involved in sport; likewise a swimmer doing laps in a pool or individuals playing cards are not engaged in sport. These and thousands of other examples of leisure and recreational activities will fall short of the criteria of sport because they lack one or more of the criteria and so must remain excluded. (The word "excluded" is used because many social activity and games associations claim to be sport associations for purposes of public and economic recognition.) Sport, on the other hand, does not have an age requirement or a predetermined level of performance skills, making certain organized age-class amateur competition just as much sport as intervarsity competition at the high school level.

To further define what sport is—or is not—the characteristic of competition or challenge must be clarified. Competition usually denotes the struggle for supremacy between two or more participants or teams within a game structure. This competition is concrete in nature because the outcome can be measured or scored. If this were the only meaning of competition, many "natural sports" such as those activities placed out-of-doors in accordance with nature's rules would also be excluded. Exclusion is not the intended purpose of laying down the criteria. Thus we find included the concept of **abstract challenge,** which allows mountain climbing, white-water canoeing and kayaking, and other natural physical activities to be sport. The abstract challenge or competition in these examples is that of the mountain or the river. Also, when one distinguishes that a socialization process should be evident in a sporting activity, the meaning is twofold. The first is that sport cannot be done singly or by oneself alone. It takes two or more participants or groups to compete, even in the abstract. If this situation is not present, the individual has once again moved to a leisure/recreational pursuit or is in the process of training for a sporting endeavour. Second, when one participates in sport, even the elementary codes of sportsmanship, or more likely one's natural desire to meet people, will require socialization to take place with fellow competitors, teammates, officials, and spectators. We may, with one reservation (the inclusion of the word "vigorous"), accept the following definition of sport given by Singer: "Sport is a [vigorous] human activity that involves specific administrative organization and historical background of rules which define the objective and limit the pattern of human behaviour; it involves competition or challenge and a definite outcome primarily determined by physical skill."[33]

Now that sport has been defined and its characteristics discussed, it is appropriate to consider the breadth of the term. Two means of visualizing this concept are presented. Eitzen and Sage, in their text *Sociology of American Sport,* differentiate the levels of sport in the following manner:

Informal Sport (Recreational)— this type of sport involves playful, physical activity primarily for the enjoyment of participants . . . [e.g., a neighbourhood touch football game, basketball or baseball games]. . . . In each example, some rules guide the competition and they are usually determined by the participants (not a regulatory body).

Organized Sport—the presence of a rudimentary organization. . . . There are formal teams, leagues, codified rules and related organizations. These exist primarily for the benefit of the players, working in fair competition [e.g., age class leagues, community club leagues, interscholastic teams up to university] . . . (those who) have not lost the original purpose of the activity.

Corporate Sport—[This type of sport] has been modified by economics and politics. . . . Here, we have sport as a spectacle; sport as big business; sport as an extension of power politics. The pleasure in the activity for the participant has [possibly] been lost in favour of pleasure for fans, owners, alumni, and other powerful groups.[34]

Another approach to the question of breadth in sport or levels of sport has been taken by Harry Edwards, sports sociologist. He presents a description of changing characteristics of sport as the sporting activity moves from playlike or recreational toward elite competition on an activity continuum from play to work. Edwards observes that the following occur:

1) activity becomes less subject to individual prerogative with spontaneity severely diminished;
2) formal rules, structural roles, positional relationships and responsibilities within the activity assume predominance;
3) separation from the rigours and pressures of daily life become less prevalent;
4) individual liability and responsibility for the quality and character of behaviour during the course of the activity is heightened;
5) the relevance of the outcome of the activity and the individual's role in it extends to groups and collectivities that do not participate directly in the act;

6) goals become diverse, complex and more related to values emanating from outside the context of the activity;

7) the activity consumes a greater proportion of the individual's time and attention due to the need for preparation and the degree of seriousness involved in the act.[35]

By these two methods one can begin to realize that the forthcoming development of an activity continuum can serve as a clarification of many of the terms discussed so far.

ATHLETICS (ELITE SPORT)

In the North American context, athletics, in the view of some theorists and much of the general public, has simply meant elite competitive sport. However, confusion exists with the term in that this particular identification is not universal. In fact, **athletics** in most of the world refers to track and field activities. This interpretation of the term is highlighted by the example of the Olympic and World Championships which use it in this manner (track and field). Within this reality it would seem reasonable that we in Canada should begin to use the phrase **elite sports competition** in lieu of athletics. For the most part, this will be the approach used in this text.

One must realize that this corporate or elite sport in the Canadian cul-ture is somewhat different from that described by Eitzen and Sage earlier. Except for some professional sports leagues and a number of specific national or international sporting events, there is proportionately less corporate sport in Canada than in the United States. Although the sports structure in Canadian universities has elements of the corporate state, it is decades away from achieving, if indeed that is the desire, the corporate characteristics described by Eitzen and Sage for its United States counterpart. Nevertheless, it would be accurate to say that Canadian university athletics and many national and international sports teams and competitions fall into the category of elite sport.

As with the term sport, there are certain changes in the notion of a phys-ical activity or game as it evolves from a recreational or an organized pursuit to that of an elite sports competition (athletics). These distinctive changes in quality are similar in nature to those mentioned in the previous term—sport—and therefore support the proposition that elite sport (athletics) is an exten-sion of organized sport. Possibly the greatest changing characteristic in this transition has to do with its more highly organized structure. This is not to infer that such factors as prowess in skills, increase in personal commitment and time, and increase in complexity of the activity as additional components do not also intensify. However, as indicated by Vanderzwaag, these organi-zational and structural changes are as follows:

1. [elite] teams are selected with greater care;
2. more attention is given to establishing and enforcing the rules in elite sport;
3. increased attention is devoted to standardization of facilities and equipment;
4. the [elite] game becomes more of a science due to the detailed analysis of skills, knowledge, and strategy of play; and
5. the entire area of public relations and publicity is highly developed.[36]

The value judgement as to whether elite sport competition (athletics) is truly sport is a personal one. It is hard for some to justify corporate or elite sport as anything but entertainment. In addition, the continuing problems relating to the abuse of acceptable ethical and moral standards of behaviour have many people concerned as to what truly is sport. However, for many more, elite sport offers a medium that is totally enjoyable and desirable, whether as a participant who pursues his individual drive for excellence; as a spectator who enjoys a feeling of identification, is enthralled by the wonderment of physical prowess, or who perceives it as interesting entertainment; or as a sports professional (coach, instructor, manager) who wishes to continue to improve and contribute to his chosen sport. Elite or corporate sport is a universal reality and it will not disappear. The problems within a sport are solvable. Sport in the abstract is just a competitive human game. It is the human factor in the application and interpretation of the game that is at times at variance. How could it be otherwise, given that all human endeavours have their supporters and detractors?

THE CONTINUUM THEORY OF PHYSICAL ACTIVITY

To conclude this chapter, it will be useful to bring into closer focus the work of Schmitz and Vanderzwaag with regard to the **continuum theory of physical activity,** which has been previously referred to on several occasions. Basically, this theory suggests that when one reflects on the various physical activities, games, and sports which for the most part constitute the work of a professional in the field of PERS, there are relatively consistent, characteristic changes that occur to the activity as it, or some modified form of it, moves from left to right on the continuum scale drawn below. Some of these changes which were discussed within the terms play, recreation, sport, and elite sport (athletics) will be reviewed at this point. In addition, there should be a general but firm understanding by the student of PERS that there is a continuous developmental relationship among the terms play, leisure, recreation, sport, and elite sport with regard to a physical activity. It has already been suggested that the concept of play is antecedent to physical recreation and sport (activitywise), and that sporting activities or games are the foundation of elite sport or athletics. Therefore, the continuum should be perceived in the following manner:

Play ⟶ Physical recreation activities ⟶ Sport ⟶ Elite sport

As Vanderzwaag indicates, this is not a simple black-and-white application but rather a melding relationship as the activity, game, sport, or physical activity changes its nature and purpose. What is so eminently important to the practitioner is that the philosophical basis, program objectives and goals, methods of instruction and communication, and content of instruction alter dramatically as the process of learning and the transformation of the activity proceeds. This can all take place within any one of the sportlike activities such as basketball, ice hockey, canoeing, golf, and hundreds more. Practical examples of the application of the theory will follow later in this section.

At this time, it should be emphasized that the word **games** is used in the context to mean "any form of playful competition whose outcome is determined by physical skill, strategy, or chance employed singly or in combination."[37] Games are the vehicle whereby play, physical recreation, sport, and elite sport (athletics) evolve. Therefore it is necessary to have a parallel structure added to the continuum:

Play ⟶ Physical recreation activities ⟶ Sport ⟶ Elite sport

⟵————————— Games —————————⟶

Probably one of the most difficult yet important procedures that an instructor in physical education, recreation, and sport has to perform regarding physical activity programming is to determine the philosophical goals and directions of that program and then place it within the context of the activity continuum. This must be done in order to be able to anticipate any degree of consistency in decision making and thus program success. If, for example, one is developing a sporting activity program such as basketball, it can be easily perceived that this sport, or a modification of it, can be learned and played in a great number of ways. Some of these ways may be playlike—bouncing or dribbling the ball, rolling it or passing it among children; recreational—having any variety of "pick-up" games, or shooting games on standard or nonstandard court space; sport—having organized teams, score keeping, officials; or elite sport (athletics)—introducing a structured competitiveness and increasing the skills, strategy, and complexity of the sport. This method of evaluation can be applied to a certain degree to hundreds of sports, games, and physical activities and it allows the PERS programmer to place the activity on the continuum fairly accurately. Thus, by definition and characteristics of the chosen position, the direction and content of the program can be determined.

To assist in the process of **program identification,** the programmer might use a question and answer technique. Examples of goal-oriented questions that could be asked follow.

1. What are the learning levels of the participants (beginning, intermediate, advanced)?
2. What are the age groups, sex, and physical limitations of the participants?
3. What are the basic reasons for participation (a leisure pastime, physical recreation, competition, instruction, socializing, or a combination of two or more of these)?
4. What time and energy expenditure do the participants wish to commit?

Once this series of questions has answers, the programmer moves to a more pragmatic or specific line of questioning.

1. What type of equipment or facilities are needed?
2. What kind and number of instructors or supervisors are needed?
3. What financial resources are required?
4. What modifications of rules and regulations might be required?

Some of these adjustments may be linked to the specificity of the activity or sport.

This format for direction setting should not be restricted to only what may be commonly recognized as formal sports, but should be used for most programming from passive leisure activities, such as card playing, to the recreational and competitive sporting scene. It is advised that whenever a game situation is present within the program, this process should be used to establish program identification on the continuum.

It cannot be too strongly emphasized that this process of development of an activity program from play, to recreation, to sport, to elite sport is not a clear distinction as the characteristics of the activity or sport could well be evolving at a different rate of time and space. The most contentious programming for the professionals, participants, and concerned observers is the gradation between sport and elite sport activities. This qualitative difficulty is often compounded because, in the abstract, sport does not differentiate age, physical prowess, or sex, and by definition therefore allowing adults to be involved in informal (recreational) sport and adolescents and children to be involved in elite sport. The latter is often inappropriate and harmful when permitted indiscriminately and so is open to justifiable criticism. If we now take as an example the activity of ice hockey and project it on the continuum from sport to elite sport, the following gradation becomes evident:

Ice Hockey

Sport ⟵————————————————⟶ **Elite Sport**

Various age-class and intramural programs	Higher tiered adolescent leagues (all ages)	Most junior and senior amateur leagues	Selected junior leagues, university intercollegiate leagues
Certain adult industrial or commercial leagues, etc.	High school interscholastic teams		National teams International competition

Of course, the activity of ice hockey can also be participated in at different levels to the left of sport in the above diagram, indicating both formal and informal recreational pastime even to the point of playlike pursuits for children.

Earlier in this chapter, play was contrasted with work in the sense that most leisure and recreational endeavours of individuals, especially adults, lie somewhere between the two. It is necessary before visually completing the continuum to explain what is meant by work in the context of the theory. **work** is thought of in two ways: first as the activity of qualified professionals working within the fields of physical education, recreation, leisure, sport, and other forms of physical activity; or, second, the performance of the professional within a given sport. With this clarification, the physical activity continuum could be visually stated in the following manner:

Play ⟵————⟶ Physical ⟵————⟶ Sport ⟵————⟶ Elite sport ⟵————⟶ Work
recreation (professional)
activities

⟵————————————— GAMES —————————————⟶

The double-ended arrows are intended to designate the interrelatedness of one set of program characteristics of a physical activity or sport with its preceding or succeeding categories. They also indicate the movement of a physical activity or sport from one category to another effected by changing its purpose and desired result.

SUMMARY

It has been the intention in this chapter to clarify, contrast, and analyze the various nomenclature and terms commonly in use in the discipline and professions of physical education, recreation, and sport studies. The terminology covered includes leisure, play, recreation, physical education, sport, and elite sport (athletics). Not only are definitions offered but some of the characteristics of each concept are presented. This is done for the reader to be able to comprehand the physical activity continuum theory presented in the final part of the chapter. This theory attempts to assist programmers in the field of PERS studies with program identification. This identification and corresponding placement of physical activity programs on the continuum leads to the establishment of clearer objectives and directions.

SUGGESTED READINGS

Ellis, M. J. *Why People Play.* Englewood Cliffs, NJ: Prentice-Hall, 1973.

Godbey, Geoffrey. *Leisure in Your Life.* Philadelphia: Saunders College, 1981.

Kraus, Richard. *Recreation and Leisure in Modern Society.* 3d ed. Glenview, IL: Scott, Foresman and Co., 1984.

Singer, Robert, et al. *Physical Education: Foundations.* New York: Holt, Rinehart and Winston, 1976.

Vanderzwaag, Harold J. *Toward a Philosophy of Sport.* Reading, MA: Addison-Wesley Co., 1972.

Vanderzwaag, Harold J., and Thomas J. Sheehan. *Introduction to Sport Studies: From the Classroom to the Ballpark.* Dubuque, IA: Wm. C. Brown Publishers, 1978.

Weiskopf, Donald C. *Recreation and Leisure: Improving the Quality of Life.* 2d ed. Boston: Allyn and Bacon, 1982.

NOTES

1. Rolf B. Meyersohn, "Americans Off Duty," in *Free Time-Challenge to Later Maturity,* Wilma Donahue et al. (Ann Arbor: University of Michigan Press, 1958), 46.

2. Christopher R. Eddington et al., *Recreation and Leisure Programming* (Philadelphia: Saunders College, 1980), 7.

3. Thorstein Veblen, *The Theory of the Leisure Class* (New York: B. W. Heubsch, 1899), 40.

4. Geoffrey Godbey, *Leisure in Your Life* (New York: Saunders College, 1981), 9.

5. The Conference Board in Canada, *Handbook of Canadian Consumer Markets, 1979* (Ottawa, ON, 1979), 132.

6. Statistics supplied by the Manitoba Sports Federation from yearly surveys of registered members (Jan. 1986).

7. Joffre Dumazedier, *Toward a Society of Leisure* (New York: Free Press, 1962, 1967), 16–17.

8. Richard Kraus, *Recreation and Leisure in Modern Society,* 2d ed. (Santa Monica, CA: Goodyear Pub. Co., 1978), 38.

9. Sebastian de Grazia, *Of Time, Work and Leisure* (New York: Doubleday-Anchor, 1962), 5.

10. Kraus, *Recreation and Leisure in Modern Society,* 2d ed., 40.

11. Bertrand Russell, quoted by Godbey and Parker in *Leisure Studies and Services: An Overview* (Philadelphia: W. B. Saunders, 1976), 175.

12. Kraus, *Recreation and Leisure in Modern Society,* 2d ed., 44.

13. James F. Murphy, "The Future of Time, Work and Leisure," *Parks and Recreation* (November 1973): 26.

14. Kraus, *Recreation and Leisure in Modern Society,* 2d ed., 44.

15. Harold J. Vanderzwaag, *Toward a Philosophy of Sport* (Reading, MA: Addison-Wesley Pub. Co., 1972), 52.

16. Max Kaplan, *Leisure in America: A Social Inquiry* (New York: John Wiley, 1960), 20.

17. Vanderzwaag, *Toward a Philosophy of Sport,* 53.

18. J. C. Griedrich von Schiller, *Letter on Aesthetic Education,* ed. C. W. Eliot (New York: P. F. Collier & Sons, 1910), 266.

19. M. J. Ellis, "Play and Its Theories Re-examined," *Parks and Recreation* (August 1971): 51.

20. Herbert Spencer, quoted in Harvey C. Lehman and Paul A. Witty, *The Psychology of Play Activities* (New York: A. S. Barnes, 1927), 13.

21. Donald C. Weiskopf, *Recreation and Leisure: Improving the Quality of Life,* 2d ed. (Boston: Allyn and Bacon, 1982), 28.

22. Jerome S. Bruner, "Child Development: Play is Serious Business," *Psychology Today* (January 1975): 53.

23. Kraus, *Recreation and Leisure in Modern Society,* 1st ed., 266.

24. Ellis, "Play and Its Theories Re-examined."

25. Godbey, *Leisure in Your Life,* 171.

26. Weiskopf, *Recreation and Leisure: Improving the Quality of Life,* 2d ed., 29.

27. Johan Huizinga, *Homo Ludens—A Study of the Play Element in Culture* (Boston: The Beacon Press, 1962), 13.

28. Kaplan, *Leisure in America: A Social Inquiry,* 19.

29. David Gray and Seymour Greben, "Future Perspectives," *Parks and Recreation* (July 1974): 49.

30. John Hutchinson, *Principles of Recreation* (New York: Ronald, 1951), 2.

31. Martin H. Neumeyer and Esther Neumeyer, *Leisure and Recreation* (New York: Ronald, 1958), 22.

32. Robert N. Singer et al., *Physical Education: Foundations* (New York: Holt, Rinehart and Winston, 1976), 28.

33. Ibid., 28.

34. D. E. Eitzen and George H. Sage, *Sociology of American Sport* (Dubuque, IA: Wm. C. Brown Publishers, 1978), 18–19.

35. Harry Edwards, *Sociology of Sport* (Homewood, IL: Dorsey, 1973), 59.

36. Harold J. Vanderzwaag, *Toward a Philosophy of Sport* (Reading, MA: Addison-Wesley Pub., 1972), 73.

37. John W. Loy, "The Nature of Sport: A Definitional Effort," *Quest* X (May 1968): 6.

CHAPTER 3
Careers

David Anderson

In discussing career opportunities within the discipline of PERS and its corresponding professions, one must be concerned that the recipient of such information understands that such careers stem not only directly from the study of the discipline but also from the combination of studies from a PERS program with a second or even a third different area of study. It is the latter, the combining of two or more disciplines as the basis of postsecondary study and preparation, which is too frequently overlooked in career counselling and could possibly narrow the vistas for satisfying employment. Some of these professions or job opportunities are listed later in this chapter; however, the following examples should clearly demonstrate this interdisciplinary approach to career preparation. A career in the field of sports journalism is open to the individual who establishes a strong foundation in English composition and style along with sport studies. To take this example an additional step, one could add communication and speech skills and prepare for a career in sports broadcasting. Still a further example of combining undergraduate fields of study toward a professional career would be joint studies of PERS and economic, business, or administrative studies, leading toward the development of opportunities in recreation or sport administration.

THE INTERDISCIPLINARY APPROACH

This form of career preparation or discipline study is often called the **interdisciplinary** approach, which simply means the study of two or more disciplines directed toward a common vocation. There are many other examples of workable combinations; in fact, the list is bounded only by one's own imagination and interests. Nevertheless, the real essence of PERS studies is to prepare students for the varied professions which do stem directly from the study of this primary discipline. In this category are such careers as physical education teacher, recreationalist, exercise physiologist, fitness instructor, sport coach, sport biomechanics specialist, and athletic therapist, to list but a few. It would be true to say that even in this short list, different emphases lead to different course selections for the undergraduate student. A student must realize that even at the undergraduate level, professional preparation varies significantly from one career to another, and therefore course grouping will vary. At this level, however, the student's curriculum would be found mainly within the programs listed in the departments, schools, or faculties designated for PERS studies. At this point it should be clear to all beginning students in PERS studies that continuous professional counselling is a significant key to the establishment of a sound undergraduate program which will lead to a desired future position.

ADDITIONAL STUDIES

Another point which must be drawn to the attention of the undergraduate student at an early stage in his or her curriculum planning is that there are many highly technical, specialized, and science-oriented careers which will require additional graduate study before entry into the profession could be attempted. In fact, one might anticipate that a number of the positions listed in figure 3.1 will require such additional preparation. As an example, a student might well find that such a common vocation as high school physical education teacher and/or sports coach will in most provinces now require teaching certification or an additional teacher-education year of study. It is also not uncommon for high school teaching positions to require a master's degree as the competition for these positions increases. Certainly department head positions often indicate this requirement. If an undergraduate wishes to pursue opportunities as a sports psychologist, exercise physiologist, biomechanics specialist, or university teacher/researcher, advanced degrees are mandatory in this day and age.

In summation of this discussion of undergraduate curriculum and professional preparation, the two categories of professional careers which should be considered by beginning students are reemphasized: (1) those professions which for the most part are developed through the curricula of PERS studies or its equivalent, and (2) those professions which are distinctively interdisciplinary in nature. Too often it is perceived by freshman students, or indicated by ill-advised counselling, that a general physical education degree (B.P.E.) or a major in PERS studies prepares one for a career which is, in fact, beyond the scope of these curricula.

Figure 3.1 will more clearly demonstrate the points already stressed. It is not meant to be completely definitive but rather to present a few common career examples. Two main groups are represented in figure 3.1. Group I contains professions which for the most part originate from, or are accommodated within, the various degrees in PERS studies (a major within a bachelor of arts or science, bachelor of physical education, or bachelor of education with a physical education major). Group II contains professions which are very much

Professional Preparation and Study Areas for Some Common Careers

CAREER	UNDERGRADUATE STUDIES	PROBABLE GRADUATE STUDIES DIRECTION
GROUP I Physical education teacher		
Elementary	PERS major, PE major, BPE plus teacher certification or BEd. (PE major), or a minor in the above where acceptable	Usually continuing study in the educational field, such as MEd. or MPEd. and Doctorate of Education or PERS
Secondary	Same as above, but no minor except in very specific employment situations	
Coaching educational institution	PERS major, PE major, BPE, BEd. (PE major) with practical experience	Master's programs in coaching do exist; however, practical experience of an advanced nature is a necessity; additional study (e.g., psychology, biosciences, administration, communication), should be considered
Noneducational institution	Same as above	
Recreationalist	Recreation studies major/ degree or PERS major with strong recreation sequence	Master's, doctoral study in field, possibly research orientation, sociological/administrative focus
University/ college professor	PERS major, PE major, BEd. (PE major)	Master's/doctorate PERS studies, specific specializations required
Sport scientist	Same as above, with strong bioscience sequence	Master's/doctorate specialized bioscience field—e.g., biomechanics, exercise physiology
Athletic therapist/trainer	Same as above	Master's in athletic therapy; doctoral study will usually follow specialization in the bioscience field

Figure 3.1

CAREER	UNDERGRADUATE STUDIES	PROBABLE GRADUATE STUDIES DIRECTION
GROUP II (a) Sport sociologist	Combination of PERS and sociology; at least one minor and one major	Master's and doctorate usually continue in the same manner as undergraduate studies with emphasis often toward theory and research methodology through sociology
Sport psychologist	Combination of PERS and psychology; at least one minor and one major	Same as above with emphasis on theory and research methodology through psychology
Recreation or sport administrator	Combination of PERS or recreation studies and administrative studies/ commerce/business administration	Master's/doctoral studies in PERS and/or administrative studies or its equivalent
Park supervisor/ director	Combination of PERS or recreation studies and environmental studies, ecology, or geography	Master's/doctoral studies continuing combination with specialization directed toward typical park settings—e.g., wilderness, urban, or semiwilderness
GROUP II (b) Sports journalist	Combination of English and communication studies and PERS	Master's/doctoral studies continuing same combination
Sports broadcaster	Same as above	Same as above with increased experience and understanding of verbal and technical communication skills
Sports facility designer	Combination of architecture/ construction/engineering and PERS	Advanced studies continuing same combination
Sports historian	Combination of study of historical methodology and PERS	Advanced studies continuing combination

Figure 3.1 Continued.

interdisciplinary in nature and in moving from II (a) to II (b) there is likely to appear a shift in emphasis away from the primary study of PERS to a second more significant field of knowledge.

The following list may suggest many other kinds of career opportunities that could be available to graduates of PERS studies.

- director of athletics
- amateur sport and recreation administrator
- professional sport coaches, managers, administrators
- instructors or directors at YMCAs, YWCAs, YMHAs
- camp counsellors, instructors, and directors
- instructors and directors in industrial recreation
- instructors and directors in commercial or private health spas
- instructors and directors in private sports clubs/resorts
- sports information and publicity
- recreation and sport instructors in the armed forces
- youth centre workers and directors
- aquatics programmers and directors
- recreation director in correctional institution
- national and provincial park recreationalist
- outdoor education or recreation instructors
- sport recreation or leisure equipment design, manufacture/sales
- private sport, recreation and leisure consultants in programming or facility design
- sport and fitness nutritionalists
- sports officiating or judging (professional or amateur)
- physical education supervisors and directors
- school principalships
- recreation programmers and directors for senior citizens, groups, or institutions
- community club supervisors
- fitness instructors, researchers, or evaluators
- Canadian Red Cross
- sports, recreation, or fitness publications, film production and sales
- Boy Scouts and Girl Guides of Canada[1]

It should be noted that recent trends suggest that employers now consider graduates of PERS studies, with majors in physical education or recreation studies, to be the equal of arts and science graduates, and in some instances superior. Recognition of this trend opens up additional work opportunities, particularly in such fields as personnel work, insurance, retailing, marketing and sales, and banking. This field of employment may not be the first choice of the graduating student, but during those periods when job opportunities in PERS professions are few and highly competitive it might offer a desirable alternative. Part V of this text, "Some Contemporary Trends within PERS in Canada," contains further discussion of career realities in the field of physical education.

THE COACHING PROFESSION IN CANADA

At this time it is appropriate to single out one profession which is directly associated with PERS studies and which in western nations has an extremely high profile, yet has great difficulty in establishing itself as a secure, consistent professional work opportunity, especially at the amateur level of sports participation. This is the profession of coaching. The truth of this situation is nowhere more evident than in Canada. In short, it is most difficult for a Canadian to acquire and maintain a permanent coaching position at the amateur level as a lifetime career, and yet its appeal to young undergraduates of both sexes is most significant and understandable. A coaching career has an element of glamour, necessitates great knowledge and skill, is achievement oriented, offers enormous self-gratification and satisfaction, and can provide significant personal and financial rewards at its upper limits.

In order to fully comprehend why this important PERS profession of coaching is so tenuous as a future career for students, it is necessary to understand the complex nature of the Canadian amateur sports delivery system which is a mixture of the European community-based sports club and the school-oriented United States (and to some degree British) programs. In the European system, sports teaching and competition is delivered to the population through a variety of institutions and agencies other than the educational system. In Canada these institutions and agencies range from municipal recreation departments to nonprofit community sports clubs to private and public sports clubs. They encompass all levels of participation from beginning instruction and recreation to elite competition. Sports such as ice hockey, baseball, tennis, figure skating, gymnastics, swimming, golf, and many others are delivered for the most part in this manner. Some sports such as soccer, track and field, and others are partially developed in this way. The degree to which a sport may be attributable to a community club system varies throughout the country.

The second facet of the Canadian amateur sport delivery system stems from our neighbours in the United States who rely heavily upon the educational system for the teaching of and participation in sporting activities. They made an early commitment to sports involvement in the educational system from public schools through college or university age levels. Canada made this choice only in selected sports such as basketball, volleyball, and Canadian football. Even from these three examples one will find variances throughout the breadth of the nation. The point to be made from all this is that the teacher/coach who wishes to choose a particular sport must first ascertain through which of the delivery systems his or her sport is developed and so prepare an undergraduate program accordingly. This dichotomy in the amateur sports system has diffused itself into the professional preparation in the field of coaching to the extent that the curricula at Canadian universities and colleges often lack direction and career commitment. Too often such preparation consists only of sequences of courses within, or added to, physical education or recreation majors. Therefore, a student who wishes to be involved in a coaching career must be fully aware of this problem and be prepared to participate, for the most part, in a career other than coaching, such as teaching or working within the recreation/leisure system. It is a travesty that such a significant profession as sport coaching has still to be granted its due in Canadian society, together with the professional recognition, independence, and permanency that it has long received elsewhere in the world. Full-time, permanent amateur sport coaching positions are few or even rare in Canada. Historical and financial limitations of the Canadian dual sports delivery system are a contributing factor to the problem. However, the root cause still lies within the social-political-educational-economic structure which only wishes to ride the crest of elation, pride, and identification when sportsmen achieve national and international levels of athletic performance in spite of great difficulties, one of the greatest of which is the shortage of professionally competent coaches. On the other hand, the same society is quick to criticize when achievement or coaching is less than expected. Canadians must eliminate this hypocrisy and establish the profession of sport coaching as a career position commensurate with society's expectations of the performance of this profession at whatever level the teacher/coach may be involved.

It should be noted that many provincial and national sport governing bodies, the National Coaching Association of Canada, and the provincial and federal governments have recognized this deficiency and in the early 1970s began the development of the National Coaching Certification Program which has shown success and great promise. However, this program is, for the most part, geared to the volunteer, amateur sports coach. Still, it does offer different levels of certification which in time, and in conjunction with postsecondary educational institutions, could be the basis for a curriculum for full-time sport coaching at the amateur and the professional levels. The National Coaching Certification Program is covered in further detail in chapters 6 and 7.

Future amateur sport coaches must face two realities: (1) that a concomitant career which furnishes basic living needs will be necessary, and (2) that the delivery system in which the sport is developed must be determined in order that an appropriate career choice can be made.

SUMMARY

The first section of this chapter attempts to distinguish for the students the many varied careers which are available to them in two broad categories: first, those professions which basically stem from the discipline study of PERS and its many subareas; second, the many other work opportunities which lie within the interdisciplinary approach to career development. Preparation usually involves study in two or more definable areas of knowledge and relates to a PERS subprofession. It is also indicated that many careers in these two categories do require additional graduate studies for entrance into the field. Finally, considerable effort is spent in describing the uniqueness of the popular amateur sport coaching profession in Canada from the historical perspective to the present realization of its position in Canadian society today.

SUGGESTED READING

Singer, Robert N., et al. *Physical Education: Foundations.* New York: Holt, Rinehart and Winston, 1976, chapter 19.

NOTES

1. This list was adapted from a similar one which may be found in Robert N. Singer et al., *Physical Education: Foundations* (New York: Holt, Rinehart and Winston, 1976), 438.

PART TWO
Philosophical and Historical Foundations

CHAPTER 4

Selected Philosophical Concepts of PERS Studies

David Anderson

It is too frequently assumed by practitioners in the field of physical education, recreation, and sport (PERS) that upon gaining some necessary theoretical knowledge, skills, and practical experience in the discipline and its profession, an individual will develop automatically a personal philosophy toward PERS. If, indeed, this were the fact, then there would be little need for one to develop and organize the study of human thought and conduct within the subject field of PERS. Further, many of the basic continuing questions and problems relating to man's involvement in physical activity and sports would remain for the most part unresolved. Since philosophical study according to Nixon and Jewett is "concerned with identifying and then formulating laws and principles that underlie all human knowledge and understanding of reality . . . ,"[1] we can accept that philosophical study in the discipline and professions of PERS is indeed necessary. We continually come under increasing pressures from all facets of contemporary society to explain what we are, what we do, why we do it, the value of what we do, and the methodology we use. As many present-day scholars in the field have stated, there are persistent problems which abound in PERS studies and programs. Therefore, it is the responsibility of all professionals to try to explain their field and reflect on the issues that arise based upon a well-considered philosophical understanding.

DEVELOPING A FRAMEWORK

Any oversimplified philosophy of physical activity and sport would do an injustice to both one's self and to the discipline and the profession. This is not to suggest that any specific knowledge and experience cannot be a significant modifier of one's philosophical growth and development. However, these must be able to be placed in a necessary framework of philosophical thought and understanding which should be structured for consistency, yet be flexible enough to absorb change or modification. From this framework, a personal philosophical position can mature through experiences in the field. It is to this end that serious study must be given to the larger philosophical questions, concepts, ideas, or thoughts that are the basis—or at least an integral part—of physical education, recreation, and sport studies. A few of these concepts are briefly described later in this chapter. Note the following statement on the importance of developing a philosophy:

> A person striving to function intelligently in society needs a philosophy of life and/or religion. In addition, a physical educator and/or coach . . . or a recreationist should have a philosophy of education. To top this off, he/she should develop still further a philosophy of physical health, [sport] and recreation education. . . .The achievement of such a total philosophy may well become a life-long task. The reflective thought required to accomplish this task, however, is a mighty cheap price to pay for a possible well-ordered life [and career].[2]

REASONS FOR PHILOSOPHICAL STUDY IN PERS

The reasons for developing a philosophical understanding in this area of study are little different from those for any other body of knowledge and should be examined along with their implication for PERS studies.

The first reason is that such understanding is necessary in order to **formulate meaningful personal objectives** which are a necessary part of a professional career and a requirement of leadership. This also applies to program and curriculum objectives. Personal choices, directions, and opportunities occur relatively early in one's professional development. For example, if a student accepts as part of his commitment (and therefore his goals) the desire to pursue a career in the subfield of leisure pursuits and recreation, or in coaching competitive sports, or in recreational or sport administration, or in teaching physical education, he is involved in professions which all require some degree of specialized professional preparation which stems from a particular set of objectives. A further example, which emphasizes the breadth of application of well-defined philosophical objectives, is the necessity for a physical education teacher to establish a curriculum of physical activity for a junior or a senior high school. Should he follow *essentialistic* goals or *progressivist* goals? Without becoming involved in explanations of these schools of educational thought, it may be said that they are significantly different in their understanding, purpose, and interpretation of the relationship between man and physical activity. Therefore, they are very different in curriculum content prescribed and methods of instruction advocated. It is, then, a most important personal and professional choice that a physical educator must make within his professional leadership responsibilities. From solid personal philosophic goals one can work, with understanding and with limited conflict, in a variety of predetermined programs or careers and can create rational justifications for various physical activity or sports programming.

Deriving from the first purpose of establishing clear objectives and goals is the development of a process for **consistent decision making.** It is only from a solid philosophical base that one can achieve the necessary consistency in judgemental decisions demanded by the variety of professions which comprise the discipline. This need for consistency is emphasized because few areas of human endeavour are more open to public scrutiny and/or critical analysis than those decisions made in the realms of physical activity, sport, and athletic competition. Ad hoc or expedient decision making is a plague which too often is part and parcel of sports and elite sport (athletics). This is not to imply that the decision-making process of professionals in the many career fields of PERS does not have to retain some degree of flexibility for spontaneous judgements in specific game situations. However, it can become confusing and disturbing to participants and observers alike if "ad hockery" becomes the norm instead of the exception. Examples of ad hockery can frequently be observed in lower age-class sports competition where often the agreed, or assumed, philosophical position with regard to team members' playing time is that of reasonable equity. Additionally, game situations are supposedly for recreational and learning experiences for all. Nevertheless, when important games or specific game situations occur which may determine the outcome or affect league standings, the less-skilled players are shunted to the sidelines so that the objective of winning can be attempted. Often the priority of winning is a secondary goal until the possibility arises. This ad hoc coaching decision is usually accompanied by little explanation to those involved and is contrary to the original concept thus causing confusion and frustration among both participants and observers. Coupled with the necessity of stable decision making, a professional must fully realize the extent of the openness or public nature of many of the major careers in PERS.

By any social, political, or economic standards which may be used to measure cultural significance, physical activity in all its forms is one of the most pervasive pastimes of modern man.

> . . . In some form physical education . . . [recreation] . . . and sport have been a feature of most every known form of cultural life, and have had a part in every major epoch in the history of civilization . . . [3]

This self-evident statement is fully substantiated through sociological research, some of which is brought to the student's attention in the chapters concerning sociological and psychological foundations. Further, in exercising purposeful judgements, one must recognize that second-guessing or armchair quarterbacking is a normal and acceptable pastime for participants and observers of any athletic game or sports contest. This critical analysis will be applied at some time to most instructors'/teachers' or coaches' decisions, whether they pertain to their own personal conduct and deportment, to player selection or recruitment, to strategies of play, to rules and regulation interpretations, to the use of teaching and motivation methods and techniques, or to various other activities. It is from well-developed philosophical principles and understanding that judgemental consistency arises and will allow an instructor, teacher, coach, or administrator in PERS to communicate more effectively, not only with participants and colleagues but also with parents and the public in general. As Zeigler states: "a consistent philosophy is the sign of a true professional,"[4] and if consistent, one's actions, decisions, and opinions concerning a vast variety of issues will at least be understood if not always accepted.

A third reason for studying the philosophical structure and meaning of PERS is that it is important for an individual to **establish and represent sound moral values** which are set forth by society and which are the basis of one's own beliefs and are therefore expressed in his or her moral behaviour. For physical educators, coaches, recreationalists, and leisurists who are deeply involved in human development and growth, interpersonal relationships, sociopsychological concerns, and personal fitness and health, the question of right and wrong or the acceptable and the unacceptable professional practice is of paramount importance and is directly related to success in the many fields of PERS. This can be exemplified by the subprofession of sports coaching within educational institutions. Coaching is constantly under scrutiny and suspect as to one's application of sociocultural standards of ethics in such areas as the degree of competitive intensity of interscholastic programs; recruiting practices; the type and quality of academic counselling directed to the student-athlete; the interpretation of educational, playing, or eligibility rules and regulations; and so on. Because of the highly publicized lack of ethics displayed by some elite sport coaches and administrators, it is often assumed by a large number of observers of educational sport that a successful coaching record is accompanied by unethical or immoral behaviour on the part of those involved. Both facets of the problem—possible unethical behaviour and the assumption of "guilt by reason of success"—are in part present in the Canadian sports scene because of the partial adoption of the American educational sport delivery system. As unjust as this is, the fact remains that such situations do occur, thereby placing an obligation on professionals involved in sports competition to construct a moral philosophy as the basis for their practices that are compatible with their own beliefs and with those of society as a whole. Physical educators, recreationalists, and other physical activity practitioners have just as compelling a need as coaches have for the formulation of ethical conduct based upon moral philosophical principles.

As indicated by Nixon and Jewett in *An Introduction to Physical Education,* the educational, personal, and therefore physical activity and sport philosophies held by the individual teacher, coach, or instructor are inseparable from the methods of instruction and techniques which they utilize. More importantly, they rest upon the basic philosophical beliefs and values which are held by the individual. It should be understood that this belief and value system is seldom explicitly organized in written form. However, it will always give guidance in one's career. In our professions we must not only have, but must be perceived to have, sound moral and ethical standards.

The last justification to be identified in this short overview of some of the reasons for philosophical study in PERS concerns the ability to identify and define the nature and significance of the art of movement, its beauty, and its appreciation. The branch of philosophical inquiry which examines this is called **aesthetics.** For centuries the human body has been viewed as an object of natural beauty and man has tried to describe and depict the ultimate "body beautiful" in the art forms of painting, sculpture, dance, literature, and poetry. In recent decades the *art of sport* has come off the bookshelves, has removed itself from the museums and archives—as important as these forms are to sport—and has become the pleasure and delight of masses of sport lovers through the technological advancement of cinematography. There is a whole new rebirth of interest in the human form and its movement.

> Concepts such as gracefulness, harmony, effortlessness, control, flow, power, rhythm and many more serve man in his acceptance of perceived physical performance, and where these concepts find most application to the arts— most notably dance and the performing arts—they take an added force in the *new vision* brought to sports activity.[5]

Sports and physical activity is now considered a performing art not only by scholars and athletic performers but also by the observers and audiences which view the products of PERS programs. It should be realized that there are two foci for athletic appreciation and understanding: the perspective of the creator/performer and the perception of the observer.

It is not the intention of the authors in emphasizing the beauty of physical skills and movement to minimize in any way the importance of the art of sport in its classical forms. Who would not have been emotionally and aesthetically thrilled at the spectacle of the opening and closing ceremonies of the Montreal Olympics and the marvellous adaptation of the music of André Mathieu to this sporting event, or similarly moved in viewing the ancient Greek sculptures of bodily perfection and harmony? However, cinematography and television have opened a whole new world of human movement and physical skills and through sport competition it is now a weekly viewing occurrence. We now frequently hear "wasn't that a beautiful move" or a commentator using such descriptions as "the effortless power of the swing" or "the rhythm of the volley" with regard to a golf or tennis swing, accompanied by slow-motion or stop-action display. These phrases are not intended as a scientific analysis of a skill pattern but rather as an artistic or aesthetic judgement of the task performed. An understanding of the philosophy of art of human movement and form can only create a greater and deeper appreciation of what is performance and beauty in physical activity and sport. The authors recommend that a student in the field of PERS who wishes to pursue a more effective understanding in this area of study become familiar with *The Beauty of Sport: A Cross-Disciplinary Inquiry* by Benjamin Lowe.

METHODS OF PHILOSOPHICAL INQUIRY IN PERS STUDIES

Philosophical inquiry into the discipline of PERS can take many forms and it is not the intention of this text to profess one method of study over another but to submit a variety of approaches. Once done, the student, practitioner, or teacher may then choose the most meaningful process. The object is to create an understanding of the importance for the individual to develop a consistent personalized philosophy which best meets his or her own beliefs and needs.

A frequent approach is to become familiar with the various schools or systems of philosophical thought that have evolved through the centuries, and in doing so develop an understanding of their principles, constructs, and ideas. From that knowledge one should extend one's understanding to the educational philosophy and ultimately to the translation of these educational tenets to a philosophy of physical activity and sport. The schools of pure and educational philosophy which seem appropriate for contemporary society because of their significance and impact would be naturalism, realism/essentialism, idealism, pragmatism/progressivism, and existentialism. One could further refine this approach by becoming familiar with the philosophical theories of individual philosophers who have been identified as major adherents to a school or system. A degree of caution should be employed in this method of study in that schools are not necessarily mutually exclusive of one another and sometimes overlap in content or method. Also, one will find that many philosophers identify with ideas or thoughts from several schools of philosophy. Lastly, no school or system of philosophic thought has ever totally dominated philosophic inquiry or any era of philosophers.

Another way of familiarizing oneself with pure philosophy, educational philosophy, and/or philosophy of PERS would be to take significant and related concepts and search for an understanding horizontally through each system or school. As an example, one might pursue the question of the relationship of man's body, mind, and spiritual being by examining the position and rationale of each school or system of philosophical thought on the question, thereby studying philosophy by ideas or concepts. Vanderzwaag in his

Toward a Philosophy of Sport has used a variation of this approach by describing the philosophy of sport in terms of pertinent topics and it is recommended reading for anyone in the field of PERS who seriously wishes to broaden and improve his or her abilities in teaching, coaching, or program development.

Still another way to approach the study of philosophy as it relates to sport and physical activity is to view it through the theoretical structure and forms of philosophical inquiry. All disciplines can be examined in this way. Since philosophy is simply the search for wisdom, truth, reality, and goodness in man's existence and conduct, it is necessary for it to have a formal structure for examination and a systematic way to understand its questions and answers. Philosophy has been conventionally divided into branches or domains. There are many subdivisions to this categorization but there seems to be wide consensus that there are four general domains. It is through these theoretical domains that philosophical concerns in PERS can be examined. Figure 4.1 gives a simplified visual presentation of the four branches and the extent of their inquiry. Further, beginning students in PERS studies should realize that this mode of philosophical inquiry is usually adopted in more advanced courses within the subject area. Therefore, the following summary is limited in depth.

The first of these domains, **metaphysics,** is the most basic and general of the branches, examines the form and substance of reality, and is speculative in approach. Many kinds of metaphysical questions are involved in PERS studies: What is the essential nature, meaning, and scope of the concepts of sport, physical education, recreation, leisure, fitness, human movement, play, and the numerous subareas of physical activity and sport (refer to chapter 2)? What is the relationship of man's mind and body and is there a spiritual or divine condition that affects this relationship? What is the role of causality, time and space, evolution, constancy and change, necessity and purpose, in human movement and physical activity?

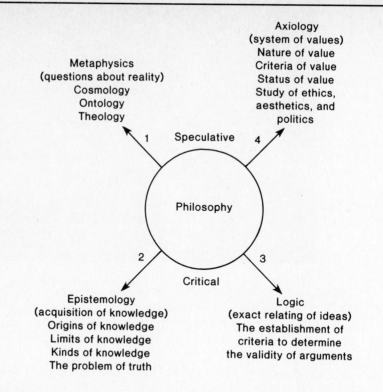

Metaphysics
(questions about reality)
Cosmology
Ontology
Theology

Axiology
(system of values)
Nature of value
Criteria of value
Status of value
Study of ethics,
aesthetics, and
politics

1   Speculative   4

Philosophy

2   3

Critical

Epistemology
(acquisition of knowledge)
Origins of knowledge
Limits of knowledge
Kinds of knowledge
The problem of truth

Logic
(exact relating of ideas)
The establishment of
criteria to determine
the validity of arguments

Figure 4.1

The second theoretical branch of philosophy is **epistemology,** which examines the acquisition of knowledge, its origin, limits, and kinds. Epistemology can be viewed as a critical and analytical outgrowth of metaphysics and is also concerned with the concept of truth. There are different theories of truth which arise from the diverse ways in which the original metaphysical question is developed and answered. For example, the *coherence theory* holds that truth is revealed by the compatibility of a new proposition (idea) to predetermined or existing systems of ideas, while the *pragmatic theory* of truth maintains that a truth is valid if it works and is useful. Does it solve problems? Regardless of these views on truth, the following are samples of epistemic questions: What are the limits, organization, or structure of PERS knowledge? What mechanisms are to be used to obtain that knowledge (chapter 1)?

Logic, the third domain, is the systematic examination of the relationship of one idea to another. It contains the formal principles of argument or reasoning and establishes criteria by which judgements can be made, therefore determining the validity or fallacy of arguments. Sports and physical activity are constantly subject to rational debate, questioning, and development whether stemming from the simplistic "second-guessing" of observers and journalists after a game, from the development of strategies in game situations, from the establishment of systematic instructional methods, or from the prioritizing of budget needs in recreational programming.

The fourth branch of philosophy, **axiology,** examines the nature and sources of values or the significance of ultimate reality. It is concerned with the development of values that are consistent with the beliefs or purpose of the other domains. Therefore, its connection with metaphysics and epistemology is intimate. The impact of this branch of philosophy is so significant and relevant to PERS studies that its three divisions should be briefly considered. *Ethics* is a division which examines the judgement of right and wrong, good and bad, virtue and vice. It is a moral philosophy and is speculative in nature, referring to formulation of goals, norms, and standards of conduct for individuals and groups. This area of philosophical inquiry would be concerned with the value, significance, or purpose of PERS as well as the moral conduct of those involved in physical activity and sport. The abuses of socially established norms of moral conduct within sport and athletics are constantly presented to us in the media—for example, drug abuse by individual performers, flagrant support of violence, or rulebreaking by professional sports organizations. Another subdivision, previously referred to in this chapter, is *aesthetics,* or philosophy of art, which examines the nature and significance of beauty and the arts. It establishes the standards of aesthetic taste and the values of artistic judgement and their criteria within PERS. The role of emotion, contemplation, expression and technique, the form of medium, artistic greatness, and similar areas in physical movement, recreational pursuits, and sport are investigated. The impact of this inquiry on many cultural leisure pursuits, outdoor recreation, and sports which involve subjective evaluation (e.g., gymnastics, figure skating, and diving) are self-evident. The last subcategory is *politics* or *social-political philosophy,* which examines the moral character of social life and political power—its origins, criteria, focus, and limits. The interrelatedness of the Canadian social-political system with sport and recreation is an ongoing process whether on the local, provincial, national, or international level. Public recreation departments, schools, and amateur community sport groups are all affected by the perceived social needs and the political jurisdictions in which they are located. Likewise, national and international sports, or for that matter, recreational or health agencies, are not only involved in the process but in turn can directly effect change upon a society or its governmental policies.

For further understanding of this method of philosophical inquiry, students are referred to R. G. Osterhoudt's *An Introduction to the Philosophy of Physical Education and Sport* or E. W. Gerber and W. J. Morgan's "Sport and The Body: A Philosophical Symposium," as well as the many articles and texts by the Canadian scholar Earle F. Zeigler.

GENERAL PHILOSOPHICAL CONCEPTS IN PERS

This section is presented in order to demonstrate a practical linkage of universal questions in philosophical inquiry to certain aspects of our understanding of the why and how of physical activity and sport. Philosophical positions concerning two prevailing initial questions which are part of PERS studies will be presented.

The first is the nature and relationship of man's body and mind. Most of the theories pertaining to this question fall into two main categories, the dualistic and the monistic. The early **dualistic** theory of the mind and body postulates that there are two separate entities or substances to be related. **Monism** approaches the problem by viewing the body and the mind as a unified substance and as such they are interdependent and one.

The second problem which permeates the discipline of PERS is the question of whether educational programs of physical activity should be based upon the concept of "education of the physical" or "education through the physical," and the implications this choice has on the objectives and goals of PERS. One's answer to this question, as well as the position one takes upon the relationship of mind to body, has a direct bearing upon the content of instructional material, the type and style of instruction, the methodology of instruction, and even on the selection of a career within which one might feel comfortable and constructive. Therefore, as previously stated, through a study of philosophical concepts such as these examples, a professional may develop a philosophical framework for beliefs and values.

Monism/Dualism

The interrelationship of man's body and mind has been a metaphysical question for philosophical inquiry from the age of Greek philosophy to the present. With the significant advancement of knowledge relating to biological sciences and sociopsychological understanding of human behaviour in the last several decades, this philosophical question has gained some degree of clarity. However, it continues to remain scientifically unresolved and one's own beliefs are still the basis of personal justification for supporting a monistic or dualistic explanation of the relationship between body and mind.

Before presenting a brief survey of thought on the body-mind problem, some mention should be made of the place of the spirit or soul of man. Identifying this third component of man (idealism) will help in understanding the interdependence of mind-body-spirit, or, as we might well describe it, the *trilogy of man*. Comprehension and acceptance of this trilogy has been growing during the latter half of the twentieth century because many of the identifiable problems in physical activity and sport arise from the lack of moral conduct, value recognition, and ethical behaviour of participants in sport. These fairly constant difficulties cannot be resolved through scientific study; rather, they may be understood only through a context which recognizes the validity of human faith and a set of values grounded in a spiritual source or societal norms. The following adapted statement may help to establish a meaning for the moral imperative within PERS programs.

> Although there appear to be tangible reasons for human movement [PERS] whose validity can be measured, the reasons that keep an individual active are not always measurable, nor associated with immediate goals, nor predicated upon the demands of biological law. The real reasons may be that indefinable human quest for *spiritual satisfaction* [emphasis added], for soul enrichment, and [or] for religious peace. . . .These movements [activities] defy logic, rational explanation or empirical justification.[6]

The principal determinant of physical activity and/or sport for the idealist is not the activity itself but rather the spiritual motive or the ultimate goal of such activity.

Idealism has given to PERS a pervading concern for the whole man and encourages the teaching of moral and spiritual, as well as biophysical, values of PERS. It is a monistic view based upon the trilogy of man and a faith in the eternal which presupposes logic and reasoning.

We now return to the original question which is the mind-body relationship. There seems to be agreement today that both the Platonic view (that mind and body are two substances totally distinct and independent) and the Cartesian theory (that the mind possesses supremacy over the physical powers) have limited application in PERS studies. However, it should be noted that the extension of the Cartesian dualistic theory formed the foundation of the early Turner development organized by Friedrich Jahn. It was based upon systematic movement and exercises and was introduced into the German school system by Adolf Speisz in the nineteenth century. Similarly, during this period of time, Per Henrik Ling introduced different forms of movement patterns based upon this dichotomy of body and mind into the Swedish school system.

Contemporary dualistic thought on this question has moved for the most part from a strict separation of mind and body to the acceptance of the interaction or interdependence of the two substances. However, the question is still one of dominance or primacy of the initial act or control of the task. Much of today's research in psychology concerning motor skills learning, training and practice procedures, and feedback systems indicates a possible dominance of a mental process at certain stages of the learning of physical movements. The practicing teacher/coach can accept the applicability of the following dualist position, especially during beginning or new learning situations. An adaptation of the twentieth century American philosopher Paul Weiss states:

> Of specific interest to present discussion is Weiss' extensive and active support of a hierarchical, dualistic conception of man. He strongly and repeatedly emphasized the power of mind over body throughout his analysis of the athlete and his body. Weiss (Sport: A Philosophical Inquiry, p. 41–46) declared that an athlete, on his journey toward attainment of excellence in sport, engages in a rigorous *training* program designed "to correct" or "to alter the body" by means of "adjusting the way in which the

body functions," until it proceeds in accord with the mind's expectation
. . . the mind uses, alters, directs, controls, restrains, restructures, disciplines and conquers the body.[7]

As strong as this statement may be, a practitioner in PERS realizes that to some degree this is the basis for physical skills and fitness learning if one is to follow a systematic and progressive task-oriented method of instruction. In accordance with such understanding, the bioscience and psychology of skills acquisition are intensely pursued by teachers and instructors alike.

On the other side of the dominance theory of dualism—that is, one in which the body leads or precedes a mental process—could not many examples be presented by performing athletes who use their body senses to create intuitive or unique movement of action or self-expression? If we look to the sense of touch and the reaction of a basketball player or a defensive lineman in football, automatically spinning from physical pressure, is this movement not instinctive and spontaneous? Is this not when the reflex act within our nervous systems takes hold, and therefore removes the necessity of constructive and thoughtful response which is so necessary in other kinds of physical learning situations? Does this process not then allow the mental process to focus upon new and evolving dynamics of play-action? The authors maintain that during actual performance of a well-tuned athlete there is a constant intuitive, creative, and instantaneous action being developed which has little relationship to immediate intellectual thought, thus (possibly) establishing the dominance of body over mind. Dualism, as expressed above, certainly moves closer to the monistic contention of denying any substantive difference between body and mind to a position of recognition that there is an undeniable interrelationship, but still allows for a difference in degree, emphasis, and initiation of action. It also allows the uniqueness of the "physical" to remain as a priority in PERS programming if so desired.

The **contemporary monistic** view of the "lived-body" or "body-subject" is expressed through the pragmatic philosophy of William James, John Dewey, and Merleau-Ponty among others, in which the total education of an individual is of paramount importance. In this view, any subject area (including PERS) sublimates itself to the final enrichment of life, to the "total person." Indeed, physical activity and sports can make a significant contribution to this end, but the mind is not one kind of substance and the body another. "Life is a process . . . and in any process, both mental and physical are present . . . there are no activities or skills in which the mind is inactive."[8] There is no doubt that in recent thinking on the body, the prevailing tendency is to see it not as a machine, not as an object or a vehicle to express the intellect (as some classical dualists see it), but rather as a multifaceted unitary being, capable of immense forms of self-expression and imagination.

The student interested in PERS studies and its related activities and professions must inevitably confront the mind-body—or mind-body-spirit—question, and the results of such inquiry will have practical applications. Such results will also bear upon one's view of the larger question of the nature of humankind.

Education of The Physical/Education through the Physical

Education *of* the physical has been the basis of PERS program development of the realist/essentialist school of educational instruction since the mid-nineteenth century. Although the objectives have, to a great degree, evolved and expanded since those early times, the focus is still upon the importance of total physical fitness of the body as a significant goal in any physical education, physical recreation, or sport program.

Early proponents of this approach stressed the development of health, strength, carriage, endurance, and flexibility and so physical education and physical recreation programs for the most part adopted the European systems of gymnastics and systems of exercise or calisthenics. Also during this period of time society saw sport, physical education, and even recreation as primary sources of training to enable their young to survive and cope with their new environment. Such training was also used in preparing youth for military purposes. This was the argument that many realists/essentialists used when trying to implement physical education or training as a necessary part of the school curriculum. They thought that the school should assume the responsibility of educating the physical body since the school was an arm of society—a society which accepted the idea that physical vigour and fitness were necessary components for individual productivity.

Today, as indicated previously, realists/essentialists have gone well beyond this justification which in the historical perspective seemed singular and lacking in depth of purpose. Now, with the explosion of scientific knowledge in the twentieth century concerning the human body and its movement and skill patterns, fitness is defined within two categories. The first, and possibly the more important, is that of cardiovascular/respiratory efficiency, muscular endurance, and strength; the second is the motor performance parameters of coordination, agility, power, balance, reaction time, and speed. With the inclusion of this latter category, one can easily comprehend the expansion of program objectives to include motor skills acquisition in sports and games. This strengthens the justification of the present day realist/essentialist program in PERS studies and the relevancy of education *of* the physical. Motor skill development is regarded not only as a means to an end in physical fitness but also as an end in itself. If an individual is to participate in PERS programs, then he or she must possess at least minimal skills if full value from such participation is to be realized. In addition, in order to understand skills and fitness development, both the student/participant and the instructor must have knowledge of the biophysical functions of the body, as well as a thorough understanding of the activity/sport itself. It is only after these primary objectives have been met that the realist/essentialist refers to the socializing qualities of physical activity and sport.

The discipline and professions of PERS should focus upon a more complete physical fitness which now includes motor skills acquisition, knowledge of the biophysical aspects of the human body, and activity and sport knowledge. Activities which require physical vigour should be included. The realist/essentialist stresses that all programs in PERS must be active and not passive since only active programs contribute to total physical fitness. Many recreational activities such as fishing, camping, certain dance forms, and other leisure activities should be excluded in structured school-centred programs (physical education). The realist/essentialist does not say that leisure activities are unimportant, but does hold that such programs could be best administered by designated recreational institutions at the community level.

As a discipline, the followers of the realist/essentialist school would like PERS studies to be identified as the discipline of the body. To achieve this status, they strongly recommend that education *of* the physical should be the main thrust in such studies. All forms of general education may develop the mind and the spirit of man, but only PERS education can develop one's body.

The foundation of the pragmatic/progressive belief in education *through* the physical had its early influence upon philosophical thought and general education in the latter part of the nineteenth century. This was followed by a broad acceptance in PERS educational curricula by the beginning of the twentieth century. It has been maintained by some educational historians that these philosophical eductional principles had greater application to and meaning for the educational process at that time than did the existing realist/essentialist educational tenets. This seems most evident in the field of PERS where rather narrow purposes for physical training (education) existed. This new concept for physical activity was that ". . . (general) education aims and objectives could be realized *through* [emphasis added] a properly conducted physical education program . . ."[9] or *through* the medium of motor activity.

It should be noted that ". . . physical education was struggling for a place in the school curriculum. . . .The identification of an additional role that physical education might play in the schools made this struggle much easier . . ."[10] by broadening program purposes.

In this brief summary of the implications of education *through* the physical upon PERS programming, only a cursory description of pragmatist/progressivist concepts can be given. Pragmatists/progressivists believe that a primary aim of education ". . . is to teach the child to live the life of the group and to acquire the disposition, the skill, and the knowledge to contribute to its welfare."[11] Thus, PERS programs would hold a central place within an instructional context because physical activity and sport provide an almost ideal sort of experience under pragmatic criteria. PERS provides

> . . . (1) an experience for achieving development and adjustment according to social standards; (2) an experience promoting social efficiency; (3) an opportunity for the development of social effectiveness and personal well-being; (4) a medium for developing the individual's potentialities in all phases of life; (5) a way of total education of being—intellectually, emotionally and developmentally.[12]

Because of the social nature of physical activity, sport, and recreation, pragmatists/progressivists see great potential in education *through* the physical.

PERS programs should contain a wide variety of physical activities because such programs provide many experiences. Also, ". . . variety itself represents an expansion of experiences."[13] It is through these experiences that participants would find workable solutions by methods of problem solving. The instructor/teacher is regarded as a facilitator who helps participants to identify problems and apply scientific methods for solving them.

A pragmatist/progressivist curriculum would emphasize group activities, involvement, and cooperation based on the interest, desire, and needs of the participants. The activities provided would not be limited to only those physical in nature. Recreational and leisure activities would be included, as long as interest is shown in them by the majority and the activities have some social value. They stress the idea of "total fitness," unlike the realists, *and* "total physical fitness," so as to create an environment where physical activity facilitates desirable mental and moral growth. It then can be understood that all forms of PERS activity contribute to the education of the whole person. Therefore, such activity is a means to an end—the end being the total individual being. Thomas Wood stated, "The great thought in physical education [PERS] is not the education of the physical nature, but the relation of physical training to complete education, and then the effort to make the physical to contribute its full share to the life of the individual, in environment, training and culture."[14]

In conclusion, it is recommended to all students in PERS studies who wish to go beyond this brief survey of some of the principles and concepts of the very different basic beliefs and approaches that are held by proponents of education of the physical and proponents of education through the physical to realize the following:

> We have to this point, briefly surveyed initial efforts to justify physical education. These ideas have persisted and are reflected in contemporary analyses of physical education. Is it now possible for you to justify physical education on the basis of these concepts? Will these arguments satisfy the criticisms you have heard leveled against physical education today? It is very important that you begin to ask yourself these questions: you may be assured that eventually you will be obliged to address this problem. Your defense will be based primarily on what physical education is to you or to your colleagues, and should be as strong and as well thought out as possible.[15]

SUMMARY

It is the intention of this chapter to establish within the student pursuing physical education, recreation, and sport studies the need for the development of a personalized philosophy of life and education which extends to physical activity and sport. Only from this can consistency in values, leadership, decision making, and programming evolve. A theoretical framework is needed for such philosophical inquiry so that one's ultimate direction is justifiable and understandable not only to the individual but to others. As indicated, this framework can be approached in a variety of ways: by the theoretical forms of philosophical inquiry, by studying the schools or systems of philosophic thought, by interrelating the ideas of individual philosophers, or by studying philosophical concepts in a comparative method.

The final section of this chapter takes this last approach and briefly discusses two philosophical questions: monism/dualism and education of the physical versus education through the physical.

NOTES

1. John E. Nixon and Ann E. Jewett, *An Introduction to Physical Education* (Philadelphia: Saunders College, 1980), 68.

2. Earle F. Zeigler, *Personalizing Physical Education and Sport Philosophy* (Champaign, Il: Stipes Publishing Co., 1975), 52.

3. Robert G. Osterhoudt, *An Introduction to the Philosophy of Physical Education and Sport* (Champaign, Il: Stipes Publishing Co., 1978), 21.

4. Zeigler, *Personalizing Physical Education and Sport Philosophy,* 52.

5. Benjamin Lowe, *The Beauty of Sport: A Cross-Disciplinary Inquiry* (Englewood Cliffs, NJ: Prentice-Hall, 1977), preface, xiv.

6. John Cheffers and Tom Evaul, *Introduction to Physical Education: Concepts of Human Movement* (Englewood Cliffs, NJ: Prentice-Hall, 1978), 22–23.

7. Klaus V. Meir, "Embodiment, Sport and Meaning," in *Sport and the Body,* ed. Gerber and Morgan (Philadelphia: Lea and Febiger, 1979), 196.

8. Robert L. Brackenbury, "Physical Education and Intellectual Emphasis?" *Quest* I (December 1963): 3–6.

9. Robert N. Singer et al., *Physical Education: Foundations* (New York: Holt, Rinehart and Winston, 1976), 5.

10. Singer et al., *Physical Education: Foundations,* 5.

11. James A. Baley and David A. Field, *Physical Education and the Physical Educator* (Boston: Allyn and Bacon, 1977), 237.

12. William A. Harper, Donna Mae Miller et al., *The Philosophic Process in Physical Education* (Philadelphia: Lea and Febiger, 1977), 189.

13. Harper, Miller et al., *The Philosophic Process in Physical Education,* 186.

14. Thomas D. Wood, "The New Physical Education," in *The Making of American Physical Education,* ed. A. Weston (New York: Appleton-Century-Croft, 1962), 154.

15. Singer et al., *Physical Education: Foundations,* 8–9.

CHAPTER 5

Canada's Sport Heritage

Barbara Schrodt

Sport is a central feature of Canadian life, and the accomplishments of Canadians in the sports world have long been a source of pride and honour in this country. The development of sports structures within Canada has also been of significance; these institutions have provided the framework within which Canadians have been able to compete, both internationally and at home.

AN OVERVIEW

This chapter contains information about Canadians who excelled in their sport and about the rise of modern organized sport in Canada. This is not a **history** of sport in Canada; that would be more interpretive, and more concerned with situating sport within the societal context of the times. Rather, the material presented here focusses on sport **chronology** (events entered according to dates) and sport **heritage** (selections from great moments in Canadian sport). This information provides some of the basic facts essential for an understanding of the development of sport in Canada. Students who want a deeper understanding of the societal factors that have influenced the rise of modern sport in Canada are directed to the references at the end of this chapter.

The first section, "Outstanding Achievements by Canadians in Sport," contains short accounts of twenty-nine individuals or teams whose accomplishments are particularly noteworthy. This is not a complete list, and other authors might have made a slightly different selection; however, the reader is presented with a broad range of sports, time periods, and kinds of contributions.

The second section is a listing of highlights in Canadian sport, including significant developments such as the formation of national organizations, the establishment of important institutions and leagues, and the accomplishments of several other Canadians (supplementing the first section). Most of the material in this section is taken from *Sport Canadiana* (Schrodt, Redmond, and Baka, 1980).

Appendix A contains the names of those Canadians who have won gold, silver, or bronze medals at the Olympic Games, and gold medals at the Commonwealth, Pan American, and World University games. In addition to being a useful reference, these lists provide some insights into the trends that have developed in our international sports achievements such as time periods, women in sport, summer and winter sports, and team and individual sports.

Finally, consideration should be given to the recommendation of T. H. B. Symons, in *To Know Ourselves: The Report on the Commission on Canadian Studies* (1975):

> The Commission believes strongly that it is high time that Canadian Educators, at all levels, recognize the importance of sports and physical culture in Canadian life. . . .This country has a rich and distinctive heritage in sports and physical culture. But Canadians seem smitten with cultural amnesia when it comes to this important aspect of our history and national life. . . .More extensive research and teaching about physical culture and sport should help Canadians to become more aware of the role of sport and of physical fitness in their lives, and of the contributions made by Canadians in this area.

OUTSTANDING ACHIEVEMENTS BY CANADIANS IN SPORT

The Nineteenth Century

George Beers: The Father of Modern Lacrosse (1843–1900)

W. George Beers was, more than any other man, responsible for organizing and popularizing the game of lacrosse. He was born in Montreal, where he became a successful dentist. He started playing lacrosse at the age of six. In 1860, when he was seventeen, he played goalkeeper in an exhibition match for the visiting Prince of Wales, and the experience inspired him to work actively in the promotion of the game. That same year he published, in pamphlet form, the first basic rules of lacrosse. His greatest achievements came in 1867, when he organized the founding convention of the National Lacrosse Association, Canada's first national sports governing organization. The first Dominion title contest was held that year. Also, due to Beers' hard work, the number of lacrosse clubs in Canada in 1867 grew from six in June to eighty in November. Then, in 1869, he published an important and influential book, *Lacrosse: The National Game of Canada*.

The game was also introduced into Britain, thanks to Beers' hard work. In 1876, he organized a team to tour Britain, with matches played in England, Ireland, and Scotland. Then, in 1883, Beers took the Montreal Lacrosse Club and the Caughnawaga Indian team to Britain for a tour that was widely popular.

An ardent nationalist, Beers campaigned to have lacrosse declared Canada's "national game." He believed that it would aid in creating unity in this new country, and that it was the ideal game for development of those qualities required of young men carving a modern society out of the wilderness. Although he did not succeed in his campaign to have the Canadian Parliament declare lacrosse Canada's national game, his active promotion of the idea gradually became accepted as fact, and the belief grew that such legislation had been passed.

The Caughnawaga Indian Lacrosse Team: First Dominion Champions (1867)

The Caughnawaga Indian village, located just outside of Montreal, was home to one of the most enthusiastic Indian lacrosse teams in the history of the game. It was reportedly the devotion of these players that inspired the formation of the Montreal Lacrosse Club, the modern game's first club, in 1856.

In 1867, the Caughnawaga team won the first Dominion championship, sponsored by the new National Lacrosse Association. Always professionals, Indian teams were soon barred from the emerging amateur championships, and in 1880, the Caughnawaga team won the first Indian World Lacrosse championship. When George Beers decided, in 1883, to take both an Indian and a white team to Britain for his second tour, he selected the Caughnawaga team. Sixty exhibition matches were played on this tour, including one before Queen Victoria.

Louis Cyr: The World's Strongest Man (1863–1912)

In the 1800s, before weightlifting became an organized sport, professional strongmen toured in circuses or troupes, presenting public demonstrations and competing in challenge matches. The greatest of these early weightlifters was Louis Cyr, a Montrealer whose legendary feats had begun at the age of seventeen when he pulled a loaded farm wagon out of the mud by hoisting it onto his back. He gained a reputation for strength while serving as a Montreal policeman, and when he left that job to become a full-time strongman, he was billed as "The Strongest Man in the World." With $5000 offered to all comers as a challenge purse, he defeated everyone who challenged him, including some of the strongest men in the world.

A popular sports hero, Cyr won acclaim wherever he went, not only for his amazing feats of strength, but also for his showmanship and his friendly manner. One of the highlights of his professional life was a tour to England in 1889 where, before the Prince of Wales in a London theatre, he performed some of his most remarkable lifts: a 250 kg (551 lb) weight with one finger; 1860 kg (4100 lb) on a platform stretched across his back; and 124 kg (273.25 lb) with one hand, to his shoulder and then above his head.

He has remained, to this day, the strongest man in history, for none of his feats have been met or bettered by any other weightlifters with the techniques that Cyr used in his day. Some of his more outstanding accomplishments follow: (1) a back lift of 1967 kg (4337 lb), believed to be the heaviest weight ever lifted by a man; the load consisted of a platform, on which were standing eighteen fat men; (2) weights lifted a few inches off the ground: 860 kg (1897 lb) with two hands, 448 kg (987 lb) with one hand, and 242 kg (533 lb) with one finger; and (3) the human merry-go-round: with two men holding onto his long-flowing hair, he would spin around so that they were lifted up by the centrifugal force, out sideways and almost horizontal, without any aid from Cyr.

Many weightlifters have attempted to duplicate Cyr's feats, and while the amount of weight now lifted by competitors does exceed Cyr's amounts in total, none has been lifted in the style "à la Louis Cyr."

Edward "Ned" Hanlan: "The Boy in Blue" (1855–1908)

Ned Hanlan, of Toronto, was the outstanding single-sculls rower of the nineteenth century and Canada's first national sporting hero. He learned to row off Toronto Island, in a makeshift shell fashioned from a two-inch plank sharpened at both ends, to which was added a seat and outriggers.

Hanlan established himself as the best sculler in Ontario, in a series of wins from 1873 to 1876. He emerged on the international rowing scene in Philadelphia in 1876, when he defeated some of the best scullers in North America in the single-sculls race. In 1877, he won the Canadian championship in Toronto Bay, and the American championship the following year on the Allegheny River. By this time, he was ready to take on the world; with the support of the Hanlan Club, a group of Toronto sportsmen who had been his backers since 1876, he travelled to England in 1879 to challenge for the English title. On the river Tyne, before tens of thousands of amazed spectators, he defeated Elliot of England by a remarkable eleven lengths. The following year, he defended his title against Trickett of Australia, the self-styled world professional champion. Thousands lined the banks of the river Thames for a match on which half a million dollars was wagered. In this race, Hanlan demonstrated the gamesmanship for which he became famous: stopping to talk to friends in the crowd, pretending to collapse from some sort of seizure, leaning back in his shell to enjoy the scenery—always able to regain the lead any time he wanted. He won the 4.25-mile race by three lengths over a frustrated and exhausted opponent, and observers felt that he could have won it by a mile.

This was to be Hanlan's flamboyant and crowd-pleasing style during the next four years, during which he successfully defended his world title six times. Known as the "Boy in Blue" because of the distinctive dark blue singlet and shorts in which he always raced, he became the master of his sport by developing a successful technique that his opponents were not able or willing to emulate. He made maximum use of the new sliding seat, with a slide of eighteen inches compared to the usual twelve; he also incorporated the extended rowlock into his technique and equipment. But he was best known for his rowing style, with a long, slow stroke and a quick, clean "catch."

Hanlan finally lost his world title to an Australian, Beach, in 1884. He continued to row into the 1890s, and in his lifetime, won more than three hundred races. During his career as a rower, he was the best-known Canadian in the world. He served Toronto as an alderman, and in 1926, a twenty-foot statue was raised in his memory on the grounds of the Canadian National Exhibition—the only statue in the world ever erected to a sculler. It is engraved with this tribute: "Edward Hanlan, the most renowned oarsman of any age whose victorious career has no parallel in the annals of sport."

The Men of Zorra: Tug-of-War Champions (1888–1893)

In a time when the tug-of-war was one of the most popular events at local fairs and field meets, a group of sturdy farmers from Zorra Township (near Woodstock, Ontario) brought fame to their proud community and to Canada. The "Men of Zorra", Billy Munro, Ira Hummason, Sandy Clark, Bob McLeod, Bob McIntosh, and their captain, Ed Sutherland, started pulling together in 1880, and their reputation spread throughout Ontario, as they successively defeated all opponents.

In 1888, they entered the North American championship in Buffalo, New York, and before ten thousand spectators, defeated all comers. A loss to a Chicago team a few months later resulted in a return match; in this, the Canadians demonstrated their superiority with a thirty-minute pull that outlasted the Americans. Then, in spite of perceived handicaps—being lighter and older than other teams—the Men of Zorra entered the world championship at the 1893 Chicago World's Fair. In the words of a newspaper dispatch filed from Chicago that day:

> Five brawny sons of Zorra, neither young nor handsome, but possessing the strength of Hectors, listlessly strolled into the Chicago Baseball Grounds this afternoon and in the presence of thousands of people, wrested the tug-of-war championship of the world from the famed Humboldts of this city. (Roxborough 1957, 36)

Thus did Zorra gain a prominent spot in Canadian sport history.

James Naismith: The Inventor of Basketball (1861–1939)

James Naismith, the man who gave the world the game of basketball, was born in Almonte, near Ottawa. He attended McGill University, and was an outstanding athlete—especially at lacrosse. While still a student there, he served as the director of physical education, and it was that experience that inspired him to train as a leader for the Young Men's Christian Association. While studying for this career at the YMCA Training College in Springfield, Massachusetts, he was given an assignment: develop an indoor game that will fill the gap between football and baseball seasons.

Naismith determined that his game would emphasize skill and discourage rough play. As an indoor game, only the hands could be used to advance the ball. To avoid tackling, the ball could only be passed (the dribble came later). To ensure that the game could be mastered quickly, a large, light

ball was used (initially, a soccer ball). And finally, the goal would be horizontal and above everyone's head, again to avoid rough play and blocking. At first, any number could play, but Naismith favoured nine players per side, the number for his favourite team sport, lacrosse. The first set of goals, intended to be boxes, turned out to be peach baskets, and it was from these that the name of basketball was derived. They were simply nailed to the walls of the gymnasium, below the balconies. As the game grew in popularity, this became a problem because enthusiastic fans would just reach down from the balcony to block shots on goal—hence, the later creation of the backboard.

The first game of basketball was played in December 1891 and was introduced into Canada the following year. It quickly gained popularity amongst American university and college students, and was one of the first team games played by girls and women in Canada, the United States, and Britain.

In its early years, with unlimited numbers of players, conditions were too chaotic; thus, by 1895, the number on a team was reduced to five. The iron hoop and cord "basket" replaced the peach basket by 1893. (Until then, it was necessary to mount a ladder and retrieve the ball every time a basket was scored!) In 1894, a special ball for the game replaced the soccer ball of the original rules.

Naismith eventually earned a medical degree and became the first physical education director at the University of Kansas. At the 1936 Olympic Games in Berlin, where men's basketball was in the program for the first time, Naismith was given a special, and well-deserved, tribute for his popular contribution to the world of sport.

Louis Rubenstein: The World's First Figure Skating Champion (1861–1931)

One of the finest all-round athletes of the late 1800s, Louis Rubenstein of Montreal was the first in a long and honourable line of champion figure skaters from Canada. Inspired by Jackson Haines, the ballet master who had popularized the art of figure skating, Rubenstein went to Europe to study with Haines in the late 1870s.

The earliest report of Rubenstein in a skating competition came in 1879, and by 1883, he was recognized as the champion of Canada. He retained that title until 1889, and during that time was twice the United States amateur champion. In 1890, the first unofficial world championships were held in St. Petersburg, Russia. Rubenstein represented Canada there, against outstanding skaters from Germany, Finland, Sweden, and Russia. In a competition consisting of nine compulsory and five optional figures, plus a ten-minute freestyle exhibition, Rubenstein displayed complete mastery of his sport; his figures were executed with grace and elegance, and he could retrace patterns three and four times without blurring the original outline. The judges were astounded by his performance, and in spite of their hostility toward foreigners, awarded him the title.

Rubenstein participated in other sports, particularly bowling and cycling. He was also active as an administrator and judge, and an indication of the breadth of his involvement can be seen from the organizations for which he served as president: Montreal Amateur Athletic Association, International Skating Union, Canadian Amateur Speed Skating Association, Canadian Wheelman's Association, Canadian Bowling League, St. Andrew's Curling and Bowling Association, Young Men's Hebrew Association, and the Montreal branch of the Royal Life-Saving Society. He also served the city of Montreal as an alderman. As Wise and Fisher (1974, 214) have noted: "No city in the world has contributed more to sport than Montreal and no Montrealer has given more to sport that Louis Rubenstein."

The Saint John Four: World Champions (1867)

In 1867, at the World's Fair in Paris, one of the principal features was a rowing regatta for the best four-oared rowing crews in the world. This included a foursome from Saint John, New Brunswick, who had been defeating all opponents from Canada and the United States since the early 1850s. These four men—a lighthouse keeper and three fishermen—were Robert Fulton, Samuel Hutton, George Price, and Elijah Ross. Like Ned Hanlan, who would dominate single sculls a few years later, the Saint John Four had developed a unique style. In their oddly constructed heavy boats, they rowed almost entirely with the arms, and without a coxswain—a technique unheard of up to that time. Ridiculed on all counts, they soon demonstrated their skill and strength, winning the races for both heavy inrigged boats and outrigged shells.

Having travelled to sinful Paris under the watchful eye of the sheriff of Saint John (who was there to protect the $6000 contribution of the Province of New Brunswick and the people of Saint John), they returned to a wildly enthusiastic hometown, a brass band, seven thousand cheering citizens, and a cash prize of $500 each.

Thereafter known as the Paris Crew, the foursome stayed together for several years, losing only to the English Tyneside crew in 1870. Coming only one month after Confederation, their Paris victory made many Europeans aware of Canada for the first time. The victory also gave strong support to the emerging feelings of nationalism in this young and proud country.

The Early Twentieth Century to World War I

Tommy Burns: World Champion Heavyweight Boxer (1881–1955)

Born Noah Brusso in Hanover, Ontario, Tommy Burns became the world heavyweight boxing champion in 1906 and held the title until late in 1908. A tenacious fighter and an extraordinarily strong puncher, Burns, at 5′7″, was the shortest man to hold that title. He defended his world crown ten times in less than three years, and in his career, lost only four of sixty fights.

Originally fighting as a welterweight, Burns was chosen by the new heavyweight titleholder, Marvin Hart, for a title bout in February 1906. Burns defeated Hart in a fight that lasted the full twenty rounds. Then, determined to prove that he deserved the title, Burns set off on a European tour to defend his crown against all challengers. He moved on to Australia, where he was followed by the American, Jack Johnson. In the title match between the two fighters, Burns was outreached and outweighed by Johnson, at 6′ and 203 lb. Instead of moving around the ring and boxing carefully, Burns foolishly chose to bear in on Johnson, and was dealt a terrible punishment from start to end. The fight was finally stopped by the police in the fourteenth round, and Johnson was declared the new heavyweight champion of the world. Although Burns lost his title and was criticized by the press, he did receive $30,000 for fighting Johnson, in what was the beginning of "big money" for boxers.

Burns retired from boxing for two years, but returned to fight until 1920, when he was knocked out for the first—and last—time. His achievements have been downplayed, chiefly because of the bias of the American public against Jack Johnson, a black. However, Johnson is now considered to be one of the greatest heavyweight boxers of all time, and Burns should therefore be recognized for the fine and courageous fighter that he was.

Walter Knox: World Professional Track and Field Champion (1878–1951)

A barnstorming, gambling athlete, Walter Knox was one of the most successful and versatile performers in Canadian sport—and possibly the greatest track and field athlete this country has ever seen. Born in Listowel, he grew up in Orillia, Ontario, a premier sporting town. He competed for thirty-eight years, from 1896 to 1933, and during this time earned 359 firsts, 90 seconds, and 52 thirds in formal competition.

In one afternoon in 1907, Knox won five Canadian titles: the 100-yard dash, the long jump, the pole vault, the shot put, and the hammer throw. At another meet, he defeated three Canadian amateur world class athletes in their specialities while each was at the peak of his athletic career—in the pole vault, long jump, and 200m sprint. In 1909, Knox equalled the world record of 9.6 seconds in the 100-yard sprint. Clearly, he could have excelled in the pentathlon and decathlon events of the Olympic Games if he had elected to retain his amateur status.

In 1913, Knox won the all-round professional championship of America. Then, in August 1914, he travelled to Manchester, England, to compete in a contest for the all-round professional champion of the world. In an eight-event match against the British champion, Knox won six events and the title.

Although he continued to compete for many years, this ceased to be his full-time occupation. He coached the Canadian Olympic track and field team in 1912 and 1920, and was to have coached Britain's team for the cancelled 1916 Games. He also coached Ethel Catherwood, the Canadian winner of the 1928 Olympic Games high jump.

Tom Longboat: The World's Best Distance Runner (1887–1949)

An Onondaga Indian from the Six Nations Reserve near Brantford, Ontario, Tom Longboat was the greatest marathoner in the world, at a time when long-distance running was an immensely popular spectator sport. He first came to the attention of the racing world in 1906, when he won the Hamilton Around-the-Bay Race by a full three minutes. He then entered the 15-mile Toronto Ward Marathon, and won that by 500 yards.

It was now time for the major test, the famous Boston Marathon. There, in April 1907, in only his third outdoor race, he won the event, leading the second-place runner by half a mile. To the amazement of all, Longboat's time was 2 hours, 24 minutes, and 20.4 seconds, breaking the previous record by 5.5 minutes.

In spite of controversy surrounding his amateur status, he ran for Canada in the 1908 Olympic Games marathon. Expected to win, he took an early and punishing lead, only to stop at the nineteenth mile. The manager of the Canadian team claimed that Longboat had taken stimulants, while Longboat's personal manager blamed it on the heat; with the passage of time, it is now suspected that he was inadequately trained, and simply ran a tactically poor race.

After his Olympic loss, Longboat raced successfully as an amateur, but turned professional later in 1908. He won a race against Pietri of Italy, and in January 1909 was matched against Alfie Shrubb, the British professional, in the start of one of the most famous rivalries in sport history. In the "race of the century," before twelve thousand spectators at Madison Square Garden, Shrubb led by a large margin at the fifteenth mile. But Longboat reduced the margin at a steady pace until the twenty-fourth mile, when he spurted past Shrubb; the Briton then collapsed and Longboat coasted across the finish line. Their rivalry continued for many years, evenly matched in wins.

At the peak of his running career, Longboat was generally regarded as the world's best distance runner, and in 1912, he set a professional record of 1:18:10 for 15 miles—7 minutes faster than his previous amateur record. He held professional records for 20 miles, and once won three indoor marathons in less than two months—a feat unmatched by any other runner. As an amateur, he had held two national track records, set several unofficial world bests on the road, and lost only three races.

His reputation suffered from charges of laziness and drunkenness, the usual racially slanted reasons given for his losses. But he was probably not an alcoholic, as had been claimed, and was not always fairly treated by his managers and handlers. He served in World War I as a dispatch runner in the trenches of France, and raced in track meets organized for the military troops overseas. After the war, he worked in Toronto until 1945, when he retired to the Six Nations Reserve.

George Lyon: The Grand Old Man of Canadian Golf (1858–1938)

An accomplished athlete, George Lyon of Toronto had been outstanding in many sports as a young man: pole vault (a Canadian record), football, soccer, baseball, curling, lawn bowling, and cricket. Then, in 1896, at the age of thirty-eight, and on a dare from a friend, he took a swing at a golf ball and a new sports career was opened to him.

Within two years, this natural athlete was Canadian amateur golf champion, a title he held until 1914. After World War I, at age sixty, he turned to the Canadian senior amateur championship, and in fifteen tournaments, he won that title ten times and placed second four times. From the age of seventy to seventy-eight, he shot his age over eighteen holes at least once every year.

Lyon's greatest single achievement took place in the Olympic Games at St. Louis in 1904, the only time that golf has been part of that program. The press ridiculed his driving form—characterized by a seemingly haphazard and ruthless wallop that was a relic of his cricket days. Playing in that competition at the age of forty-six, he was considered nothing more than a middle-aged upstart, and when he reached the finals, he was definitely the underdog. But with a steady game and very long drives, he took the championship round by three strokes. The length of his drives was his strongest point, and in one of the rounds for that tournament, he drove the ball 299 metres (327 yards).

R. Tait McKenzie: Educator, Sculptor, Surgeon, Author (1867–1938)

A native of Almonte, Ontario, and a graduate of McGill University, Tait McKenzie is one of the most honoured figures in physical education in Canada and the United States, and is commemorated by the professional physical education organizations of both countries. He combined his training in medicine and his interest in physical activity to develop innovations in physical therapy, and to pioneer in the field of physical education in universities. His book *Exercise in Education and Medicine* (1909) was a landmark of the time, and he devised techniques for the rehabilitation of disabled soldiers during

World War I. McKenzie began his career in physical education as the director of physical education at McGill University, and later became the first director of physical education at the University of Pennsylvania.

McKenzie was renowned for his accomplishments as a sculptor. Described as the greatest sculptor of athletes since the ancient Greeks, he produced over two hundred major and minor works: statues and statuettes, medals and medallions, masks, plaques, monuments, and memorials. Some of his better-known pieces are *The Joy of Effort, The Four Masks,* the *Olympic Shield* (for which he won the bronze medal in art at the 1936 Olympic Games), *Brothers of the Wind, The Competitor, The Sprinter, The Ice Bird,* and *The Onslaught.* Later in his life, he restored the Mill of Kintail, outside of Almonte, and continued to work on his sculpting there. The Mill has been designated a heritage site, and is now a museum containing more than seventy of his works.

Twice president of the American Physical Education Association, McKenzie was also active in the Boy Scout movement, and in the development of the Philadelphia playground system.

Fred "Cyclone" Taylor: Ice Hockey's First Great Star (1883–1979)

The outstanding player of hockey's formative years, "Cyclone" Taylor was born in Tara, Ontario. He played as an amateur in Listowel, Ontario, and Portage la Prairie, Manitoba.

Taylor was a member of hockey's first professional team, the Portage Lakes, from Houghton, Michigan (1906). He played for Ottawa (1908–09), Renfrew Millionaires (1910–11), and Vancouver Millionaires (1912–21). While with the Renfrew team, he received a salary of $2800 for the season, a very large amount for that time. In his professional career, he won five scoring titles, and scored 194 goals in 186 league games. He was a member of two Stanley Cup teams (1908 and 1915).

Swift and agile, Taylor was a star wherever he played, and always attracted huge crowds and commanded high salaries. One of his favourite tricks was to score while skating backwards toward the goal. He received his nickname from Governor-General Earl Grey in Ottawa in 1907. Taylor also played lacrosse, as did many hockey players of that era, and was a member of the Ottawa team that won the Mann Cup in 1908.

The Golden Age of Canadian Sport

The *Bluenose*: Canada's Most Famous Ship (1921–1946)

One of the finest fishing schooners ever built, the *Bluenose* was launched in Lunenburg, Nova Scotia, in 1921. A "saltbanker," she was designed to both fish the Grands Banks off Nova Scotia and compete in the schooner races held amongst the ships of the North Atlantic fishing fleets. She was 44 metres long and carried 10,000 square feet of sail on two masts.

The highly competitive contests between the fishing boats of the Canadian Atlantic and New England regions had a long tradition, and in 1920 this custom was formalized with the establishment of the prestigious race for the International Fisherman's Trophy; in its first year, the trophy was won by an American schooner. The skippers of these fishing boats had long been irritated by the attention and money spent on the nonworking sloops and schooners of yacht races such as the America's Cup, and schooners racing for the Fisherman's Trophy were required to work at least one season on the Grand Banks. Thus, Angus Walters, skipper and part-owner of the *Bluenose,* took her out to the Banks for the 1921 season. Then, in October, she won the right to represent Nova Scotia in the race for the International Fisherman's Trophy.

The *Bluenose* defeated the American schooner *Elsie* from Gloucester, Massachusetts, in two straight races over the 40-mile course. She successfully defended her title for the next two years, and again in 1931. The final series for the Fisherman's Trophy was run in 1938, and the *Bluenose* was once again victorious. In her racing career, the only major race series she lost was for the Lipton Cup in 1930. With the outbreak of World War II, these schooner races ceased, and the *Bluenose* was sold in 1942 to a West Indies trading company. Then, in 1946, she sank after hitting a reef off the coast of Haiti.

The *Bluenose* was dearly loved by Canadians, and particularly by Nova Scotians, who affectionately called her "Stormalong" and "Old Weatherlegs." She was a beautiful ship, and she could withstand strong winds. But most of all, she was a symbol of a proud era of sailing ships, and a defiant challenge to mechanical progress.

In 1963, a replica, *Bluenose II,* was launched in Halifax, and is sailed as a nostalgic reminder of the original. Also, the sculptured profile of the *Bluenose* has graced the reverse side of the Canadian ten-cent coin since 1937, a daily reminder to Canadians of the glory of a great ship.

Lionel Conacher: Canada's Athlete of the Half-Century (1900–1954)

Lionel Conacher of Toronto was an outstanding all-round athlete in the days before specialization. Nicknamed "The Big Train," he excelled in every sport he tried: football, lacrosse, baseball, boxing, wrestling, ice hockey, and track and field. His accomplishments spanned twenty years, and included the Ontario 125-lb wrestling championship at age sixteen and the Canadian light heavyweight boxing championship at age twenty. He was a member of the Toronto lacrosse team that won the 1922 Ontario Amateur League championship and the Toronto basketball team that won the 1926 Triple A championship.

Professionally, Conacher played for four National Hockey League teams over eleven years, and was a member of the teams that won the Stanley Cup in 1934 and 1935. While playing for the Toronto Argonauts Football Club (from 1921 to 1925), he led his team to a 1921 Grey Cup victory by scoring fifteen of his team's twenty-one points.

For these and other achievements, Conacher was named Canada's Athlete of the Half-Century by a 1950 poll of Canadian Press sports journalists. He was Ontario athletic commissioner, and worked to provide recreational facilities in city parks. He entered politics in 1937, and was a member of the Ontario Legislature, and later a member of Parliament, for Toronto.

The Edmonton Grads: The Greatest Basketball Team on Record (1915–1940)

In 1914, Percy Page, a teacher at McDougall Commercial High School in Edmonton, started coaching the girls' basketball team. The next year, the graduates of that school formed a team that would come to dominate women's basketball like no other team in the world. Page coached the team for all twenty-five years of its existence, and in that entire time, all but two players were graduates of McDougall High.

The record of the Edmonton Grads is astonishing, especially in respect to its time span. In 1915, its first year, the team won the top trophy for Alberta girls' basketball, and from then until 1940, took every provincial championship except one (and that was lost on the technicality of an ineligible player who was still attending school). In all matches for the Western Canadian championship, the Grads were never defeated. They won the national title every year from 1922 to 1940, losing only two games in these championships series. In playing the United States for the Underwood Trophy, the Grads represented Canada eighteen times and won all eighteen competitions. And in four North American championships series, they lost the first, in 1933, but won the next three.

Their domination of world competition began in 1924, when the Grads travelled to Paris to participate in a series of exhibition games and the European championship, played in conjunction with the Olympic Games. In this series, they defeated six European teams, won the European title, and were subsequently declared the world champions by the international federation for women's athletics. They repeated their European sweep in 1928, and again in 1936. In these three European tours, the Grads played twenty-four games, and won all of them; it is generally agreed that if women's basketball had been part of the Olympic Games program in the 1920s and 1930s, four more gold medals would have been added to Canada's Olympic honours roll.

The roster of players lists only forty-eight names over twenty-five years, for an annual turnover rate of two per year. By the time the Grads disbanded, they had won 108 titles at local, provincial, national, international, and world levels. It is calculated that they played 416 official games, winning all but 29, for an amazing success rate of 93 percent.

The success of the Grads has largely been credited to their coach, Percy Page, and to his coaching and recruitment system. He required that they practice twice weekly (except for the summer months), and he concentrated on fundamental skills. They were noted for their good sportsmanship as well as for their playing ability, and they were the pride of Edmonton and all of Canada. Perhaps their finest compliment came from James Naismith, the inventor of basketball, who called them "the finest basketball team that ever stepped out on a floor."

Bill "Torchy" Peden: King of the Six-Day Cyclists (1906–1980)

"Torchy" Peden was born in Victoria, and in the mid-1920s took up the sport of bicycle racing. He competed in amateur races for three years, with only marginal success, but in 1928 won national titles at one and five miles. This earned him a position on the Canadian Olympic Games team headed to Amsterdam. Although he did not do well there, he stayed on in Europe, determined to learn the tricks of the trade. Successful at last, he returned to North America, became a professional in 1929, and joined the circuit of six-day bicycle racers. He stayed with this sport until 1948, and became its greatest individual star. He was given his nickname because of his red hair.

Six-day races had been popular since the 1890s, and consisted of nonstop racing in hockey arenas with banked sides; the races started at midnight Sunday and continued to midnight Saturday, and demanded continuous grinds of 144 hours. Cyclists were exhausted and frequently injured, and the sport became a cruel, inhuman spectacle. As a result, New York passed a law stating that a cyclist could only race twelve hours in every twenty-four. Promoters then formed teams of two cyclists, each riding for twelve hours, so that races could still be continuous. By the time Peden started to race, these events were extremely popular with spectators in New York and Montreal, and the top twenty cyclists in the circuit were making between $20,000 and $60,000 a year. Even a newcomer could be assured of $100 a day, and the best racing teams made $5000 a week, with extras from the sprints that were added to break the monotony of the main race.

Peden held several records during his professional career, including the English record for 103 miles, at 1:39:39. In 1931, he set a United States record for one paced mile, at 73.5 mph. Of the 148 races that he entered between 1929 and 1948, he won 38, a record that stood until 1965. His brother Douglas was his teammate in many of his victories.

After World War II, the popularity of six-day bicycle races faded in North America. Based in Chicago, Peden tried to revive the sport, but was not successful; public tastes had changed and the appeal of hippodrome sports had been lost.

Fanny "Bobby" Rosenfeld: Canada's Woman Athlete of the Half-Century (1905–1969)

"Bobby" Rosenfeld was born in Russia and raised in Barrie, Ontario. The complete athlete, she excelled in track and field, ice hockey, basketball, softball, and tennis.

In the 1920s, Rosenfeld played on several Ontario and eastern Canada championship basketball teams, and won the Ontario grass courts tennis title in 1924. But she is best known for her track and field accomplishments. In 1925, she was the one-woman team that won the Ontario track and field title for her club, taking the discus, 220y sprint, 120y hurdles, long jump, and placing second in the 100y sprint and javelin. In 1928, Rosenfeld set Canadian records for the long jump, standing broad jump, and discus that lasted into the 1950s. At one time, she reportedly was coholder of the world record time of 11 seconds for the women's 100y sprint.

The highlight of her athletic career was the 1928 Olympic Games in Amsterdam, in which women's track and field was included for the first time. Rosenfeld was a member of the Canadian team that took the unofficial women's track and field championship by one point over the United States. She was lead runner on the winning 4 × 100m relay team, and placed second in the 100m sprint; she also finished fifth in the gruelling 800m race.

After the Amsterdam Olympics, Rosenfeld was afflicted by arthritis, and did not continue in track and field. However, she did recover to play softball in Ontario's leading league. She was also the top player in her favourite sport, ice hockey, in 1931–32. When arthritis struck again in 1933, Rosenfeld gave up active competition in sport, and became a sports writer for the Toronto Globe. In 1950, in a poll of Canadian Press sports journalists, "Bobby" Rosenfeld was named Canada's Woman Athlete of the Half-Century.

Percy Williams: The World's Fastest Human (1908–1982)

In 1928, Percy Williams of Vancouver won the 100m and 200m sprints at the Olympic Games in Amsterdam. This performance still ranks as one of the most outstanding achievements by a Canadian in international track and field competition.

Williams was an unusual runner, able to combine a fast start with a smooth midrace pace, and then a final drive in the last few yards. His success was due, in no small part, to his coach, Bob Granger, who saw Williams' potential, pressured him to train, improved his running style, and gradually persuaded him to aim for victory at the Olympic Games.

It was no small task for Williams to even qualify for the Canadian team at a time when the power structure of track and field favoured central Canada. An unknown in his own country, he had to overcome the added obstacles of inadequate finances and regional discrimination in both 1927 and 1928.

In Canadian trials in 1928, he equalled the world record time of 10.6 seconds for 100m, as he won both the 100m and 200m races. Then, in Amsterdam, he surprised and pleased the crowd by defeating strong runners from the United States and Britain to take the sprints "double gold." Returning to Canada, Williams was given a hero's welcome. After receptions in Quebec City, Montreal, Hamilton, and Winnipeg, he finally reached Vancouver, the city that he had put on the map. His reception was the largest ever seen there, and the motorcade through the downtown streets was cheered by tens of thousands of Vancouverites. Williams was presented with a sports car and a $16,000 trust fund for his further education.

Continuing to compete, Williams ran for Canada in the first British Empire Games in Hamilton in 1930. Unfortunately, while winning the 100y sprint, he badly tore a thigh muscle, which never did heal completely. Consequently, when he raced in the 200m event in the 1932 Olympic Games in Los Angeles, he was eliminated in the semifinals.

This was to be the last time that Percy Williams competed, and he was seldom seen in connection with organized sport. He became somewhat of a recluse, granting very few interviews and appearing in public on only rare occasions. Then, crippled with arthritis and handicapped by the effects of three strokes, Williams took his own life in 1982. Vancouver citizens who remembered the glory that he had brought to Canada were deeply saddened to learn that the life of the great athlete is not always a joyous one. But this did not erase those few great moments, in 1928, when he was "the world's fastest human."

Toward Another Golden Age: Post-World War II

Marilyn Bell: The Underdog Champion (b. 1937)

Marilyn Bell (now Marilyn DiLascio) was born in Toronto, and won fame as a marathon swimmer. In 1954, at the age of sixteen, she became the first person to swim across Lake Ontario. Braving numbing cold and fighting off lamprey eels, she swam 64 kilometres (40 miles) in 21 hours, from Youngstown, New York, to the Canadian National Exhibition Grounds in Toronto. With this remarkable achievement, she captured the hearts of Canadians, particularly those Torontonians who had been following her progress through the city's radio stations and newspapers, and who were waiting to greet her as she reached the lakeshore.

An unheralded entry in this race, she had quickly left behind the American, Florence Chadwick, who was considered to be the world's best distance swimmer and who had been promised an award of $10,000 if she completed the crossing. Chadwich dropped out after 15 miles, and Bell received the prize.

The Lake Ontario swim was not Bell's first major marathon; just eight weeks earlier, she had become the first woman to complete the 25-mile Atlantic City swim. She continued to meet challenges: in 1955, she became the youngest person to cross the English Channel, and in 1956, the first woman to swim across the Straits of Juan de Fuca.

At eighteen, she withdrew from marathon swimming, but for a brief moment she was a household name and the greatest swimming star in Canadian sport.

The Edmonton Eskimos: Football's Dynasty

Established in 1910, the Edmonton Eskimos football club was reborn as a publicly owned enterprise in 1948, and since then has appeared in more Grey Cup finals than any other team in the Canadian Football League's modern era (from the early 1950s).

The Eskimos earned their spot in football history with two major winning streaks, something that no other CFL team has been able to match. The first streak started in the mid-1950s, when they won three straight Grey Cups, in 1954, 1955, and 1956. (Many Canadians still recall that exciting moment, in 1954, when Jackie Parker, the Edmonton quarterback, scooped up a fumble in the final minute of the Grey Cup game against Montreal, raced 90 yards to score a tying touchdown, and set up the winning convert.)

During this first great period, some of the outstanding players, in addition to Parker, were Normie Kwong, Johnny Bright, and Rollie Miles. The team remained very strong until 1960, and then faded during the next decade.

In the early 1970s, under coach Ray Jauch, the Eskimos returned to power, winning three straight Western titles (1973–1975), and the Grey Cup in 1975. Then, with coach Hugh Campbell and players such as Tom Wilkinson, Warren Moon, Dave Cutler, and Jim Germany, the Edmonton Eskimos began a string of victories unprecedented in CFL history: the Western title from 1977 to 1982 and five straight Grey Cup victories from 1978 to 1982. The achievements of this great football club may be impossible to match.

Nancy Greene: "The Tiger" (b. 1943)

As an alpine skier, Nancy Greene (now Nancy Greene Raine) began racing seriously at the age of sixteen. Born in Ottawa, she was raised in Rossland, British Columbia, and was selected to the Canadian Olympic ski team in 1960. Inspired by the victory of teammate Anne Heggtveit that year, Greene was determined to do the same. An aggressive but inconsistent style led to many injuries in the early 1960s, but with more control, she began to achieve better results and to realize her potential.

In 1967, she was a serious contender for the newly established Women's World Cup, but after leading in the first few races, she found herself well back in third place, with only a mathematical chance of winning. Determined to prove that she had what it took, she raced aggressively in the last three events of the series, and emerged victorious—ahead by only .07 seconds.

The following year, two major goals lay ahead: a repeat of her World Cup victory and success in the Winter Olympics at Grenoble. In the Olympic competition, she finished a discouraging tenth in the downhill, but recovered to take the slalom silver medal. Buoyed by this achievement, she entered the giant slalom confident of a win. Skiing a perfect run, she led by a full four seconds to win the gold medal. Greene returned home to a cheering crowd of fifteen hundred fans in Montreal, and thousands more who greeted her in cities all across Canada. It was then on to the 1968 World Cup series, and this time there was no doubt; she scored eight straight victories to take the championship a second time.

In the spring of 1968, Greene retired from competitive skiing, and moved on to a life of endorsements, speeches, television appearances, and other commercial endeavours. She was prominent as a sports ambassador, and served on the federal task force on sport for Canadians. In 1969, she married Al Raine, national ski team coach, and the Raines became deeply involved in the development of ski resort facilities at Whistler, British Columbia.

Gordon Howe: "Mr. Hockey" (b. 1928)

Gordie Howe, born in Floral, Saskatchewan, played professional hockey from 1942 to 1980, and in that time, amassed one of the most remarkable records in the game of hockey. Possessed of exceptional skating ability, he was also strong and tough, and his punishing elbows were as renowned as his ability to score goals. His wrist shot was once clocked at 183 km/h (114 mph).

Howe played junior hockey in Saskatoon and Galt, and then turned pro. He played professional hockey for thirty-two seasons, twenty-six with the National Hockey League and six with the World Hockey Association. One of the game's greatest right wingers, he scored 1081 goals and was credited with 1518 assists, in 2421 regular and play-off professional games. Between 1952 and 1963, he received the Hart Trophy for most valuable player and the Art Ross Trophy for leading scorer, six times each. He also held the NHL records for most seasons, most games, most goals, and most assists.

After playing for the Detroit Red Wings from 1946 to 1971, Howe retired. However, when the WHA was formed in 1973, he came out of retirement to join his sons on the Houston Aeros team. He retired permanently in 1980 at the age of fifty-two, the finest athlete the game of hockey had ever seen.

Harry Jerome: World Record Holder (1940–1982)

In terms of world records, Harry Jerome was one of the greatest sprinters that Canada ever produced. Born in Prince Albert, Saskatchewan, and raised in North Vancouver, British Columbia, Jerome was the first man to share, with other sprinters, both the 100m and 100y world records. He equalled the 100m record of 10 seconds flat in 1960, and the 100y record of 9.3 seconds in 1961. Then, in 1966, he once again equalled the 100y record of 9.1 seconds. As a member of Canada's track and field team, he won a bronze medal for the 100m sprint in the 1964 Olympic Games in Tokyo, a gold medal in the 1966 Commonwealth Games in Kingston, Jamaica, and another gold at the Pan American Games in Winnipeg.

In the 1960 Olympics in Rome, where he was expected to win, he tore a hamstring muscle and did not complete his race; two years later, at the Commonwealth Games, he tore the thigh muscle very badly, and again did not complete his race. For these two incidents, he was unfairly labelled a quitter, but surgery successfully repaired his thigh, and he was able to make the remarkable comeback that produced his 1966 world record time and Commonwealth Games gold medal.

After retiring from competition, Jerome worked in sport development programs for young people, and designed the British Columbia Premier's Sports Awards program for elementary school students. In 1982, just one week after Percy Williams died, Harry Jerome was suddenly struck by an illness and died soon after. He remained one of the greatest sprinters in Canadian track and field history.

The Montreal Canadiens: "Les Glorieux"

The Montreal Canadiens, founded in 1910, is one of the four founding teams that formed the National Hockey League in 1917. The Canadiens have established a dynasty of excellence surpassing that of any team in professional sport in North America. By the time the team celebrated its seventy-fifth anniversary in 1984–85, it had won twenty-two Stanley Cups. And when it was not winning the Stanley Cup, it was still very strong; from 1947–48 to 1984–85, it missed the playoffs only once.

Eighteen of the Montreal Canadiens' Stanley Cup wins came during the "glory years," beginning with the 1943–44 season. While Hector "Toe" Blake was team coach (1955–1968), the Canadiens finished first in the league nine times, and won the Stanley Cup eight times, including an unmatched five Cups in succession (1956–1960). Some of the more outstanding players have been Jean Beliveau, Ken Dryden, Bernie Geoffrion, Doug Harvey, Guy Lafleur, Newsy LaLonde, Howie Morenz, Jacques Plante, Maurice Richard, and Georges Vezina.

Much of the Canadiens' success can be attributed to the strong support of its fans. Throughout its history, the team has been a symbol of pride for the people of Montreal and Quebec.

Maurice Richard: "The Rocket" (b. 1921)

Maurice "Rocket" Richard, born in Montreal, was an outstanding and colourful member of the Montreal Canadiens at a time when that team reigned supreme in the National Hockey League. He played for the Canadiens from 1942 to 1960, and set several records, including his most famous one of fifty goals in fifty games during the 1944–45 season. When he retired, his 544 goals in regular season play was also a record, and in 1985, his record of 82 goals in Stanley Cup playoffs still stood.

An aggressive player and a brilliant goal scorer, Richard excelled under pressure. However, he was notorious for his short temper and violent behaviour, and spent an inordinate amount of time in the penalty box. It was his temper that triggered a sequence of events in 1955 that sparked the worst sports riot in Canadian history. Richard had been fighting an opponent in a game against the Boston Bruins in the Montreal Forum, and when the referee attempted to separate the two players, Richard punched the referee in the face twice. The next day, Clarence Campbell, the League president, announced that Richard had been suspended for the rest of the season and the playoffs.

The suspension touched off a violent fan reaction in the Forum the next night when Campbell appeared at the game. Tear gas was set off and chaos resulted. The game was stopped and the Forum evacuated, but the crowd outside on St. Catherine Street turned ugly and rioted. Extensive damage was done to stores and cars for several blocks over a five-hour period. The next day, in television and radio broadcasts, Richard successfully appealed to the fans to calm down, and peace was restored to the city. Although this was a very unfortunate incident, the outrage generated by his suspension is indicative of the devotion that Richard inspired during his eighteen years with the Montreal Canadiens.

Barbara Ann Scott: "Queen of the Blades" (b. 1928)

Barbara Ann Scott (now Barbara Ann King) was born in Ottawa, and began figure skating at the Minto Club when she was six years old. At age nine, she began a daily seven-hour training routine, and one year later, became the youngest Canadian to earn a gold medal for figures. By 1940, she was Canadian junior champion, and held the national senior title from 1944 to 1948; she was North American champion from 1945 to 1948.

In 1947, she competed in the World Championships in Stockholm. In becoming the first Canadian to win an official world figure skating title, she scored two perfect 6.0 marks in her 4-minute free skating routine. The next year, she repeated her World Championship victory, and capped off her career with an Olympic Games gold medal, again the first for Canada in figure skating. Scott's achievements provided a much-needed boost to the morale of Canadians, still struggling with the aftermath of World War II. She was feted and adored for her victories (seventy thousand people lined the streets of Ottawa for her homecoming parade). Also, her fans tried to give her a yellow convertible; however, it was ruled that if she accepted the car, she would forfeit her Olympic medal, and she therefore declined the gift.

Barbara Ann Scott made an extremely important contribution to her sport. Her strong, athletic performances moved women's figure skating away from the swoops and glides of the pre-war period, and into the era of multiple double—and later, triple—jumps. She will be remembered as the woman who changed figure skating forever.

Marlene Stewart Streit: "Little Miss Maple Leaf" (b. 1934)

Marlene Stewart Streit was born in Cereal, Alberta, and raised in Fonthill, Ontario. She burst upon the women's golf scene in 1951, when she defeated Ada McKenzie, the reigning queen of Canadian women's golf, in the Ontario Ladies' Amateur Championship. This victory, won when Streit was seventeen, was the start of a long and illustrious career, during which she became the world's best woman amateur golfer. She won nine Canadian closed and eight open titles, as well as several open championships in the United States.

Her greatest achievement came in winning the amateur titles of Britain in 1953, of the United States in 1956, and of Australia in 1963 (after a period of semi-retirement to raise a family). With her several Canadian championships, she became the only woman to win all four crowns. Streit golfed competitively for many years, and in 1979 was captain of the Canadian team that won the Commonwealth championship in Australia—the first team to defeat Britain for this title.

Her success as a golfer was due to her natural athletic talent and to her willingness to practice endlessly. She was a perfectionist, and employed a remarkable ability to concentrate during play. Although she would have been successful on the professional circuit, Streit never did consider this as an option; she preferred marriage and raising a family to life in a suitcase.

HIGHLIGHTS IN THE HISTORY OF SPORT IN CANADA

1683 Jean de Brébeuf, Jesuit missionary, recorded his observations of Indians playing *baggataway* (the forerunner to lacrosse) at Georgian Bay, Ontario.

1763 Ojibway Indians used a game of *baggataway* as a cover to enter and capture Fort Michilimackinac, massacring the English soldiers garrisoned there.

1807   The Montreal Curling Club was founded; this was the first curling club on the American continent, and its establishment is generally seen as the birth of modern, organized sport in Canada.

1818   The St. John's Regatta (Newfoundland), the oldest continuing sporting event in North America, was reportedly first held, at Quidi Vidi Lake.

1834   A team of Caughnawaga Indians demonstrated the game of lacrosse before a large crowd of Montreal spectators.

1836   The running of the King's Plate was first held, the longest continuously-run horse-racing event in North America. With the accession of Queen Victoria to the throne the following year, this race was renamed the Queen's Plate.

1837   The Royal Nova Scotia Yacht Squadron was established in Halifax, the first yacht club in Canada and claiming to be the oldest in North America.

1839   The Toronto Athletic Games were held, the earliest record of an organized track and field meet in Canada.

1843   The Montreal Snow Shoe Club was officially established, the first of its kind in the world. That year, snowshoe races were conducted for the first time, at St. Pierre.

1844   The first Montreal "Olympic Games" were held; events included lacrosse matches, rifle shooting, track and field activities, climbing the pole, and quoits.

1851   The first YMCA in North America was opened in Montreal.

1852   The first covered skating rink in the world was opened, in Quebec City.

1856   The Montreal Lacrosse Club was established, the first lacrosse club in Canada.

1859   A tour of eastern Canada by an English cricket team was the first time that a team from another continent had visited Canada for sports competition.

1862   The Victoria Skating Rink was opened in Montreal, the largest in the world; 200 feet by 80 feet, it was later used for ice hockey, and became the standard rink size for that sport.

1867   The National Lacrosse Association was constituted, and the first Dominion lacrosse title contested. The winners of the match, the Indians of Caughnawaga, were declared "world champions."

1869   George Beers published *Lacrosse: The National Game of Canada*. This book helped establish the myth that the Canadian Parliament had passed legislation in 1867 decreeing lacrosse to be Canada's national game; in fact, no such legislation was ever passed.

1872   The British military garrison left Canada. This brought an end to one of the most important influences in the development of sport in Canada, particularly in cricket and equestrian sports.

1873 The first Montreal Snowshoe Carnival was held, and it included a torchlight procession across Mount Royal.

1880 The Canadian Association of Amateur Oarsmen was constituted in Toronto, the first national amateur sports governing body in Canada.

1881 The Montreal Amateur Athletic Association, the "grandfather" of all Canadian multi-sports organizations, was incorporated as a confederation of athletic clubs; original member clubs included the Montreal Lacrosse Club, the Montreal Snow Shoe Club, and the Montreal Bicycle Club.

1882 The traditional "scrum" of the English game of rugby was abolished in Canada, due mainly to the influence of the American "snapback" system; this represented the starting point in the separation between the English and the North American games.

The Canadian Wheelmen's Association was formed; it claims to be the oldest continuing sports governing body in Canada.

1883 The first Montreal Winter Carnival was held, featuring sleigh races, curling, horseraces, tobogganing, snowshoe meet, and construction of ice palace. The Carnival continued to 1889.

1884 The Amateur Athletic Association of Canada (AAA of C) was constituted as the authoritative body to establish standards of a national amateur code and to mediate disputes over the eligibility of participants; it was the first truly national governing body of sport in Canada. This same year, the AAA of C held its first track and field championships; these became the Canadian championships in 1893.

1890 George Dixon of Halifax won the world professional bantamweight boxing championships; in 1891, he won the world featherweight crown.

1892 Basketball was introduced to Canada through the YMCA programs.

1893 Lord Stanley, Governor-General of Canada presented the Stanley Cup, a challenge cup to be held by the leading ice hockey club in Canada. The following year, the Montreal Amateur Athletic Association won the first Stanley Cup game.

1898 The Amateur Athletic Association of Canada changed its name to the Canadian Amateur Athletic Union (CAAU).

1901 Governor-General Lord Minto presented the Minto Cup for amateur lacrosse teams; by 1904, this trophy was awarded for the professional championship.

1905 A team from Dawson City, Yukon, travelled for four weeks, covered 4000 miles by dogteam, boat, and train, to challenge the Ottawa Silver Seven for the Stanley Cup; Ottawa won the two-game series, 9–2 and 23–2.

1906   The original Canadian Intercollegiate Athletic Union (CIAU) was constituted, with universities and colleges from Ontario and Quebec.

The federal Lord's Day Act was passed, making commercial sports on Sunday illegal.

1907   The Central Olympic Committee of CAAU was formed, to organize the representation of Canada at the Olympic Games. In 1909, this became the Canadian Olympic Committee.

1908   Sir H. M. Allan presented the Allan Cup for amateur ice hockey; the Stanley Cup became a professional trophy.

1909   The Canadian Amateur Athletic Union became the Amateur Athletic Union of Canada (AAU of C); this resulted from amalgamation with the Amateur Athletic Federation of Canada, which had been formed in 1907.

Governor-General Earl Grey presented the Grey Cup for amateur rugby in Canada; the University of Toronto team was the first to win the Cup.

1910   The Maritimes Intercollegiate Athletic Union was founded; charter members were Dalhousie, St. Francis Xavier, King's, Acadia, New Brunswick, and Mount Allison.

The National Hockey Association was formed; in 1917, it was disbanded and the National Hockey League was established with teams from Montreal, Ottawa, and Toronto.

1911   Canadian athletes participated in the "Festival of Empire" games, on the occasion of the coronation of King George V. Canada was awarded the Earl of Lonsdale Cup as overall winners. These games were considered a forerunner of the British Empire Games.

The Patrick brothers opened Canada's first artificial ice rink in Victoria in December; in January 1912 their Vancouver rink was opened.

1918   The Federal Minister of Health banned all sport in Canada due to the Spanish flu epidemic; this ban extended from mid-October until early November.

1919   In Paris, the Inter-Allied Games were held, partly to keep morale high while Allied troops were waiting to return home; Canadian athletes performed well, particularly in basketball, track, and soccer.

1923   The first radio broadcast of an ice hockey game was made in February; in March, Foster Hewitt gave his first play-by-play broadcast, from Toronto.

Sam Langford, born in Weymouth Falls, Nova Scotia, fought his last boxing match this year. Known as the "Boston Tar Baby," he is considered to be one of the best heavyweight boxers ever to fight, but was never able to fight for a world title because of prejudice against blacks.

1924   The Montreal Forum was opened.

Charles Gorman, of Saint John, New Brunswick, won the world mass-start outdoor speed skating championship; he repeated this win the following year.

1925   A Canadian women's track and field team competed in an international meet in London, England, the first such participation for Canadian women.

Leila Brooks of Toronto broke six world speed skating records in international competition this year.

1927   The first Wrigley Marathon Swim race was conducted at the Canadian National Exhibition in Toronto.

George Young of Toronto won the 30-mile Catalina Island Swim in California, with a prize of $25; he completed the distance in fifteen hours.

1930   Hamilton hosted the first British Empire Games, now called the Commonwealth Games; competitions were held in track and field, rowing, boxing, wrestling, swimming, and lawn bowling.

1931   Box lacrosse became the official game of the Canadian Amateur Lacrosse Association. The construction of Toronto's Maple Leaf Gardens was completed.

1934   Jimmy McLarnin of Vancouver won the world welterweight boxing championship for the second year in a row.

1936   Philip Edwards earned the distinction of winning more Olympic medals than any other Canadian (five bronze) while participating in the 1928, 1932, and 1936 Olympics in track events.

1937   Howie Morenz, one of the greatest hockey players of the era, died as a result of injuries suffered in a game. He was an excellent skater, stick handler, and scorer, and a popular idol in Montreal, where he played with the Canadiens.

Dorothy McKenzie Walton, of Swift Current, Saskatchewan, won the All-England women's badminton singles crown, emblematic of the world's amateur championship.

1940   Gerard Côté, of Saint-Hyacinthe, Province of Quebec, won the Boston Marathon in a record time of 2:28:28; he also won this race in 1942, 1943, and 1948.

1943   Johnny Longden, born in England and raised in Taber, Alberta, won the Triple Crown on *Count Fleet*. When he retired in 1966, he had ridden 6032 thoroughbred winners, a record for that time.

1949   The Canadian Olympic Committee, having assumed more control of its own affairs during World War II, officially became an independent, autonomous organization known as the Canadian Olympic Association, (COA), following some conflict with the AAU of C over the separation.

Cliff Lumsden of Toronto won his first of five world marathon swimming championships in the Canadian National Exhibition 15-mile swim. In 1956, he became the first person to swim the Straits of Juan de Fuca, off Vancouver Island.

1950 Ontario passed the Lord's Day (Ontario) Act, permitting commercial sport by local option of municipalities. This led the way for other provinces to relax their Sunday sport restrictions.

Lionel Conacher (Canadian football, ice hockey, lacrosse, baseball, wrestling), from Toronto, was named Canada's Athlete of the Half-Century; Fanny "Bobbie" Rosenfeld (track and field, ice hockey, basketball, softball), also from Toronto, was named Canada's Woman Athlete of the Half-Century.

1951 The Canadian Sports Advisory Council, forerunner of the Sports Federation of Canada, was formed to serve as the spokesman of national sports governing bodies.

1953 The British Empire and Commonwealth Games Association of Canada became an autonomous national sports organization, no longer under direct supervision of AAU of C.

Doug Hepburn of Vancouver won the world heavyweight weightlifting championship, in Stockholm.

1954 At the V British Empire and Commonwealth Games in Vancouver, Roger Bannister of England defeated John Landy of Australia in the "Miracle Mile." Spectators also witnessed Englishman Jim Peter's unsuccessful attempts to complete the marathon distance.

1955 The AAU of C established a committee to facilitate Canadian participation in the II Pan American Games held in Mexico City; this was Canada's first showing at these games.

Canada's Sports Hall of Fame was established at the Canadian National Exhibition grounds in Toronto.

The CIAU (Central) was divided into two sectional organizations: Ontario-Quebec Intercollegiate Athletic Association and Ottawa-St. Lawrence Intercollegiate Athletic Association.

1958 The Pan American Games Committee of the COA was established to govern Canadian participation in Pan American Games competition.

1959 Ernie Richardson formed the famous Richardson curling rink from Stroughton, Saskatchewan, which won four Macdonald Briers in five years, four Scotch Cups, five Provincial Championships, a Masters title, and a Tournament of Champions. This family group of two brothers and two cousins is probably the best-known curling rink in Canadian curling history.

1961   The Fitness and Amateur Sport Act was passed by Parliament, its objective being to encourage, promote, and develop fitness and amateur sport in Canada.

The CIAU become a national organization; member unions were Maritimes, Ontario-Quebec, Ottawa-St. Lawrence, and Western Canada Intercollegiate Athletic Associations.

The Trail Smoke Eaters won the World Ice Hockey Championship, the last time that a Canadian team won this title.

1962   Don Jackson won the World Figure Skating Championship in Prague, the first men's singles crown to be won by a Canadian.

1963   Don McPherson, of Windsor, Ontario, won the Canadian, North American, and World figure skating championships, the first Canadian man to win all three in one year.

1964   *Northern Dancer,* owned by E. P. Taylor, was the first Canadian-bred horse to win the Kentucky Derby; she went on to win the Preakness and the Queen's Plate that year, and was named Horse of the Year.

1965   A Canadian team entered the World University Games for the first time.

1966   George Knudson from Winnipeg won the individual title in the World Cup golf tournament in Tokyo; as a professional golfer, he won nineteen tournaments between 1961 and 1969, the best record by a Canadian.

Elaine Tanner of Vancouver set a world record of 2:33:3 for the 220y individual medley; that same year, she won four gold medals at the Commonwealth Games in Jamaica.

1967   Winnipeg hosted the V Pan American Games, in Canada's Centennial year.

The first Canada Winter Games were held in Quebec City.

The National Hockey League expanded from six to twelve teams.

Ferguson Jenkins, from Chatham, Ontario, began a six-year string of twenty or more pitching victories per season, as the best Canadian-born baseball player in the major leagues.

1968   The professional North American Soccer League was established.

Sandra Post, from Oakville, Ontario, won the U.S. Ladies' Professional Golf Association Championship; she also was named Rookie of the Year.

1969   The *Report of the Task Force on Sport for Canadians* was presented to the federal government; the report strongly influenced Canadian government involvement in sport, with most recommendations being implemented.

The first Canada Summer Games were held in Halifax-Dartmouth.

Hockey Canada was constituted as a nonprofit organization to organize Canadian teams for international competition.

The Montreal Expos entered the National Baseball League.

Russ Jackson, born in Hamilton, Ontario, retired after eleven seasons with the Ottawa Rough Riders football team. He was an outstanding quarterback, and the only Canadian in the CFL to excel at this position; he won the Schenley outstanding player award three times.

1970   The federal government released *A Proposed Sports Policy for Canadians,* which outlined a redirection of the Fitness and Amateur Sport Directorate program.

The Administrative Centre for Sport and Recreation was created, and subsequently renamed the National Sport and Recreation Centre, Inc.

The AAU of C was dissolved, ceasing operations as a national multi-sports governing body.

The Olympic Trust of Canada was formed, with responsibility for raising and administering funds required to fulfill the objectives of the Canadian Olympic Association.

1971   The Coaching Association of Canada was formed.

Sport Participation Canada (Participaction) was formed as a nonprofit, private company designed to increase the physical fitness of all Canadians by convincing them of the need for more physical activity.

Jean Beliveau, from Victoriaville, Quebec, retired after eighteen seasons with the Montreal Canadiens hockey team. During that time, he set a record, as a centre, of 507 regular-season goals, played on ten Stanley Cup teams, and was one of the most popular players in the NHL.

1972   The WCIAU was dissolved; two autonomous intercollegiate organizations were formed: the Canada West University Athletic Association and the Great Plains Athletic Conference.

The *Comité Organisateur des Jeux Olympiques* (COJO) was established to organize the 1976 Summer Olympic Games in Montreal.

In the first ice hockey series between Canada (an NHL team) and the USSR, Team Canada won 4:3:1. In a final game that was reportedly watched on television by 80 percent of the Canadian population, Paul Henderson scored the winning goal with 34 seconds left to play.

The World Hockey Association was established with twelve teams.

1973   Game Plan was initiated by Sport Canada, COA, and national sports governing bodies to develop Canadian athletes for the 1976 Olympic Games.

Karen Magnussen of North Vancouver won the world figure skating championship; one year earlier, she had won the Olympic Games silver medal.

Bruce Robertson of Vancouver won the 100m butterfly race at the World Aquatic Games in Belgrade; this was Canada's first world championship in swimming since 1912.

Ron Turcotte, from Drummond, New Brunswick, rode Secretariat to win the Triple Crown of thoroughbred racing, the first such win since 1948.

1974 The first Canadian rodeo finals were conducted in Edmonton.

1975 The Quebec government took the control of major facility construction for the Olympic Games away from Montreal, and established a special Olympic Installations Board.

The first National Netball Tournament was held, in Toronto.

John Primrose of Edmonton won the World Trapshooting Championship in Munich. He repeated this victory in 1983.

1976 The Olympiad for the Physically Disabled was held in Etobicoke, Ontario. Canadians won twenty-six gold, thirty silver, and twenty-nine bronze medals.

In the first Canada Cup ice hockey tournament, Team Canada won, over the USSR, Czechoslovakia, Finland, and the United States.

The Toronto Blue Jays were established as a franchise of the American Baseball League; the team commenced play in 1977.

Sandy Hawley, from Oshawa, Ontario, in setting a North American record for 515 thoroughbred racing wins in one year, became the first jockey to surpass five hundred wins.

1977 After an absence of seven years, Team Canada again participated in the ice hockey World Championship and placed third.

1978 The CIAU and CWIAU were amalgamated into a single body: the Canadian Intercollegiate Athletic Union.

The XI Commonwealth Games were held in Edmonton, Alberta; this was the third time that the Games were held in Canada. Canadians won forty-five gold, thirty-one silver, and thirty-three bronze medals, for their best showing to date in the Commonwealth Games and an unofficial victory over all other competing nations for the first time.

Wayne Gretzky of Edmonton began his professional career as a hockey player, with scoring prowess that rewrote the record book. By 1984, playing for the Edmonton Oilers, he had twice exceeded two hundred goals in a season (1981–82 and 1983–84) and set a record of ninety-two goals in a single eighty-game season; he held or shared more than thirty NHL records.

Graham Smith of Edmonton won the 100m individual medley race at the World Aquatic Championships; earlier that year, he won an unprecedented six gold medals at the Commonwealth Games in Edmonton.

1979   The remaining World Hockey Association teams merged with the NHL, and teams now operated in seven Canadian cities.

Bobby Hull, the "Golden Jet," retired after twenty-two seasons with NHL and WHA hockey teams. One of the highest-scoring left wings in hockey history, he gave credibility to the new World Hockey Association when he accepted a ten-year, $2 million contract with the Winnipeg Jets in 1972.

Bobby Orr, from Parry Sound, Ontario, retired after an illustrious hockey career with the Boston Bruins (1967–76) and the Chicago Black Hawks (1976–79). The only defenseman to receive the NHL award for leading scorer, he was voted the greatest athlete in Boston history.

Helen Vanderburg of Calgary dominated world synchronized swimming competition with an unprecedented sweep of all major championships: Pan American Games solo and duet, Pan Pacific Games solo, and FINA Cup solo and duet, following her 1978 World Championships in solo and duet.

1980   Canada, along with twenty-five other countries, boycotted the XXII Summer Olympic Games in Moscow because of the invasion of Afghanistan by the USSR.

Terry Fox, of Port Coquitlam, British Columbia, who lost his right leg to cancer at the age of eighteen, began his Marathon of Hope run across Canada from Newfoundland. He was forced to stop in Thunder Bay, Ontario because cancer had spread to his lungs, but his inspiring run raised $23.5 million for cancer research. He died in 1981, but his memory lives on in several annual Terry Fox fund raising marathons.

1981   The International Olympic Committee awarded the 1988 Winter Olympics to Calgary.

Susan Nattrass of Edmonton won her sixth world women's trapshooting championship. The first woman from any country to be named to an Olympic Games trapshooting team, she won her first world title in 1974, and set a world record of 195/200 in 1978.

1982   A "Best Ever" fund of $25 million was established by the federal government to prepare Canadian athletes for the 1988 Winter Olympics; in 1984, this was extended to Summer Games athletes preparing for the Olympics in Seoul, South Korea.

Debbie Brill, born in Mission, British Columbia, and originator of the "Brill Bend" high jumping technique, set a world indoor record of 1.99m. She was ranked among the world's best women high jumpers for more than a decade.

Cindy Nicholas, from Toronto, completed her nineteenth marathon swimming crossing of the English Channel, having won the coveted Queen of the Channel title in 1979 and 1981. She set several records for Channel crossings.

Steve Podborski from Toronto won the World Cup alpine skiing down-hill title, the first Canadian man to win this championship.

Laurie Skreslet of Calgary was the first Canadian to reach the top of Mt. Everest, in the Canadian expedition. He was followed, two days later, by Pat Morrow of Kimberley, British Columbia.

1983 The World University Games were held in Edmonton, Alberta.

1984 In ice hockey, Canada won the Canada Cup tournament with a surprise victory over the USSR in the semifinals and a sweep of the finals against Sweden.

Hervé Filion, born in Angers, Quebec, reached the 9000-wins plateau, as harness racing's most prolific race money winner. He had been season leading money winner seven times.

1985 Steve Fonyo, of Vernon, British Columbia, completed his Journey for Lives run, from St. John's, Newfoundland, to Victoria, British Columbia. He had lost his left leg to cancer at age twelve and he raised $13 million for cancer research.

1986 Ben Johnson, born in Jamaica and resident of Toronto, gained the title of "fastest man in the world," running 100m in 9.95 seconds, for a sea-level world record.

Carolyn Waldo of Calgary won three gold medals in synchronized swimming at the World Aquatic Championships, in solo, duet, and team; she was the first synchronized swimmer to score a perfect 10 in the solo event.

Sharon Wood, born in Halifax and resident in Canmore, Alberta, became the first North American woman to reach the summit of Mt. Everest.

1987 Rick Hansen of Vancouver, a paraplegic since 1975, completed his re-markable Man in Motion journey around the world in a wheelchair, for the purpose of raising money for spinal-cord injury research and in-creasing public awareness of the potential of disabled people.

REFERENCES

Batten, Jack. *Champions: Great Figures in Canadian Sport.* Toronto: New Press, 1971.

Canadian Encyclopedia. Edmonton: Hurtig Publishers, 1985.

Cochrane, Jean; Hoffman, Abby; and Kincaid, Pat. *Women in Canadian Life:Sports.* Toronto: Fitzhenry and Whiteside, 1977.

Cosentino, Frank. *Ned Hanlan.* Toronto: Fitzhenry and Whiteside, 1978.

Cosentino, Frank, and Leyshon, Glenn. *Olympic Gold: Canadian Winners of the Summer Games.* Toronto: Holt, Rinehart and Winston, 1975.

Cosentino, Frank, and Morrow, Donald. *Lionel Conacher.* Toronto: Fitzhenry and Whiteside, 1981.

Ferguson, Bob. *Who's Who in Canadian Sport.* 2d ed. Toronto: Summerhill Press, 1985.

Frayne, Trent, and Gzowski, Peter. *Great Canadian Sport Stories.* Toronto: McClelland and Stewart, 1965.

Howell, Maxwell, and Howell, Reet, eds. *History of Sport in Canada.* Champaign, IL: Stipes Publishing Co., 1985.

Howell, Nancy, and Howell, Maxwell. *Sports and Games in Canadian Life.* Toronto: Macmillan of Canada, 1969.

Kearney, James. *Champions: A British Columbia Sports Album.* Vancouver: Douglas and McIntyre, 1985.

Kidd, Bruce. *Tom Longboat.* Toronto: Fitzhenry and Whiteside, 1980.

McDonald, David. *For the Record: Canada's Greatest Women Athletes.* Rexdale, Ontario: John Wiley and Sons, 1981.

Roxborough, Henry. *Canada at the Olympics.* 3d ed. Toronto: McGraw-Hill Ryerson, 1963.

————. *Great Days in Canadian Sport.* Toronto: The Ryerson Press, 1957.

————. *One Hundred–Not Out.* Toronto: The Ryerson Press, 1966.

Schrodt, Barbara; Redmond, Gerald; and Baka, Richard. *Sport Canadiana.* Edmonton: Executive Sport Publications, 1980.

Symons, T. H. B. *To Know Ourselves: The Report on the Commission on Canadian Studies.* Ottawa: The Association of Universities and Colleges of Canada, 1975.

Winners: A Century of Canadian Sport. Toronto: Grosvenor House, 1985.

Wise, S. F., and Fisher, Douglas. *Canada's Sporting Heroes.* Don Mills, Ontario: General Publishing Co., 1974.

Further information about the history of sport in Canada can be obtained from articles published in journals in this field. Some of the more useful journals are

- International Journal of History and Sport
- CAHPER Journal
- Canadian Journal of History of Sport
- Journal of Sport History
- Urban History Review

Finally, the serious student of the history of sport in Canada is strongly advised to refer to the many theses and dissertations that have been written on a wide range of topics in this field.

CHAPTER 6

The Canadian Amateur Sport and Recreation Delivery System

Eric F. Broom

The Canadian amateur sport and recreation delivery system is a complex structure of public, voluntary, private, and commercial organizations which provide environments for public participation in physical activities. Public sector organizations include schools, colleges, universities, municipal recreation or leisure services departments, and provincial and federal government agencies. Within the private sector are voluntary organizations such as sport clubs, governing bodies of sport, sport federations; commuunity organizations such as Boys' Clubs and Girls' Clubs; private organizations such as country clubs; and commercial organizations such as fitness centres and racquets clubs.

DEFINING THE SPORT AND RECREATION DELIVERY SYSTEM

The delivery system is made up of a number of self-contained or interlocking systems which encompass organizations at local, municipal, regional, provincial, interprovincial, and national levels, and comprises a vast network of agencies which interrelate, to greater or lesser degree, to form the total system. Figure 6.1 illustrates some of the organizations in the delivery system.

The Canadian Amateur Sport and Recreation Delivery System

LEVEL	EDUCATION				SPORT GOVERNING BODIES (SGB's)	MULTI-SPORT AGENCIES	RECREATION AGENCIES	FITNESS	GOVERNMENT
	Physical Education	High School Athletics	Community Colleges	Universities					
INTERNATIONAL	Intn'l Council for Health, Physical Educ. & Rec. (ICHPER)			World Student Games (FISU)	Intn'l SGB's e.g., FIG (gymn.) IIHR (hockey) FINA (swimming) FIFA (soccer)	Intn'l Olympic Cttee. (IOC) Pan Am Games Br. Commonwealth Games Olympiad for Physically Disabled			
NATIONAL	Cdn Assoc. for Health, Physical Educ. & Rec. (CAHPER)	Cdn School Sports Federation	Cdn Colleges Athletic Association (CCAA)	Cdn Interuniversity Athletic Union (CIAU)	Nat SGB's e.g., CASA (swimming) CAHA (hockey) CGF (gymn.) CSA (soccer)	Cdn Olympic Assoc. Sports Fed. of Canada Nat. Sp. & Rec. Ctr. Coaching Assoc. of Canada (CAC) Canada Games	Cdn Parks/ Rec. Assoc. YMCA YWCA Red Cross	Participaction YMCA YWCA	Dept. of National Health & Welfare Fitness & Amateur Sport Branch —Sport Canada —Fitness Canada

	Provincial physical education associations	Provincial schools sports federations	Provincial colleges athletic associations	Provincial/regional interuniversity athletic associations	Prov. SGBs e.g, CASA Ont. section (swimming) OHA (hockey) OGF (gymn.) OSA (soccer)	Federations of prov. SGBs e.g., Sport BC Sport Alberta Prov. sport admin. centres	Provincial recreation assoc., prov. parks assoc., prov arenas assoc.	Shape Up Alberta	Provincial ministries of culture, sport, recreation, & fitness
PROVINCIAL									
MUNICIPAL	Physical education programs Intramural programs	High school teams	College teams	University teams	Local assoc. Clubs Leagues Teams Individuals	Community sport councils, e.g., Etobicoke Sport Council	YMCA/ YWCA Red Cross Boys'/ Girls' Clubs	Health clubs Employee fitness Municipal recreation programs	Municipal recreation departments

Figure 6.1

A **sport and recreation delivery system** may be defined as a system which provides opportunities for people to engage in physical activities at a level and frequency compatible with ability and desire. A complete delivery system is therefore comprehensive in nature, ranging over the full spectrum of opportunity for the beginner and the recreational participant at one extreme to the elite athlete at the other.

Much of Canada's amateur sport delivery system was inherited from Britain in the latter part of the last century. Sport within the education system, be it in schools, colleges, or universities, came from the same mould as the British model, as did sport clubs and governing bodies. The municipal recreation delivery system was modelled on similar developments in the United States. Influences which helped establish and develop Canada's delivery system were undoubtedly British and American, but over the years environmental influences—geography, climate, philosophy, ethnicity, economics, and more recently, politics—have modified the system. The basic frameworks remain, but refinements have produced an amateur sport and recreation delivery system that is uniquely Canadian.

THE EDUCATION SPORT DELIVERY SYSTEM

Within the **education sport delivery system** are physical education programs, intramural programs, and interschool sports in elementary and high schools, as well as sport programs in community colleges and universities. The delivery system is shown diagrammatically in figure 6.2.

The Public School System

Under Article 93 of the British North America Act of 1867 jurisdiction for public education is granted to each individual province. There is no federal Ministry of Education. Each provincial Department of Education delegates considerable responsibility for the operation of schools to locally elected and appointed school boards whose authority is determined by provincial legislation.

Physical education, like other subject areas in schools, is governed by the province but is generally controlled by local school boards. The local aims and objectives are usually in line with the provincial aims. However, the program content and corresponding activities are usually left to the discretion of the physical education teacher, although most provinces publish curriculum guides. Provincial autonomy has produced distinctive educational systems and curricula, with no two being exactly alike.

The Early Years

The first official recommendation for a physical education program in schools was made by Egerton Ryerson in 1846, and in 1852 a course of exercises was published for the guidance of teachers. In the early 1860s cadet training (which from its initiation was closely associated with schools) developed rapidly, encouraged by a federal government grant of $50 in 1865 to all schools conducting "drill and gymnastics."

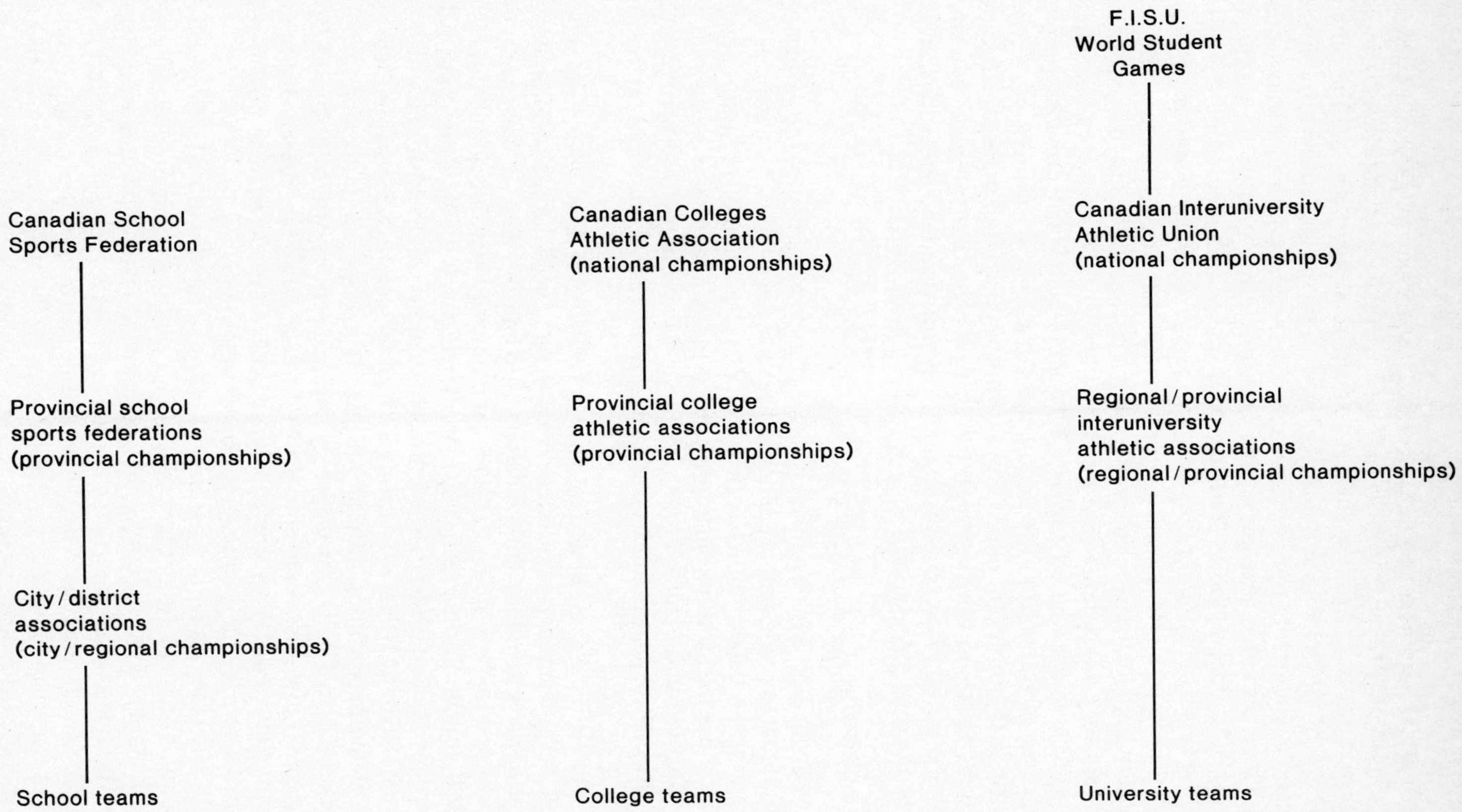

F.I.S.U.
World Student
Games

Canadian Interuniversity
Athletic Union
(national championships)

Regional/provincial
interuniversity
athletic associations
(regional/provincial championships)

University teams

Canadian Colleges
Athletic Association
(national championships)

Provincial college
athletic associations
(provincial championships)

College teams

Canadian School
Sports Federation

Provincial school
sports federations
(provincial championships)

City/district
associations
(city/regional championships)

School teams

Figure 6.2 The education sport delivery system

In 1909 Lord Strathcona established the Strathcona Trust Fund which made available annual grants to provinces which (1) incorporated physical training as an integral part of the curriculum in all schools above the primary grades, (2) formed cadet corps, and (3) provided teacher training in physical education. The grants were administered by the National Department of Militia, which provided army sergeants to teach "physical drill" to teachers in training at normal schools. Their teaching was supplemented by the use of the 1904 British *Syllabus of Physical Exercises for Public Elementary Schools,* which was based on the Swedish Ling system of gymnastics, and later the 1933 syllabus which focussed more on British team games. These syllabi were also used extensively in schools. During the early years of the century Canada had few professionally trained physical educators, and most provinces availed themselves of grants from the Strathcona Trust.

Up to the midpoint of the present century Canadian physical education was somewhere midway between the British belief that physical education should be for fun, fitness, and character development and the American emphasis on competitive sport.

Elementary Schools

The 1970s will go down in history as the decade of daily physical education. Up until that time elementary school physical education had a low priority in education, the major emphasis being on the high school program. Several major conferences and publications drew attention to the low status of physical education in Canadian elementary schools in relation to other countries and made strong recommendations urging an increased emphasis on the subject.

The National Conference on Fitness and Health held in Ottawa in 1972 made it very clear that professionals in the related fields of health and physical education were convinced that more activity time and better quality programs were needed in the schools. A specific recommendation for thirty minutes of physical education on a daily basis in elementary schools came out of the conference on The Child in Sport and Physical Activity held at Queen's University in 1973. CAHPER's position paper of 1974, which recommended that every elementary school child should have the opportunity in school to experience effective daily instruction in physical activity, was followed in 1976 by the report of its task force entitled *New Perspectives for Elementary School Physical Education Programs in Canada,* which made specific recommendations for improving elementary school programs.

In 1979 the results of a national survey indicated that daily physical education in Canadian elementary schools was being very favourably received by the majority of children, teachers, administrators, and parents where programs had been developed. Throughout the 1980s progress continued to be made, but much remains to be done before daily physical education is universal in Canadian elementary schools. Some of the major problems encountered include inadequate facilities and inadequately prepared teachers. These obstacles in particular resulted in a refinement of the theme to **daily quality physical education.**

made, but much remains to be done before daily physical education is universal in Canadian elementary schools. Some of the major problems encountered include inadequate facilities and inadequately prepared teachers. These obstacles in particular resulted in a refinement of the theme to **daily quality physical education.**

The elementary school physical education program forms a major building block in the foundations of the Canadian delivery system for physical education and sport. In the absence of a uniformly high-quality program at this level the structure will lack the solid base it requires on which to build.

High Schools

Canadian high school physical education programs, which were virtually static for the first half of the present century, have undergone major change in the second half following three midcentury decades when the emphasis was primarily on fitness. In the 1940s Canada, a country at war, needed a youth fit to fight and the decade was characterized by fitness-oriented programs made up largely of dull, repetitive, rigourous calisthenics. Throughout the early 1950s traditional programs of calisthenics, team games, and formal gymnastics prevailed, but the beginnings of a more liberal approach was also apparent. Toward the end of that decade *Sputnik* burst upon the world and, in concert with America, Canada once again became primarily concerned about the fitness of its youth.

In 1960 this concern was reinforced by the Kraus-Weber research which compared the fitness of North American and European children, the findings of which were unfavourable to the former. Two events in the previous year—the poor results of the Pan American Games team and the rebuke of Canadians for their low level of fitness by the Duke of Edinburgh at the Canadian Medical Association Conference—had already stimulated much Parliamentary debate. Reflecting these concerns the federal government in 1961 passed *An Act to Encourage Fitness and Amateur Sport.* Through this <u>Act</u> funds were made available in 1967 to develop the Centennial Fitness Awards, a series of tests to measure fitness at different levels, which later became the Canada Fitness Awards. Since its introduction the awards program has been well-supported by elementary and junior high school students. Throughout the decade physical educators and the medical profession continued to express concern over Canadians' sedentary, spectator-oriented lifestyles.

Beginning in the early 1970s the national focus switched to the need to keep active throughout the life span. The driving force behind this social change was Sport Participation Canada through its Participaction program. High school physical education programs responded by emphasizing lifetime sports or activities which can be continued in postschool years.

The typical Canadian high school physical education program consists of three segments: basic instruction, intramural, and interschool. Each segment plays its own role in the delivery system.

Basic Instruction Program

Through the **basic instruction program** all students receive an introduction and basic instruction in a range of physical activities. Across the country the typical time allocation for this program is two hours per week. However, because of different methods of scheduling, the classes may be twice per week all year, twice in every seven school days, or every day for one semester and not at all in the second semester. Since 1980 the physical education requirements have been eroded in almost all provinces, and by the middle of the decade most provinces had dropped the requirement in the twelfth grade and a number in the eleventh grade.

The desire of the teacher to offer a range of activities has, of necessity, resulted in relatively short periods of time being devoted to any one activity. Within each unit of activity it is difficult for the average student to reach a modicum of proficiency, and units of the same activity in subsequent years tend to be repetitive.

It is anomalous that the value of physical education as a school subject should be more widely recognized at the lower level of the school system while at the same time it is given less importance at the upper level.

Intramural Program

The **intramural program** is intended to provide opportunities for competition for all students. Unlike the basic instruction program, the intramural program is voluntary and participation rates show wide variability. The school intramural program is usually student organized, with teacher guidance. Intramural competition takes place before and after school hours and at lunchtime. In too many cases the program growth is restricted by the availability of facilities, and when intramural requirements conflict with those of the interschool program the latter usually gains priority.

Interschool Program

The third component of the high school delivery system is the **interschool program,** through which opportunities for a higher level of instruction and competition are made available to students. As with the intramural program, the interschool program is extracurricular and is conducted after regular class periods.

The interschool sport program has been a part of the total school program in Canada since the late nineteenth century. At that time Canadian private schools adopted the program from English schools which regarded interschool sport competition as a valuable contributor to a full education. In a similar manner to England, the program spread from the private to the public school system.

From the inception of interschool sport programs, boys have had greater opportunity to participate than girls. This was primarily reflected in a boys' program which offered more sports than were available to girls. Starting in the mid-1970s a succession of highly publicized court cases, in which girls sought the right to play on boys' community sports teams, drew attention to the inequity throughout the whole system. There simply were not enough girls' teams available.

There is no doubt that the number of girls playing sport has increased markedly since the 1970s, but girls' participation overall remains smaller than boys'. Public attitudes toward girls' participation and the lack of desire of some girls to take part, although both show positive change, have resulted in limited opportunities. These factors, combined with the absence of legislation comparable to Title IX in the United States, have dictated that progress toward equal opportunity for girls and boys to participate in sport in Canada has not yet been fully attained.

As in other components of the public school system, the interschool sport program shows some variation from province to province in size, organization, and popularity. Three studies of interschool sport programs in Ontario, British Columbia, and Nova Scotia provide a cross section of programs across the country (Macintosh 1977; Hindmarch 1979; Fiander 1985).

In both Ontario and Nova Scotia small high schools have the highest proportion of active student participation, with the population decreasing in inverse ratio to school size. In Ontario, for example, small schools on average have 50 percent participation and large schools 33 percent. Overall, the larger schools have the largest number of active participants. Nova Scotia also reported that rural high schools had higher participation rates than urban schools in interschool sport programs, but the latter had higher rates of participation in community-based programs.

In both Ontario and British Columbia less than 10 percent of students are involved in the administration of interschool sport programs, and the former province indicated that almost 80 percent of the total school population are spectators at interschool sport events at least once a year. The two earlier studies of Ontario and British Columbia reported no drop-off in participation rates, but the Nova Scotia study, which made comparisons between 1979 and 1983, found a dramatic reduction in participation. The average number of students involved in intramural programs per school dropped from 462.9 to 180.0 in four years, and the total number of participants provincewide in interschool sports declined from 56,534 in 1979 to 20,344 in 1983.

Almost 50 percent of participants in the interschool programs play more than one sport, the average being two to three activities. Further, interschool athletes comprise a large proportion of intramural program participants. In both Ontario and Nova Scotia, males made up 60 percent of participants in the interschool programs, and females 60 percent in the intramural programs. Ontario reported a need for a wide participant base to the interschool program, and that the major reason for nonparticipation was that students thought they were not good enough.

The average number of hours spent practicing each week in Ontario ranged from 3.6 for girls' senior volleyball to 7.0 for boys' senior football. Most sports reported competitive seasons ranging from six to ten weeks duration. These time requirements were considered acceptable by administrators, teachers, and students, with the exception of high-performance female athletes who would have preferred increased time involvement. Nova Scotia indicated that interschool athletes were not excused from physical education classes.

The total time commitment for coaches in the Ontario study was found to range from six to fifteen hours per week. In general, football demanded the largest time commitment and the coaches of girls' teams were involved for less time than the coaches of boys' teams. Coaching in all provinces is a voluntary activity, carried out after normal school hours. In Ontario it was not seen as having a negative impact on teaching effectiveness, and in British Columbia coaches saw themselves as teachers first and coaches second. However, the comparison of Canadian teachers coaching in a voluntary capacity with teachers in the United States receiving extra remuneration for coaching has long been a bone of contention. On occasion, teachers in several provinces have withdrawn services for after-school activities, including sport, in protest against school board actions.

Almost all coaches in Ontario were teachers. In British Columbia and Nova Scotia, schools were reluctant to use nonteachers as coaches, primarily because of legal implications, but were obliged to do so because of a shortage of teacher-coaches. In order for a school to offer opportunities in a range of sports in the interschool program, teachers, in addition to those in physical education, must volunteer to coach a team. The average commitment a volunteer teacher makes to coaching is somewhat less than ten years. In normal circumstances the turnover is compensated by newly appointed young teachers, but the restricted hiring practices of most provinces during the first half of the 1980s resulted in a serious shortage of coaches for the interschool program. In consequence, teams in some sports were not offered.

The funding for interschool sport programs is derived from a number of sources. In some provinces (but by no means all), school boards provide grants to individual schools. School boards in Ontario, for example, either make a grant or pay directly the costs of selected items such as officials and transportation. In other provinces, school boards do not universally provide financial assistance. By way of contrast, the general practice in the United States is for school boards to provide almost total funding for interschool programs, whereas in Canada such funding at best is only partial.

The average high school interschool sport budget in 1975–76 in Ontario was $7079, and in Nova Scotia in 1979 and 1983 it was $8227 and $13,017 respectively. In Ontario the proportion allocated to boys' and girls' programs was approximately two-thirds to one-third, which reflected the numbers of athletes of each sex in the programs. Over time the girls' program budget showed a slight proportional increase. As pointed out in the Ontario study, the program's most valuable resource is the teacher-coach, whose voluntary services, if remunerated, were estimated at a hypothetical dollar value of $27,000 per school on an annual basis.

In order to counter rising costs, all schools engage in a range of fund-raising programs. British Columbia schools, for example, raise considerable amounts through participation in a raffle organized by the Provincial High School Sports Federation. Principals in Nova Scotia expressed widespread willingness to accept commercial sponsorship.

Participation in interschool athletics does not appear to be detrimental to academic achievement. In the Ontario study, as reported by students, interschool athletes perform significantly better academically as a group than do other students. An explanation for this difference is that interschool athletes come more often from an upper-middle socioeconomic background than does the rest of the student population, and this group was found to achieve significantly higher academic levels than other groups.

In the Nova Scotia study, school principals saw a definite connection between school spirit, to which they felt the interschool sport program made a major contribution, and academic achievement. Ontario teachers and administrators saw the program as reasonably consistent with the traditional objectives of enjoyment, health, fitness, and social interaction. In all three provinces the interschool program was perceived by principals, teachers, parents, student councils, and participating students as a most valuable experience which contributed to the total school program. The Ontario study reported that interschool sport programs were seen very positively in retrospect by former participants and by a substantial number of former nonparticipants. In disturbing contrast, school principals' opinions, as reported in the Nova Scotia study, were that the community, school boards, and the provincial Department of Education were rated low or not at all in their support of interschool sport programs.

Special Schools and the Young Elite Athlete

The level of competition provided by the interschool sport program, as reported in the Ontario study, appeared to meet the desires of participants, with the exception of a minority of female athletes who wanted a higher level of competition. A problem which remains largely unaddressed, and which grows steadily more severe, is the determination of the respective roles of the school and community leagues and clubs in the delivery of sport programs, both recreational and elite. At the present time an overall lack of communication and cooperation results in considerable duplication of programs and conflicts for student athletes who either compete for both school and club, with attendant excessive time demands, or for club alone which results in diminution of association with school.

The school system has neither the objectives nor the resources to develop elite athletes. On the other hand, sport clubs, provincial and national governing bodies of sport, and provincial and federal governments have the development of sport excellence as a major objective. The student athlete who aspires to excellence is too often caught in the middle of the jurisdictional and philosophical conflict and torn by divided loyalties.

Further, the decentralized nature of the total system—home, school, and club—presents aspiring young high-potential Canadian athletes with additional obstacles. Unlike many Communist and Western countries, Canada has not developed a sport school system, neither residential nor day school. In consequence, the young elite Canadian athlete is forced to spend considerable time travelling between club, school, and home, whereas residential sport schools completely eliminate such travel and day sport schools do so between club and school.

In addition to the problem of excessive travel time, the young elite Canadian student athlete is faced with a generally inflexible school schedule. By way of contrast, their counterparts attending a residential sport school in a Communist country enjoy a system in which the education schedule is adapted to meet the time requirements of sport at different times of the year. Education is not neglected; in fact, academic standards are strictly adhered to. However, the classes are flexible and are structured around the needs of sport.

Canadian society—particularly the education fraternity—has been slow to embrace the sport school model. A notable exception, Seneca College (a junior college in Ontario) in cooperation with the North York Board of Education has, since 1978, operated a combined elementary school and high-performance gymnastics program for girls, modelled on the socialist state sport school. In 1981 the program was expanded to include tennis, figure skating, and rhythmic gymnastics, and a similar cooperative arrangement was established with a local high school. By 1985 there were forty-nine female students in the program. The goal is to place athletes on national teams. Each day the students, all of whom are nonresidents, receive schooling from teachers in portable classrooms located on the college campus, and coaching from full-time coaches. Education and coaching are each allocated approximately five hours daily. By integrating education and high-level sport training at one location, extraneous travel is eliminated.

In the Vancouver area several individual high schools have offered flexible academic schedules with reduced course loads to talented athletes and performing artists since 1981. By 1986 there were seven such schools. The schools, at the request of parents and in cooperation with local sport clubs or associations, develop an individualized schedule for each student which frees them from school work for two to three hours each day. All arrangements for training, which is usually at nearby facilities, are made by the clubs. Two of the schools each have approximately fifty students on flexible programs, the others much smaller numbers. In all cases athletes vastly outnumber performing artists. Experience has shown that students on these flexible programs have consistently met their educational requirements.

The Earl Haig Secondary School in Willowdale, Ontario, which operates in similar fashion to the Vancouver schools, established the Academic Centre for Gifted Athletes (ACGA) in 1983. In 1986 the program was fully enrolled with one hundred students and also had a waiting list. Students receive one credit for time spent training and a second credit for sport-related courses which include kinesiology, sport psychology, coaching theory, and business management. The majority of the athletes in the program indicate that they wish to become involved in sport after their competitive careers, primarily in coaching. Academic schedules are structured to avoid interference with training schedules and teachers ensure that classes missed because of competition are made up. Academic standards are not lowered and in 1985–86 the average grade for ACGA students was 75% (Cruickshank 1986).

There is no doubt that the modified education arrangements being made in Canada are assisting talented young athletes to strive for excellence. However, in several respects, all but a very few programs fall short of those in Communist states.

The major overall deficiency is the relatively small number of talented young athletes who are able to enroll in such programs because of their paucity. Further, very few programs include intensive, high-level coaching as part of the school program. Instead they enable the student to devote daily blocks of time, either in regular school hours or after school, to training. Responsibility for coaching is left to the clubs which, in most sports, find it necessary to levy heavy fees. Many children, among whom there must be those with sports talent, are excluded from club programs because of an inability to pay.

Athletic talent is not related to socioeconomic status but, in too many cases in Canada, the opportunity to develop that talent is determined by it. The small number of programs and the isolation of school and club inevitably result in additional travel time and cost between home, school, and club. Finally, the ability to have sufficient flexibility in the education program to enable students, following lengthy absence from school for competition, to make up missed classes is difficult to attain in regular schools. These problems notwithstanding, programs which facilitate the concurrent pursuit of education and sport training are likely to be widely sought and established in Canada in the early 1990s.

Young athletes striving for excellence frequently devote twenty to thirty hours each week to sport training, and additional hours to travel. Essential competitions are sometimes scheduled in term time and unless the education schedule is made flexible to accommodate the sport needs of the young athlete, the tendency will be for the youngsters to neglect education. The consequences of this would be tragic. If talented young athletes are to fully develop their sport potential, and at the same time receive a sound education, it will be necessary for education and sport authorities to work closely together. Such cooperation has not been apparent on a wide scale to the present.

Other Support Groups

In each province a provincial School Sports Federation provides a range of support services to interschool sport programs. Services include communication—journals, bulletins, newsletters; coordination—conferences, seminars, administration of provincial championships; development—clinics for coaches and officials, athlete training camps; arbitration—arm's length interpretation of eligibility; and fund raising—organization of provincial lotteries to assist school fund raising. Each federation employs several full-time professional staff, and volunteer teachers make up committees which develop policies. The provincial federations are affiliated to the national body, the Canadian School Sports Federation. Refer back to figure 6.2, which shows the structure diagrammatically.

The national association for the broad field of physical education, the Canadian Association for Health, Physical Education, and Recreation (CAHPER), was established in 1933. Its first president, Dr. Arthur S. Lamb from McGill University, became known as the "father of physical education" in Canada. C. R. "Blackie" Blackstock, who had a forty-four year association with CAHPER, was the first executive secretary, and served for twenty-five years in that position. He was affectionately known as "Mr. CAHPER." The association's highest honour, the R. Tait McKenzie Honour Award, is in memory of the renowned Canadian physical educator, medical doctor, and sculptor.

Since 1971 a national office with professional staff has been located in Ottawa. The board of directors is comprised of the elected representatives of each of the twelve provincial and territorial branches. In addition, CAHPER business is carried out by a series of committees and special interest groups (SIGs) through which members engage in a wide variety of projects.

CAHPER serves its members by publishing a regular journal and newsletter and organizing an annual conference in different parts of the country. Throughout its existence CAHPER has provided national leadership in a wide range of developments in physical education. Its mission in the mid-1980s focussed upon the advocacy of physically active lifestyles for all Canadians, with particular emphasis on educational settings through the promotion of daily physical education for all school students, the dissemination of research findings and other resource material to practitioners, and the provision of input into programs of teacher preparation.

Summary of the Sport Delivery System in Public Schools

That segment of the delivery system which has the capacity to most influence the lifelong physical activity involvement of young people, namely the public schools, is beset by a series of contradictions and paradoxes.

At the elementary school level the delivery system has been strengthened by an increasingly widespread recognition of the importance of daily physical education, but implementation is hindered by inadequacies in facilities and teachers with insufficient preparation in the subject. Within the high schools the system has been progressively weakened by the removal of the requirement to take physical education after the tenth grade and the relatively small numbers of students who opt for the subject in the two senior grades. At one and the same time the federal government and one or more ministries in every provincial government are strongly encouraging increased participation in physical activity for the total population as a preventive health measure, while the education ministries in the provincial governments are reducing the physical activity involvement of senior high school students.

Declining school enrollments, coupled with reduced school budgets, have resulted in a curtailment of new young graduates entering the system. This lack of new blood has impoverished physical education programs and created a shortage of coaches which, compounded by the increasing withdrawal of teachers' voluntary services, is resulting in the demise of some interschool teams. Although there is a serious attempt to redress the longstanding inequality of opportunity for female students in the interschool program, progress may well be delayed by the shortage of coaches, particularly women, and rapidly rising program costs. It is ironic that provincial governments, under whose jurisdiction education lies, provide little or no funds for interschool sport but, in concert with the federal government, channel considerable sums toward the pursuit of excellence in sport outside schools.

There is considerable overlap between schools and community sport programs and, as we shall see later in this chapter, generally poor cooperation between school boards and governing bodies of sport.

If the school segment of the delivery system is to avoid stagnation some key issues must be addressed. Is physical education and sport educational? Does the school have a role in the pursuit of excellence in sport? As attitudes and practices regarding physical activity and sport in Canadian society undergo rapid change, the school system appears unsure of its role. Reappraisal of roles and commitment to responsibilities is an urgent requirement.

Universities

All Canadian universities offer intramural programs for the benefit of their students. These programs, in which large numbers of students take part, encompass a wide range of sports activities. The programs are funded by grants from the university and student society, membership and entrance fees, and increasingly from commercial sponsors. In all but the smallest universities, intramural programs are administered by faculty or other salaried personnel, but a very large proportion of operations, such as organizing and refereeing, are carried out by students on either a paid or voluntary basis.

Interuniversity sport competition has been an important part of Canadian universities since their inception. A conference, under the title of Canadian Intercollegiate Athletic Union, was established by universities and colleges in Ontario and Quebec in 1906, and the Maritimes Intercollegiate Athletic Union followed in 1910. The former body, which became known as the CIAU (Central), divided into two sectional organizations in 1955: the Ontario-Quebec Intercollegiate Athletic Association and the Ottawa-St. Lawrence Intercollegiate Athletic Association. However, prior to the mid-1950s, in all parts of the country except Ontario and Quebec (and the Maritimes to a lesser extent) where Canadian competition was more readily available, competition was more often with American universities. Geography was a major obstacle to all but a small amount of Canadian interuniversity competition; distances to the south were shorter than to the east or west. The advent of jet air travel and the rapid expansion of postsecondary institutions in the 1950s led to a major increase in Canadian interuniversity competition.

In response to these developments the Canadian Intercollegiate Athletic Union (CIAU) was formally established in 1961 as a national governing and coordinating body. The Canadian Women's Intercollegiate Athletic Union (CWIAU) was formed in 1969 and in 1978 the two bodies amalgamated to form the Canadian Interuniversity Athletic Union (CIAU). In order to make scheduling and costs more manageable, four geographically aligned regional associations were established in 1969: Atlantic, Quebec, Ontario, and Western Canada. In 1971 rising travel costs resulted in subdivision of the western region into two autonomous associations—Great Plains, covering Manitoba and Saskatchewan, and Canada West, incorporating Alberta and British Columbia— thus giving the CIAU five regional associations. The structure is shown diagrammatically in figure 6.2.

The CIAU has forty-four member universities, all the major degree-granting universities save one. Simon Fraser University is not a member of the union because of its recruiting and scholarship policies. Teams from that university compete in an American conference, the National Association of Intercollegiate Athletics (NAIA).

Within each regional association, universities compete in a limited number of designated sports for regional championships, the winners of which take part in national championships. A limited amount of interregional competition takes place, the results of which are important in determining national rankings and the award of wild-card invitations to national championships. The inclusion of a sport in the CIAU national championship program was determined initially by the number of universities across the country that have teams in that sport, but now is more dependent on the amount of available funding.

Interuniversity sport has traditionally been funded by annual student athletic fees, which are levied on all students and which vary considerably between institutions; admission fees to athletic events; and university grants. Almost from the beginning of expanded Canadian competition, and the virtual elimination of American competition, the western universities in particular (and those in the eastern Maritimes to a lesser extent) experienced repeated financial problems. Only by dismemberment of the Western Association, and the formation of two new associations, the Great Plains and Canada West, were travel costs made manageable in 1971. By 1978 the Canada West universities in particular, and also those in the Atlantic conference, were again in financial difficulty, due primarily to increased air travel costs. This was relieved by the federal government's introduction of the Travel Equalization Program. This program subsidizes interprovincial transportation costs of geographically distant universities, thereby encouraging continuance of participation in interuniversity sport. The universities in question are those in the Canada West and Great Plains associations and Memorial University.

Initially the total equalization grant was set at $500,000 annually, but this level of support was never realized. Before implementation in 1979 the grant was reduced to $378,000, in 1985 to $300,000, and in 1986 to $285,000. The latter grant was for one year only pending a proposal from the CIAU at Sport Canada's request to show how the money could be used in the future by universities to develop elite athletes in Olympic sports only, rather than being used as a travel subsidy for complete teams. Elimination of the travel equalization grant, as proposed by Sport Canada, would make it very difficult for universities in the two western conferences and Memorial University to continue to participate in interuniversity sport in its present form.

In the 1970s travel costs accelerated rapidly, and in the seven year period, 1972–73 to 1977–78, thirty-six sport programs were deleted from the six Canada West institutions. Despite the federal equalization grants, a further four programs were lost in the next four years. The smaller universities were particularly vulnerable. For example, in the decade 1975–1985 Brandon reduced its interuniversity program from fourteen sports to three, and Winnipeg from six to three.

Throughout the 1980s all interuniversity sport programs were adversely affected by increasing costs and declining budgets, particularly those in the four western provinces and Newfoundland. By 1985 many university programs were operating at between 60 and 70 percent of their 1980 budgets. Some of the steps that university athletic departments have taken in an attempt to generate increased revenue include renting out facilities to nonuniversity groups; organizing summer camps and other instructional programs for the general public; and soliciting corporate sponsorship, the latter often through the appointment of a full-time marketing manager.

Until 1970 Canadian universities were vehemently opposed to any form of athletic scholarship, fearing the abuses that had developed in the United States. In 1971 the federal government initiated a student-athlete financial aid program, which was followed by similar programs in each of the provinces. The development and extent of these programs are detailed in chapter 7.

The CIAU recognizes three levels of student-athlete assistance, and these awards may be received by student-athletes without jeopardy to their eligibility status. Second- and third-party awards are made by provincial and federal governments respectively in support of high-performance athletes. First-party awards, which were approved by the CIAU in 1981–82, are administered by university awards offices. The value of the awards varies from university to university; however, they may not exceed $1000. Irrespective of any award, only full-time students are eligible for CIAU competition.

Community Colleges

The community college sport structure is somewhat similar to that of the universities. There are eight conferences (Maritimes, two in Quebec, Ontario, Manitoba, Saskatchewan, Alberta, and British Columbia) which are members of the Canadian Colleges Athletic Association (CCAA). The structure is shown diagrammatically in figure 6.2. In total there are some 120 community colleges in Canada, 90 of which are members of the CCAA.

Quebec differs from all other provinces in that all students in higher education are required to attend a community college or *College d'Enseignement General et Professional* (CEGEP). Students may then either proceed directly into the work force or after two years of study transfer to a university to complete a degree. In all other provinces, students may chose to enrol in nontransfer courses at a college, study for up to two years at college and then transfer to a university, or enter university in the first year of a degree program. In consequence, the community college organization in Quebec is much larger than in any other province.

The national championships organized by the CCAA are contested in six sports: badminton, basketball, curling, and volleyball for both men and women, and hockey and soccer for men. Travel costs associated with championships are fully funded by Sport Canada. Provincial championships are held in the same six sports. In most cases these championships receive provincial government funding assistance.

The level of development of community college sport varies considerably from province to province. Quebec, on the one hand, attaches great importance to this strata of the delivery system, and with close to sixty colleges, good quality, easily accessible competition results in an overall high standard of achievement. On the other hand, the ten colleges in British Columbia, five of which are in the distant interior of the province, receive no government funding and in the early 1980s suffered severe funding cutbacks due to college budget reductions. As a result, the five interior colleges withdrew from provincial and national competition.

Summary of University and Community College Sport Delivery Systems

The years between eighteen and twenty-five that young people spend at a university are a time when those among them that are aspiring elite athletes approach athletic maturity. Canadian universities have the necessary resources to develop athletic excellence: a large proportion of young athletes with elite potential; facilities that are among the best in the country; highly competent coaches; support services, such as sport medicine, athlete testing, and research capabilities; and a well-established competition program. Interuniversity sport should, therefore, be a cornerstone in the amateur sport delivery system.

Since the early 1970s, the universities in the four western provinces (particularly British Columbia) and Memorial University have encountered repeated financial problems caused by increasing air travel costs and decreasing university and Sport Canada support. A large number of sports have been eliminated from the interuniversity program, and once that level of competition is lost the talent base in that sport is dissipated. Rebuilding that talent base is a lengthy, arduous process. Yet program reduction continued into the second half of the 1980s, and the threat to the survival of Canadian interuniversity sport in those provinces remained undiminished. The university as a nursery of sport talent is irreplaceable in the Canadian delivery system and further erosion can have only the most serious consequences. The community college sport delivery system is a microcosm of the university system and suffers from similar problems.

THE AMATEUR SPORT DELIVERY SYSTEM

The **amateur sport delivery system** in Canada is made up of a group of autonomous core organizations—clubs and provincial and national governing bodies of sport—which together constitute the spine of organized amateur sport. With very few exceptions each individual sport has a similar structure, which is essentially pyramidal in nature.

At the base of the structure are clubs or teams which compete primarily within locally organized leagues. The clubs in each sport are members of a governing body of that sport, an organization which is recognized as the controlling agency for that sport in a geographically designated area. Governing bodies are primarily organized at provincial and national levels, but may also be local and regional. Within the governing body structure each level is affiliated with the level above, thus forming a unified structure from base to apex.

At each level the governing body's function is to provide governance and services to member organizations. Although most governing bodies, and a very few clubs, employ salaried personnel to perform administrative, technical, and coaching duties, the vast majority of club and governing body officers are democratically elected volunteers. Amateur sport is, and has always been, dependent on volunteer workers. Without the many hundreds of thousands of hours they devote to the running of their sport organization the amateur sport delivery system would be completely unable to operate.

Outside the governing body structure, but providing support services to it, are sport federations and administration centres at both provincial and national levels and, at the latter level, organizations such as the Coaching Association of Canada. In addition, national governing bodies in the Olympic sports are members of the Canadian Olympic Association (COA). Extensions of the Canadian system provide a two-pronged affiliation to the International Olympic Committee (IOC). The COA, like other national Olympic committees, is a member of the IOC, and each Canadian national governing body is a member of the international sport federation in that sport. Each of these federations, in the Olympic sports, is represented on the IOC. The amateur sport delivery system is shown diagrammatically in figure 6.3.

Amateur Sport Clubs

Within the sport delivery system the club is widely regarded as playing a key role. The **club** is the basic unit of organization outside the school system.

> The origin of the 'club' system of sport was a phenomenon of urbanization resulting from an uprooting of the traditional rural approach to recreation. Urban living imposed different restrictions on individuals and yet, concomitantly, it also offered more opportunities for individuals with common interests to assemble together and organize competition amongst themselves. (Jobling 1976, 74)

The club system was first developed in Britain as a consequence of urbanization associated with the Industrial Revolution. As Redmond has said, ". . . Britain may be described as the main crucible in which modern sport was forged for mass production and consumption and later distributed on a worldwide basis through the international network of Empire (now Commonwealth)" (Redmond 1978, 76).

In the history of sport in Canada in the nineteenth century the single most significant factor was the British influence. Initially Montreal, at that time the centre of a vast commercial empire, became the "cradle of Canadian sport" (Wise and Fisher 1974, 21). A group comprising leading businessmen, professional men, and military officers, all with a background of sport gained in the British public schools, were instrumental in developing a club structure for sport in Montreal. As Metcalfe has said in his detailed analysis of organized sport in early Montreal, ". . . the predominant position of the British, white collar (upper) middle class, first as participants and always as organizers is striking" (Metcalfe 1976, 96–97). On the west coast, British naval officers performed the same role, as did the Royal Canadian Mounted Police on the prairies. Overall, the military garrisons provided the leadership and organizational skills across the country.

The preeminence of Montreal in the development of Canadian sport is indicated by the large number of "first" clubs in Canada, in a range of sports, that were established in that city. Examples include the Montreal Curling Club (1807), which was the earliest sport club in Canada; Montreal Snow Shoe Club (1840); Montreal Olympic Club (1842–43); Montreal Lacrosse Club (1856); Montreal Football Club (1868); and Montreal Golf Club (1873).

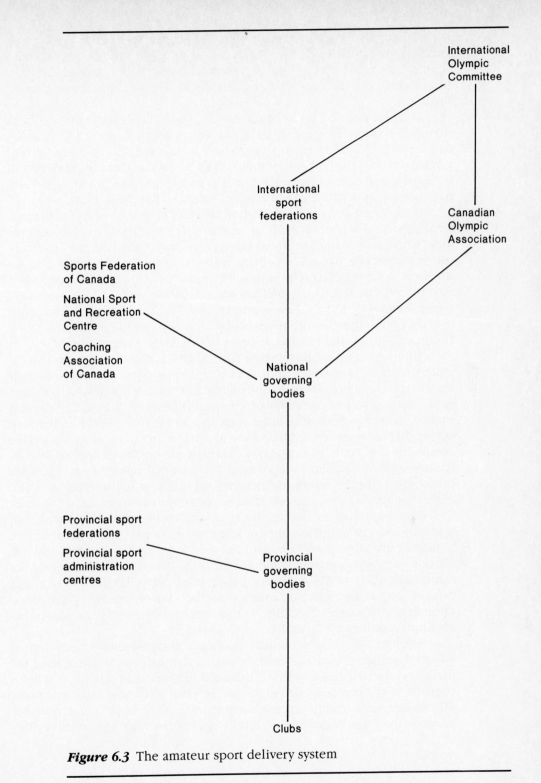

Figure 6.3 The amateur sport delivery system

Other "first" clubs in Canada were the Halifax Yacht Club (1837); Victoria Cricket Club (ca. 1850); Victoria Rowing Club (1865); and Toronto Tennis Club (1874). As in England, some clubs built their own clubhouses and grounds, but the number doing this in Canada was proportionally much smaller.

Mention must be made of the YMCA. From its beginning in the back streets of London, England in 1841, the Young Men's Christian Association developed rapidly in North America, where it built and operated hundreds of gymnasia before the end of the century. The YMCAs on this continent had all the appearance of a multisport club and in both Canada and the United States have been a cornerstone of physical recreation to the present day.

In the present-day Canadian sport delivery system, the base of the pyramid outside of schools is made up of teams of young boys, and increasingly girls, who start playing as early as eight years of age. Hockey and soccer are the primary sports played, but much smaller numbers of youngsters also get involved in other sports. The teams, which are usually organized and operated by enthusiastic parents, affiliate within age and geographic divisions in house leagues or local minor sport associations. These minor associations provide opportunities for thousands of young boys, and unfortunately fewer young girls, to get their first experience of organized competition.

Minor sport teams, in common with all clubs, at a minimum provide facilities, coaching, and competition in varying degrees commensurate with their level of development. These are the essential services without which athletes could not participate or fully attain their performance potential. Voluntary sport clubs range from little more than a group of like-minded individuals who gather together at a public park or similar facility in order to take part in competition, to complex organizations which own and operate their own facilities, employ salaried coaches, and have annual operating budgets approaching a quarter-million dollars. Among older established private sport clubs, budgets of more than one million dollars annually are not uncommon.

The key resources of an amateur sport club are the volunteers who devote many hours to its operation in both administration and coaching capacities. Volunteer officials usually become involved with a club through familial affiliation (a child becomes a club member) and, in many cases, terminate the association when the child leaves the club. Many club officials attend training courses for administrators or coaches. In the case of coaches, certification through the National Coaching Certification Program is increasingly becoming a requirement by clubs.

Amateur sport clubs' annual operating budgets range from several hundred dollars to a quarter-million dollars. Irrespective of the size of the budget, clubs struggle to achieve balanced finances, and all devote what is considered by many to be excessive time in a variety of fund-raising projects. The major source of club income is membership fees, which range from $10 annually for a low-organization club to $1500 for a high-performance club.

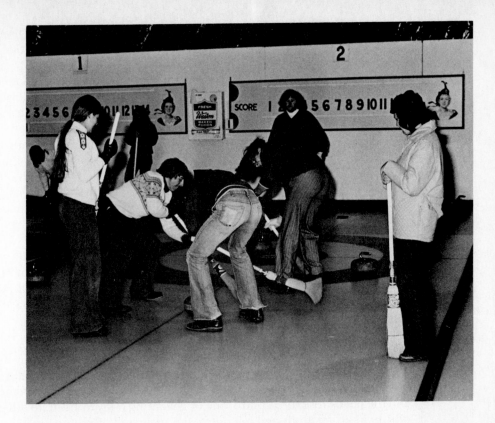

The high fees in some sports are a major deterrent to participation. Athletic talent is not related to socioeconomic status, but in too many cases the opportunity to develop that talent in some sports is determined by it. High fees are necessary because athletes in these elite clubs receive coaching for at least twenty hours a week, and the resulting coaching expenses and facility rentals are high-expenditure items. High-performance clubs, particularly in such sports as gymnastics, swimming, and figure skating, are more professionalized than other clubs in the sense that they employ salaried coaches often on a full-time basis and, in a small number of cases, own their own facilities. With very few exceptions the facilities used by amateur sport clubs in Canada are under the jurisdiction of local recreation departments or school boards.

Access to school and recreation department facilities by amateur sport clubs is controlled by policies drawn up by autonomous local school boards and recreation departments, and there is considerable variance from one community to another. In some communities all school sport facilities are programmed and managed by the municipal recreation department in nonschool time, and clubs have access at minimal or no cost. In others, school boards manage all school facilities. Policies range from access at little cost to high rental fees and inflexible regulations. In still other communities, recreation departments, in their efforts to provide facilities for recreational use, experience difficulty allocating the amount of time clubs require, particularly at prime times.

In general, access to adequate facilities at desired times and at reasonable cost is a major problem for amateur sport clubs. Overall, the level of cooperation between school boards, recreation departments, and amateur sport clubs could be improved to the benefit of the sport delivery system.

If the increased participation in amateur sport and physical recreation activities is to be sustained, it is imperative that responsible sport groups be permitted easy and affordable access to school sport facilities. Within the delivery system some communities may well be deficient in some specialist sport facilities. In the case of general sport facilities it is not so much a shortage, but rather a shortage of facilities that are accessible. Access to all school facilities would go a long way to remedying the situation.

An enlightened approach to the design of school sport facilities is to provide dimensions which can accommodate both school children of a specific age and adults. Unfortunately, a very large majority of school facilities have been designed for a specific school-age population and this places some limitations on wider public use.

Sport Governing Bodies

As we have seen, the organization of sport clubs was largely a product of urbanization. With improved transportation, competition spread further afield and the need arose for a controlling or governing body to arbitrate differences of rule interpretations and to control the incursion of professionalism.

The first governing body in Canada, the National Lacrosse Association, was formed in 1867, and others followed soon after. A major influence in the formation of national governing bodies in the years after Confederation was national pride, and this was reflected in a desire for national championships and international competition.

Many of the early national governing bodies were national in name only, with organization and jurisdiction only in parts of the country. With time, however, the classical pyramidal-structured sport organization became fully developed. From clubs at the base, the organization structure progresses to regional associations to provincial and national governing bodies.

In the early days the primary function of a governing body was to govern—to establish the rules and to arbitrate when disputes occurred. All officers were voluntary and honorary; they ran their sport in their spare time without remuneration and often without expenses. This independence continued essentially until beyond the midpoint of this century.

In the second half of the present century the development of amateur sport has burgeoned. Unprecedented growth of national competition, and more particularly international competition, increased the costs of developing and promoting an amateur sport beyond the means of the sport itself. External assistance was an urgent requirement.

The assistance came from the federal government in 1961 in the form of *Bill C131, An Act to Encourage Fitness and Amateur Sport,* which is discussed in detail in chapter 7. Under the <u>Act</u>, national governing bodies received grants for such things as team travel to international competition, coaches' training, conferences, newsletters, and other developmental activities. Through a cost-sharing agreement with the provinces, provincial governing bodies received similar grants from provincial government sport agencies. The administrative structure of both provincial and national governing bodies was strengthened, and the delivery system made more effective.

An unforeseen consequence of government funding assistance was the heavily increased administrative load placed on volunteer officials, to the extent that the duties could not be adequately performed by them. In the words of the *Report of the Task Force on Sport for Canadians* in 1969, Canadian amateur sport could no longer be completely run by "kitchen table administration." In 1970 the federal government response, through its agency Sport Canada, was a program of grants to national governing bodies to cover the costs of an executive director and support services for each sport. All sports welcomed the assistance, but a large majority resented the centralization of their executive directors in the National Sport and Recreation Centre in Ottawa. The centralization, a requirement of Sport Canada, created a physical separation between the executive directors and the elected voluntary governing body officials.

Almost seventy national governing bodies have established a national office in the National Sport and Recreation Centre in Ottawa, with administrative, technical, and clerical staff supported by Sport Canada grants. At the provincial level, grants from provincial governments support similar offices and personnel, usually housed in provincial sport administration centres.

The functions of governing bodies, at both national and provincial levels, have increased dramatically since the 1950s, and particularly since the onset of government funding assistance in 1961. They now include identification, testing, selection, and coaching of athletes; training camps at home and abroad; organization of major competitions in Canada and transportation to competitions abroad; hosting touring teams; athlete financial support programs; training and certification of coaches and officials; and advisory services, promotions, and publications. To fulfill these obligations governing bodies employ full-time salaried administrators, technical directors, and coaches.

Two major concerns have ensued. The expanded activities of governing bodies have resulted in financial requirements beyond the means of all but a very few. Membership fees, which are the primary source of income, do not meet expenditures. At the national level (and it is no different at the provincial level) it has been determined that government grants contribute between 60 percent and 75 percent of all dollars spent by the governing bodies. In the halcyon days of the 1970s, government grants increased with demand, but by the early 1980s a limit to increase had been reached. Governing bodies, of necessity, had to improve their revenue generating capacities and pursue private sector sponsorship. Governing bodies, both national and provincial, which were completely independent prior to 1961, had, in less than twenty years, developed a high level of dependency on governments for their operating funds.

The second concern is largely a consequence of the first. Government funds do not come without some measure of control on programs and policies. In addition, full-time employees who carry on the day-to-day business of the governing body become influential because of their centrality. Among some volunteer elected officials there is concern that a sport's control of its operations and destiny is being progressively eroded.

In 1980 the Canadian Amateur Hockey Association (CAHA), the largest governing body in the country, took an unprecedented step in changing the volunteer makeup of its executive officers. The CAHA believed that the office of president had become too demanding for a part-time volunteer and restructured its senior administration along the lines of a business corporation. A full-time, salaried president is responsible for day-to-day administration and he reports to a chairman and board of directors who are part-time elected volunteers.

In 1986–87 Sport Canada introduced a career-structure salary assistance policy which provided incentives for national sport organizations to give more responsibility to senior professional staff. A higher level of funding support became available, in a pilot project with high-performance Olympic sports, to those organizations which had given over the management responsibility, including a significant role in policy development, to the director general. The Canadian Track and Field Association (CTFA) met these requirements in 1986 when its senior professional officer assumed the titles of president and chief executive officer and the volunteer part-time officials became chairmen and directors of the board. The CTFA restructuring is likely to be emulated by other large Olympic National Sport Organizations (NSOs).

Multi-Sport Agencies

The primary function of multi-sport agencies is to provide support or special services to national and provincial governing bodies. In the Canadian amateur sport and recreation delivery system the major multi-sport agencies are as follows.

Amateur Athletic Union of Canada

Historically, the first national multi-sport agency in Canada was the Amateur Athletic Union of Canada (AAU of C) which was founded in 1885, largely through the efforts of the Montreal Athletic Association, itself an amalgam of three single-sport clubs, established in 1881. The primary purpose of the AAU of C was to protect the amateur ideal in the face of incursion by rapidly developing professional and commercial sport.

The AAU of C developed into the most powerful organization in Canadian sport in the first half of this century. It was the authority for granting of official sanction to stage national championships, drawing up rules defining amateur status. It also was the Canadian representative on most international sport associations and governed Canada's participation in the Olympic Games. The AAU of C began to lose its almost total control of Canadian amateur sport immediately before, but more so after, World War II, when individual sports withdrew to form autonomous single-sport governing bodies. In 1949 the Canadian Olympic Association, which previously had been an AAU of C committee, established its autonomy, and in 1970 the AAU of C was dissolved.

Canadian Olympic Association

The Canadian Olympic Association (COA) is the representative of the Olympic movement in Canada whose purpose is to promote Olympism and amateur sport in the country. This autonomous nonprofit organization raises funds through the Olympic Trust, and receives federal government grants to coordinate Canadian Olympic and Pan American Games teams and provide funding to a number of development programs.

The COA's membership comprises representatives from the national governing bodies of the Olympic sport disciplines in Canada, and selected leaders from Canadian business, industry, and community affairs. An executive director and staff manage the day-to-day operations of the association out of Olympic House in Montreal.

Sports Federation of Canada

Following a series of annual conferences of national governing bodies in the late 1940s, the Canadian Sports Advisory Council was formed in 1951 to act as a clearing house for ideas, to formulate ways and means for the advancement of amateur sport, and to hold annual meetings which would act as a forum for the exchange of members' views. In 1971 the organization changed its name to the Sports Federation of Canada. The primary role of the federation continues to be a forum for discussion of issues and concepts in Canadian sport at national level, and many developments in the delivery system have first been raised among its more than eighty national governing body members.

Two further multi-sport support organizations, the National Sport and Recreation Centre and the Coaching Association of Canada, play major roles in the sport delivery system and are, therefore, worthy of note. These organizations are two of a small group known as arm's-length organizations which were created—and are funded—by the federal government to conduct specific programs. Each organization is autonomous, controlled by a board of directors and free from direct government control.

National Sport and Recreation Centre

The National Sport and Recreation Centre was created in 1970 after a federally appointed task force on sport for Canadians reported that national sport and recreation associations suffered from a lack of unity and inadequate administration. Based in Ottawa the centre provides a wide variety of administrative services to some ninety associations, close to seventy of whose administrative offices are located in the centre complex. An indication of the development of the centre is the increase in administrative, technical, and clerical staff, which grew from 65 in 1970 to 532 in 1984.

Coaching Association of Canada

The Coaching Association of Canada (CAC) is a national, nonprofit organization. Its major aims are to increase coaching effectiveness in all sports and to encourage the development of coaching by providing programs and services to coaches at all levels.

The CAC was formed in 1971 on the recommendation of the federal government's task force on sport. Its policies are developed and supervised by a board of directors and executive committee drawn from several sectors of the Canadian sport community. It is managed by a professional staff in its national office, which is located in the National Sport and Recreation Centre in Ottawa.

Among the association's programs and services are the National Coaching Certification Program; scholarships and grants for university students in coaching studies at the graduate level, and for apprentice coaches studying under master coaches at the elite level; an audiovisual, library, and resource centre; a world-recognized documentation centre; major national symposia on coaching-oriented topics; and consultant services to many sport agencies.

Provincial Sports Federations

At provincial level, sports federations, the first of which was founded in the early 1960s, provide a range of services to their member associations, similar to the National Sport and Recreation Centre in Ottawa. The provincial sports federations are known as Sport B.C., Sport Nova Scotia, Sask Sport, etc., and their members are provincial governing bodies of sport. Each federation is controlled by a board of directors and employs professional staff for day-to-day operations. Most provinces have a sport administration centre which accommodates the administrative offices of provincial governing bodies, and which is managed by the provincial sports federation.

Summary of the Amateur Sport Delivery System

Up to the midpoint of the present century, all levels of the amateur sport delivery system in Canada were autonomous, independent, and run at a low-key level by part-time volunteers. Since midcentury the massive expansion of national and international competition, and the concomitant services required for supporting the pursuit of high performance, have dramatically increased the roles and responsibilities of two levels of the system, namely national and provincial governing bodies. In the process these two levels have become largely dependent on government funding, and have lost some degree of autonomy.

In the lower tier of the system, the clubs which constitute the essential base upon which the sport structure is built are still run to a very large extent by part-time volunteer officers. With very few exceptions these clubs do not receive funding assistance from municipal or other levels of government. The lack of assistance to clubs, in the form of grants and reduced facility rental fees, remains the major unresolved problem in the amateur sport delivery system.

THE RECREATION DELIVERY SYSTEM

> Recreation is seen as an expression of leisure and is an essential life-enriching experience. It is the medium through which the individual may improve the quality of life, and includes all those things people choose to do in their free time, alone or in a group, and from which they get enjoyment and personal satisfaction. (Ontario undated, 1:1)

In contrast to the delivery systems in schools, amateur sport clubs, and governing bodies of sport, the Canadian **recreation delivery system** has been strongly influenced by the United States. Only since the 1960s has a Canadian recreation identity begun to emerge. Inspiration in the early part of the century came from the Playground Association of America. Provision for recreation in Canadian communities was often initiated by the local Council of Women, followed by a broadly representative playground association. These community or neighbourhood associations, supplemented by service clubs, eventually led to the establishment of a civic department—usually a section of the parks department—responsible for playground and other recreation programming. In addition, many Canadian recreators, both academic and professional, received much of their education in American universities, and this association is clearly reflected in the development of Canadian municipal recreation.

The delivery of recreation in Canada is through a complex system of interrelated enterprises. This delivery system is made up of public, voluntary, private, and commercial agencies. In the ideal system, agencies would constantly interact with each other and all would relate closely to other public delivery systems such as education, health, and amateur sport. However, these systems have developed independently of each other, and jealously guard their autonomy. In consequence, complete consultation and cooperation have not been achieved and the potential of the system not fully realized.

Municipal Recreation

Municipal recreation in Canada, which had its beginnings in the 1930s, grew slowly at first but began to gather strength in the late 1940s and expanded rapidly in the 1950s. During the early stages of municipal recreation, the initiative for developing all recreation programs was taken by citizens. These volunteers planned and operated their own activities with encouragement and support from local councils. The programs that were developed reflected particular interests and attitudes of a local community, and the wide diversity of programs established at that time remains today. Although all but the smallest communities now employ professional staff, the volunteer involvement remains high, particularly in medium and small communities.

The size of the municipality is the primary determinant of the type of administrative structure established to provide recreation services. Throughout Canada there are three major administrative models. Large urban centres usually have a recreation committee made up of appointed councillors (Vancouver is the exception where the recreation committee members are elected), a recreation department with full-time staff, and relatively little direct citizen participation. Smaller towns have a committee of council, a small department with full- and part-time staff, and rely heavily on volunteers. The smallest communities have no paid staff and depend entirely on volunteer help. In addition to the central recreation committee most larger communities also appoint community recreation centre management committees. These latter committees develop policies for the operation of local community centres.

The municipal recreation committee is not a corporate body and cannot own property. All recreation facilities are vested in the name of the municipality, and at all times the recreation committee is the agent of the municipal council. The committee cannot incur debt beyond the items of expenditures identified in its current budget and approved by council, and monies in the budget are held in the municipal bank account.

The major source of revenue for municipal recreation programs is municipal taxes. Other local sources are registration or admission fees, rental charges, concessions, and donations. Grants from provincial and federal governments may be awarded. Such grants are primarily toward the cost of constructing facilities but in a few instances are also for programs.

A municipal recreation committee acts on behalf of the city council, to whom it is responsible, in undertaking assigned duties according to city bylaws and established procedures. It also advises the council on recreation matters in the community. The duty of the recreation committee is to ensure that adequate opportunities exist for all citizens in the community to engage in satisfying and constructive recreation activities appropriate to their age, capabilities, and personal interests (Ontario undated, 3:2).

Other public agencies are also involved in the provision of recreation programs and services. These include such specialist organizations as school boards, colleges and universities, and library, museum, and gallery boards. Some school boards have agreements with municipal recreation committees for the joint use of school facilities. The best of these agreements provides for the transfer of responsibility for the management of all school facilities, after school hours, to the municipal recreation department. Such an arrangement ensures maximum use of school facilities for public recreation. However, a large number of municipalities fall short of the ideal.

The provision of opportunities for recreation depends, to a large extent, on the provision of facilities. In the Canadian delivery system, the provision of the vast majority of recreation facilities is the responsibility of the municipal level of government. Two municipal agencies—the recreation committee and school board—either recommend to city council or act on their behalf in such provision. All provincial governments contribute to the capital costs of school and recreation facility construction. Grants toward school buildings are based on long-standing formulas. For recreation facilities, grants became widely available in the early 1970s. The proportion of total cost covered by grant varies in size from province to province, and in the case of recreation facilities, have not been continuously available in all provinces.

The federal government contributes to capital expenditures for sport facilities only to those used for major multipurpose sports events, such as the Olympic, Commonwealth, Pan American, World Student, and Canada games. Some cities, notably Winnipeg, Montreal, Edmonton, and Calgary, have benefitted greatly from hosting major international competitions, as have municipalities in every province from hosting the biannual Canada Games. The federal government does give capital and program grants to municipalities for nonsport-related recreation activities.

In municipalities that have a recreation department the primary role of the staff is to maintain, manage, program, and staff facilities such as community centres, arenas, swimming pools, playing fields, tennis and other racquet courts, running tracks, golf courses, boating facilities, and a range of facilities for other activities, as well as parks and open spaces. In small communities without professional staff, these responsibilities, albeit involving a much smaller range of facilities, are covered by volunteers.

The programs available in municipal recreation centres encompass a wide range of physical, social, and cultural activities for all ages from young children to senior citizens; for able-bodied citizens and those with a variety of handicaps; and for complete beginners to those who wish to practice skills already learned. Instructors and leaders are provided by the recreation department, and by organizations and groups which use the facilities.

Traditionally in Canada, recreation has not been afforded the same status as other public services such as health and education. However, at the first provincial recreation ministers' conference, held in Edmonton in 1974, it was unanimously resolved that:

> because: society is rapidly changing and leisure time is increasing; and recreation includes all those activities in which an individual chooses to participate in his or her leisure time of a physical, artistic, creative, cultural, social and intellectual nature; and recreation is a fundamental need for citizens of all ages and interests and is essential to the psychological, social and physical well-being of people; therefore be it resolved that: recreation be recognized as a social service in the same way that health and education are considered social services and that recreation's purpose shall be:
> > to assist individual and community development,
> > to improve the quality of life, and
> > to enhance social functioning (Alberta 1974, 1)

Voluntary agencies were the forerunners of the recreation delivery system, and include such long-established organizations as the YMCA and YWCA; Boy Scouts and Girl Guides; Boys' and Girls' Clubs of Canada; and and settlement houses. Many voluntary agencies have strong connections with the church. Although some voluntary agencies raise considerable sums from membership fees, they rely heavily on self-generated fund-raising programs, and donations and grants from both the private and public sectors.

Private Agencies

Private recreation agencies include (1) country clubs, which usually offer a range of sports activities, and (2) clubs, which provide opportunities to learn or play one or a small number of sports. The curling club has been a feature of all but the smallest of Canadian communities for many years and has become a social institution. Golf clubs have also been long established in larger cities, but in recent years groups of enthusiasts have formed clubs and built courses and clubhouses in many smaller towns. In areas where neither population density nor terrain would support a commercial enterprise, local groups also operate small ski hills.

Private clubs are nonprofit organizations which are administered by boards of directors that are elected from the club members. All expenditures must be met by membership fees and club services such as dining and bar facilities, pro shop, and instruction.

Commercially Operated Recreation Centres

Among the commercial organizations that are more oriented toward physical activity are bowling alleys, racquet sports centres, and fitness centres. Commercial bowling alleys are a phenomenon of the 1950s. Tennis, squash, and racquetball centres, either separately or with two or more sports combined, developed rapidly in the 1970s. Fitness centres, incorporating one or more of a number of fitness training methods, first made an appearance in any numbers in the late 1970s. Unlike public recreation agencies, commercial centres receive no subsidies and must generate profit to remain in business.

Employee Recreation Programs

Organized employee recreation programs are more often associated with large commercial or industrial firms. Research in Canada and abroad has demonstrated that involvement in company-provided fitness programs significantly reduces worker absenteeism, resulting in improved productivity. Although Canada lags behind the United States and Japan in the provision of employee fitness programs, there has been considerable growth since 1978 in such programs, both within firms and through company contributions to employee membership fees in community or commercial fitness programs.

Recreation Associations

Each province has a provincial recreation association which acts as a voice for recreation issues and concerns, and as a service organization to its members. Members include individuals (both practitioners and volunteers), recreation departments, and voluntary, educational, and commercial organizations. In some provinces there are independent provincial organizations for parks, arenas, aquatics, recreation directors, facility managers, and research which, in some cases, are affiliated by membership in a provincial federation. In other provinces the provincial recreation association embraces the wide range of special interests. Associations whose primary function is to provide services to members are usually required to be self-supporting, while associations who also provide educational and developmental services to a wider population usually receive provincial government grants to offset costs.

At the national level, the Canadian Parks and Recreation Association performs a similar service function for provincial associations. Membership is open to individuals, municipal recreation departments, and voluntary and commercial organizations.

Summary of the Recreation Delivery System

Although the earliest voluntary recreation agencies were established in response to poor social conditions in the mid-1800s, it was only a century later that recreation began to gain widespread acceptance as a social service in the same vein as education and health. In that time the Canadian recreation delivery system has expanded to include a myriad of agencies—public, voluntary, private, and commercial—which provide opportunities for physical, as well as social and cultural, recreation for a wide range of interests and populations.

The municipal recreation department, which has assumed a central role in the system, is a major provider of facilities which are a basic prerequisite for opportunity to participate. An equally important provider of facilities is the school board, which up to now has not always accepted a responsibility for provision of recreation. In ideal situations these two public agencies work closely together to maximize the availability of publicly owned recreation and sport facilities. However, the ideal is far from universal, and the challenge that remains is to attain complete cooperation and coordination between municipal recreation departments, school boards, amateur sport clubs, and other voluntary agencies.

SUMMARY

It has been shown in this chapter that the Canadian amateur sport and recreation delivery system is a complex structure made up of a large number of organizations with the overall common objective of creating environments in which citizens may engage in physical activities of their choice. Although some organizations from the outset developed in association with others, most developed in complete independence. Therefore, it is not surprising that full cooperation and coordination is yet to be attained. However, if we are to make the fullest use of our resources—human, fiscal, and facilities—full cooperation must be our aim. Only then will the delivery system provide opportunities for all—infants and senior citizens; males and females; beginners and high-performance athletes; rich and poor. Such a system would enhance the quality of life of all Canadians.

REFERENCES

Alberta, Province of. First National Conference of Provincial Recreation Ministers. *Resolutions.* Edmonton, Alberta, 1974.

Cruickshank, Ian. "A European Concept Comes to Canada." *Coaching Review* (Coaching Association of Canada, Ottawa) (September 1986).

Fiander, Paul R. *Extra Curricular Activities in Public Senior High Schools in Nova Scotia as Perceived by the Principal.* Halifax, Nova Scotia, 1985.

Hindmarch, R. G., et al. *B.C. High Schools Interscholastic Athletic Programs: A Survey.* Vancouver, British Columbia, 1979.

Jobling, Ian F. "Urbanization and Sport in Canada, 1867–1900." In *Canadian Sport: Sociological Perspectives,* edited by R. S. Gruneau and J. G. Albinson. Don Mills, Ontario: Addison-Wesley (Canada), 1976.

Macintosh, Donald J., et al. *The Role of Interschool Sports Programs in Ontario Secondary Schools.* Ontario: Ministry of Education, 1977.

Metcalfe, A. "Organized Sport and Social Stratification in Montreal, 1840–1901." In *Canadian Sport: Sociological Perspectives,* edited by R. S. Gruneau and J. G. Albinson. Don Mills, Ontario: Addison-Wesley (Canada), 1976.

Ontario, Province of. *Municipal Recreation Bulletin,* Issues 1 and 3. Toronto: Ministry of Tourism and Recreation, (undated).

Redmond, Gerald. "Some Aspects of Organized Sport and Leisure in Nineteenth Century Canada." *Loisir et Societe* (Spring, 1978).

Wise, S. F., and Fisher, D. *Canada's Sporting Heroes.* Don Mills, Ontario: General Publishing Company, 1974.

CHAPTER 7

Government in Sport and Recreation

Eric F. Broom

Direct and substantial government involvement in amateur sport, which started in 1961 at the federal level and somewhat earlier in some provinces, came later in Canada than in most developed nations. This was particularly so in comparison to European countries, both western and eastern. Despite this late start, and slow development of government assistance up to 1970, both federal and provincial governments made very rapid advances in their sport aid programs in the next decade. To a large extent the greatly increased involvement was due to the award of the 1976 Olympic Games to Montreal. This chapter will trace the development and detail the extent of government involvement in amateur sport and recreation in Canada.

EARLY GOVERNMENT INVOLVEMENT

Up to 1960 the interest of the federal government in amateur sport was superficial. Any involvement was cautious, low-key, and catalytic. It was centred on the themes of physical fitness for national security through the Strathcona Trust (1909) and the National Physical Fitness Act (1943); rehabilitative training for the unemployed through the Youth Training Act (1939); and fostering national prestige through international sport as reflected by grants to the Canadian Olympic Committee, which were first made in 1920, to help defray Olympic team expenses.

Prior to the 1930s, provincial government involvement in amateur sport was minimal, although a number of provinces did make small annual grants to sport organizations. For example, provincial rifle associations were grant-aided by Manitoba as early as 1884, and the Alpine Club of Canada was aided by Alberta from 1906. Other provinces assisted these and other sport associations in later years. Throughout the 1930s, 1940s, and 1950s, provincial governments continued to make small grants to an increasing number of provincial governing bodies of sport. Regular grants were also made to the organizations in charge of Canada's participation in the Olympic, Pan American, and Commonwealth games. During this period there were few, if any, systematic policies, and as a result there existed a rather haphazard and occasional method of funding.

In 1934 British Columbia, motivated by welfare considerations during the Depression, became the first government in Canada to promote sport and recreation on a wider scale. Originally designed for the thousands of unemployed men in relief camps in the province, the program later expanded to encompass the whole community. The program, formally designated the Provincial Recreation Program and popularly known as Pro-Rec, functioned until 1953. Once federal funds became available in 1937 it was used as a model for similar programs in Alberta, Saskatchewan, Manitoba, and New Brunswick.

National Physical Fitness Act of 1943

In response to the high rejection rate of military recruits because of inadequate physical fitness, the federal government passed the **National Physical Fitness Act** in 1943. Between 1944 and 1954 the federal government, under this Act, made cost-sharing grants to the provinces which assisted the development of provincial fitness and recreation programs; school programs and degree courses in physical education; and the 5BX and 10BX physical fitness programs developed by the Royal Canadian Air Force. The federal Fitness Branch, which was established to administer the program, also convened meetings of national governing bodies of sport, which eventually led to the founding in 1951 of the Canadian Sports Advisory Council (CSAC), now the Sports Federation of Canada.

Despite these indirect achievements, the ten-year tenure of the federal program was characterized by frustration and a general sense of disappointment. Inadequacies in legislation, objectives, and funding, as well as inconsistent leadership and direction, all contributed to its demise, but these were merely reflections of the insurmountable obstacle—a less than full commitment by the federal government. When, in 1954, the Act was repealed almost without discussion, no widespread provincial lobby emerged in protest, but the unilateral termination of the joint funding program exacerbated provincial distrust of cooperation with the federal government.

In addition to contributing to the lack of accord between the two levels of government, the program also led to alienation between national sport associations and the federal government. A poorly worded announcement from the director of the Fitness Branch, Ian Eisenhardt, who had previously headed the Pro-Rec program in British Columbia, led sport officials in 1945 to believe that government was planning to exert influence on the development of sport. The ensuing nationwide outcry against government control of sport, exaggerated though it may have been, led to the withdrawal of the announcement and a statement that the federal government had no intention of interfering with amateur sport. In the next fifteen years the federal government adhered to this approach to sport organizations. Government assistance to sport was almost nonexistent.

The Doldrums

The fifteen-year void in federal assistance to amateur sport associations was accompanied by a seven-year period in which there was no national involvement with the provinces when federal assistance was discontinued in 1954. Each province went its own separate way. While programs in a few provinces such as Alberta and Ontario matured, expanding in budget and services offered, such was not the case in other regions. Services, such as grants to sport associations, were minimal and by 1960 most provinces were in need of renewed federal stimulus if their sport and recreation programs were to expand. The paucity of government assistance, both federal and provincial, resulted in the 1950s being a lean decade for sport and recreation in Canada.

Throughout the 1950s the Canadian Sports Advisory Council struggled, without adequate funding, to keep the concern for physical fitness and amateur sport before the government. The CSAC was aided in its efforts by Dr. Doris Plewes, who was retained in the Department of National Health and Welfare as a consultant on physical fitness after the demise of the national physical fitness program in 1954.

In the late 1950s the subject of sport and fitness was frequently raised in the House of Commons, and in 1959 two completely separate events served to focus public and federal government attention. First, H.R.H. Prince Philip, in an address to the Canadian Medical Association, rebuked Canadians for their complacency toward physical fitness. Second, newly elected Prime Minister John Diefenbaker visited the Canadian team at the Pan American Games in Chicago, and promised increased support for amateur sport.

Fitness and Amateur Sport Act, 1961

Despite the national concern for physical fitness, the most frequent reference in Parliamentary debates throughout 1959, 1960, and 1961 was to the value of sport in the furtherance of national prestige. With this background it was somewhat surprising that in September 1961, when the federal government introduced *Bill C131, An Act to Encourage Fitness and Amateur Sport,* the focus was clearly upon physical fitness. At the last moment "physical fitness through amateur sport" was changed to "physical fitness and amateur sport." This significant amendment notwithstanding, the first major federal government assistance to amateur sport was ushered in, not in its own right, but clinging to the coattails of physical fitness.

The government's cautious approach was a reflection of the embarrassment it suffered in 1945 as a result of Ian Eisenhardt's announcement and the deep-seated belief that government involvement in sport was politically risky. The intent was to assist sport; fitness was a convenient and acceptable cover.

To advise the minister on the operation of the <u>Act</u>, the government established the National Advisory Council on Fitness and Amateur Sport, which consisted of thirty appointed members from all areas of Canada. In addition, the Fitness and Amateur Sport Directorate, a small body of civil servants, was formed within the Department of National Health and Welfare to administer the program.

The program which developed as a result of the 1961 Fitness and Amateur Sport Act had three major thrusts. The first, a program of grants to national governing bodies of sport and other agencies for such things as national championships, international competition, leadership programs, and conferences, started slowly but has developed into the major federal government program. A second thrust provided support for research, fellowships, and graduate scholarships. The third program—grants to the provinces—was initially the most important.

Federal-Provincial Agreements

From 1962–63 to 1967–68 nine provinces and two territories participated in the federal-provincial cost-sharing program, and Quebec entered in 1968–69. During the nine years (1962 to 1971) that the program was in operation there were five separate agreements. The matching agreement came into effect in 1963, and was based on an allocation of $35,000 to each province, plus a per capita proportioning of the balance, with a 60 percent federal to 40 percent provincial matching provision.

It was originally intended that the funds allocated annually to the federal-provincial agreement should be 50 percent of the total Fitness and Amateur Sport program budget. This level of allotment was made in the first two years of the agreement, with $500,000 in 1962–63 and $1 million in 1963–64. However, as the total budget increased, the allocation to this program remained fixed at $1 million annually. The full allocation was not claimed by the provinces until 1967–68, and only in 1968–69, when Quebec entered the program, was $1 million exceeded.

The reaction of most provinces to the federal-provincial agreements was to establish or expand departments to more effectively administer new sport programs. Federal funds were catalytic, and once the cost-sharing program got under way provincial governments began making grants to provincial governing bodies of sport. Development of provincial sport associations was slow initially, but by the mid-1960s they had gained a new lease on life. Buoyed by the new grants, the associations strengthened structures, trained coaches and leaders, and launched programs.

Despite the cooperative nature of the agreements several contentious issues persisted throughout the life of the program. The provinces were disenchanted about the federal insistence that all projects receive preapproval from Ottawa, and that federal approval did not always match provincial priorities. These issues became very sensitive because at this time provinces were seeking increased control of their own destiny and any federal infringement of provincial prerogative was strongly opposed.

With the unilateral federal withdrawal from the cost-sharing program in 1954 still fresh in their memories, the provinces were also wary of investing in new programs simply because the federal government offered grants. They recognized that a cessation of federal funding would leave them with the difficult choice of accepting a 60 percent increase in program costs or eliminating established programs.

This caution notwithstanding, provincial funding to sport increased steadily during the 1960s and by the end of the decade the federal contribution to most provinces represented only a small percentage of overall expenditures on sport and recreation. Only the Atlantic provinces and the Northwest Territories remained heavily dependent on federal funds.

In 1970, contrary to the advice of the Task Force on Sport for Canadians, the federal government unilaterally terminated the cost-sharing program. They felt the program had accomplished its objective of stimulating greater provincial government involvement in sport and fitness and they were dissatisfied with the low level of public recognition obtained by the federal government from the program. Strong provincial pressure resulted in a federal concession of a phaseout year until 1971, with a 50 percent reduced grant of $500,000. After the termination of the full program in 1971, federal monies continued to be allocated to the Atlantic provinces, the Northwest Territories, and the Yukon but, with one exception, these grants stopped in 1976. To the present the Atlantic provinces continue to receive federal funds, under a cost-shared program, the purpose of which is to help improve the competitive position of athletes from the region which lags behind other parts of the country. Initially the grant assisted student-athletes to attend a special summer training camp, but was subsequently broadened to include training grants to non-student-athletes. In 1985–86 the federal contribution to this program was $99,400.

The nine-year period (1962–1971) when the federal-provincial agreements were operational for a majority of provinces represented the closest cooperation achieved by the two levels of government in the field of sport and fitness. There is no doubt that the agreements influenced provincial governments to strengthen their sport programs. On the other hand they did little to develop cooperation. Following the termination of the program, relations between the two levels of government became very badly strained. The provinces were particularly dismayed because the unilateral federal action occurred at a time when, after several years of difficult negotiations, the program at last appeared to be running smoothly.

Fitness and Amateur Sport Directorate

During the early years of the program there was a deliberate policy to maintain a low profile for the Directorate, which was in keeping with current thinking: keep the bureaucracy small so as not to destroy the voluntary element of amateur sport. For the first six years the Directorate played a predominantly supportive role to the National Advisory Council and the federal-provincial agreements. Gradually, however, in addition to awarding annual grants to national sport associations, the Directorate developed a program of its own. Early examples, all launched in 1967, were major roles in the first Canada Winter Games, the Pan American Games, the Montreal Symposium on Recreation, and the Centennial Fitness Award Program, which later became the Canada Fitness Award Program.

The Canada Games, first held in Quebec City in 1967, is a biannual competitive multi-sport festival which alternates winter and summer. This event stimulated the provinces to increased participation in sport, which manifested itself in funding to prepare provincial teams and, in cooperation with municipal and federal governments, to the capital and operating costs of the Games.

Although the 1961 Fitness and Amateur Sport Act had decreed that up to $5 million be made available each fiscal year, the amount was not appropriated immediately. The budget for the first two years of operation, 1961–62 and 1962–63, was fixed at $1 million annually, and that amount was to be increased each year by $1 million until the full allocation of $5 million became available in 1966–67. Government restrictions delayed the proposed rate of increase in funding, and the full allocation of $5 million was not authorized in the 1960s.

Despite the reduced funds, requests did not equal the amount available during the decade. The low level of demand was related to two major factors: (1) delay in the early years in developing acceptable criteria for grants to sport associations, and (2) many sport associations seeking grants not being sufficiently organized to ensure proper safeguarding and budgetary control of public monies. These explanations would also be pertinent to the underutilization of provincial allocations, as would the reluctance of some provinces to develop programs dependent on federal funds.

The federal government's role during the decade of the 1960s is perhaps best summarized by the Federal Green Paper, *Toward a National Policy on Amateur Sport:*

> Only as recently as 1961, with the passing of the Fitness and Amateur Sport Act, did the federal government commit itself to an ongoing involvement in sport. Through most of the 60's, however, its role remained ill-defined. As a consequence, organizations were created and patterns of spending established which caused dissatisfaction among politicians, sports people and the permanent officials. However, during this period, one theme did emerge: "Do something about the sorry performance of most Canadians in international competitions." (Campagnolo 1977, 3)

FEDERAL GOVERNMENT: SPORT AND RECREATION SINCE 1969

Concern within the federal government over Canada's poor results in international sport resulted in the appointment in August 1968 of a three-member Task Force to investigate amateur sport in Canada. The appointment fulfilled a preelection promise made by the Prime Minister in early June. At that time Trudeau said he had come to the realization that the federal government must do more for sport, and he particularly mentioned Canada's national sport, hockey.

Task Force on Sport for Canadians

The *Task Force Report,* tabled in February 1969, reflected the tenor of the Prime Minister's concern by devoting some 50 percent of its contents to professional sport, primarily hockey. Further, a major recommendation of the Task Force Report, that a nonprofit corporation to be known as Hockey Canada be established for the purpose of managing and financing the national hockey teams of Canada, was implemented even before the report was tabled.

This preoccupation with hockey and professional sport notwithstanding, the *Task Force Report* represented a watershed in Canadian amateur sport. The report drew attention to deficiencies in several major areas—administration, technical programs, promotion, and most important, leadership and coordination. Overall, the report called for increased interest and involvement in sport by the federal government.

Most of the recommendations of the Task Force Report were implemented—a large proportion with great speed—and the majority of these will be discussed later. Of particular interest are those that were not realized. This latter group of recommendations are those which required cooperation between federal and provincial governments. They include reevaluated federal-provincial agreements; cooperative programs for planning, funding, and providing new facilities; and increasing the use of existing facilities. Further, although not listed as a recommendation, the Task Force Report indicated that some agreement should be reached with the provinces that would permit better coordination of national and provincial policies in sport and fitness.

A Proposed Sports Policy for Canadians

A *Proposed Sports Policy for Canadians,* Minister John Munro's response to the *Task Force Report,* was unveiled in March 1970. It contained a number of major contradictions, the most crucial pertaining to the issue of mass participation or excellence. Pervading the first half of the document was a philosophy of sport for all—"putting the pursuit of international excellence in its proper perspective—as a consequence and not as a goal of mass participation" (p. 23). In the program section of the paper, in addition to notice of intent to provide initial support for a national coaches association, which developed into the Coaching Association of Canada, and the germ of what was to become Sport Participation Canada, were two major new proposals which offered administrative support to national governing associations and grants-in-aid for promising athletes.

While the principle of administrative support met with universal governing-body approval, the two-level classification system, and the corresponding major difference in extent of financial and services support, inevitably disappointed some. A much more contentious issue was that office space and support services were to be provided only in Ottawa, and to qualify for the executive director grant that person had to operate from the Ottawa office. Each sport association wished to locate its executive director at its discretion, in a part of the country where its sport was strongest. The minister's requirement prevailed, but the associations' resentment resulted in severe curtailment of intended consultation between sport bodies and federal officials.

The grants-in-aid program was intended to assist athletes to meet the increasing costs of training and competition. This program, a major objective of which was to reduce the "brawn drain" to American universities, was clearly directed at the elite athlete. The orientation of these two programs was in conflict with the philosophy of mass participation expressed earlier in the policy paper.

Sport Canada: Recreation Canada Report

A second policy paper, entitled *Sport Canada: Recreation Canada,* which announced progress on earlier proposals and also new federal government initiatives, was released in May 1971. The sequel to the Task Force Report recommendation that a nonprofit corporation, to be known as Sport Canada, be established to provide a focus for the administration, support, and growth of sport in Canada emerged at this time. What the Task Force had in mind was an autonomous Sport Canada, similar in concept to the Canada Council. However, the decision was made to keep the two agencies (Sport Canada and Recreation Canada) into which the directorate was split as in-house government organizations. It has been suggested that Canadian sport was considered too immature to handle autonomy, and that the program was simply too attractive and popular to be released by the government.

Sport Canada was to be primarily concerned with participation in organized competitive sport at both the national and international levels; Recreation Canada with participation in physical recreation and in coordinating activities of government agencies at all levels.

During the period 1970–71, when the two reports were released, the government made an unannounced decision that other organizations necessary to implement the federal role should not be developed within a government department, but through "arms-length" organizations. Four such organizations were set up: Hockey Canada, the National Sport and Recreation Centre, the Coaching Association of Canada, and Sport Participation Canada.

Hockey Canada was established by the federal government early in 1969 with a directive to operate, manage, and develop national teams to represent Canada in international hockey, and to foster and support the playing of hockey in Canada. As with all other sports, these functions had heretofore been the responsibility of the national governing body—in this case, the Canadian Amateur Hockey Association. However, the unique problems in hockey engendered by the participation of professional players in international hockey and by the influence of commercial hockey at municipal level led to this unprecedented involvement of the federal government in the control of amateur sport. The Canadian Amateur Hockey Association has representation on Hockey Canada, but this has not prevented an almost continuous altercation between the two bodies.

The National Sport and Recreation Centre was established in Ottawa in 1970 and incorporated in 1974 to accommodate the executive directors appointed by national governing bodies and to provide support services. In 1987 the centre provided residence to almost seventy federally recognized national sport bodies and fitness agencies. In addition the centre provided a range of support services for resident organizations and some thirty nonresident sport and recreation groups.

The Coaching Association of Canada was formed in 1971, on the recommendation of the Task Force on Sport, to encourage the development of coaching and to improve its effectiveness. It has instituted the National Coaching Certification Program; graduate coaching scholarships; coaching apprenticeships; the Sport Information Resource Centre (SIRC), which has developed into one of the finest documentation centres in the world; and provides technical and audiovisual services to sport associations.

Sport Participation Canada, better known as **Participaction,** was established in 1971 to promote the fitness of all Canadians through a media motivational campaign. In common with the other arms-length organizations, it is an autonomous, nonprofit body which receives a substantial annual grant from the federal government.

The federal government saw the establishment of these arms-length organizations as a demonstration of its lack of desire to "control" amateur sport. Certainly, each organization is sufficiently removed from government to be able to appoint competent business and professional leaders to its board. However, the Canadian Olympic Association has questioned the extent to which these organizations are autonomous, claiming rather that they are mere extensions of government.

The *Sport Canada: Recreation Canada* paper also formally announced a new focus for federal programs. In place of the pre-Task Force federal-provincial agreements, research grants, scholarships for future physical educators, and grants for clinics were sport demonstration tours, continued support of the Canada Games, the Canada Fitness Award, grants-in-aid to student athletes, and a proposal which failed to materialize for a Canada Olympic Trials in the non-Olympic years between the Canada Games.

These programs were developed to carry the message of sport and physical recreation directly to the Canadian people, and were the means by which the federal government sought to attain a higher degree of visibility for its involvement with sport.

Demonstration Tours

The first project, known as the **Cross Canada Sports Demonstration Tour,** consisted of demonstrations by a group of international athletes which were designed to motivate high school students to participate in sports. In 1981 the project was renamed **Sport Action,** and the twenty-odd presentations of fitness and sport activities were seen by more than half a million Canadians that year.

Canada Games

Another high profile program—**the Canada Games**—was inaugurated in Quebec City in 1967. Canada Games are held every two years, alternating between winter and summer competitions, and are restricted to athletes who have not yet achieved national status. The federal government contributes to each Games one-third of the capital costs (the remainder being shared equally by the host province and municipality) and virtually 100 percent of the operating costs including transportation. This program has been the only successful cooperative venture between federal and provincial governments, other than grants to the Atlantic provinces, since the dissolution of the federal-provincial agreement in 1970.

Canada Fitness Award

A third program of this type was the **Canada Fitness Award** which was launched in 1970 following a successful experiment with a Centennial Fitness Award in 1967. The awards within this incentive program were achieved by more than 3.5 million boys and girls between seven and seventeen years of age in the first five years of the program.

Student Athletes Grants-in-Aid

The *Task Force Report* had recommended that some form of bursary be made available to outstanding athletes in much the same way that musicians and painters were assisted by the Canada Council. In contrast to the university-directed and price-bidding American system, the grants-in-aid program for student-athletes was to be administered by Sport Canada, with standardized value awards. Athletes are ranked by their sport association, and the recipients of grants are chosen from among the applicants by a national selection committee. With grant-aided athletes free to attend the educational institution of their choice, many problems associated with recruiting in the United States are avoided.

The **grants-in-aid program** was implemented to enable student athletes to continue their education while remaining financially free to pursue excellence in their sport. Awards were first made in 1970–71 in small numbers, but for the next three years approximately one million dollars was allocated each year from the federal government's summer student program. At the height of this program in 1973–74 some six hundred grants were made annually. However, since the introduction of the Athlete Assistance Program in that year, the grants-in-aid program was gradually reduced in scope as the new program expanded, and was discontinued in 1981–82.

Game Plan

Between the release of the *Proposed Sports Policy for Canadians* and the *Sport Canada: Recreation Canada* paper, Montreal, against all expectations, was awarded the 1976 Summer Olympic Games. This ensured a continuation of the major federal thrust in support of elite sport and the minister called for the development of more athletes, more coaches and officials of all kinds, and particularly more technical directors. The potential of the 1976 Olympic Games to provide a boost for Canadian sport could not be ignored, and a National Conference on Olympic '76 Development was held late in 1971 from which stemmed initiatives to maximize the benefits to be gained.

This program, known as **Game Plan,** was launched by the Canadian Olympic Association in 1972. Its overall objective was to place Canada in the top ten nations on a total points basis in the 1976 Olympic Games. Between 1973 and 1976 Game Plan, which included twenty-four sports, initiated programs such as talent identification for national teams; the Athlete Assistance Program, which provided training and living support for six hundred carded athletes; expanded opportunities for competition in both North America and abroad; national and international training camps; the hiring of national coaches and other support personnel; and the establishment of national team training centres. In the three-year period Game Plan spent about $9.5 million.

The major goal of Game Plan was to increase significantly the number of world-class Canadian athletes. In the **Athlete Assistance Program,** athletes are classified, or carded, in relation to their world ranking. "A" athletes are those ranked in the top eight in the world in individual events, or top four in team events; "B" athletes are those with an individual ranking between nine and sixteen, or a team ranking of five to eight; "C" athletes are those who have demonstrated the potential to achieve "A" or "B" card status in Olympic sports only. In 1973, when the program was launched, Canada had 47 carded athletes; by 1976 there were 126; and by 1987 there were 793 carded athletes; 107 at "A" level, 80 at "B" level, 384 at "C" level, 148 at "C-1" level, which is a first year probationary award, and 74 Development Cards for young athletes of outstanding potential.

rose from twenty-first position in the 1972 Summer Olympic Games to tenth in 1976—its best performance since 1932. The 1976, 1980, and 1984 Summer Olympic Games were all marred by boycotts, the last two being the most seriously affected, and in 1980 Canada did not participate. However, in 1984 in Los Angeles, Canada achieved its best ever results, winning 44 medals, including 10 gold, and having finishes in the top 8 in 120 events out of a total of 220. Overall, Canada placed fourth in the Games.

Following the Los Angeles Olympic Games the monthly stipends of carded athletes were increased: "A" athletes from $500 to $650, "B" athletes from $475 to $550, and "C" athletes from $400 to $450. In 1986–87, financial assistance through the Athlete Assistance Program was almost $4.98 million.

In 1980 the Athlete Assistance Program, which up to then had been confined to the thirty-five Olympic sports, was extended to include a further thirty-five non-Olympic sports. Also until 1980, Canadian athletes attending American universities had received grants, but that eligibility was phased out as ongoing recipients graduated.

In 1982 Sport Canada introduced the Extended Athlete Assistance Program which was designed to assist retiring Canadian athletes who had fulfilled a long-term training commitment and who had represented Canada in international events. Retiring athletes are eligible for tuition fees and living allowance at a Canadian educational institution for a period of time dependent upon the length of their international career.

Within the Canadian sport system, Game Plan had one unique characteristic. It attempted to bring together the key amateur sport sponsoring agencies (specifically the federal government, the governments of the ten provinces and two territories, and the Canadian Olympic Association) to coordinate financing and planning. The COA made a major contribution to Game Plan, particularly the athlete support program, but the uncertainty of their revenue-generating program prevented a complete commitment. Among the provinces only Ontario contributed its full assessment, and in December 1975 the provinces agreed among themselves to discontinue their involvement. Game Plan thus became primarily a Sport Canada program.

These problems notwithstanding, Game Plan was successful but less so, it may be argued, than if federal-provincial cooperation had been achieved. The original Game Plan was focussed specifically upon the 1976 Olympic Games, but the program is now ongoing and aligns itself to each major multi-sport festival in turn.

An Expanded Role: Excellence and Fitness

Coupled with the drive for excellence in sport was a thrust for improved national physical fitness, in an effort to reduce rapidly escalating health care costs. In line with the expanded role, the Fitness and Amateur Sport Directorate was upgraded to branch status and reorganized in 1973. As further evidence of the increasing importance attached to this area of government activity, Prime Minister Trudeau, in September 1976, appointed Iona Campagnolo as the first Minister of State for Fitness and Amateur Sport.

The principal objective of the branch was to raise the fitness level of Canadians and to improve participation in physical recreation and amateur sport. With the new organizational structure and the increased budget, much progress was made toward implementing activities to meet the branch's three subobjectives:

1) to increase the appreciation for and understanding of fitness, physical recreation and amateur sport.
2) to improve the Canadian delivery system of fitness, physical recreation and amateur sport.
3) to improve the quality of participation of Canadians in physical recreation and amateur sport. (*Fitness and Amateur Sport Annual Report 1976–77*, 5)

In 1977 Recreation Canada, to more fully reflect its orientation, became Fitness and Recreation Canada, and in 1980 a further internal reorganization resulted in another name change to Fitness Canada. At this time it was felt that recreation fell more under provincial and municipal mandates than federal, and the emphasis of the federal thrust would be to improve the fitness levels of Canadians by increasing participation in physical activity and encouraging healthy life-style behaviours.

By 1985 the mandates and goals of Fitness Canada and Sport Canada had become much more specific, and this is reflected in the organizations' structures, which are shown in figure 7.1. Fitness Canada had three major objectives:

1. To increase the motivation of Canadians to engage in physical activity leading toward fitness and a healthy life-style;
2. To increase the availability and accessibility of quality programs which facilitate participation in physical activity and a healthy life-style;
3. To improve the general environment, organizational infrastructure and program delivery systems for physical activity in Canada. (*Fitness and Amateur Sport Annual Report 1985–86*, 9)

Government of Canada: Fitness and Amateur Sport

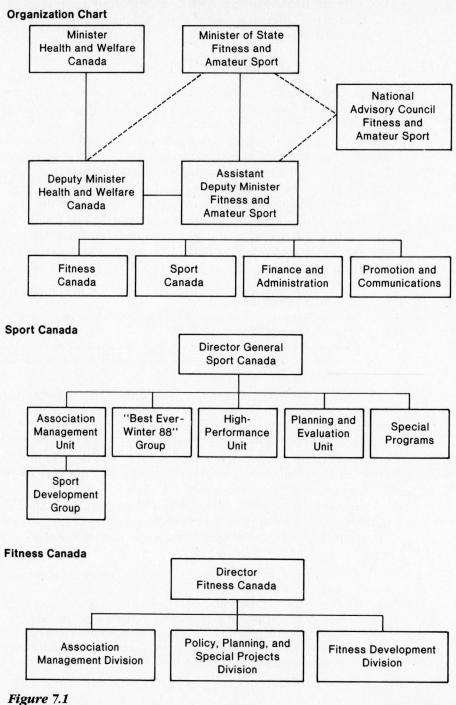

Figure 7.1

In 1985–86 Fitness Canada consolidated a new organization structure consisting of three divisions with responsibilities in the areas of association management, fitness development, and policy, planning, and special projects (figure 7.1). Assisting the development of effective delivery systems to support the promotion of fitness on a national basis through consultation and liaison with national organizations is the primary responsibility of the Association Management Division. The Fitness Development Division initiates research, leads the development of policies and the setting of national goals and priorities for fitness on behalf of Fitness Canada, and coordinates the development of strategies and plans to respond to public needs. Planning, evaluation, and control processes within Fitness Canada, as well as coordinating total federal policy on fitness matters, are the responsibility of the Policy, Planning, and Special Projects Division.

Throughout the 1980s Fitness Canada's efforts have been directed primarily at particular populations: older adults, the disabled, youth, low income Canadians, and employee fitness. Specific programs or initiatives in support of these thrusts include a professional development practicum in which, since 1981, fifty-eight recent graduate interns have developed administrative skills under experienced supervision; the establishment of the Secretariat for Fitness in the Third Age in 1982 to increase physical activity among Canada's older population; National Physical Activity Week, which was started in 1983; and an increased emphasis on youth fitness associated with the 1985 International Year of Youth. Additional programs or initiatives include the establishment of the Canadian Fitness and Lifestyle Research Institute in 1985; Skills Program for Management Volunteers; employee fitness initiatives including publications, consultation, and an annual Employee Fitness Awards Banquet which, at its inception in 1985, honoured twenty Canadian companies for their leadership in fitness programs in the workplace; a national program of fitness appraisal certification and accreditation, and in 1986 the development of a program to train master trainers of fitness leaders; and the Canadian Summit on Fitness in 1986 which provided a forum to discuss issues and to develop long-range goals and strategies to enhance the future of physical activity and fitness in Canada.

In addition, Fitness Canada has furthered close cooperation with the provinces and territories. Following the first federal-provincial meeting of fitness and recreation ministers, initiated by the federal minister Otto Jelinek in 1985, it was agreed to establish a number of federal-provincial task forces on fitness, more specifically on National Physical Fitness Week, promotions, youth, employee fitness, leadership, and older adults.

Sport Canada's mandate in 1985 was

a) To provide leadership, policy direction and financial assistance for the development of Canadian sport at the national and international levels; and

b) To support the highest possible level of achievement by Canada in international sport.

Its major goals were:

1. To coordinate, promote and develop high performance sport in Canada in conjunction with recognized national sport organizations;
2. To assist in the development of domestic sport in Canada in those areas requiring coordination at the national level;
3. To provide administrative and technical leadership, policy direction, consultative services and financial resources for the development and maintenance of an effective sport delivery system at the national level (that is, to assist national sport organizations to function effectively as the primary agents for sport excellence and domestic sport development in Canada);
4. To develop federal government sport policies. (*Fitness and Amateur Sport Annual Report* 1985–86, 20)

To facilitate the drive toward excellence Sport Canada was restructured in 1981 to include a High-Performance Unit, the function of which was to address the area of technical planning and evaluation in order to bring about improved performances of Canada's high-performance athletes. A further restructuring took place early in 1984, as shown in figure 7.1. The Sport Development Group was established to provide Sport Canada liaison with the non-Olympic national sport organizations and to address the issue of sport development in Canada. In addition, the "Best Ever–Winter 88" Group was formed to develop Sport Canada's "Best Ever" planning system.

"Best Ever" Program

Sport Canada's "Best Ever–Winter 88" program was introduced early in 1983, and a similar program for summer Olympic sports one year later. The intent of the program was to assist the national sport organizations to prepare Canada's "best-ever" teams for the 1988 Olympic Games, and to develop a high-performance system measured season-to-season by competition results at international events.

In addition to providing extra funding support for the national organizations in Olympic sports, Sport Canada introduced several other programs under the "Best Ever" mandate. Guidelines and general criteria for support for high-performance sport centres were drawn up in 1983. A **high-performance sport centre** is a training locale where high-level athletes are able to train in good facilities under the guidance of expert coaches with adequate medical and sport science support services. Centres should also cater to the educational, occupational, and sociocultural needs of the athletes, and a majority of the twenty-two centres established in the initial year of the program were located at universities. By 1986 some sixty high-performance sport centres were in existence.

Through the High-Performance Sport Centre Program, Sport Canada also developed general guidelines in 1983 for sport science centres which act as research and testing centres for high-performance athletes and their coaches. As of September 1986 five centres had been approved at the universities of Calgary, Alberta, Victoria, York, and the Fitness Institute in Toronto.

A further development in the drive toward sport excellence occurred in 1986 with the establishment of the National Coaching Institute at the University of Victoria which is cooperatively funded by the federal and provincial governments and the university. This pilot project offers an intensive twelve-month program in coaching theory, coaching practice, and sport science to a limited number of individuals with the overall objective of increasing the number of high-calibre coaches in Canada. In 1988 a second Institute was established at the University of Calgary.

In 1984 Sport Canada, in conjunction with the national sport organizations in each of the Olympic sports, initiated a Quadrennial Planning Program designed to develop, implement, and monitor four-year plans to provide optimal support to athletes as they prepared for the 1988 Olympic Games and beyond. The management of national sport organizations increased in scope and complexity with the additional responsibilities of quadrennial planning, marketing, fund raising, and the supervision of larger staffs. Sport Canada assisted associations through the Professional Development Program for senior managers and by providing funding incentive for the appointment of directors general in those associations which gave over to their senior manager a significant policy development responsibility.

The "Best Ever" concept was strongly supported, not only by Sport Canada but also by the sport agencies of most provincial governments which also developed programs under the same name. The common objective engendered close cooperation between the federal and provincial government sport agencies which led to a more precise clarification of roles for all organizations which compose the sport delivery system.

Other Sport Canada initiatives are the Science and Medicine in Sport Program which coordinates the science, medical, and paramedical activities related to the preparation of high-performance athletes; a Sport Science Support Program and an Applied Sport Research Program, both of which provide funding for projects which will enhance the Canadian sport system, and in particular the high-performance system; the Program of Drug Use and Doping Control in sport; the Women's Program which seeks to improve the status of women in physical activity and sport; the Program for the Disabled which supports the promotion of participation by disabled Canadians in fitness-related activities and in the pursuit of excellence in competitive sport. In 1986 this program assisted the organization of the "Jasper Talks, A National Symposium on Strategies for Change in Adapted Physical Activity in Canada."

Funding

Funding of the federal program which developed as a result of the Fitness and Amateur Sport Act of 1961 started slowly, but flowed more freely after 1970. In the first eight years, 1961–1969, funding increased from zero to $4 million annually; in the next ten years, 1969–1979, from $4 million to $25 million; and in the next eight years, 1979–1987, from $25 million to $58 million.

were established in 1971 it was acknowledged that in combination the preoccupation with sport overshadowed recreation. It was intended that the new structure should redress the situation, and that budgets would be allocated in a balance between the two. Such a redress has not occurred. There seems little doubt of the intent to upgrade the federal contribution to the development of physical recreation. However, programs at the elite sport level were more easily identified and the target date of the 1976 Olympic Games more immediate than the longer-term and more intangible recreation problems.

Throughout the life of the program the largest proportion of funding by far has gone to sport. For example, in 1976–77, $20.8 million was allocated by Sport Canada and $3.9 million by Recreation Canada, and in 1986–87, $50.5 million by Sport Canada and $7.6 million by Fitness Canada.

In 1986–87 Sport Canada assisted

(1) some sixty-seven national sport governing bodies with contributions totalling more than $27 million in "core" funding to pay the salaries of full-time employees such as executive and technical directors, program coordinators and national coaches, to help defray travel and other costs associated with clinics, seminars and annual meetings.
(2) the administration of amateur sport through grants totalling $4.5 million towards the operating costs and programs of the National Sport and Recreation Centre, Inc. in Ottawa;
(3) the Coaching Association of Canada with a grant of $2.7 million and an additional $525,000 to the Sport Information Research Centre;
(4) the Canadian Olympic Association with a grant of $501,000, and the Canadian Interuniversity Athletic Union with $1.0 million;
(5) the Athlete Assistance Program with a grant of $4.98 million.

In the same year contributions from Fitness Canada included:

(1) grants to National Associations such as Canadian Association for Health, Physical Education and Recreation, $480,000; Canadian Parks and Recreation Association, $126,000; Canadian Intramural Recreation Association, $546,000; and the YWCA of Canada, $141,000;
(2) Participaction which received $1.7 million;
(3) projects for the Disabled which, in conjunction with Sport Canada, were granted $783,000;
(4) (Fitness and Amateur Sport Annual Report 1985–86)

In the decade following the 1976 Olympic Games the costs of achieving excellence in sport increased dramatically. Although the federal government's contribution to sport development rose from $18 million in 1976 to $60 million in 1986 it alone did not meet the need. Prior to 1984, when Sport Canada began to strongly encourage self-generated revenue, national amateur sport associations received 80 percent of their funding from the federal government. By 1986 this had decreased to 70 percent with much of the remainder coming from the corporate sector.

In 1986 Otto Jelinek, the Minister of State, Fitness, and Amateur Sport, established the Sport Marketing Council, comprised of some of Canada's most influential business people. The council's mandate is to help national sport associations to become more financially secure through mutually beneficial arrangements with members of the corporate community. The minister's objective was to maintain current levels of government funding to amateur sport and for corporate sector funding to match the government contribution by the end of 1988.

Sport Canada also introduced marketing support guidelines in 1986, designed to help national sport and recreation associations raise a larger proportion of their financial requirements from the private sector. Under the Marketing Support Program, assistance is available to organizations which demonstrate strong potential to obtain corporate sector sponsorship and/or undertake major fund-raising activities.

Lotteries

The Criminal Code was amended by the federal government in 1969 to legalize lotteries in Canada. In July 1973 Parliament passed the Olympic (1976) Act, which concerned the creation of a lottery, as well as special issues of Olympic stamps and coins. Subsequently, the Olympic Lottery of Canada Corporation was established, and the nine drawings of the Olympic Lottery between April 1974 and August 1976 generated $256.3 million, of which $230 million went toward the cost of the 1976 Summer Olympic Games, and $26.3 million to the provinces based on 5 percent of gross revenue from tickets sold in each province.

The announcement in May 1976 that Ottawa intended to set up a national lottery called Loto Canada to be run by a Crown Corporation met with an angry response from the provinces, who were expecting the federal government to vacate the lotteries field following the Olympic Games. Loto Canada was established by an act of Parliament on June 7, 1976.

For a three-year period, starting in December 1976, 82.5 percent of Loto Canada revenue was allocated to help cover the 1976 Olympic Games deficit, and to defray the costs of the 1978 Commonwealth Games in Edmonton; 12.5 percent to the provinces, in proportion to the number of tickets sold in each province; and 5 percent to Sport Canada. One hundred ninety-eight million dollars went to the Olympic Games, $4 million to the Commonwealth Games, $30 million to the provinces, and $12 million to Sport Canada.

When Loto Canada was established in 1976 the federal government announced a firm commitment that revenue from the lottery would be allocated to the Olympic deficit for three years only. In response to questions in the House, the government was noncommital about extending the operations of Loto Canada beyond December 1979.

The uneasy truce that existed between the federal and provincial governments in the lotteries field exploded early in 1978 when it became known that the federal government intended that Loto Canada continue into the 1980s. Early in 1979 Minister Iona Campagnolo introduced Bill C-41 in the House of Commons which would set up a new distribution plan for Loto Canada funds beginning in January 1980. The new plan would support events of national importance: at least 30 percent of net revenue to fitness, amateur sport, and recreational activities and at least 30 percent to arts and cultural activities. It was expected that each beneficiary would receive a minimum of $20 million annually. The passage of the bill was interrupted by the May 1979 general election.

In the election campaign, national Conservative leader Joe Clarke announced that if the Conservative party were elected the federal government would withdraw from Loto Canada and allow the provinces to operate exclusively in the lottery field. The Conservatives were elected and as of December 31, 1979, Loto Canada fell under provincial jurisdiction. Through the new Interprovincial Lottery Corporation the provinces agreed to remit annually to the federal government a guaranteed sum starting in 1980 at $24 million indexed to inflation, and commitments to pay $29.8 million worth of federal projects.

The Liberal government, which was reelected in January 1980, was most unhappy with the transfer of Loto Canada, but their plans to return to the gaming business met with intense provincial government opposition and were long delayed. Late in 1980 the federal government pledged $200 million to the 1988 Winter Olympic Games in Calgary, to be raised from coin and stamp sales and a national sports pool. The weekly sports pool, it was claimed, did not repudiate the federal-provincial agreement because it required some skill and was therefore not a lottery. Participants were required to predict the outcomes of major league games—initially baseball, but it was also intended to utilize hockey and football results. Revenue from the program was to be used for projects in the arts, culture, fitness and amateur sport, medical research, the 1988 Calgary Olympic Games, and capital projects of national interest in the arts and sport.

A bill providing for the establishment of a new Crown corporation, to be known as the Canadian Sports Pool Corporation (CSPC), was tabled in March 1982, and the Act creating the corporation came into force on October 20, 1983. Final approval was delayed until mid-February 1984. Tickets went on sale on May 1 and draws were held each week from the end of May until September 30. Strong opposition to the sports pool came from the three professional sport leagues and particularly from the united provinces, and public response was poor. In the four-month life of the sports pool the average weekly deficit was between $1 million and $1.25 million and the total loss was $46.5 million.

On September 14, 1984, a Conservative government was returned to office. One week later it was announced that the Sports Pool Corporation would be closed down and the last draw would be on September 30. The Sports Pool and Loto Canada Winding Up Act was tabled on November 8, 1984, and on June 11, 1985, Otto Jelinek, the minister of state for fitness and amateur sport, announced an agreement between federal and provincial governments. Over the next three years the provinces were to pay a total of $100 million in annual installments to the federal government toward the costs of the 1988 Winter Olympic Games in Calgary. In exchange the federal government was to amend the Criminal Code to ensure exclusivity in the gaming field to the provinces.

Planning and Policies

Since 1961 a great deal of effort has been expended in developing the framework for a Canadian sport system. However, Canada still lacks a national sport plan. In a move to remedy this failing, Iona Campagnolo released a Green Paper, *Toward a National Policy on Amateur Sport: A Working Paper,* in October 1977, which presented the federal viewpoint and invited sport bodies and individuals to respond. In this paper the federal government finally made a clear commitment to excellence in sport.

A major criticism of the federal paper was that the lack of federal-provincial cooperation might result in a federal policy, but not in a national policy. Further, it was widely felt that a working paper on fitness and recreation should have been issued simultaneously so that the total federal involvement could be discussed. In addition, the collective provincial governments were frustrated by their inability to arrange a federal-provincial ministers meeting to discuss the proposals in the three-month period in which the federal government would accept responses.

The short response time was explained by the intention of issuing a White Paper on a national sport policy by midsummer 1978. After an unexplained long delay the White Paper, *Partners in Pursuit of Excellence: A National Policy on Amateur Sport,* was released in late April 1979, midway through a general election campaign. Proposed in the paper were some radical structures for sport: a federal amateur Sports Council, in the form of a Crown Corporation, a National Sport Trust, and a national Congress of Sport.

The document was intended, in the first instance, as a framework for discussion, from which a national plan upon which all partners—governments, sport governing bodies, and service and multi-sport organizations at federal and provincial levels—were agreed could flow. The Liberals were defeated in the election, and the proposals were not enacted.

A Green Paper, *Toward a National Policy on Fitness and Recreation,* was released by Iona Campagnolo in early April 1979 as a discussion paper, and a steering committee was struck to gather more information and report back in 1980. This action was seen as a method of keeping the paper alive, rather than have it die on the floor in Parliament because of the impending election.

In the nine months that the Conservative party were in office, little of significance occurred other than the transfer of lottery jurisdiction to the provinces which, as explained earlier, resulted in a loss of millions of dollars annually to the federal treasury. Following the reelection of the Liberals a new minister responsible for fitness and amateur sport, Gerald Regan, issued another White Paper, *A Challenge to the Nation: Fitness and Amateur Sport in the Eighties,* in June 1981. The paper contained no mention of the Sports Council or the Congress of Sport. Instead it proposed a National House of Sport, which was to be an extension of the existing National Sport and Recreation Centre, and also would include Sport Canada and a new National Sport Technical Services Organization. It was also to include the Coaching Association of Canada, the Sport Information Resource Centre, the Sport Medicine Council, and the new Technical Planning and Evaluation Section of Sport Canada. It was eventually decided not to pursue these developments.

Federal-Provincial Coordination

A theme which has persisted in federal-provincial relations in sport and recreation from the latter years of the National Physical Fitness program in the early 1950s to the present has been an inability to cooperate. One of the very few exceptions to the rule has been the highly successful Canada Games program.

The establishment of the Federal-Provincial Liaison Section within Recreation Canada in 1976 represented an effort to improve cooperation and coordination between the two levels of government. In 1979 a new federal-provincial/territorial fitness committee was established to provide for the cooperative planning of fitness programs. The committee meets twice a year.

In April 1978 the federal and provincial ministers responsible for sport, fitness, and recreation met to define more clearly their areas of jurisdiction. The ministers agreed that the federal government had the responsibility for the development of high-performance athletes and sport at national and international levels, and that the provincial governments had primary responsibility for recreation. Further, the federal government proposed to gradually withdraw from the recreation field. The ministers also agreed on the need to consult on a regular basis and to engage in two-level decision making on an amateur sport policy. The ministers met again in October 1980, at which time the federal ministers offered to collaborate with the provinces in articulating a national recreation policy. An Interprovincial Recreation Statement was approved by the provinces in 1981, but did not receive federal approval.

An indication of improved cooperation was the establishment at the 1981 Federal-Provincial Ministers Conference of a joint committee to prepare a comprehensive plan of action for the development of high-performance athletes. The resulting "Blueprint for High-Performance Athlete Development," which detailed the responsibilities of the two levels of government and sought through improved cooperation and coordination to maximize the use of available resources, was approved by the 1982 ministers conference.

The "Best Ever" programs, developed at both national and provincial levels in the mid-1980s, engendered close cooperation between the two levels of government. A shared objective of producing high-performance athletes, and the anticipated publicity and acclaim, in common with the Canada Games, provides all parties with the desired public recognition.

PROVINCIAL GOVERNMENTS: SPORT AND RECREATION SINCE 1969

Despite the deep resentment of the provinces to the unilateral federal termination of the federal-provincial cost-sharing agreement in 1970, the provinces quickly filled the funding void and the ensuing decade was characterized by widespread expansion of provincial government sport and recreation programs.

Programs and Services

During the 1970s and 1980s the range of programs and services offered by provincial governments has shown great similarities. The differences have been in extent rather than kind, with Ontario, Quebec, and Alberta surpassing other provinces in annual budgets on a per capita basis.

As a general rule provincial government sport and recreation departments play a facilitating rather than a providing role. In line with this principle, grants to provincial sport associations for clinics, workshops, competition, and conferences showed a dramatic increase during the 1970s. Whereas grants over the decades of the 1940s, 1950s, and 1960s were often provided in a rather irregular, sporadic fashion, during the 1970s more detailed funding programs became evident. Provincial governments have always given high priority to assisting sport and recreation leadership; in addition to funding training programs for volunteers, most provinces also provided assistance to governing bodies for the hiring of full- or part-time administrators, technical directors, and coaches.

In 1974 the National Coaching Certification Program was inaugurated and all provinces, with the exception of Quebec, became heavily involved. The program has two major sections: technical sections, which are specific to each sport, developed and administered by the national and provincial governing bodies of sport; and a theory section, common to all sports, which is administered by provincial government sport departments. Both sections of the program receive high funding priority.

One of the longest established provincial government programs is financial assistance to community sport and recreation directed through municipal recreation structures. All provincial governments expanded this aid during the 1970s, thus promoting the development of a wide range of activities at the grass-roots level.

During the 1970s financial support of the Provincial Games assumed a top priority among almost all provincial government sport programs. By 1978, all provinces, with the exception of Nova Scotia, had a Provincial Games competition in operation. Some provinces hold both winter and summer Games each year, while others hold such Games in alternate years. The Northwest Territories, the Yukon Territory, Quebec, and Newfoundland cooperate every two years to organize the Arctic Winter Games.

The biannual Canada Games hold a special interest for all provinces. What began as a friendly competition between provinces in 1967 rapidly became events in which provincial identity could be expressed through sport. To some provinces, at least, winning became very important. The provinces provided teams with heavy financial support in order to ensure that athletes representing them were well prepared, competitive, and appropriately dressed. Provinces have shown great willingness to equally fund the capital and operating expenses of a Canada Games with the federal and municipal governments when the festival was within their province. In addition to providing an ideal level of competition for young aspiring athletes, the Games offer opportunities for public exposure to politicians at federal, provincial, and municipal levels. As a result, they have been well supported by all three levels of government and are one of the most successful sport programs in the country.

A major area of emphasis of most provinces during the 1970s, more particularly British Columbia, Alberta, and Ontario, was financial assistance toward the capital costs of sport and recreation facilities. Most construction occurred in the last two-thirds of the decade. Quebec and Alberta, with federal assistance, also constructed major facilities for the 1976 Olympic Games, the 1978 Commonwealth Games, and the 1988 Winter Olympic Games.

All provincial governments have assisted the establishment and development of provincial sport federations. Since the formation of the first of these collectives in the mid-1960s, provincial governments have awarded regular substantial grants to enable these bodies to provide a range of services to their member sport associations.

Most provinces in the 1970s became more active in the promotion of physical fitness. A variety of funding patterns emerged—for example, some provinces grant-aided autonomous agencies such as Action B.C. and Shape Up Alberta. Other provinces appointed fitness consultants within their sport departments, and in 1978–79 Ontario established a Fitness Services Branch.

Services to special groups, especially for the disabled population, was another area in which provincial governments became active in the 1970s. Alberta was an early leader in this field and established a Recreation for Special Groups Section within its sport department in the early 1970s. The Ontario government has been a strong supporter of the Ontario Games for the Disabled since they were established in 1975. These services gained momentum in all provinces in 1981, the International Year of Disabled Persons.

All ten provinces established programs of financial awards to assist athletes to strive for excellence. British Columbia was among the leaders in this development. Initially the awards were confined to university students and were small in both number and value. By the late 1970s the programs had developed into High-Performance Athlete Assistance programs similar to the federal government program, usually, but not always, with the intent of assisting athletes to attain Sport Canada carded status. Quebec, Ontario, and British Columbia have the largest budgets for these programs, with those of the Maritime Provinces remaining very small.

In addition to the High-Performance Athlete Assistance Program, three western provinces established programs of University Sports Awards. The British Columbia program, which started in 1980, made available 550 awards of $1000 annually. Alberta and Manitoba established similar programs in 1981, the former with awards of $1000 to university students and $500 to junior college students, the latter with awards ranging from $600 to $1000.

Provincial "Best Ever" Programs

Sport Canada's "Best Ever" iniative acted as a catalyst for the development of provincial government "Best Ever" programs. Ontario launched a "Best Ever" program in September 1984, and British Columbia, Alberta, and other provinces followed soon after. All provincial "Best Ever" programs had the same central objective—to place as many athletes as possible on the 1988 Olympic Games teams. In addition, all provincial programs aimed to train more and better-qualified coaches, and to develop and enhance training facilities along with sport medicine and sport science support services. Some programs, such as Ontario's, also sought to increase overall participation and provide more opportunities for female and disabled athletes.

All provincial "Best Ever" programs required provincial sport associations to develop quadrennial plans and undergo annual evaluation. The planning process was often assisted by government staff and a much higher level of cooperation was developed between the agencies, as was the case between the two senior levels of government as indicated earlier in the chapter.

Lotteries

In all provinces and territories, a phenomenon of the 1970s was the addition of large lottery revenues to help finance provincial government sport programs. The provinces planned to expand their own lotteries, believing that federal withdrawal from lottery operation would occur in 1976. They were incensed by the federal government's decision to remain in the lottery field, and, with the exception of Quebec, were extremely negative to Loto Canada and its objective of paying off the Olympic facilities debt. The uneasy alliance of federal and provincial governments in the lottery field continued until December 1979 when lotteries became exclusively under provincial jurisdiction, and the conflict was resumed over the federal government's Sports Pool in the early 1980s as detailed earlier in the chapter.

With the exception of Saskatchewan, where the provincial government awarded the lottery licence to Sask Sport (the provincial sport federation), lotteries are administered by provincial government agencies. At the discretion of each provincial government, revenues from provincial and regional lotteries may be allocated to amateur sport, fitness, recreation, culture, heritage, and other areas. Some provinces deposit all lottery revenue into the consolidated revenue account and do not earmark any of it for sport. Lotteries generate in excess of $200 million a year and, in general, sport is a major beneficiary.

Planning and Policies

Throughout the 1960s provincial priorities were strongly influenced by the dictates of the federal cost-sharing program. However, the autonomy attained in 1970 and the increased involvement and expenditure since then resulted in a greater degree of planning by provincial governments. Almost all provinces commissioned reports in the 1970s, some more than one, and in 1983 the province of Alberta developed a Sport Development Policy for its involvement in sport. This was followed by a Sport Development Strategy in 1984 and a Recreation and Parks Policy in 1986. Ontario established similar provincial policies for community recreation services in 1984 and sport and fitness in 1985. These policy statements are indicative of a more systematic provincial government approach to their involvement in sport, recreation, and fitness.

SUMMARY

The past thirty-odd years have witnessed a 180 degree change of direction in government involvement in sport. At the federal level the change is illustrated in progressive stages by the remarks of the Honourable Paul Martin in 1949 that sport was entirely a provincial and municipal responsibility; the interest of Parliament in the late 1950s and early 1960s to do something for Canadian sport, but the belief that such action would be politically risky and therefore bringing in the 1961 Physical Fitness and Amateur Sport Act under the cover of assistance to fitness; the deliberately low-key role of the Fitness and Amateur Sport Directorate between 1961 and 1967, and the emergence and subsequent growth of a federal program starting in Centennial year; the impetus to sport provided by the 1969 *Task Force Report on Sports for Canadians,* and John Munro's encouragement and policies; the goals and successes of Game Plan; the claim by Iona Campagnolo, with which few would disagree, that the collaboration between sport and government had made possible the highly visible successes of Canadian athletes at Montreal and Edmonton; and the unabashed theme of the federal Green Paper, *Toward a National Policy on Amateur Sport* (1977), and the White Paper, *Partners in Pursuit of Excellence: A National Policy on Amateur Sport* (1979)—let's go for sport excellence.

Provincially the change of direction is less dramatic, but it has occurred nevertheless, and it has gathered momentum since 1970. The evidence is the increasing proportion of budgets and personnel devoted to sport, and more particularly, the rapid growth and importance of Provincial, Regional, and Canada games—each at its own level a mini-Olympic Games—and the development of "Best Ever" programs.

An equally dramatic change of direction has occurred in sport. The pendulum has swung from the nationwide outcry against government control of sport that greeted Major Eisenhardt's innocuous statement in 1945 (that his newly formed National Physical Fitness Branch would in future serve as the link between sport bodies and government) to the symbiotic relationship between government and sport that exists today.

Governments, at both levels, no longer regard involvement in sport as politically dangerous. Governments no longer feel they must hide their intentions with sport behind the skirts of fitness and recreation, and there are at last indications that governments are beginning to define their respective responsibilities for sport, fitness, and physical recreation. In the mid-1980s the inability of the federal and provincial governments to cooperate, except for intermittent periods of uneasy coexistence, appears to be breaking down. Closer cooperation is developing, particularly in high-performance sport programs. This augurs well for the development of a system through which elite Canadian athletes can attain their potential.

At the lower developmental levels of sport a great deal remains to be done. Ultimately the height reached by the apex of the sport system pyramid is dependent on the strength and breadth of the base, which was dealt with in chapter 6 on the amateur sport and recreation delivery system.

REFERENCES

Alberta, Province of. *Sport Development Policy, Alberta Recreation and Parks.* Edmonton, Alberta, 1983.

Alberta, Province of. *Sport Development Strategy, Alberta Recreation and Parks.* Edmonton, Alberta, 1984.

Broom, Eric F., and Baka, Richard S. *Canadian Governments and Sport.* Calgary: University of Calgary Press, 1979.

Canada. *Bill C-131, An Act to Encourage Fitness and Amateur Sport.* 1961.

Canada. *Report of the Task Force on Sports for Canadians.* Ottawa: Queen's Printer, 1969.

Canada. *A Proposed Sports Policy for Canadians.* Ottawa: Health & Welfare, 1970 (Minister John Munro).

Canada. *Sport Canada: Recreation Canada.* Ottawa: Health & Welfare, 1971 (Minister John Munro).

Canada. *Fitness and Amateur Sport Annual Reports.* Ottawa: Fitness and Amateur Sport, 1976–77, 1982–83, 1984–85, 1985–86, 1986–87.

Canada. *A Working Paper: Toward a National Policy on Amateur Sport.* Ottawa: Fitness and Amateur Sport, 1977 (Minister Iona Campagnolo).

Canada. *Partners in Pursuit of Excellence: A National Policy on Amateur Sport.* Ottawa: Fitness and Amateur Sport, 1979 (Minister Iona Campagnolo).

Canada. *A Challenge to the Nation: Fitness and Amateur Sport in the 80's.* Ottawa: Fitness and Amateur Sport, 1979 (Minister Gerald Regan).

Canada. *Blueprint for High Performance Sport.* Ottawa: Fitness and Amateur Sport, 1982.

PART THREE

Anatomical, Physiological, and Biomechanical Foundations

CHAPTER 8

Human Anatomy

D. Gordon E. Robertson

A beginning student in PERS studies should be aware that it is desirable, if not imperative, that a thorough understanding of human anatomy or anatomical kinesiology should precede the study of biomechanics of human motion (chapter 11); or for that matter, before consideration of the information within human and exercise physiology (chapters 9 and 10). Much of the analysis of human movement, and in particular the examination of a sport skill, includes the analysis of the cause-and-effect relationship of one human body to another or to the manipulation of a sport object such as a bat, ball, racquet, or any one of numerous other implements including the human body itself. The understanding of the cause-and-effect concept in human movement is the essence of good sport skills teaching. Instruction will have little meaning to the learner or the insructor without the latter having a full grasp of the science of human anatomy. It is a prerequisite, much as simple arithmetic is a prerequisite to the study of mathematics. Such also is the relationship between the knowledge of human anatomy and the study of human biomechanics and physiology.

Therefore, this chapter deals with some of the elementary concepts and terminology of the science of anatomy. **Anatomy** is the science that studies the structure of animals and plants. In this chapter basic information for the study of human anatomy will be presented with examples drawn primarily from the human musculoskeletal system. The musculoskeletal system consists of the body's bones, muscles, ligaments, and joints. Other anatomical systems, such as the visceral, cardiopulmonary, hormonal, and neural, will be introduced in later chapters.

The concepts of anatomical position, cardinal frame of reference, and centre of gravity will be introduced first. Second, nomenclature for describing the relative positions of anatomical structures will be defined. Third, nomenclature relating to the study of human motion, called applied anatomy, anatomic kinesiology, or applied kinesiology, will be outlined. The chapter concludes with a discussion of the concept of levers and how this relates to the musculoskeletal system.

ANATOMICAL TERMINOLOGY

Anatomical Position

Due to the complexity of the skeletal system and because of the irregular shapes of human bones, it is difficult to describe the positions or orientations of body parts and define joint movements. A system has been developed to describe the positions of the joints and joint movements relative to a standard orientation of the body parts. This position, called the **anatomical position,** is shown in figure 8.1. Notice that the palms are positioned forward and that the rest of the body is in an erect standing posture.

Frames of Reference, Planes, and Axes

To define the positions or movements of the various joints and body parts it is necessary to define a frame of reference. In the study of anatomy, a **frame of reference** is a system of three orthogonal axes from which the location of points or the angles of line segments may be measured. Orthogonal means that the three axes must all be at right angles (90 degrees) to each other.

There are two types of frames of reference. One is called an **absolute** or **Newtonian** frame of reference because it is essential to Newtonian mechanics and is used to define positions in absolute rather than relative terms. Newtonian frames of reference, which are usually fixed to the ground, will be described in chapter 11.

The other frame of reference is called the **cardinal,** relative, or anatomical frame of reference because it is located within and moves with the body. Anatomists have for centuries recognised the existence of **planes** of reference within the human body. Figure 8.1 shows a cardinal frame of reference and its three associated principal or cardinal axes and planes. The *sagittal plane* divides the body into left and right halves. Its axis is called the *mediolateral axis.* The *frontal plane* divides the body into front and back halves. Its axis is called the *anteroposterior axis.* The *transverse plane* divides the body into upper and lower halves. Its axis is the *longitudinal* or *vertical axis.* These axes and planes are usually made to intersect at the body's centre of gravity.

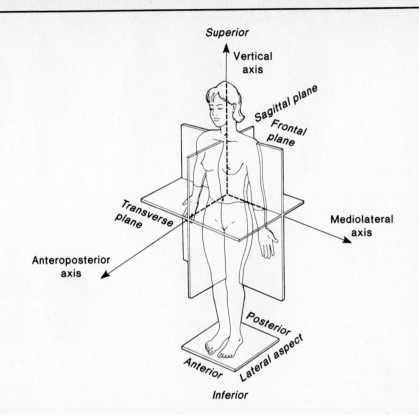

Figure 8.1 The anatomical position and cardinal planes and axes. The axes intersect at the body's centre of gravity.

SOURCE: Hay & Reid, *The Anatomical and Mechanical Bases of Human Motion,* Prentice-Hall, 1982, p. 10, fig. 6.

Centre of Gravity

The **centre of gravity** is the point at which the body could be balanced. In general, the centre of gravity is in the vicinity of the navel; however, it is not a fixed point within the body. It is shifted whenever a body part, including internal organs, are moved. For example, the centre of gravity shifts upward from its anatomical position when the arms are raised or shifts downward when one squats. Furthermore, the centre of gravity does not always lie within the body. For instance, when a person is in a piked position, as can be the case in such activities as diving and gymnastics, the centre of gravity is likely to be somewhere in front of the navel (outside the body).

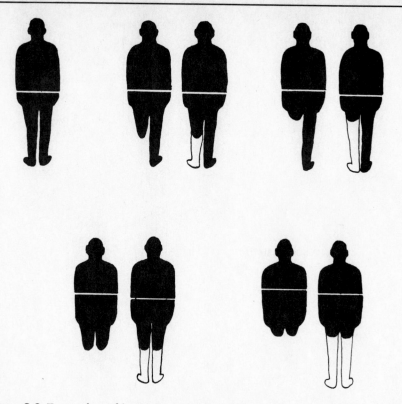

Figure 8.2 Examples of how the height of the centre of gravity varies with amputations of the leg and with the addition of prostheses

SOURCE: Cooper, Adrian, & Glassow, *Kinesiology,* 5th ed., C. V. Mosby, 1982, p. 51, fig. 4.9 (from Hellebrandt, F. A., J. Amer. Med. Assoc. 142: 1353, 1950).

Other factors that influence a person's centre of gravity are age, sex, physical dimensions, and the mass and positioning of clothing or devices that the person is wearing. Age is a factor due the differing proportions of the body parts in infants as opposed to adults. This is one of the reasons that seat belts are inappropriate for infants and young children: their centre of gravity is higher relative to the buttocks because their heads are proportionally greater than an adult's.

Amputations, atrophy (particularly in paraplegics or quadriplegics), and skeletal deformities change the location of the centre of gravity quite markedly, which may cause the individual to be much less stable than a normally proportioned person. Figure 8.2 illustrates how the centre of gravity varies with various leg amputations and added prostheses. Note that the addition of the prosthetic limb partly compensates for the lost mass and the consequent raising of the centre of gravity.

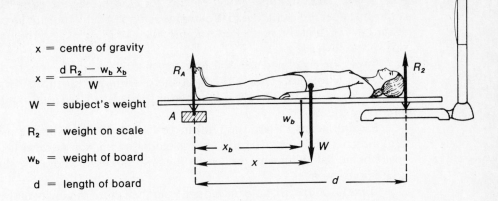

x = centre of gravity

$$x = \frac{d\,R_2 - w_b\,x_b}{W}$$

W = subject's weight

R_2 = weight on scale

w_b = weight of board

d = length of board

where d = the known distance between the supporting edges and x_b = the unknown horizontal distance from A to the line of action of w_b. (In accord with the established convention, counterclockwise moments are considered to be positive and clockwise moments to be negative.)

Figure 8.3 The reaction board method for locating the centre of gravity for a prone position

SOURCE: Hay & Reid, *The Anatomical and Mechanical Bases of Human Motion*, Prentice-Hall, 1982, p. 210, fig. 122(*c*).

When determining the actual location of the centre of gravity, each person and each orientation should be considered individually. Unfortunately, the methods used are typically quite laborious, require specialized equipment, and so are beyond the scope of this text. Figure 8.3 shows a simple method for locating the centre of gravity of a person in a prone position with only a tape measure, balance scale, and a flat board. For the purposes of defining joint angles and movements it is sufficient to assume that the centre of gravity occupies a position midway between the navel and the back.

Directional Nomenclature

Just as navigators have names to define directions on a map, so too do anatomists have a system for identifying directions within the body. These directions are related to the cardinal axes and anatomical position described previously. The following is a glossary of terms for specifying directions of anatomical structures. Figure 8.1 shows some of these terms.

Anterior means toward the front of the body in the anteroposterior direction. The anterior surface of the hand, for example, is the palm; the face is the anterior side of the head. **Posterior** is opposite to anterior and means toward the back of the body. For example, the calf muscle is on the posterior side of the lower leg.

Superior is defined as toward the top of the head in the longitudinal or vertical direction. **Inferior** is the opposite of superior, meaning toward the foot. For example, the shoulder is superior to the hand, whereas the knee is inferior to the hip.

Medial means toward the midline or longitudinal axis in the mediolateral direction. For instance, the nose is medial to the ear. **Lateral** is the opposite of medial and means away from the midline of the body. The shoulder is lateral to the neck.

Distal is a term that means farther from the centre of gravity of the body; **proximal** means toward the body's centre of gravity. Distal and proximal are terms not related to an axis as are the previous terms. Examples of distal body segments are the hands and feet. The navel is considered the most proximal part of the body.

The terms **deep** and **internal** mean inward from the surface of the body. **Superficial** and **external** mean closer to the surface of the body. Thus, the skin is superficial while the muscles are deep.

Two special terms are used in reference to the foot. The term **plantar** means in the direction of the sole of the foot. **Dorsal** means toward the superior surface of the foot from its anatomical position.

MOVEMENT NOMENCLATURE FOR APPLIED ANATOMY

Applied anatomy refers to the branch of anatomy which analyzes and describes the anatomical structures involved in movements. Applied anatomy, which used to be called **kinesiology,** has in the past dealt mainly with describing the muscles involved in simple non-athletic motions. This is due to the difficulty of obtaining accurate three-dimensional information about internal anatomical structures and internal skeletal movements during athletic contests. Improvements in computer technology and spatial (three-dimensional) imaging systems, such as infrared cinematography, stereoroentgenography (stereo X-ray), and magnetic resonance imaging (MRI), could remove this barrier in the future. However, it will always be difficult, if not impossible, to apply these technologies outside the laboratory.

When describing human movements or the arrangement of body parts in a static posture it is important that there be no confusion between one person's description and another's. Anatomists have developed a traditional system of terms which provides a means of identifying human movements and joint positions. The various terms will be presented according to their primary plane of motion assuming the body is in its anatomical position. Note that when a body part moves in a single plane the rotation axis is an axis which is perpendicular to the plane. Thus, a sagittal plane rotation implies a rotation about the mediolateral axis. Be aware that some texts use other names for some of the terms presented.

Sagittal Plane Movements

This plane theoretically bisects the body through the centre of the skull, spinal column, rib cage, pelvis, and lower limbs (figure 8.1). Motion through the cardinal sagittal plane involves the cervical, thoracic, and lumbar regions of the spinal column. There are also many parallel non-cardinal sagittal plane movements that can be found in many joints and limbs, such motions are found extensively in sport skills. Skills such as the takeoff in the long jump or many balance beam routines (walk-overs) are just two accepted complex skills which use both the cardinal and parallel sagittal planes in their execution. For a clearer understanding of human movement in this plane, an explanation of terms follows.

Flexion is a sagittal planar motion of a joint which reduces the joint's angle from its anatomical position. **Extension** is the opposite of flexion and is an increasing of a joint's angle in the sagittal plane from its anatomical position. Many joints have the ability to flex and extend, including the wrist, elbow, shoulder, knee, hip, trunk, finger, and neck. Figure 8.4 gives an example of flexion and extension of the hip and whole leg and flexion of the knee.

Hyperextension is a motion in the same direction as extension but occurs when the joint's angle exceeds its angle in the anatomical position. For example, tilting the neck backwards from being erect in the anatomical position is called neck hyperextension. Some joints are incapable of hyperextension without discomfort or injury occurring. The knee and elbow are examples of joints that can only be hyperextended due to external loading while the fingers, back, neck, hip, and shoulder joints can be hyperextended by voluntary muscular contractions without any concomitant discomfort or damage.

Similarly, **hyperflexion** is a flexion that exceeds the normal range of motion of a joint and is often associated with persons having abnormal flexibility or with externally applied forces, some of which may cause injury. A serious example of hyperflexion is when the neck of a hockey player is flexed excessively after sliding into the boards headfirst with the neck flexed. This type of impact has caused quadriplegia (paralysis of all four limbs) in a number of hockey players.

The ankle joint has special names for its movements because, unlike the other segments, its long axis is perpendicular to the longitudinal axis of the body. **Dorsiflexion** (figure 8.5) is similar to flexion because the ankle's angle is reduced from the anatomical position. Extension of the ankle joint is called **plantar flexion** because the foot moves in the plantar direction.

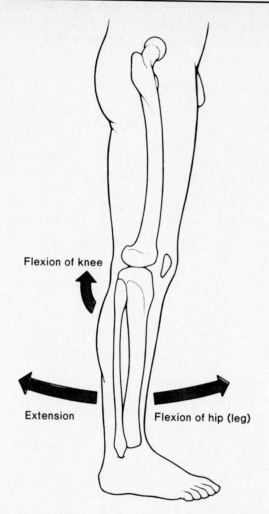

Flexion of knee

Extension

Flexion of hip (leg)

Figure 8.4 Extension and flexion of the hip (leg) and flexion of the knee

SOURCE: From Kent M. Van De Graaff, *Human Anatomy.* Copyright © 1984 Wm. C. Brown Publishers, Dubuque, Iowa. All Rights Reserved. Reprinted by permission.

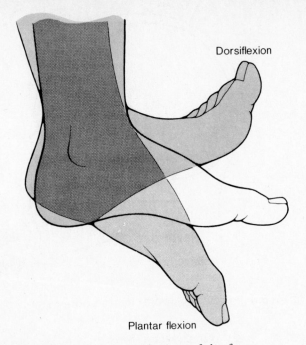

Dorsiflexion

Plantar flexion

Figure 8.5 Dorsiflexion and plantar flexion of the foot

SOURCE: From Kent M. Van De Graaff, *Human Anatomy.* Copyright © 1984 Wm. C. Brown Publishers, Dubuque, Iowa. All Rights Reserved. Reprinted by permission.

The terms protraction and retraction (figure 8.6) refer to sagittal or frontal planar translations (linear movements) of body parts along any axis parallel to the ground. **Protraction** is the movement of a body part away from its location in the anatomical position. **Retraction** is a movement of the part back toward its anatomical position along an axis parallel to the ground. The shoulder blade (scapula), collarbone (clavicle), and jaw (mandible) are capable of these movements.

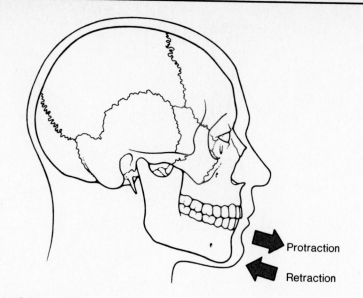

Figure 8.6 Protraction and retraction of the jaw

Frontal Plane Movements

This cardinal plane bisects the body laterally through the ear, shoulder, spinal column, pelvis, hips, knees, and ankles (figure 8.1). Capabilities for movement through the frontal or lateral planes of the body are somewhat less when compared to the two other planes of motion. Body areas involved are the upper and lower limbs and the cervical and thoracolumbar spinal regions. Remember that the principle of parallel non-cardinal motion mentioned earlier in the chapter applies also in the frontal plane as it will in the following discussion of the transverse plane. Examples of motions in the frontal plane particular to sport movement would be the use of the upper and lower limbs to enhance body stability or balance in certain gymnastic routines. For a clearer understanding of human movement in this plane, an explanation of terms follows.

Abduction is a frontal plane motion that increases the angle of a joint from its anatomical position. Its opposite is **adduction** which decreases the angle of a joint toward the anatomical position. For instance, raising the arm laterally is called shoulder abduction while lowering the arm is called shoulder adduction. Joints which can perform these movements include the hips, shoulders, fingers, and wrists. Figure 8.7 shows hip abduction and adduction.

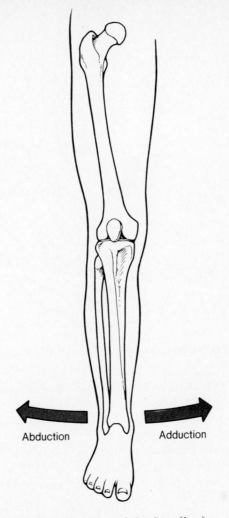

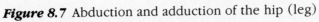

Abduction   Adduction

Figure 8.7 Abduction and adduction of the hip (leg)

SOURCE: From Kent M. Van De Graaff, *Human Anatomy.* Copyright © 1984 Wm. C. Brown Publishers, Dubuque, Iowa. All Rights Reserved. Reprinted by permission.

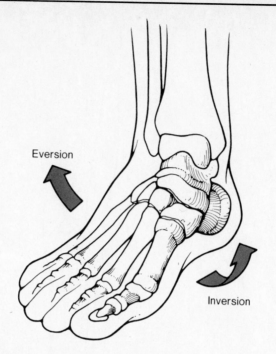

Eversion

Inversion

Figure 8.8 Inversion and eversion of the foot

SOURCE: From Kent M. Van De Graaff, *Human Anatomy.* Copyright © 1984 Wm. C. Brown Publishers, Dubuque, Iowa. All Rights Reserved. Reprinted by permission.

Lateral bending is the term used for frontal planar movements of the spinal column. Right lateral bending of the neck, for example, would be to move the head laterally toward the right shoulder. The reverse motion would be called left lateral bending.

The terms varus and valgus are used for frontal planar motions of the knee. These movements, which are not produced by voluntary contractions of the knee musculature, require external loadings such as experienced during the landing phase of running. **Varus** is when the knee's angle decreases medially (i.e., bowlegged). **Valgus** is when the knee angle decreases laterally (i.e., knock-kneed).

Rotations of the ankle in the frontal plane (figure 8.8), which correspond to rotations about the long axis of the foot, are called **inversion** when the rotation moves the plantar surface of the foot medially and **eversion** when the plantar surface is rotated toward the lateral side. The ankle is usually only capable of these movements when an external force is applied as during the landing phase of running or when the ankle "turns over" while walking.

Transverse Plane Movements

As described earlier, the cardinal transverse plane of motion theoretically divides the body into superior (upper) and inferior (lower) halves of the anatomically positioned body (figure 8.1). Remember that there can be a close theoretical relationship between transverse motion and the centre of gravity even though the position of a person's centre of gravity can be changed on the basis of variables already mentioned in the chapter. Rotations or twisting motions found in calisthenics, exercises, gymnastics, and diving routines are examples of body motions through the transverse plane. Again, for a clearer comprehension of the movement abilities in the transverse plane, an explanation of terms follows.

Medial rotation and **lateral rotation** are transverse rotations which rotate a joint or segment toward or away from the midline of the body, respectively. These movements are usually associated with ball and socket joints such as the shoulder and hip. Figure 8.9 shows these movements for the arm. The ankle joint is also capable of these movements to a lesser degree. Rotations of the spinal column about the transverse axis are called **left** or **right rotation.**

Pronation and supination (figure 8.10) are the terms used to describe the equivalent movements of the forearm about the transverse axis. **Supination** occurs when the forearm muscles rotate the palm toward the anatomical position, forming what looks like a soup bowl with the hand. **Pronation** is when the forearm rotates the palm away from the anatomical position. Supination and pronation of the ankle are more complicated rotations which will be described later along with other triaxial movements.

Horizontal flexion, also called *horizontal adduction,* of a limb (arm or leg) is a movement in which the limb rotates medially in the transverse plane. **Horizontal extension,** also called *horizontal abduction,* is the opposite movement whereby the limb is rotated laterally in the transverse plane. These movements are usually accompanied by other rotations when performed at the hip; the shoulder joint can perform these motions in isolation (figure 8.11).

The terms **elevation** and **depression,** which are actually translations (linear movements) of joints and not rotations, are used to describe the movements of either the shoulder blade (scapula), jaw (mandible), or knee (patella) in the superior and inferior directions, respectively. They may also be used to describe the very small movements that each joint is capable of when internal or external forces attempt to pull or push the bones a part in the transverse direction.

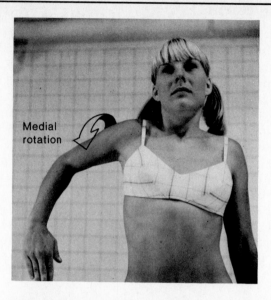

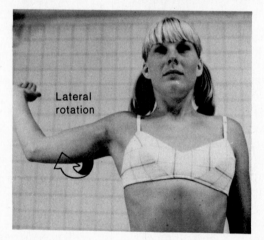

Figure 8.9 Medial (internal) and lateral (external) rotation of the shoulder (arm)

SOURCE: Logan/McKinney, *Anatomic Kinesiology,* Wm. C. Brown Company Publishers, 1982, p. 78, figs. 4.44 and 4.45.

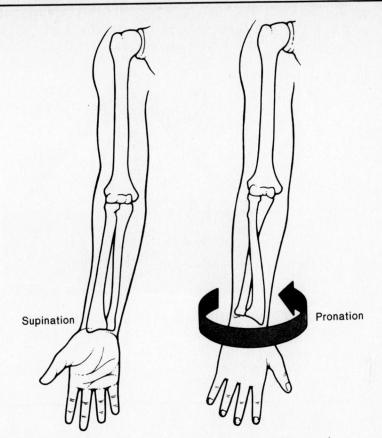

Supination

Pronation

Figure 8.10 Pronation and supination of the elbow (forearm)

Source: From Kent M. Van De Graaff, *Human Anatomy.* Copyright © 1984 Wm. C. Brown Publishers, Dubuque, Iowa. All Rights Reserved. Reprinted by permission.

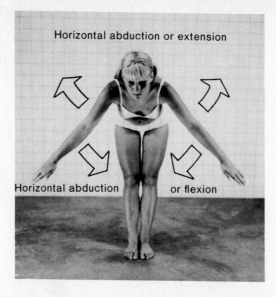

Figure 8.11 Horizontal flexion (horizontal adduction) and horizontal extension (horizontal abduction) of the shoulder (arm)

SOURCE: Logan/McKinney, *Anatomic Kinesiology*, Wm. C. Brown Company Publishers, 1982, p. 78, fig. 4.43.

Triaxial Movements

The planes of motion mentioned so far in no way describe all human motion. In fact there are numerous routines or complex skills in sports when the upper and lower limbs move diagonally through one or more of the three planes. Most ballistic movements involving throwing, striking, and kicking techniques employ this motion. Therefore, some joints are capable of performing triaxial or three-dimensional movements. Ball and socket joints (shoulders and hips) are particularly suited to triaxial movements. Note that it is impossible to rotate, simultaneously, a joint about two axes without involving the third. **Circumduction** (figure 8.12) is an example of a triaxial movement. It occurs when a joint or combination of joints is rotated in a conical pattern. Such joints as the thumb, hip, shoulder, and spinal column are capable of circumduction.

Pronation and **supination** of the ankle joint are also triaxial motions. Supination involves plantar flexion, inversion, and internal rotation of the foot. Ankle pronation requires simultaneous dorsiflexion, eversion, and outward rotation of the foot.

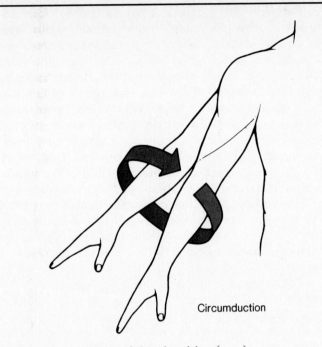

Circumduction

Figure 8.12 Circumduction of the shoulder (arm)

LEVERS OF THE MUSCULOSKELETAL SYSTEM

Following an understanding of the kinds of motions of which one's body is capable, there must be some further consideration of what substances and mechanisms are responsible for these motions. The rest of this chapter explains how motion is theoretically developed in the human body through the levers of the musculoskeletal system. In human anatomy the lever is the bone, the fulcrum is the joint at which movement takes place, and the force is supplied either by the contraction of skeletal muscles or by the pull of gravity on the whole or part of the body mass.

Skeletal muscles consist of bundles of fibres called **myofibrils** (Latin: *myo,* muscle; *fibrilla,* fibril) which are surrounded by a protective sheath. Muscles terminate at both ends in strong, relatively stiff material called **tendons.** Tendons connect the muscles with bones and always attach across one or more joints. Both ends of a muscle cannot be attached to the same bone because its contraction would cause no muscle shortening or motion. Clearly, this would be a waste of the body's resources; biological systems always try to avoid such inefficiencies. Muscles detached from a bone or otherwise prevented from contracting become atrophied (i.e., reduced in size).

Two terms are used to distinguish opposite ends of a muscle. The term **origin** refers to the proximal end of a muscle while **insertion** identifies the distal end. Some muscles have multiple ends or heads. For example, the biceps (Latin: *bi,* two; *capit,* head) brachii (the large elbow flexor that people flex while drinking) has two origins both on the shoulder blade (scapula). The triceps brachii (major elbow extensor) has three heads—one on the scapula and the other two on the humerus (the bone between the shoulder and elbow).

Muscles cross joints so that when they contract or shorten they draw two or more bones together. The lines of action of most muscles do not cross directly through the centres of rotation of joints. The **line of force** (*line of pull*) of a muscle is defined as the line of action of the muscle taken from either the muscle's origin or insertion. Such a line is shown in figure 8.13. If this line crosses through the joint centre the effect of the muscle contraction would be to compress the two bones together and cause no net movement. This function is used to prevent a joint from being pulled apart as, for example, when one carries a briefcase full of anatomy texts. The usual action of muscles, however, is to cause both rotation and compression of bones.

The ability of a muscle to cause rotation is affected by its force level and its angle of pull with respect to the bones that it attaches. A muscle's angle of pull changes as the joint angle that it crosses changes. The greater its angle of pull (other factors being equal), the greater will be its turning effect. The **angle of pull** of a muscle is defined as the angle between the line of pull of the tendon and the line of the bone to which it attaches.

There must be some perpendicular distance between the line of force of the muscle and the joint centre of rotation for the muscle to cause any rotation. This distance, called the **moment arm,** is one of the major factors which determines the ability of a particular muscle to exert force against external objects or the environment. In this respect the muscle and its associated bones may be considered a lever system. The muscle's ability to contract against a bone, which acts as the lever, defines a quality that is usually called strength.

The term **strength** may be defined as the maximum force or moment of force that a muscle or group of muscles can create voluntarily. The concept of moment of force will be defined more precisely in the biomechanics chapter; for now, it will be defined as the muscle's ability to cause rotation or as the product of the muscle's force times its moment arm with respect to a joint. This quality—strength—is determined by many factors, such as muscle length, fibre composition, fatigue state, speed of contraction, level of recruitment, and cross-sectional area; these factors will not be considered in this chapter.

The following section will describe the musculoskeletal system as a mechanical leverage system. First, the three classes of levers will be presented with both mechanical and human levers as examples of the various classes.

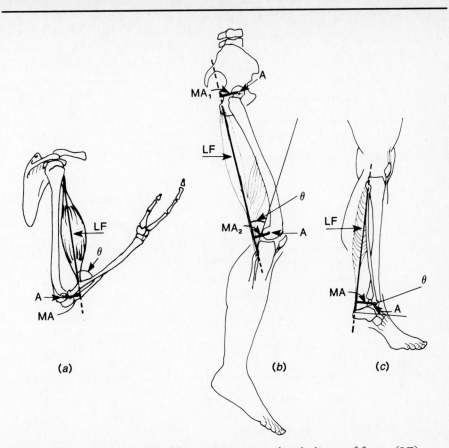

Figure 8.13 Angles of pull (θ), moment arms (MA), lines of force (LF), and axes of rotation (A) of the (*a*) biceps brachii, (*b*) biceps femoris, and (*c*) soleus muscles

SOURCE: Gowitzke & Milner, *Understanding the Scientific Bases of Human Movement,* Williams & Wilkins Publ., 1980, p. 124, fig. 5.6.

Then the concepts of mechanical advantage and speed advantage will be discussed in the context of the musculoskeletal system.

Classes of Levers

The lever is one of the six simple machines of mechanics—the others are the incline plane, the wheel and axle, the wedge, the pulley, and the screw. A lever system consists of an applied force, a lever, a fulcrum, and a load. Levers have been classified into three groups depending upon the arrangement of

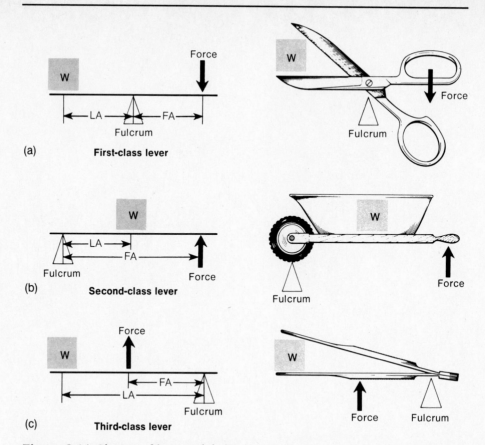

Figure 8.14 Classes of levers: (*a*) first class, (*b*) second class, and (*c*) third class (LA = load arm, FA = force arm)

SOURCE: From John W. Hole, Jr., *Human Anatomy and Physiology,* 3d ed. Copyright © 1984 Wm. C. Brown Publishers, Dubuque, Iowa. All Rights Reserved. Reprinted by permission.

the applied force, fulcrum, and load. The three arrangements and their associated names are presented in figure 8.14. The terms **force arm** and **load arm** in this figure refer to the moment arms of the applied force and load taken from the point of rotation at the fulcrum, respectively.

First-Class Levers

An example of a muscular first-class lever is the calf (gastrocnemius) muscle when the foot is free to move. Figure 8.15 shows the foot in an inverted position to better illustrate its first-class leverage. Very few muscles are arranged as first-class levers because muscles can contract for only a short distance before their force output drops off.

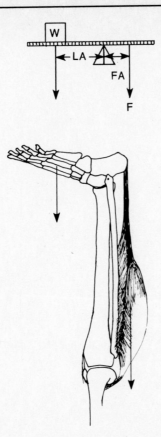

Figure 8.15 Gastrocnemius muscle acting as a first-class lever when the foot is free to move

SOURCE: Gowitzke & Milner, *Understanding the Scientific Bases of Movement*, Williams & Wilkins Publ., 1980, p. 111, fig. 4.16 (*a*).

Second-Class Levers

Ironically, the gastrocnemius muscle is also an excellent example of a second-class lever; however, to act in this manner the ball of the foot must act as the fulcrum as when standing on tiptoe. The load in this case, as illustrated in figure 8.16, becomes the line of force or line of gravity of the body which must fall in front of the tendon of the gastrocnemius's insertion on the back of the foot (at the calcaneus). Because the gastrocnemius has second-class leverage in this situation, it is capable of lifting very heavy loads relative to its size. However, it cannot lift the load through a large distance since it does not have a speed advantage.

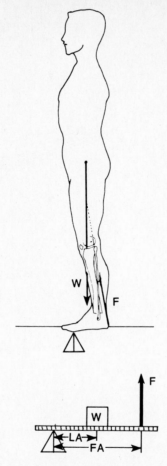

Figure 8.16 Gastrocnemius muscle acting as a second-class lever during standing

SOURCE: Gowitzke & Milner, *Understanding the Scientific Bases of Human Movement,* Williams & Wilkins Publ., 1980, p. 125, fig. 5.7.

Third-Class Levers

Most muscles have third-class leverage. Two examples are pictured in figure 8.17—one is the biceps brachii muscle during flexion of the elbow; the other is the biceps femoris muscle during knee extension. In both of these cases a small shortening of the muscle will cause a relatively large movement of the forearm and lower leg, respectively.

An important feature of the quadriceps femoris group is its connection with the patella. The patella has the effect of increasing the moment arm of

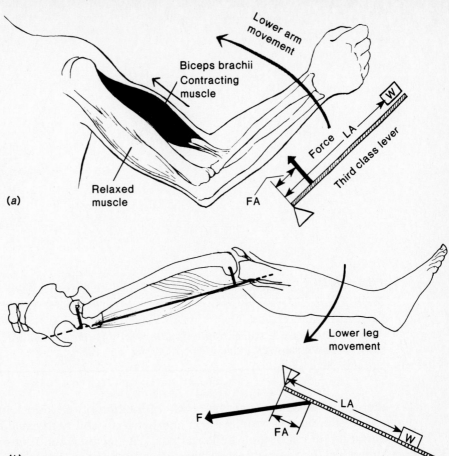

Figure 8.17 (*a*) biceps brachii and (*b*) biceps femoris muscles acting as third-class levers (note FA of (b) is not a moment arm because it is not perpendicular to line of force)

SOURCE: (*a*) From John W. Hole, Jr., *Human Anatomy and Physiology,* 3d ed. Copyright © 1984 Wm. C. Brown Publishers, Dubuque, Iowa. All Rights Reserved. Reprinted by permission. (*a*); and (*b*) Gowitzke & Milner, *Understanding the Scientific Bases of Human Movement,* Williams & Wilkins, 1980, p. 124, fig. 5.6 (*b*).

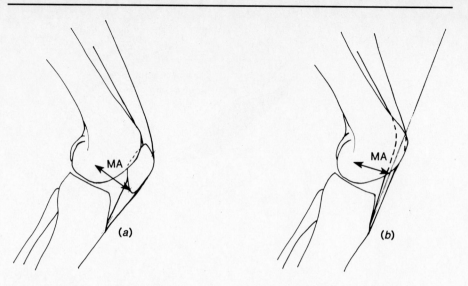

Figure 8.18 Change in the moment arm of the quadriceps femoris muscle group (*a*) before and (*b*) after removal of the patella (MA = moment arm)

SOURCE: Gowitzke & Milner, *Understanding the Scientific Bases of Human Movement,* Williams & Wilkins, 1980, p. 112, fig. 4.17 (*a*), (*b*).

the quadriceps away from the centre of rotation of the knee joint. This increases the group's turning effect and hence its ability to extend the knee. Surgical removal of the patella, called a patellectomy, seriously reduces the strength of the knee extensors; therefore, postoperative strengthening of these muscles is extremely important for rehabilitation (figure 8.18).

Mechanical Advantage versus Speed Advantage

Mechanical advantage is determined as the ratio of the moment arm of the force to the moment arm of the load. When this ratio is greater than 1 the lever is said to have a mechanical advantage. Conversely, when the ratio is less than 1 the lever is at a mechanical disadvantage; this is called a speed advantage.

In the case of a mechanical advantage the amount of force required to cause the load to move is reduced, but the force must be applied over a proportionally longer distance. For example, if the mechanical advantage is 2 (force arm is twice as long as the load arm) then the force need only be half as large as the load for it to be moved. However, the force will have to be applied over a distance twice as large as the distance the load will be moved. All second-class levers have a mechanical advantage; no third-class levers have a mechanical advantage; and first-class levers may or may not have mechanical advantage depending of the lengths on the force and load moment arms.

Speed advantage is the inverse of mechanical advantage and occurs whenever the force moment arm is shorter than the load moment arm. In this case, the force required to move a load must be greater than the load. However, it will be able to move the load through a proportionally greater distance and, hence, with greater speed. For example, if the force moment arm is 1 unit and the load moment arm is 10 units, the lever will have a speed advantage of 10. Thus, when the force applied is ten times that of the load the load will be moved ten times faster than the speed of the force. This is the situation for all third-class levers and some first-class levers. Most human muscles are arranged as third-class levers because a muscle can shorten only a small distance relative to the distance that the bones are required to be moved. Through evolution and natural selection, the body has sacrificed mechanical advantage in most of its muscle groups to achieve speed of movement.

CHAPTER 9

Physiological Basis for Exercise: The Motor Team

Edward C. Rhodes

The human organism is extremely complex and strikes a fine balance and interdependence on the various parts. The basis of human life is contained in the cell. Every living cell is a complex structure involved in the life processes within specialized confines (e.g., muscle cell, nerve cell, bone cell, fat cell). Each cell has some common general characteristics while also demonstrating unique specialized activities that enable the body to function normally. The development of the electron microscope has allowed scientists the opportunity to delve into the complexities of the cell and study at the molecular level. However, it will take decades before many of the mysteries are fully understood. Many of the physiological mechanisms will be discussed in the following sections.

Chapter 8 introduced the reader to some elementary concepts concerning the terminology of anatomy such as the anatomical position, the centre of gravity, planes of movement, directional nomenclature, and the bones and muscles as a lever system. This chapter will further develop one's knowledge of the structure and function (anatomy and physiology) of man and explore how man moves by the **motor team.** The motor team will include the skeletal system (bones and joints), the muscular system (engines for movement), and the neurological component (brain, spinal cord, and nerves going to the muscles). Functioning as a unit, the nervous system (computer) exerts control over the muscles which move the bones at fixed joints.

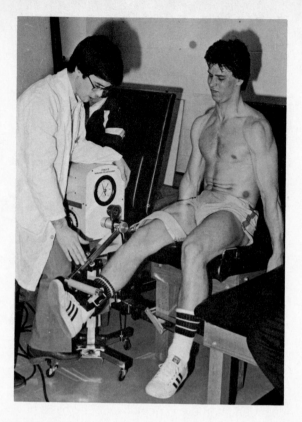

Throughout the discussion emphasis will be placed on the applied aspects of physical activity so that the prospective teacher or exercise specialist of human movement will be able to bridge the gap between a basic understanding of the human body and what happens during exercise stress.

An understanding of how the body autorenovates (repairs and adapts) during recovery after exercise will also be of prime importance. Emphasis will focus on the acute (short term) adjustment of the body to exercise, as well as the chronic (long term) changes that take place. The body is a very prodigious machine and the adjustments and adaptations during exercise are truly amazing.

THE SKELETAL AND ARTICULAR SYSTEMS

The skeleton is a supporting structure or framework. It allows us to stand erect and accomplish extraordinary feats of artistic grace, physical endurance, and athletic endeavour. It is comprised of 206 separate bones that are viable, living structures of the human body. Five general functions of the skeleton follow.

1. It protects vital organs and certain soft tissues of the body (e.g., brain, heart, lungs).
2. It offers support to the body.

3. It manufactures red blood cells. This function (hematopoiesis) occurs primarily in the red bone marrow.
4. It stores some mineral salts (phosphorus and calcium) for bodily needs.
5. It provides levers for movement.

Anatomy of Bones

Bones can be classified into the following four categories.

1. **Long bones** of the body consist of a shaft (diaphysis) and two extremities (epiphyses). Examples of long bones of the body are the humerus and femur.
2. **Short bones** have an irregular shape and are not merely shorter versions of long bones. They are exemplified by the carpals of the wrist and the tarsal bones of the foot.
3. **Flat bones** are usually found where there is a need to protect some of the soft tissues of the body. They are also evident at locations where extensive muscle attachment is needed. Good examples are flat bones of the skull.
4. **Irregular bones** are bones of peculiar and differing shape. Good examples of this type of bone are the vertebrae.

Types of Bone Cells

Three basic types of cells exist in bone. They are **osteoblasts** (builders of bone), **osteoclasts** (bone destroyers), and **osteocytes** (mature bone cells). Bone is not just an inert white mass, but is constantly undergoing change and turnover of cells. Initially bones are made of cartilage; through a process called *endochondral ossification* the cartilage is slowly replaced by bone cells. This process primarily takes place in the long bones of the body. Bones are constantly remodeling themselves by the work of osteoclasts. Eventually, as bone grows and remodels itself, osteoblasts become surrounded by bone matrix and become fully formed bone cells. At this point the osteocytes are primarily involved in the maintenance of bone (see figure 9.1).

Homeostatic Mechanisms and Bone

Bones are storage depots for about 99 percent of the total calcium in the body. It is extremely important that ionized calcium (Ca^{++}) is kept at basal levels in the blood plasma and in the interstitial fluid. Lack of proper levels of Ca^{++} can result in the following:

1. an uncontrolled excitation of nerve fibers with resultant transmission of impulses to the muscle causing spasm; sometimes this is linked to muscle cramps that often occur after extreme physical work;
2. a weakness of cardiac muscles which could result in a decrease in the blood supply to tissues; and
3. an interference with blood coagulation.

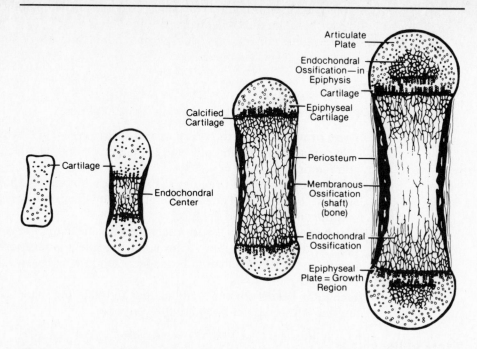

Figure 9.1 Bone formation and growth from a cartilagenous form in the embryonic stage to an almost mature bone

Division of the Skeleton and Bone Identification

The skeleton is divided into two parts. The **axial portion** (axis; 80 bones) consists of the skull, vertebral column, sternum, and ribs. The second part of the skeleton is the **appendicular portion** (appendages; 126 bones). Figure 9.2 shows both anterior and posterior view of the axial and appendicular skeleton.

Effects of Activity on Growth of Bone

Wolff's law states that bones will adapt to suit the stresses and strains placed upon them. Like muscle, bone atrophies internally with disuse. There is a general loss in weight and mineral loss (decalcification) in bones due to inactivity. The condition is much like osteoporosis (loss of Ca^{++} and a weakening of the bone). Essentially, the bone becomes porous and less dense. Studies involving long-term bed rest (physical confinement) and weightlessness (space travel) demonstrate alterations in bone metabolism. As such, Wolff's law comes into effect and osteoclastic activity, with reduced osteoblastic involvement, causes bone to become more porous and spongy. Both tensile and compressive forces are essential for normal bone growth and development. The stress and strain on bones, particularly through exercise, can help to maintain the integrity of the bone. On some of the first space flights

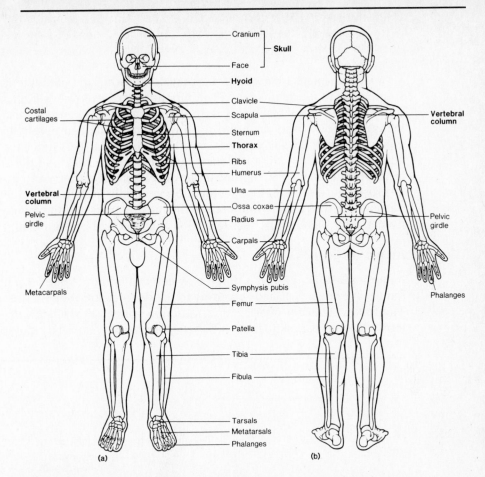

Costal cartilages

Cranium ⎤
⎬ **Skull**
Face ⎦

Hyoid

Clavicle

Scapula

Sternum

Thorax

Ribs

Humerus

Ulna

Ossa coxae

Radius

Carpals

Vertebral column

Pelvic girdle

Metacarpals

Symphysis pubis

Femur

Patella

Tibia

Fibula

Tarsals

Metatarsals

Phalanges

Vertebral column

Pelvic girdle

Phalanges

(a)

(b)

Figure 9.2 (*a*) Anterior view and (*b*) posterior view of the human skeleton. The bones of the axial skeleton are shaded to differentiate them from the bones of the appendicular skeleton.

astronauts were losing from 5 percent to 20 percent of their bone mass. However, during later flights, exercises were performed while in space, and this activity attempted to offset the degenerative process and reduce the loss of active bone. Further studies have demonstrated direct relationships exist between muscle mass and bone strength.

Electrical potentials are established in bone cells and seem to have a direct bearing on the cellular activity. The stimulation of exercise causes the direct response of increasing osteoblastic activity and helping the bone to counteract the stress. Tensile forces seem to be more important in allowing proper growth and development than compressive ones. Extreme compressive forces may cause the growth zone of the bone (epiphyseal region) to lessen its activity. However, exercise is important as a stimulus to bone. It helps to promote the normal growth and development of bone cells. The question is, How much exercise is beneficial and when does it become harmful?

Growth plate injuries can be prevalent during the adolescent growth spurt (nine to fourteen years). The monitoring of exercise is a must at this time. Excessive physical stress is an individual variable and overuse can be manifest in one individual and not in another. Enlarged epiphyses in the elbows of Little League pitchers have been reported. This indicates the excessive strain of throwing too many curve balls. The knee and the shoulder are other vulnerable joints prone to the development of traumatic epiphysitis. Overuse injuries in children are manifest generally in skeletal problems. Understanding the proper alignment of the moving parts and the monitoring of potential problems (e.g., sore knees) is a must for all practitioners.

Classification of Joints

An **articulation** (joint) is a union between two or more bones. Traditionally joints have been classified according to the degree of movement they permit. The following major classifications describe joints: (1) *synarthrosis*—an immovable joint (e.g., skull bones); (2) *amphiarthrosis*—a slightly movable joint

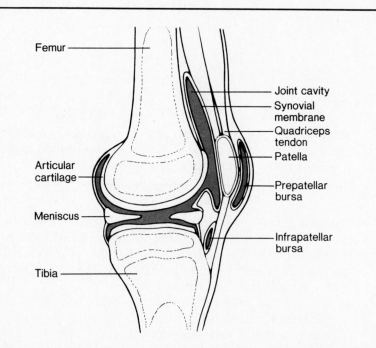

Figure 9.3 A diarthrotic joint is represented by this diagrammatic lateral view of the knee joint. What structural features do all diarthrotic joints have in common?

(e.g., tibiofibular; and (3) *diarthrosis*—a freely movable synovial joint. Synovial joints are freely movable and comprise the types of joints primarily involved in the study of human movement.

Anatomy of Synovial Joints

Synovial joints are comprised of a joint cavity enclosed by a capsule of dense fibrous connective tissue and lined with a vascular connective tissue called the synovial membrane. This membrane secretes synovial fluid. Synovial fluid is the major source of nutrition for the cartilage. The bones are covered with an articular cartilage. Ligaments bind the joints together. They are bands of dense connective tissue with sites of origin from bone to bone. Figure 9.3 shows the anatomy of a typical diarthrodial joint. The relationship of a tendon sheath to bone is shown in figure 9.4.

Types of Synovial Joints

The types of freely movable joints are usually classified according to the shape of their articulating ends.

1. **Ball and socket joint—** a ball-shaped head fits into a concave socket. This type of joint provides the widest range of movement in all planes (e.g., shoulder and hip).

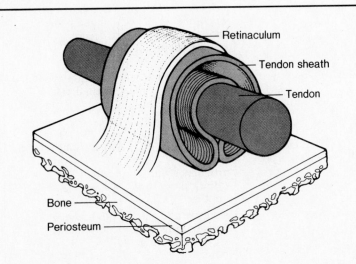

Figure 9.4 A tendon sheath facilitates the gliding of a tendon as it traverses a fibrous or bony tunnel. Tendon sheaths are closed sacs, one layer of the synovial membrane lining the tunnel, the other folding over the surface of the tendon.

Table 9.1 Types of articulations

TYPE	STRUCTURE	MOVEMENTS	EXAMPLE
Synarthroses	Articulating bones in close contact, bound by a thin layer of fribrous tissue or cartilage	None	Suture between bones of the skull; epiphyseal plate
Amphiarthroses	Articulating bones separated by fibrocartilaginous disks or bound by interosseous ligament	Slightly movable	Intervertebral joints; symphysis pubis and sacroiliac joint; between tibia-fibula and radius-ulna
Diarthroses	Joint capsule containing synovial membrane and synovial fluid	Freely movable	
A. Gliding	Flattened or slightly curved articulating surfaces	Sliding	Intercarpal and intertarsal joints
B. Hinge	Concave surface of one bone articulates with convex surface of another	Bending motion in one plane	Knee; elbow; joints of phalanges
C. Pivot	Conical surface of one bone articulates with a depression of another	Rotation about a central axis	Atlantoaxial joint; proximal radioulnar joint
D. Condyloid	Oval condyle of one bone articulates with elliptical cavity of another	Biaxial movement	Radiocarpal joint
E. Saddle	Concave and convex surface on each articulating bone	Wide range of movements	Carpometacarpal joint of the thumb
F. Ball and socket	Rounded convex surface of one bone articulates with cuplike socket of another	Movement in all planes and rotation	Shoulder and hip joints

2. **Pivot joint**— usually a pivotlike process rotates within a smooth fossa around a longitudinal axis (e.g., radioulnar joint).
3. **Hinge joint**— usually movement is limited to a single plane (flexion and extension) whereby a bony prominence fits into a fossa (e.g., elbow).
4. **Condyloid joint**— an oval-shaped surface (convex) fits into a concave or elliptical cavity. Motion is possible in two planes (biaxial) at right angles to each other (e.g., wrist: radial bone and carpals).
5. **Saddle joint**—a unique joint between the first metacarpal (thumb) and the trapezium (carpal). Often called reciprocal reception because it is like two saddles fitting together.
6. **Gliding joint**—a joint between two opposing plane surfaces, one gliding over the top of another. This type of joint has flat or slightly concave-convex surfaces (e.g., articular processes of vertebrae).

Table 9.1 summarizes the classification of joints.

A great deal of trauma is placed on bone during our everyday lives. Joints are subject to stresses and strains and at times injuries do occur. Sometimes extreme trauma can cause ligaments binding the joint to be stretched or actually torn. The joint capsule can also be traumatized. Bones can be broken and need to be reset. However, exercise plays a vital role in maintaining the integrity of joints and bones. As bone is a viable tissue it often strengthens itself in a parallel fashion with muscle during repeated bouts of exercise stress. Ligaments can also exhibit increased tensile strength. Musculature around the joints also strengthens and helps to stabilize the joint. However, the basic question still arising is, What type of exercise regimen allows for the proper setup of the cells and autorenovation to take place without destruction (fatigue fractures) occurring and a resultant weakening of bone? For example, excessive running on hard surfaces over a period of time can cause deleterious effects. Therefore, threshold levels do exist and care must be taken to allow for the best adaptive regimen of training without causing an overuse syndrome in bone.

THE MUSCULAR SYSTEM

In studying the motor team, the actual forces for movement are created by the muscles. These forces depend on the ability to transform the chemical energy "locked up" in a high-energy compound (ATP) into the mechanical energy of contraction. The little "pistons" in the muscle generate force acting through **connective tissue** (tendons) to the bones which move about the joint axis. The movement allowed is subject to the anatomical structure of the joint and the potential interference of the soft tissues around the joint (muscles, ligaments, tendons). This is generally thought of as flexibility (range of motion). Neuromuscular mechanisms (proprioceptors) can also be involved in controlling the range of motion about joints.

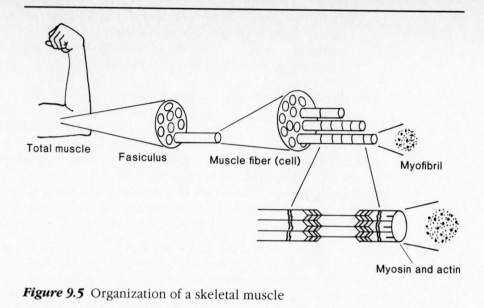

Total muscle   Fasiculus   Muscle fiber (cell)   Myofibril

Myosin and actin

Figure 9.5 Organization of a skeletal muscle

Structure of Skeletal Muscle

There are approximately 600 skeletal muscles in the human body. Seventy-five percent of skeletal muscle weight is water, 20 percent is protein, and the remaining 5 percent is other substances (ATP, minerals, myoglobin, inorganic salts, etc.). The proteins are myosin (52 percent), actin (23 percent), and tropomyosin (15 percent).

The muscle cells (cylindrical fibres) are wrapped in fibrous connective tissues. Each muscle fibre is surrounded by the **endomysium.** Approximately every 150–200 fibres form a bundle (fasciculus) which is surrounded by the **perimysium.** The entire muscle belly is enclosed by a third connective layer, **the epimysium.** These connective tissues blend together to form the strong dense tendons which penetrate into the outer covering of the bone (periosteum). It is often the tendons or connective tissues in the muscle that are involved in muscular soreness rather than the contractile proteins.

Functional Contractile Unit

The ultrastructure of muscle has been revealed through research with the electron microscope. Figure 9.5 shows the organization of skeletal muscle. The muscle is composed of long cylinders called fibres. Each fibre is composed of long **myofibrils** which are comprised of smaller **myofilaments.** The proteins actin and myosin make up approximately 85 percent of the myofilaments.

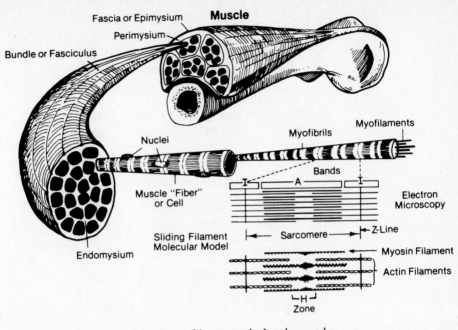

Figure 9.6 Structural design of human skeletal muscle

The actual functional component of the muscle is the **sarcomere.** Figure 9.6 shows a typical sarcomere. The muscle appears striated (striped) under low magnification. The dark banding is primarily because of the myosin or thick filament. The Z lines are connected to the actin filament and separate each sarcomere. Recent studies on the ultrastructure of muscle are unravelling the complexity of the cell and showing the involved process by which chemical energy is transposed into mechanical forces of movement. The theory most prevalent is called the *sliding filament theory of contraction* and proposes that the filaments slide past one another without alteration in their length. Figure 9.7 gives representation of the structural arrangement of the protein filaments. They are linked by cross-bridges on the myosin and undergo oscillatory movements, combining and recombining with sites on the actin filaments. The energy for this cross-bridge movement is brought about by the splitting of **ATP** (adenosine triphosphate), a high-energy compound. When the myosin and actin combine, a special enzyme, myosin ATPase, splits the ATP which causes a conformational change and a subsequent oscillation and movement of the filaments. The continued availability of energy and the ATPase activity will often determine the duration and intensity of the work output.

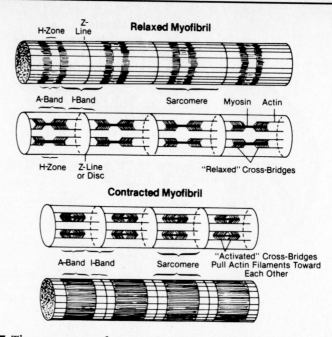

Figure 9.7 The sequence of events that produce motion during the contraction of a muscle fiber. Note the change in the arrangement of the cross-bridges and the length of the sarcomeres from the resting to the activated state.

The Energy Processes

All human cells must be continually supplied with chemical energy to perform their specific function. ATP is a special carrier of energy for use by the cells (see figure 9.8). This energy-rich compound is the ubiquitous source of energy for all of our billions of living cells. However, the primary focus in this chapter is directed more toward the muscle cell and energy needs as we perform either short bursts of work or long-lasting activity sessions. The energy in food we eat is not transferred directly to the cells but is captured in molecules of ATP and later transferred to the filaments of the muscle cell. The high-energy compound is split and the released energy is used to drive these tiny "pistons". Therefore ATP is the energy currency of the cell.

There is very little ATP actually stored in the cell. Therefore the amount of ATP and the subsequent splitting to ADP (adenosine diphosphate) can be altered very quickly with an increase in cellular function. ATP cannot be supplied by other cells or through the blood but must be recycled continuously by the muscle cell itself. ATP is needed to carry on muscular work. The question is, Where will it continually come from?

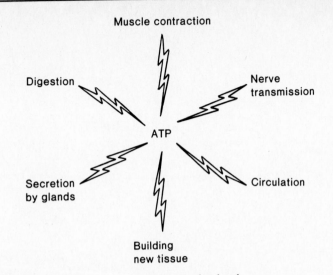

Figure 9.8 ATP is the energy currency in the body

With very little ATP stored in the cell we must first look for other reservoirs to reload our stores. There is another direct source of quick ATP: a high-energy phosphate compound called **creatine phosphate** (CP). The muscle cells' supply of CP is approximately five times greater than that of free ATP. However, there is not a great abundance of either one. CP essentially reloads ADP to ATP. Free energy is released when the bond between the creatine and phosphate molecules split. The phosphate couples with the ADP to form a new ATP:

$$CP + ADP \longrightarrow ATP + C.$$

The actual transfer of energy as phosphate bonds is known as **phosphorylation.** The supplier of energy for phosphorylation is primarily the oxidation of fats and carbohydrates, supplied to the body through digestion.

The energy processes of the muscle cell are usually defined as either anaerobic or aerobic. Energy transferring processes that do not involve oxygen are termed **anaerobic,** while energy transfers where oxygen is involved in the degradation process are **aerobic.** Therefore, the actual muscle has available for its use immediate, short-term, (anaerobic), and long-term (aerobic) sources of energy.

In investigating these energy sources, the concept of specificity of exercise will be strongly supported. Energy processes in the muscle cell can be schematically represented in diagrams such as figures 9.9 and 9.10. The circulatory system delivers the fuels to the muscles in times of low-energy requirements and much of the fuel is stored as glycogen (carbohydrate sources)

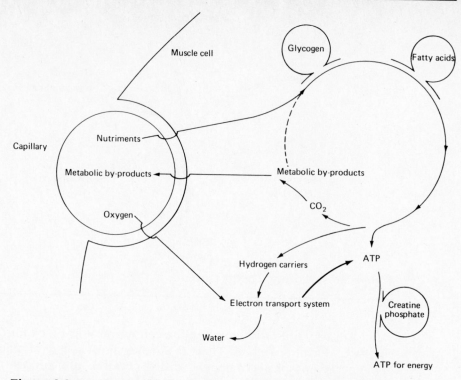

Figure 9.9 Energy metabolism and the resultant manufacturing of ATP

and lipids (free fatty acids and triglycerides). During bouts of heavy exercise the muscle cells make use of these stored fuels, while the circulatory system can provide additional fuels and, of course, **oxygen.** The muscle cells use the fuels and oxygen in the metabolic processes. As a result of the metabolic processes' attempt to generate ATP, by-products are produced and removed from the cell by way of the circulatory system. Many of these products are later either excreted from the body or reconverted into useful materials.

Immediate Sources of Energy

For many power activities such as high jumping or one maximum lift of weights, there is a high-energy demand for a short period of time. ATP must move into place quickly on the myosin cross-bridges and be split rapidly to allow the muscle to contract. However, there are not great amounts of free ATP stored in the muscle for this burst of energy. The high-energy compound creatine phosphate is also available to reload the ATP. The skeletal muscles will have approximately four to six seconds of energy available through these sources.

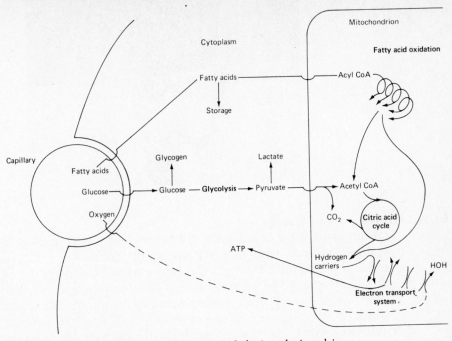

Figure 9.10 Biochemical pathways and their relationships

Short-Term Sources of Energy

For activities of high-energy needs, lasting from ten seconds to two minutes, it will be important to use carbohydrates as a fuel. During the digestive process carbohydrates are broken down to glucose ($C_6H_{12}O_6$). The muscle cell stores the glucose as a distinct molecule known as glycogen. During this period of highly intense work, glycogen can be degraded by a nonoxidative process known as **glycolysis,** (see figure 9.10).

The term glycolysis refers to the degradation of glycogen to another compound called pyruvate. There are approximately ten steps in this process and extremely strenuous exercise (e.g., sprinting 400 metres) can increase the flow of molecules through glycolysis up to 100-fold. The formation of ATP is limited and "dead-end" molecules increase quite dramatically. These so-called dead-end molecules, of which lactate (from lactic acid) is the most pronounced, can eventually become rate limiting on the chemical processes. As lactate accumulates it disrupts the metabolic balance of the cell and limits the glycolytic mechanisms. Everyone knows the feeling of running hard and then feeling fatigued and not being able to keep the pace. This is very likely because of lactate formation and the resultant interference with the ability to produce more ATP.

Long-Term Sources of Energy

For events of long duration the oxygen system will contribute most of the energy for the generation of ATP. For events lasting more than two minutes there is an increased percentage of the available energy being supplied through the oxygen (aerobic) system. Many athletic events require a steady pace, with the energy requirements being totally supplied by oxidative energy pathways. A marathon race (26 miles 385 yards or 42 kilometres) is a good example of this. The runner usually maintains a steady pace for the entire event. World-class runners would complete the performance in around two hours and ten minutes. Recently, a more exhaustng aerobic event has been performed: the triathlon. Athletes are involved in three events: swimming (2.4 miles); cycling (110 miles); and concluding the endurance spectacle, a marathon. This type of an "iron man's performance" requires the utmost in fuel efficiency, energy yield, and stamina.

The metabolic processes that utilize oxygen in yielding energy take place in the **mitochondria** (powerhouse) of the muscle cell. During this process great amounts of ATP are generated by coupling the utilization of oxygen with the oxidation of hydrogen carriers in the electron transport system of the mitochondrion (see figure 9.10). Oxygen is a final acceptor of the electrons as they are passed down the chain; it also combines with the hydrogen ions to form metabolic water. Oxygen must be present—without it the process "backs up," the flow of electrons ceases, and no ATP is produced. The continued supply of hydrogen atoms for the oxidative phosphorylation process comes from the degradation in the cell of carbohydrates and free fatty acids. The processes are extremely complicated biochemical reactions. The system is essentialy life-sustaining in our oxygen environment. Many of our body functions are designed to provide the oxygen (circulorespiratory system), and to dissipate heat (integumentary system) and clear waste products (execretory system) after cellular metabolism.

Oxygen, therefore, becomes essential and many laboratory measurements in exercise physiology deal with the consumption and utilization of oxygen.

The aerobic capacity, often termed VO_2 max, is indicative of the maximum amount of oxygen a person can consume which is directly related to the energy or ATP produced. During recovery after strenuous exercise, whereby the subject has extended into the immediate and short-term sources of energy, the supplies must be recharged. The "huffing and puffing" done after exhaustive exercise is the repayment phase known as the oxygen debt. The subject must reload the borrowed energy for the next session. Frequently, high oxygen consumption will help the athlete in sports where he or she must perform repeated bouts of high-intensity work and have short recovery periods (e.g., ice hockey).

NEURAL INVOLVEMENT OF THE MOTOR TEAM

Bone-joint and muscle implications to human movement have been briefly studied. The last aspect to consider at this stage will be the neural mechanisms and their controlling influence on human motion. Some of the basic concepts will be explained; in later courses the student will gain a more in-depth understanding of the mechanisms. The neural control patterns consist of the **central nervous system** (CNS; brain and spinal cord) and the **peripheral nervous system** (long nerves innervating the muscle fibres). The correct recruitment of precise motor units (nerve innervation and muscle fibres) to perform a complex motor skill, such as a golf swing or the shooting of a hockey puck at high velocity, requires a series of coordinated neuromuscular patterns. These patterns flow from the brain (motor cortex) down the spinal cord and send the appropriate motor impulses to the specific muscle fibres. Receptors in the muscles and joints (muscle spindles, Golgi tendon organs, pacinian corpuscles) are always monitoring the changes in muscles and informing the central nervous system as to how the performance is progressing. The neural circuitry of the human body is somewhat comparable to present-day computers but much more advanced and complex. The nervous system is constantly monitoring external and internal environments; these sensory impulses are automatically and rapidly transmitted for specific processing by the sensorimotor cortex.

Figure 9.11 represents a general scheme of the basic organization for the control of motor activity. The basic functional unit (cell) for the nervous system is a neuron. The brain and spinal cord are composed of millions of neurons. They demonstrate the properties unique to the nervous system such as irritability and conductivity. Irritability refers to responding to a stimulus. Conductivity means conducting an electrical impulse. The brain is like a giant computer, so complex that man has not yet come close to understanding the intricacies of neural involvement. To attempt to deal with the complexity of what is known about the human brain is beyond the scope of this book. However, figure 9.11 represents some of the major links in the control and feedback of our movement analysis. The feedback loops are accentuated by the motor or efferent impulses travelling to the muscles and the afferent or sensory information being fed back by receptors. The area of the brain initiating the movement is called the **motor cortex.** This area is composed of nerve

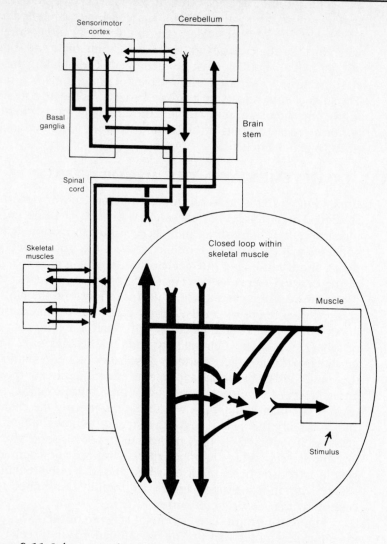

Figure 9.11 Schematic diagram of motor control pathways

cell bodies just a few millimetres thick. The motor cortex is part of the gray matter of the brain and is linked to the sensory cortex which receives all the discrete sensory information. In order to perform a complex motor activity, continual sensory information must be supplied about the movement so that adjustments may take place. The impulses travel from the motor cortex down through the basal ganglia and brain stem to the spinal cord (see figure 9.11). The tracts of nerves for the more discrete motor movements are called the pyramidal tracts (pyramids). They pass down from the motor cortex of the brain and eventually cross over in the **medulla oblongata** so that the left

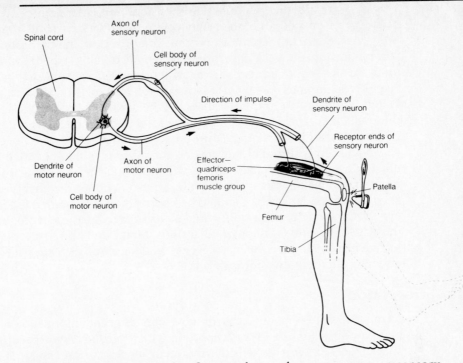

Spinal cord

Axon of
sensory neuron

Cell body of
sensory neuron

Direction of impulse

Dendrite of
sensory neuron

Receptor ends of
sensory neuron

Dendrite of
motor neuron

Axon of
motor neuron

Effector—
quadriceps
femoris
muscle group

Patella

Cell body of
motor neuron

Femur

Tibia

Figure 9.12 The knee-jerk reflex involves only two neurons—a sensory neuron and a motor neuron

cerebral cortex controls the right side of the body and vice versa. The tracts which pass down and control movement are also known as the **corticospinal tracts** (cortex to spine). These nerves form a junction (synapse) with the alpha motoneurons that control the various skeletal muscles. There are also extra-pyramidal tracts that do not originate from the motor cortex of the brain but from other areas. They seem to be more responsible for postural control and tonic-firing nerves.

The **alpha efferent motoneuron** is the last link of the nervous system to the working muscle. The wave of excitation originating in the motor cortex of the brain finally reaches the neuromuscular junction. At this point, a chemical transmitter substance (acetylcholine) floods across the synapse and causes a change in permeability in the postsynaptic membrane of the muscle. This results in a continued flow of excitation and eventual contraction of the muscle fibres. The entire process is extremely involved and accentuates our evolution as an electrochemical being. Figure 9.12 shows the knee-jerk reflex, which involves only two neurons—one sensory neuron and one motor neuron.

Each muscle fibre generally receives only one nerve fibre; however, a motor nerve may innervate many muscle fibres. The terminal axon and the muscle fibres innervated by that terminal axon are known as a **motor unit.**

Physiological Basis for Exercise: The Motor Team

This is essentially the functional unit for neuromuscular control. The fibres of the motor unit are all of the same type in that they have similar metabolic properties. Some of the motor units are comprised of muscle fibres that are fast-contracting, deliver a high force, and fatigue quickly (type II) while other units are slow-contracting, exhibit low tension, but are very slow to fatigue (type I). Sometimes these motor units are referred to as slow oxidative (type I) and fast glycolytic (type II) fibres. As the student's knowledge increases, these different motor units will be more fully understood along with the implications for athletic training. However, it seems that fiber type is not changed very significantly through training and therefore is more dependent on natural endowment. Potentially, an individual with more fast-contracting motor units should be a better sprinter while a person endowed with a preponderance of slow oxidative fibers should be a better marathon runner. It does, however, depend on the ability of the nervous system to fire these motor units and the state of training of the particular units. Motor unit firing patterns and selective recruitment are the major factors in determining speed, strength, and endurance in different motor skill tasks.

Proprioception

As the CNS sends out messages for movement to occur, information must also be relayed back to the CNS to report on the movement. **Proprioceptors** are special receptors that are sensitive to stretch, tension, and pressure. They relay information to both conscious and unconscious parts of the brain concerning the dynamics of movement. Thus, we are constantly being fed back information with regard to our movement, and subsequent alterations can be performed. When coordinated movement takes place thousands of muscle fibres are relaxing and contracting in a very precise manner. Muscles must work in conjunction with other muscle groups. The agonist groups (prime movers) must contract while the antagonists (opposing) must relax. The CNS will interpret this information from sensory organs and try to contract and relax the musculature to perform the desired, precise movement.

Muscle spindles are small organelles lying parallel to the regular muscle fibres. They respond to changes in length and tension of muscle fibres. Basically they respond to the stretch of the muscle and cause a reflex contraction of the same muscle fibres so as to reduce the stretch. Figure 9.13 illustrates a muscle spindle unit. This stretch reflex is fundamental in maintaining posture and adjusting the desired force of contraction when a stretch is applied to the muscle. **Golgi tendon organs** (GTOs) are another type of special receptor important in human movement. They are also servomechanisms responsible for detecting the force applied to the tendons of a muscle. They can respond to excessive tension or stretch on the tendons of the muscle and protect the connective tissue from overload. They usually cause the muscle fibres to relax. A third type of receptor is the **pacinian corpuscle.** They can be found in the joints and tendons and are sensitive to quick movements and pressure. They primarily detect the changes that have occurred and not the quantity of pressure.

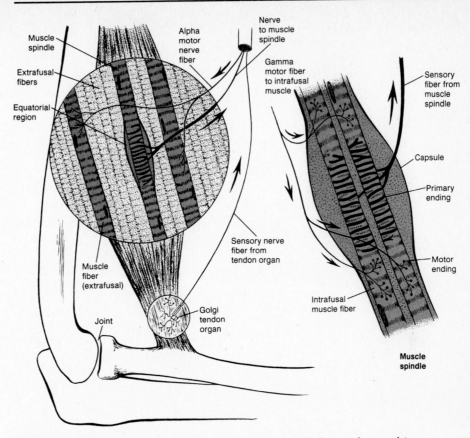

Figure 9.13 The structure of muscle spindles and their relationship to skeletal muscles

Most of the sensory information (feedback) is amassed by a complex part of the brain, located behind the brain stem, called the **cerebellum.** It is involved with monitoring the intricate feedback circuits and coordinating other areas of the brain involved in motor control. This organ is intricately involved in fine muscular control and coordination. The cerebellum receives impulses from a vast supply of sensory receptors (from muscles, joints, tendons, skin, hearing, vision, and balance) and processes this information to allow for the fine-tuning of movement.

The CNS with its complicated feedback circuits is the most important element of human movement. However, it is the area that exercise physiologists know the least about. Much of the research over the past ten years has taken place out in the ''engine room'' (muscles). The final link will be to understand the nervous system, how it organizes itself, and the effect of training and learning on the component parts.

CHAPTER 10

Support Systems to the Motor Team

Edward C. Rhodes

This chapter will focus on primarily three support systems to the motor team: the respiratory system, the cardiovascular system, and the digestive system. In order for the muscle cells to continue to contract, oxygen (O_2) must be delivered to aid in the production of energy while carbon dioxide (CO_2), produced by the active cells, needs to be eliminated. The cardiorespiratory system primarily accomplishes these objectives. In many physical activities, endurance is a factor in learning and performance. Consequently, in these activities a teacher, instructor, or coach must have a significant understanding of the cardiorespiratory (CR) system. The greater the factor of endurance is to the execution of a physical activity or skill, the greater the knowledge the coach or athlete should have regarding the functions of this body system. It is also extremely important that the proper nutrients be provided to the working muscles (digestion and circulation).

THE RESPIRATORY SYSTEM

The basic process of **external respiration** (breathing) involves the exchange of oxygen between the lung air sacs (alveoli) and the capillary network of the circulatory system. Internal respiration was previously described in chapter 9 and involves the use of oxygen in the production of energy. Atmospheric air is composed of 20.93 percent O_2, 0.03 percent CO_2, and 79 percent nitrogen (N_2).

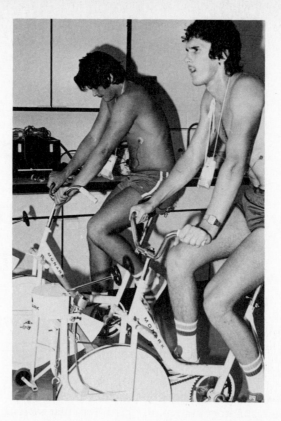

Air must be drawn into the lungs and the O_2 in the air exchanged with CO_2 which is transported back from the metabolically active tissues of the body. Figure 10.1 depicts this exchange process by which the regulation of the gaseous states of the body are controlled.

This exchange of gases is of much importance to physical activity and sports specialists because many of the parameters of the respiratory system are easily measured or predicted, therefore allowing one to estimate the energy cost of many exercise or movement patterns. In order to fully understand gas exchanges within the human body, it is also necessary to observe the interaction of the cardiovascular system and the role of tissue metabolism to the respiratory system.

The lungs provide the surface area for the exchange of the gases between the blood and the external environment. Although the entire volume of the two lungs is usually between four and seven litres, the actual surface area is predicted to be approximately half of a tennis court (see figure 10.2). It is also estimated that there are 600 million discrete alveoli within this huge surface area for exchange. During rest, approximately 250 ml of oxygen leave the alveoli and enter the blood while about 200 ml of CO_2 diffuse in the opposite direction. During maximal exercise stress this amount could be increased 25-fold.

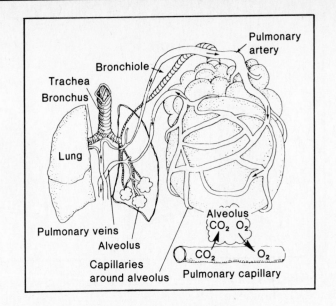

Figure 10.1 Exchange of O_2 and CO_2 in the lung

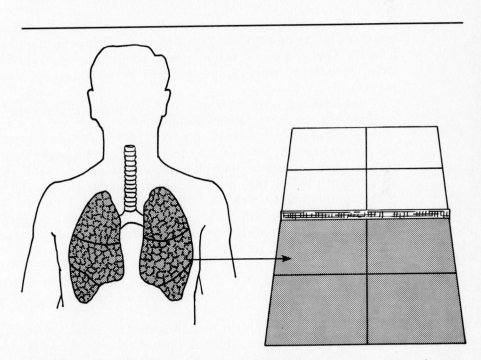

Figure 10.2 Approximately 80m² is provided in the lungs for gas exchange

Support Systems to the Motor Team

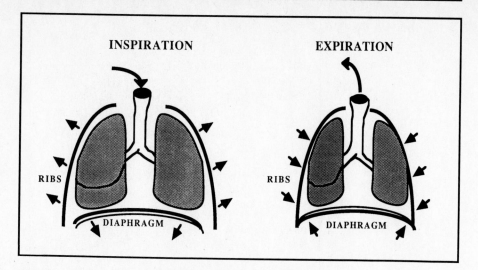

Figure 10.3 In mechanical aspects of breathing, movement of the rib cage and diaphragm increase and decrease the volume of the thoracic cavity, creating positive and negative pressures within the lungs

The actual mechanics of breathing are controlled by a dome-shaped muscle called the **diaphragm.** The diaphragm is assisted by other respiratory muscles. When the air is drawn into the lungs the process is called **inspiration.** When the elastic lungs are squeezed and air forced out, **expiration** occurs (see figure 10.3).

The most important factor relative to breathing patterns is sustaining a high level of airflow. The airflow will depend primarily upon the resistance of the respiratory passages to the flow of air. Most healthy individuals experience very little resistance to breathing; however, obstructive lung disease such as asthma or emphysema could reduce ventilation. The exchange of gases at the alveolar level is the critical part of the respiratory cycle. The diffusion of O_2 into the capillary and CO_2 from the capillary to the alveoli is accomplished by **pressure gradients.** The partial pressure of the gases is calculated by multiplying the barometric pressure times the percentage of the particular gas in atmospheric air. For example, the partial pressure of oxygen is the following: 20.93% $\times$ 760 mm Hg = 159 mm Hg. This pressure will be responsible for the diffusion of O_2 into the blood. The pressure differences between the gases in the plasma and the tissues will establish the gradients for diffusion (see figure 10.4).

The transport of O_2 in the blood is mainly in combination with an iron-containing compound called **hemoglobin.** When oxygen combines with this iron-protein molecule in the red blood cell it forms oxyhemoglobin. Each litre of blood carries 200 millilitres (ml) of oxygen: 197 ml combined with

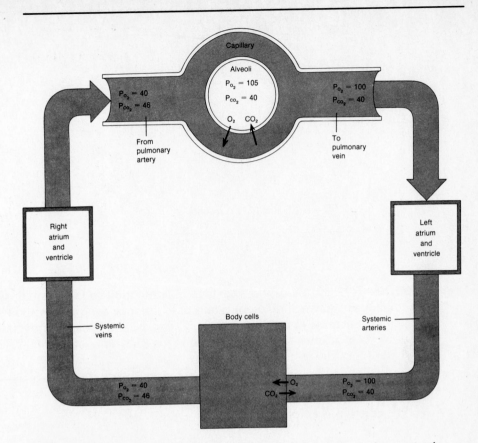

Figure 10.4 The P_{O_2} and P_{CO_2} of blood as a result of gas exchange in the lung alveoli and gas exchange between systemic capillaries and body cells

hemoglobin and 3 ml physically dissolved in the plasma. Often if an individual's diet is deficient in iron it may reflect on the hemoglobin levels and result in a decreased oxygen-carrying capacity. Figure 10.5 shows hemoglobin saturation according to oxygen pressure. Another iron-protein compound, **myoglobin,** is found in cardiac and skeletal muscle. It also binds with oxygen inside the cell to form **oxymyoglobin.** It functions as an additional source of oxygen and acts as a shuttle mechanism to move oxygen through the cell.

The CO_2 produced in the cells must find its way out of the body and be expired to the atmosphere. The removal of CO_2 is by the following three mechanisms.

1. A small amount is carried in physical solution in the plasma of the blood (3–5 percent).
2. Approximately 20–25 percent of the CO_2 combines with hemoglobin.
3. The majority of the CO_2 (65–70 percent) is carried by bicarbonate ions (HCO_3^-).

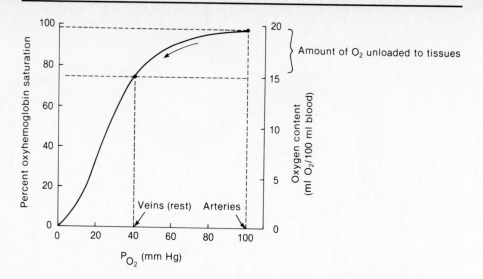

Figure 10.5 The percent oxyhemoglobin saturation and the blood oxygen content are shown at different values of P_{O_2}. Notice that there is about 25 percent decrease in percent oxyhemoglobin as blood passes through the tissue from arteries to veins, resulting in the unloading of approximately 5 ml O_2 per 100 ml to the tissues.

The reaction is as follows:

$$CO_2 + H_2O \xrightarrow{\text{carbonic anhydrase}} H_2CO_3 \xrightarrow{\hspace{1cm}} H^+ + HCO_3^-$$

The regulation of pulmonary ventilation is a very complex phenomenon that is not completely understod by respiratory physiologists. The rate and depth of breathing is finely adjusted in response to the metabolic needs of the body. As shown in figure 10.6, many factors integrate in sending information to the medulla oblongata of the brain to help regulate the ventilatory rate. The major factors include proprioceptors in the joints and muscles, receptors in the lung tissues, peripheral chemoreceptors, temperature, and the chemical state of the blood and cerebrospinal fluid in the brain.

During increased physical activity the muscle cells need increased amounts of O_2. Therefore, it is critical that ventilation increases proportionately to maintain alveolar gas concentrations in order for the O_2 and CO_2 to be exchanged. Outstanding aerobic athletes have recorded gas ventilations as high as 200 litres per minute at maximum exercise. This would require a breathing frequency between forty and fifty times per minute and a volume of air between 3.5 and 4.0 litres per breath. Generally the work of the lungs

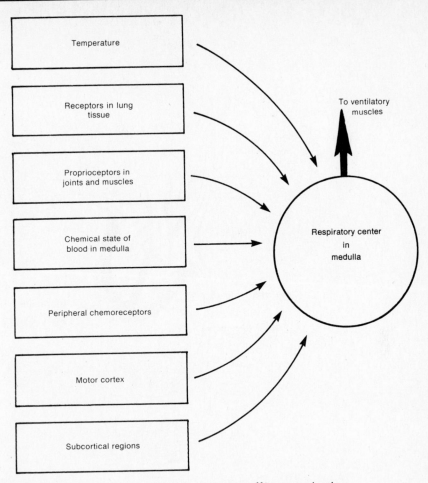

Figure 10.6 Many factors interplay in controlling respiration

and the exchange process is not limiting to the exercise situation. However, if an athlete suffers from exercise-induced asthma it may definitely affect performance.

THE CARDIOVASCULAR SYSTEM

The cardiovascular system (heart and vessels) provides the delivery system for the working muscles. The effectiveness of these working muscles with regard to their speed, duration, and resistance capabilities is heavily dependent upon the efficiency of one's cardiovascular system. All physical activity and sports specialists should realize that cardiac output can be greatly increased during and through exercise. Cardiac output is directly proportional to the intensity of the exercise or training program.

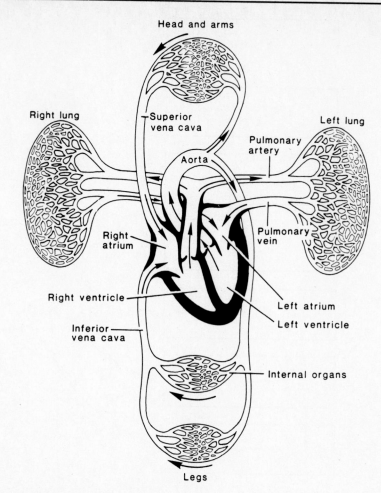

Figure 10.7 The Vascular Systems

SOURCE: From J. H. Wilmore and David L. Costill, *Training for Sport And Activity,* 3d ed. Copyright © 1988 Wm. C. Brown Publishers, Dubuque, Iowa. All Rights Reserved. Reprinted by permission.

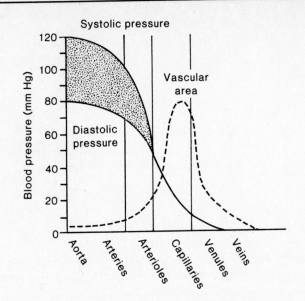

Figure 10.8 Fall in blood pressure throughout the vascular system

The cardiovascular system transports the nutrients and oxygen to the cell and removes the waste products of metabolism. The system is composed of a continuous enclosed circuit consisting of a pump, a high-pressure vessel circuit for delivery, exchange vessels, and a low-pressure return system. The functional component (capillary system) is composed of thin-walled vessels which allow O_2, nutrients, and CO_2 to diffuse freely across cellular membranes. The diffusion will depend on the concentration gradients established. Figure 10.7 provides a schematic representation of the cardiovascular system.

The fluid medium (blood) is comprised of two parts: (1) the cellular component of red blood cells, white blood cells, and platelets, and (2) the plasma or fluid component. As the blood is pumped through the vessel compartment it exerts pressure on the arterial walls (blood pressure). The blood pressure is usually greatest in the arteries when the heart is pumping (systolic pressure) and drops as the blood moves into the capillary network and the heart is relaxing and refilling (diastolic pressure). Figure 10.8 demonstrates potential blood pressure changes in the system.

The heart (pump) is the most essential organ within the entire system. It continually contracts its muscle (myocardium) on an average of seventy beats per minute. A well-trained aerobic athlete may have a resting heart rate of 40 and a maximum heart rate of 200. The heart muscle is capable of maintaining its own rhythm (inherent rhythmicity). There is a specialized tissue,

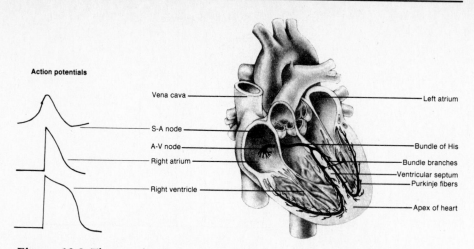

Figure 10.9 The conduction tissue of the heart. The appearance of action potentials in the S-A node, atria, and ventricles is also shown.

the sinoatrial (SA) node, situated in the wall of the right atrium (see figure 10.9). This node controls the inherent discharge of the electrical impulse that spreads throughout the myocardium and initiates the contraction of the heart muscle. The graphic record of the heart's electrical activity is known as the **electrocardiogram** (ECG), which is shown in figure 10.10.

The regulation of the heart rate is controlled both by nervous and hormonal involvement. The sympathetic nerves of the autonomic nervous system to the SA node act to accelerate the heart contraction. This is generally known as **tachycardia.** The parasympathetic innervation of the autonomic nervous system to the heart slows the heart rate, a state known as **bradycardia.** Through endurance training there is a significant bradycardia, or lowering of the heart rate, at rest. Hormones will also influence the beating and contractility of the heart.

With a limited amount of blood in the body, metabolic demands must be met by shunting the blood rich in oxygen and nutrients to the active tissue. This is accomplished by the ability of the vasculature to either constrict or dilate depending on the need. Many local factors will control the regional blood flow.

The total functional capacity of the cardiovascular system is primarily indicated by the **cardiac output** (Q) of the heart. The compoments of the cardiac output are the **stroke volume** (SV) and the **heart rate** (HR); therefore,

$$Q = SV \times HR.$$

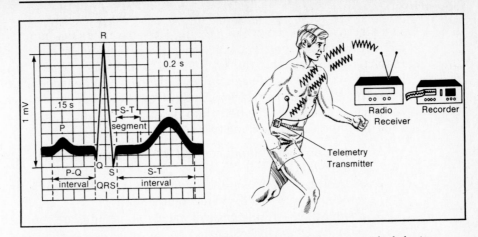

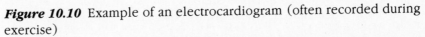

Figure 10.10 Example of an electrocardiogram (often recorded during exercise)

The SV is the volume of blood ejected with each contraction of the ventricles. With athletic training, the cardiovascular system becomes more efficient. The heart becomes a stronger pump that can generate a larger stroke volume. The muscle tissue is supplied with more oxygen-rich blood and also extracts a greater proportion of the oxygen from the blood. This will ultimately allow for higher energy production and increased work.

NUTRITION AND HUMAN PERFORMANCE

To this point we have studied the movement team of nerve-muscle-bone and the cardiorespiratory system as it pertains to oxygen delivery. The digestive system is also of ultimate importance for optimal physical performance. It provides the fuels for biological work and the essential elements for the synthesis of new tissue and the repair of existing cells.

It has been said that essentially, we are what we eat. However, as Edington and Edgerton in *The Biology of Physical Activity* state, ". . . through training and exercise we can definitely modify what we make out of what we eat. That is, a sedentary person may convert food into fat, while an exercising or trained person converts identical food into other components of the body for increased performance capabilities." Consequently, a physical activity or sports professional should have a sound grasp of the interrelatedness of nutrition and physical activity. A brief description of the digestive system will be followed by an understanding of the necessary nutrients and concepts related to performance.

Digestion

The digestive system consists of a long muscular tube beginning at the lips and ending at the anus. The component parts include the mouth, pharynx, esophagus, stomach, and the small and large intestines (figure 10.11). Also involved in the system are certain large glands located outside the digestive tube. These include the salivary glands, liver, gallbladder, and pancreas—all of which empty their secretions into the digestive tube. The processes involved in digestion are the following:

1. **ingestion**—the introduction of food into the system (chewing and swallowing);
2. **secretion**—enzymes are secreted for the chemical breakdown of large molecules into smaller water-soluble forms;
3. **absorption**—resultant small water-soluble units are absorbed by the blood or lymphatic system;
4. **assimilation**—utilization of these small units by all cells of the body; and
5. **elimination**—solid wastes are rejected by the system.

The food products that are ingested usually fall into one of three categories: (1) carbohydrates, (2) fats, or (3) proteins. Also ingested for normal body function are vitamins, minerals, and water.

It is not the scope of this text to cover the anatomy and physiology of digestion but to emphasize the energy fuels for human movement.

Fuels for Action

Atoms of carbon, hydrogen, and oxygen combine to form carbohydrate compounds. The most simple carbohydrate is a molecule of **glucose** ($C_6H_{12}O_6$). Most complex carbohydrates are readily digested to the form of glucose. Usually glucose is stored as a **glycogen** molecule. Glycogen molecules are composed of many glucose molecules linked together. The main function of glycogen is to serve as an energy fuel for the body. However, the body does not store great amounts of glycogen. Approximately 375–500 grams of carbohydrate are stored throughout the body. Of this, approximately 275–300 grams are in the form of muscle glycogen, 90–100 grams are liver glycogen, and only 20 grams are present as blood glucose.

Carbohydrates are essential for the proper functioning of the central nervous system. The CNS (brain and spinal cord) uses blood glucose exclusively as a fuel and does not store glycogen. Because glucose is so important as an energy source for the brain, blood sugar must be maintained within narrow limits. If the blood sugar drops (hypoglycemia), feelings of hunger, dizziness, and weakness prevail.

During high-intensity exercise, stored muscle glycogen and blood glucose are major contributors within the energy processes. They are the only fuels that provide energy when the oxygen supplied is not sufficient to satisfy

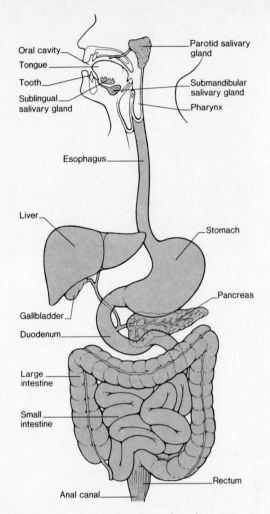
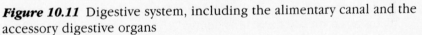

Figure 10.11 Digestive system, including the alimentary canal and the accessory digestive organs

the energy needs. It is possible to extend work by ingesting a slight glucose solution (< 5% glucose). The intake of this glucose, when the muscle and liver supplies are almost empty, will help to maintain the blood sugar level. This in turn will help supply the CNS and working muscles with valuable glucose. By manipulating the depletion of glycogen and the intake of carbohydrates in the diet it is possible to store more glycogen in the muscle cell than normal. Also a diet deficient in carbohydrates could deplete both muscle and liver glycogen and seriously affect both short- and long-term work.

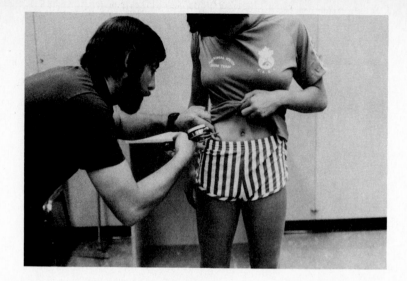

Fats are also important energy sources for active skeletal muscles. A molecule of fat possesses a higher ratio of hydrogen to oxygen than do carbohydrate molecules; otherwise the structural atoms are very similar. Approximately 99 percent of body fat is in the form of triglycerides. A triglyceride molecule consists of a glycerol molecule attached to three clusters of carbon-chained groups called **fatty acids.**

Fat is an ideal fuel for work because each molecule carries large quantities of energy per unit weight. It is also easily transported to the cell and is readily utilized for energy. Fat contains more than twice the energy storage compared to an equal quantity of carbohydrate. This is due to the greater quantity of hydrogen in the fat molecule; it is the hydrogen atom that provides the electrons in the electron transport system for the coupling of energy. Fat is relatively water-free and concentrated as compared to glycogen which stores 2.7 grams of H_2O per gram of glycogen. If exercise continues for an hour or more there is a gradual increase in energy derived from fat. As individuals train aerobically, there is a general "glycogen sparing" and an increase in fatty acid metabolism. World-class marathoners metabolize close to 70 percent fat in their event.

Approximately 15 percent of the body weight of males is fat while closer to 25 percent of the weight of the average female is fat. These values can vary considerably for athletes, with reported values of less than 5 percent for some marathon runners. Most of the fat is available as an energy source, particularly during prolonged, moderate exercise. Also, excessive intake of carbohydrates or proteins can be readily coverted to fat for storage.

FOOD	PROTEIN RATING
Eggs	100
Fish	70
Lean beef	69
Cow's milk	60
Brown rice	57
White rice	56
Soybeans	47
Brewer's hash	45
Whole-grain wheat	44
Peanuts	43
White potato	34
Dry beans	34

Figure 10.12 Rating scale for dietary protein

Proteins are known as the building blocks of the human body. Although very similar to carbohydrates and fats in that they contain carbon, hydrogen, and oxygen, they also contain sulfur, phosphorus, iron, and nitrogen which is approximately 15 percent of the molecule. The building blocks are really **amino acids** which are linked in long chains with different chemical combinations to form an infinite number of protein structures. There are twenty different amino acids that are required by the human body and they combine with side-chain configurations of organic acids. This makes the protein molecule potentially infinite with different combinations of amino acids. For example, hemoglobin contains some 574 amino acid combinations. Of the twenty required amino acids, nine cannot be synthesized by the human body and must be provided by food intake. They are often referred to as essential amino acids. These essential amino acids can be provided to our bodies by either plant or animal origin. Eggs have been given a rating of 100 or perfect in supplying essential amino acids. Vegetables must be taken in combinations to supply the needed amino acids. Vegetarian diets can supply all the essential nutrients; however, a lactovegetarian diet (add milk, cheese and related products) assures complete nutrition. Figure 10.12 shows the protein rating of various foods.

Anabolism is the process of building tissue in the body. Amino acids are the major contributors to the synthesis of cellular components. During periods of rapid growth in childhood or training periods, it is important to supply the body with the essential amino acids. However, a well-balanced diet will do this and generally supplementation is not required. The recommended

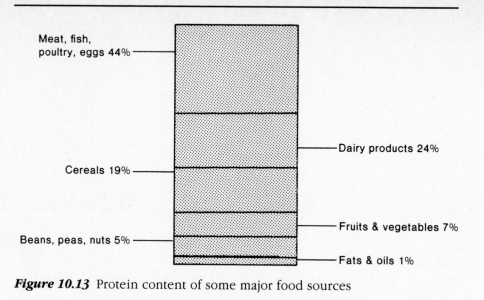

Figure 10.13 Protein content of some major food sources

daily intake of protein is 0.9 grams per kilogram of body weight. As an athlete increases his or her calorie expenditure, the subsequent increased intake will provide for any protein needs. There is no benefit from eating excessive amounts of proteins. In fact, excessive intake can be harmful by placing extra strain on the liver and the urinary system. Figure 10.13 shows the protein content of some major food sources.

Vitamins, Minerals, and H_2O

To supplement the carbohydrates, fats, and proteins provided to the body through food intake, cells also need micronutrients such as vitamins and minerals. These accessory nutrients are involved in highly specific roles in facilitating energy transfer.

Vitamins are not manufactured by the human body but must be supplied by either the diet or dietary supplementation. They are organic substances needed by our bodies in small amounts. Fourteen different vitamins have been isolated and recommended for dietary intake. They are classified as either water soluble or fat soluble.

- **H_2O Soluble:** pyridoxine (B_6), thiamine (B_1), riboflavin (B_2), niacin, pantothenic acid, biotin, choline, folacin, cobalamin (B_{12}), and ascorbic acid (C)
- **Fat Soluble:** A, D, E, and K

Table 10.1 lists the vitamins, their recommended daily allowance, dietary sources, their major body functions, plus problems from a deficiency or excess of each.

Generally speaking, all vitamins are available if an individual consumes a well-balanced diet. There seems to be little evidence to indicate that athletes expending extra energy need special foods or supplements. If intake of food is increased in proportion to exercise and the food is obtained through a well-balanced diet, proper vitamin intake is assured. Excess intake of vitamins can have serious toxic effects and should be avoided.

Vitamins are very important to the body. They help metabolic reactions both to release the energy found in the food molecule and to control tissue synthesis. These vitamins can be used repeatedly in all the metabolic reactions. Therefore, there is no research evidence to indicate athletes need excess amounts to enhance energy release and subsequently improve performance.

Minerals composed of metallic elements account for approximately 4 percent of the body's weight. The most important minerals are those found in enzymes, vitamins, and hormones. Many are found free or in combination with organic compounds in the body. There is generally little necessity for supplementation of minerals to the diet. Most minerals are readily available in common foods and in water. Occasionally deficiencies exist in minerals such as iron. Women are more predisposed to iron deficiencies than men; the deficiency can often be rectified by a diet rich in iron-containing foods such as liver, kidney, green vegetables, and uncooked fruits. Table 10.2 lists information about the minerals needed by the body.

The mineral nutrients are primarily needed for their role in cellular metabolism. They play an important part in constructing the enzymes that regulate the chemical reactions within the cells. Figure 10.14 shows some of the minerals involved in anabolism and catabolism during the energy processes.

Minerals also form important components of hormones. The formation of an especially important hormone, insulin, requires the mineral zinc. Some of the more important minerals and their involvement in bodily functions follow.

The body contains approximately 4–5 grams of **iron.** The iron is combined in three main structural components: hemoglobin, myoglobin, and the cytochromes. Athletes should definitely include iron-rich foods in their diet. Iron deficiency anemia can develop if iron is not available. It is characterized by loss of appetite, sluggishness, and an inability to exercise. Iron deficiency anemia is more prevalent in women athletes and often they must be put on dietary iron supplements.

Calcium, in combination with phosphorus, helps to form the bones and teeth. It is the most abundant mineral in the body. It is also involved in nerve transmission, muscular contraction, and blood clotting.

Table 10.1 Vitamins: recommended intake, dietary sources, functions, and deficiencies.

VITAMIN	RDA FOR HEALTHY ADULT MALE (mg)	DIETARY SOURCES	MAJOR BODY FUNCTIONS	DEFICIENCY	EXCESS
WATER-SOLUBLE					
VITAMIN B-1 (THIAMINE)	1.5	Pork, organ meats, whole grains, legumes	Coenzyme (thiamine pyrophosphate) in reactions involving the removal of carbon dioxide	Beriberi (peripheral nerve changes, edema, heart failure)	None reported
VITAMIN B-2 (RIBOFLAVIN)	1.8	Widely distributed in foods	Constituent of two flavin nucleotide coenzymes involved in energy metabolism (FAD and FMN)	Reddened lips, cracks at corner of mouth (cheilosis), lesions of eye	None reported
NIACIN	20	Liver, lean meats, grains, legumes (can be formed from tryptophan)	Constituent of two coenzymes involved in oxidation-reduction reactions (NAD and NADP)	Pellagra (skin and gastrointestinal lesions; nervous, mental disorders)	Flushing, burning, and tingling around neck, face, and hands
VITAMIN B-6 (PYRIDOXINE)	2	Meats, vegetables, whole-grain cereals	Coenzyme (pyridoxal phosphate) involved in amino acid metabolism	Irritability, convulsions, muscular twitching, dermatitis near eyes, kidney stones	None reported
PANTOTHENIC ACID	5–10	Widely distributed in foods	Constituent of coenzyme A, which plays a central role in energy metabolism	Fatigue, sleep disturbances, impaired coordination, nausea (rare in man)	None reported
FOLACIN	.4	Legumes, green vegetables, whole-wheat products	Coenzyme (reduced form) involved in transfer of single-carbon units in nucleic acid and amino acid metabolism	Anemia, gastrointestinal disturbances, diarrhea, red tongue	None reported
VITAMIN B-12	.003	Muscle meats, eggs, dairy products, (not present in plant	Coenzyme involved in transfer of single-carbon units in nucleic acid	Pernicious anemia, neurologic disorders	None reported

		Food Sources	Function	Deficiency	Toxicity
BIOTIN	Not established. Usual diet provides .15–.3	Legumes, vegetables, meats	Coenzyme required for fat synthesis, amino acid metabolism, and glycogen (animal-starch) formation	Fatigue, depression, nausea, dermatitis, muscular pains	None reported
	Not established. Usual diet provides 500–900	All foods containing phospholipids (egg yolk, liver, grains, legumes)	Constituent of phospholipids. Precursor or putative neurotransmitter acetylcholine	Not reported in man	None reported
VITAMIN C (ASCORBIC ACID)	45	Citrus fruits, tomatoes, green peppers, salad greens	Maintains intercellular matrix of cartilage, bone, and dentine. Important in collagen synthesis	Scurvy (degeneration of skin, teeth, blood vessels, epithelial hemorrhages)	Relatively nontoxic. Possibility of kidney stones
FAT SOLUBLE					
VITAMIN A	1	Provitamin A (beta-carotene) widely distributed in green vegetables. Retinol present in milk, butter, cheese, fortified margarine	Constituent of rhodopsin (visual pigment). Maintenance of epithelial tissues. Role in mucopolysaccharide synthesis	Xerophthalmia (keratinization of ocular tissue), night blindness, permanent blindness	Headache, vomiting, peeling of skin, anorexia, swelling of long bones
VITAMIN D	.01	Cod-liver oil, eggs, dairy products, fortified milk, and margarine	Promotes growth and mineralization of bones. Increases absorption of calcium	Rickets (bone deformities) in children. Osteomalacia in adults.	Vomiting, diarrhea, loss of weight, kidney damage
VITAMIN E	15	Seeds, green leafy vegetables, margarines, shortenings	Functions as an antioxidant to prevent cell-membrane damage.	Possibly anemia	Relatively nontoxic
VITAMIN K	.03	Green leafy vegetables. Small amount in cereals, fruits, and meats	Important in blood clotting (involved in formation of active prothrombin)	Conditioned deficiencies associated with severe bleeding; internal hemorrhages	Relatively nontoxic. Synthetic forms at high doses may cause jaundice

Table 10.2 Minerals: recommended intake, dietary sources, and functions

MINERAL	AMOUNT IN ADULT BODY (g)	RDA FOR HEALTHY ADULT MALE (mg)	DIETARY SOURCES	MAJOR BODY FUNCTIONS	DEFICIENCY	EXCESS
CALCIUM	1,500	800	Milk, cheese, dark-green vegetables, dried legumes	Bone and tooth formation Blood clotting Nerve transmission	Stunted growth Rickets, osteoporosis Convulsions	Not reported in man
PHOSPHORUS	860	800	Milk, cheese, meat, poultry, grains	Bone and tooth formation Acid-base balance	Weakness, demineralization of bone Loss of calcium	Erosion of jaw (fossy jaw)
SULFUR	300	(Provided by sulfur amino acids)	Sulfur amino acids (methionine and cystine) in dietary proteins	Constituent of active tissue compounds, cartilage, and tendon	Related to intake and deficiency of sulfur amino acids	Excess sulfur amino acid intake leads to poor growth
POTASSIUM	180	2,500	Meats, milk, many fruits	Acid-base balance Body water balance Nerve function	Muscular weakness Paralysis	Muscular weakness Death
CHLORINE	74	2,000	Common salt	Formation of gastric juice Acid-base balance	Muscle cramps Mental apathy Reduced appetite	Vomiting
SODIUM	64	2,500	Common salt	Acid-base balance Body water balance Nerve function	Muscle cramps Mental apathy Reduced appetite	High blood pressure
MAGNESIUM	25	350	Whole grains, green leafy vegetables	Activates enzymes Involved in protein synthesis	Growth failure Behavioral disturbances Weakness, spasms	Diarrhea

IRON	4.5	10	Eggs, lean meats, legumes, whole grains, green leafy vegetables	Constituent of hemoglobin and enzymes involved in energy metabolism	Iron deficiency anemia (weakness, reduced resistance to infection)	Siderosis Cirrhosis of liver
FLUORINE	2.6	2	Drinking water, tea, seafood	May be important in maintenance of bone structure	Higher frequency of tooth decay	Mottling of teeth Increased bone den Neurologic disturbances
ZINC	2	15	Widely distributed in foods	Constituent of enzymes involved in digestion	Growth failure Small sex glands	Fever, nausea, vomiting diarrhea
COPPER	.1	2	Meats, drinking water	Constituent of enzymes associated with iron metabolism	Anemia, bone changes (rare in man)	Rare metabolic condition (Wilson's disease)
SILICON VANADIUM TIN NICKEL	.024 .018 .017 .010	Not established	Widely distributed in foods	Function unknown (essential for animals)	Not reported in man	Industrial exposures Silicon—silicosis Vanadium—lung irritation Tin—vomiting Nickel—acute pneumonitis
SELENIUM	.013	Not established (Diet provides .05–.1 per day)	Seafood, meat, grains	Function in close association with vitamin E	Anemia (rare)	Gastrointestinal disorders, lung irritation
MANGANESE	.012	Not established (Diet provides 6–8 per day)	Widely distributed in foods	Constituent of enzymes involved in fat synthesis	In animals: poor growth, disturbances of nervous system, reproductive abnormalities	Poisoning in manganese mines: generalized disease nervous system
IODINE	.011	.14	Marine fish and shell-fish, dairy products, many vegetables	Constituent of thyroid hormones	Goiter (enlarged thyroid)	Very high intakes depress thyroid action
MOLYBDENUM	.009	Not established (Diet provides .4 per day)	Legumes, cereals, organ meats	Constituent of some enzymes	Not reported in man	Inhibition of enzyme

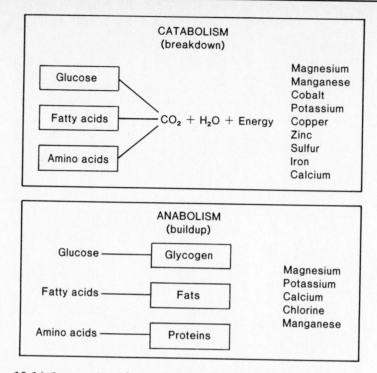

Figure 10.14 Some minerals involved in bodily processes

As well as having a combined function with calcium in forming bones and teeth, **phosphorus** is an essential part of the high-energy compounds adenosine triphosphate (ATP) and creatine phosphate. ATP is the ubiquitous form of energy for all biological work. Phosphorus is also involved in the buffering of acids after energy metabolism.

Sodium, potassium and **chlorine** are in the body as charged particles called ions. They are often referred to as **electrolytes.** They are involved in establishing electrical gradients across cell membranes and the conduction of action potentials. These electrolytes are also involved in balancing body fluid exchange with the H_2O compartments of the body.

During exercise in hot weather for prolonged periods of time, the body in an effort to dissipate heat through evaporative heat loss will lose great amounts of H_2O in the form of sweat. Some mineral salts, primarily sodium and potassium, will also be lost to the body in this sweat. This loss of body water and electrolytes can lead to severe neural dysfunction, cramps, heat exhaustion, and heat stroke. It is crucial that the athlete replaces the H_2O immediately during exercise in a hot environment. It is recommended to supplement the fluid being ingested with small amounts of electrolytes; however, the most important aspect is rehydrating. A great deal of the electrolytes can be added later through the diet.

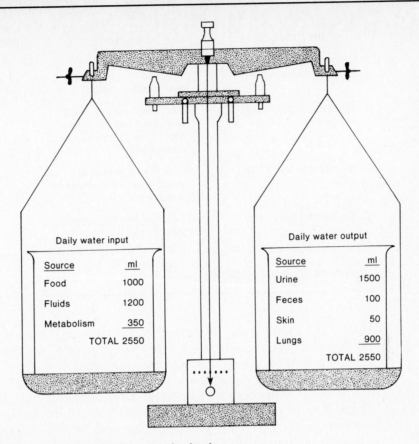

Daily water input

Source	ml
Food	1000
Fluids	1200
Metabolism	350
	TOTAL 2550

Daily water output

Source	ml
Urine	1500
Feces	100
Skin	50
Lungs	900
	TOTAL 2550

Figure 10.15 H_2O balance in the body

The **water compartments** contribute approximately 60 percent of an individual's body weight. Most body water is contained in two main compartments: intracellular (inside the cell) and extracellular (outside the cell). The extracellular component is comprised of the fluid that bathes the cells, the blood plasma, lymph, glandular secretions, saliva, and fluid in the eyes.

The homeostatic mechanisms strive to maintain H_2O balance in the body. As shown in figure 10.15, the intake of H_2O is finely balanced with the output of H_2O. The intake aspect is from liquids, food, and metabolism. The average person consumes between 1200 and 1500 millilitres of H_2O each day. If the individual is active, this amount can increase drastically. Most foods contain great amounts of H_2O. Fruits and vegetables are a good example of such foods. Metabolic water is formed during energy metabolism through the degradation of fats and carbohydrates. In fact, the role of oxygen in energy production pathways is to accept hydrogen in a long chain of events and form metabolic

FOOD CATEGORY	EXAMPLES	RECOMMENDED DAILY SERVINGS
1. Milk and milk products	Milk, cheese, ice cream, sour cream, yogurt	2
2. Meat and high-protein	Meat, fish, poultry, eggs— with dried beans, peas, nuts, or peanut butter as alternatives	2
3. Vegetables and fruits	Dark green or yellow vegetables: citrus fruits or tomatoes	4
4. Cereal and grain food	Enriched breads, cereals, flour, baked goods, or whole-grain products	4

Figure 10.16 A well-balanced diet

H_2O. It is estimated that 25 percent of the daily requiremt of H_2O is met through this pathway. Glycogen stores an appreciable amount of H_2O and when it is used for energy this H_2O becomes available.

Water is a truly remarkable commodity in the body and is essential for life. It serves as the body's transport medium. Nutrients and gases are transported through this aqueous solution. It has heat-stabilizing qualities and lubricates the joints. It also gives structure and form to the body. Without adequate amounts of H_2O, death could occur in days.

The balance of H_2O intake and output is finely controlled by brain mechanisms. The body is able to sense the loss of fluid and by thirst mechanisms it attempts to restore the fluid compartments and their electrolytic components. Loss of H_2O primarily occurs through the urine, skin, feces, and H_2O vapor in expired air. Under normal conditions the kidneys of the body excrete about 1 to 1.5 litres per day. The amount of insensible H_2O loss via droplets in exhaled air is between 200 and 300 ml per day. Between 100 and 200 ml of H_2O are lost through fecal matter. The potential greatest loss of H_2O is through perspiration. Usually 500–700 ml of sweat are secreted each day. During heavy exercise it has been reported that 10–12 litres of sweat have been produced. Dehydration can occur very quickly in exercise in hot environments. This is why the athlete must be very careful when copiously sweating and should make every attempt to rehydrate.

To supply the body with the required nutrients that have been discussed, it is extremely important to follow sound nutritional guidelines. Many athletes seem to think they need special diets and dietary supplements while they train. The general consensus of researchers is that athletes do not require additional nutrients beyond those obtained in a *well-balanced diet.* As the energy expenditure increases as the athlete trains, the increased caloric intake will take care of his or her nutritional needs. Usually once the basic nutrient requirements of the body are met, the extra energy needs can be supplied from foods based on the athlete's preference. If a person follows the *Canada Food Rules Guide,* published by Health and Welfare Canada, with the four food-group plan (figure 10.16), he or she would satisfy the requirements of a balanced diet.

CHAPTER 11
Selected Principles of Biomechanics

D. Gordon E. Robertson

In any physical activity or educational sports program within a school, community, or club situation, there are usually three main individual and/or group objectives cited: fitness, enjoyment (including friendships), and sport skills learning. It is the last characteristic which is the focus of this chapter. In order to attain this goal, the physical educator, instructor, coach, or recreationist must be thoroughly aware and competent in a variety of analytical motor skill techniques. Whether the analysis is that of a learner's beginning sport skills movement or that of improving the skills of an adept sports performer, this motor skills examination always precedes the communicative process of learning. Consequently, biomechanical analysis is a vital tool for all instructors of physical activity who are involved at any level of motor skills learning, correction, or improvement of the efficiency of human motion. Quality teaching in any physical activity or sports instruction always includes scientific biomechanical analysis. Some fundamental principles of the science of biomechanics and of its analytical techniques are examined in the following pages.

THE MECHANICS OF RIGID BODIES

Literally, **biomechanics** is the study of the mechanics of biological organisms. It is the science which attempts to predict and describe the motions of living bodies. Its scope is broad, encompassing three subareas: (1) the **mechanics of fluids,** which includes such diverse areas as lung, blood, swimming, and aquatic biomechanics; (2) the **mechanics of deformable solids,**

which examines the strength of bones, ligaments, and other tissues; and (3) the **mechanics of rigid bodies,** which examines objects that are nondeformable or nearly so.

It is the latter branch that will be presented in this text as it is the branch which is most often utilized by sport science researchers. It is the most simplistic of the three subareas because it assumes that objects do not bend, stretch, or compress. Nevertheless, it provides a reasonably accurate means by which the mechanics of human motion can be studied. Of course, the body is not actually rigid, despite the strength of its bones; but when studying gross movements of the limbs and body the assumption of rigidity is sound. Furthermore, it is not yet feasible to determine the changes induced by the movements of body fluids or muscle masses or to quantify the bending of the bones. This would only be possible by employing expensive equipment and potentially hazardous radiation, such as X rays or gamma rays, to monitor the internal movements of biological tissues.

Rigid body mechanics is divided into the areas of statics and dynamics. **Statics** is the study of objects or structures that are at rest (i.e., not moving). As such, it is not an area of particular concern to the biomechanist. **Dynamics** is the study of objects in motion and therefore has more relevance to the biomechanical study of humans.

Dynamics itself is subdivided into kinematics and kinetics. **Kinematics** is the study of motion without regard to the causes. It is the study of motion patterns and motion description. Kinematics does not take into account the mass of objects. Kinematics restricts itself to characterizing motions by identifying various properties of the motion. It serves as a means by which comparisons can be made of the performances of various individuals or of the same individual performing various skills. Kinematic quantities include position, distance, speed, displacement, velocity, acceleration, and their angular counterparts. Time, although an essential element to kinematics, is not itself a kinematic quantity.

Kinetics is the study of the causes of motion and is primarily concerned with the study of forces. A muscle generates force by contracting and attempting to pull together its two ends. Each muscle attaches by tendons to bones on either side of one or more joints. Muscular contractions can cause or resist rotations of these joints. The kinetic analysis of human movement is mainly concerned with how to quantify the forces produced by muscles (i.e., muscle strength and power) and what movements these forces produce in the joints and the bones. Kinetic quantities also include such measures as the work, impulse, moment, and power produced by forces.

The problem with analyzing human muscle forces is that these forces cannot be directly measured without surgery; thus, indirect methods are employed. By first quantifying the kinematics of a motion and then by applying Newton's laws, the causes of the motion (i.e., the kinetics) can be computed. Therefore, both kinematics and kinetics are essential to mechanically evaluate human movements.

In the following pages the fundamental concepts of mechanics will be defined. These will be followed by descriptions of linear and angular kinematic quantities. Next, the laws of mechanics will be presented followed by various other mechanical principles that are used to evaluate human performances.

FUNDAMENTAL CONCEPTS OF NEWTONIAN MECHANICS

The scientific principles underlying the study of human motion are based on the fundamental principles of Euclidean geometry, Newtonian mechanics, and the calculus. The calculus was originally invented by Newton to handle his mechanics problems. In this text we shall avoid the use of calculus but some knowledge of Euclidean geometry is expected of the reader.

Einstein has shown that some of the principles of Newtonian mechanics are in error. However, these errors are *relatively* small and are only relevant in special circumstances, such as travelling near the speed of light. When compared to biomechanics, where the errors are large in measuring the body's dimensions, the errors associated with Newton's laws are insignificant. (The measurement of body dimensions is called anthropometry.)

International System of Units

It is essential for scientists to use a common system of units so that research can be communicated among the scientific community without the need for converting from one unit to another and without distortion of the results. In the past, both the metric and Imperial systems were widely used to report results in the scientific literature. Today, however, most journals and publishers will only accept metric or, more properly, the International System of Units (*Le Système international d'unités,* abbreviated "SI").

Selected Principles of Biomechanics   **237**

The SI system precisely and unambiguously defines a wide variety of physical and chemical quantities, most of which are beyond the scope of this text. A few of the most important quantities used in biomechanics are listed in Appendix B with their associated units and abbreviations. The reader may obtain a more comprehensive list from the Canadian Standards Association. Appendix B contains a list of the acceptable prefixes and their abbreviations and some rules for properly reporting SI units.

Space, Mass, and Time

There are three fundamental quantities or dimensions in biomechanics—space, mass, and time. These dimensions are empirical concepts; that is, they are based on experience and experiment, and cannot be derived from other fundamental dimensions. These dimensions form the foundation from which all other mechanical dimensions can be derived and upon which laws of motion can be defined.

In Newtonian mechanics space, mass, and time are assumed to be independent of each other. This implies that time does not vary with position, nor mass with speed (rate of change of position with time), nor space with time, etc. Einstein has shown that this assumption is not true but for most biomechanical purposes this assumption is reasonable.

Space

The term **space** refers to the concept that an object occupies a volume and has a position. The basic SI unit of space is the metre (m). Other units include the kilometre (km) and the millimetre (mm). It is common practice to measure human dimensions in centimetres (cm). Volume is commonly measured in cubic metres (m³) or litres (L).

Any position in space, P, may be defined by three coordinates representing three lengths, x, y, and z, measured along three reference axes, X, Y, and Z. These axes form what is called a **Cartesian frame of reference.** Cartesian (named after René Descartes) is the name given to any axis system where the axes are oriented at right angles to each other. The point of intersection of the three reference axes is called the **origin** (figure 11.1).

In Newtonian mechanics, an absolute or Newtonian frame of reference is used such that the origin of the reference system is set at a point that is fixed in space and does not move. Such a point is rather impractical to find but a point fixed to the earth or a structure connected to the earth is usually sufficient for all but the most precise purposes.

There are two possible orientations of a three-dimensional reference system—right-handed and left-handed. These are illustrated in figure 11.1. The right-handed axis system has been accepted as the standard orientation. This is called the **right-hand rule.** This rule holds that if one axis is oriented upward and another axis points horizontally in the forward direction, movements to the right, up, and forward are defined as positive, while movements directed to the left, down, and backward are negative along their respective axes.

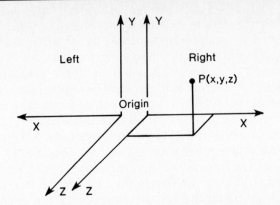

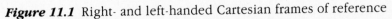

Figure 11.1 Right- and left-handed Cartesian frames of reference

The concepts of a line and a plane are simplified versions of space. The position of an object in a plane requires two coordinates while position along a line requires only one coordinate. Thus, a line is termed one-dimensional, a plane two-dimensional, and space three-dimensional. Planar motion refers to motion that takes place in only one plane, whereas spatial motion refers to motion that is not limited to one plane. Linear motion refers to movement along a single straight line.

Mass

Mass is a concept that was developed to explain the resistance that objects have to changes in their motion. Experience has shown that objects of equal mass require the same amount of effort to be put in motion. This fact eventually led to the formulation by Isaac Newton of the *first law of motion*. The measurement of human body mass and its distribution within the body is a part of the field called anthropometry. **Anthropometry** is concerned with the measurement of various body dimensions, such as height, weight, girth, segment length, or body density, and the relationships among these factors and athletic performance. The basic SI unit of mass is the kilogram (kg). The metric tonne (T) is the same as 1000 kilograms or a megagram (Mg).

Time

In Newtonian mechanics, **time** is assumed to tick away at a constant rate. Actually, time slows down (dilates) if one travels at speeds approaching the speed of light. This assumption of the invariance of time, however, is valid for all terrestrial human movements. The term **temporal analysis** refers to the analysis of the timing or duration of events with respect to each other. **Chronometry** is the measurement of time by various instruments such as stop watches, interval timers, or stroboscopes. The basic SI unit of time is the second (s). Of course, other units such as the minute (min), the hour (h), and the millisecond (ms) are used.

Selected Principles of Biomechanics   **239**

Force

Another important concept in biomechanics is that of force. Force is not considered an independent quantity as are space, mass, and time. In fact, Newton's laws of motion define mechanical forces in terms of the fundamental concepts of space, mass, and time. These laws have enabled physicists and others to develop mathematical and physical principles upon which the movements of bodies can be predicted and explained.

A **force** may be defined as an influence that one body has upon another. A simpler description might be that a force is a push or a pull. There are essentially three types of forces in nature. They are (1) gravitational forces, which are relatively weak; (2) electromagnetic forces, which are intermediate in strength; and (3) two types of nuclear forces, one of which is strong and one weak. In biomechanics, electromagnetic forces and gravitational forces are mainly dealt with.

Electromagnetic forces are the forces that hold molecules together to form structures or biological tissues such as muscles and bones. These forces are the forces that allow muscles to contract by the attraction and repulsion of special proteins (actin and myosin) within the muscle. Gravitational forces, which will be discussed later in this chapter, are too weak to be of any consequence with the exception of the gravitational attraction of the earth on the bodies in its vicinity. The relatively large mass of the earth makes its gravitational force significant.

The SI unit of force is a derived unit called the newton (N). A **newton** of force is the force required to accelerate a one kilogram object at the rate of one metre per second squared:

$$1 \text{ newton} = 1 \text{ N} = 1 \text{ kg} \cdot \text{m/s}^2.$$

Notice that this relationship implies that force is dependent upon mass (kg), space (m), and time (s).

LINEAR KINEMATICS

Distance versus Displacement

In biomechanics the word **distance** takes on a special meaning; it is the length of the path travelled by a body. As such, distance cannot have a unique direction since the path may be winding. This makes distance a scalar quantity.

A **scalar** quantity is a quantity that possesses a magnitude and may have a positive or negative value. Other examples of scalar quantities are time, temperature, work, energy, power, volume, and mass. Scalar quantities add algebraically; that is, 10 kg plus 5 kg equals 15 kg or 550 joules of energy minus 60 joules results in 490 joules.

Displacement is the term used to describe the straight line which connects a point's position from one instant in time to another. It must include both the length and direction of this line. Displacements do not add algebraically as do distances, unless all the displacements to be added are along the same straight line. Instead, displacements add according to the *parallelogram law* and are therefore called vector quantities.

Vectors are quantities that possess magnitude, direction, and add according to the parallelogram law. Examples of other vector quantities include force, moment of force, momentum, impulse, velocity, and acceleration. A complete description of the parallelogram law will be given later in this chapter. In written text, students should indicate vectors by underlining. In this chapter, the common practice of **boldfacing** vectors will be followed.

The question arises: Which quantity should be used for describing human movements, distance or displacement? The answer depends upon the motion that is being analyzed. It is always better and safest to quantify the total movement of an object or person by distance since distance measures the actual path that the person travelled.

For example, in a marathon race where the route travelled is often quite circuitous and can actually start and end at the same point, distance would be the only appropriate measure. The distance would be some amount greater than 26 miles 385 yards depending upon the exact route taken by the particular runner. The displacement could be ridiculously low, considering only the difference between the runner's starting and finishing positions.

Displacement, based upon the previous example, would seem to be a relatively useless measure. However, it does have a very important role in biomechanics when used in the proper situations. Displacement should only be used when the amount of movement from one position to another is reasonably small. It is the better measurement in these situations since it will indicate the direction of travel and not just the amount.

It is often difficult to quantify the exact path (i.e., distance) that a person travels from one instant to another. On the other hand, the displacement can easily be determined knowing only the initial and final positions. The length of the displacement vector can then be determined by applying the Pythagorean theorem, $R^2 = X^2 + Y^2$, to obtain the length of the vector and using a trigonometric relationship to obtain the direction. Also, trigonometric operations are quickly and easily performed by calculators or computers. Distances would have to be measured by some instrument, such as a planimeter or a trundle wheel. These instruments are laborious and time-consuming to use.

Displacement measurements also lend themselves well to the quantification of human movement by cinematography or television. Both of these media record movements at discrete points in time which for most television systems is every 30th of a second and for cine cameras can range from a 24th to a 500th of a second or even faster. In addition, displacement measures are more appropriate for the recording of human movements by digital computers (the majority of computers are digital) which are incapable of storing the continuous signals that would be required for distance measurements.

Speed versus Velocity

Speed is defined as the rate of change of distance over time and is therefore a scalar quantity, as is distance. No direction need be associated with speed because the movement may not be in a straight line. To compute speed, divide the distance travelled by the time taken to travel the distance. That is:

$$\text{speed} = \text{distance} / \text{time}. \qquad \text{[m/s] or [km/h]}$$

The common unit of measure for speed is metres per second (m/s) but kilometres per hour (km/h) is often used. (The symbols within the square brackets in this equation and all subsequent equations are the acceptable SI abbreviations for the units of the answer.)

Velocity is defined as the rate of change of displacement per unit of time. As such, it must be a vector quantity since displacement is a vector. A velocity will always have an associated direction which indicates the direction of movement of the person or object. Velocities are measured in the same units as speed. The equation for the magnitude of the velocity vector, v, is:

$$v = s / t \qquad \text{[m/s]}$$

where s represents the length of the displacement vector in metres and t is the time taken in seconds. The direction of the velocity will be the same as the direction of the line that connects the initial to the final position of the object or person.

Acceleration

Acceleration is defined as the rate of change of velocity. It may also be defined as the rate of change of the rate of change of displacement. Since displacements and velocities are vectors, accelerations are vectors and will therefore always have associated directions. In the following discussion, we will deal only with the equations of acceleration for objects in simple linear motion since more advanced mathematical skills are needed to deal with planar or spatial motions.

If an object's velocity in a particular direction (e.g., X direction) changes from an initial velocity magnitude of v_{x_0} m/s to a final velocity magnitude of v_{x_1} m/s, the equation for the magnitude of the acceleration vector will be

$$a = (v_{x_1} - v_{x_0}) / t \qquad [m/s^2]$$

where t represents the time taken to make the change in velocity. The direction of the acceleration vector along the X-axis will depend upon the magnitudes of the two velocity vectors. If the magnitude of a is positive then the acceleration will be in the positive X direction; if negative then the acceleration will be toward the negative X direction. Note that the direction of the acceleration may be different from those of the two velocities. For example, if an object is moving at −10 m/s and slows to −8 m/s in 1 s then the acceleration will be 2 m/s in the positive X direction, which is the same acceleration as when an object increases velocity from 6 m/s to 7 m/s in 0.5 s in the positive X direction.

The concept of acceleration is difficult to grasp yet it is the most important kinematic quantity to understand because it is directly related to the cause of motion—force—as defined by *Newton's second law*. This law states that whenever an object undergoes an acceleration then a force must be present causing the acceleration.

Accelerations are difficult to determine by observation alone. The brain is incapable of performing the required mathematical operations as the movement is taking place. Therefore, it is necessary to record the motion in some way and then apply the appropriate operations to compute the acceleration pattern.

The direction of acceleration of an object, which is the same as the direction of the total applied force, must not be confused with the direction of movement of the object. The direction of movement is equivalent to the direction of the object's velocity and can be the same or quite different from that of the object's acceleration.

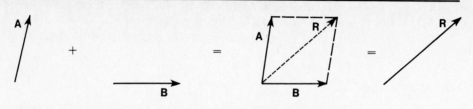

Figure 11.2 Parallelogram Law for the addition of vectors

For example, if a ball is thrown straight up its acceleration and velocity will both be directed upward while in the person's hand. After being released from the hand, the ball will continue for a time with an upward velocity until the top of its flight. Then, for an instant, it will have zero velocity, followed by an increasing downward velocity until it strikes the ground. Its acceleration, on the other hand, will remain constant throughout its flight and be directed always straight down toward the ground.

Another example, which illustrates how the directions of acceleration and velocity are independent, is the motion of a sprinter. After the starting gun is fired and a brief delay due to human reaction time, a sprinter will start accelerating forward, gradually increasing velocity in the same direction. At some point in the middle of the race the sprinter will reach maximum forward velocity. For a time the sprinter will maintain at this velocity and, therefore, have an acceleration of zero.

As local muscle fatigue sets in and reduces the muscles' abilities to create adequate force, the sprinter's velocity may begin to reduce and deceleration will occur. Yet the sprinter's velocity will continue to be directed forward. It may appear to an observer watching from the side that a particular sprinter is accelerating past other sprinters at the end of a race. However, what may be happening is that the other runners are decelerating faster and only appear to be accelerating.

In a recent study of Ben Johnson, the Canadian and world 100m sprint champion, it was found that he accelerates up to a maximum velocity of, approximately, 12 m/s at the 60 metre point in the race. From 60 to 100 metres he essentially maintains this velocity and does not decelerate until after crossing the finish line. Other less well trained athletes may well begin decelerating before reaching the finish line.

Parallelogram Law for the Addition of Vectors

This law defines the rule by which vectors may be added together. The law states that the sum of two vectors, called the **resultant, R,** is equal to the diagonal of the parallelogram which has sides equal to the two vectors. It is best described graphically as illustrated in figure 11.2. Note that the word resultant is used to describe the sum of any number of vectors and is always a vector itself. Furthermore, the resultant of a sum of vectors can be of zero magnitude, called a zero vector.

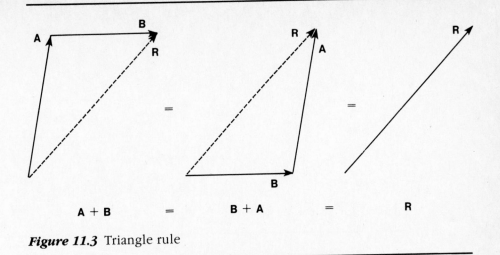

$$A + B \qquad = \qquad B + A \qquad = \qquad R$$

Figure 11.3 Triangle rule

A simplification of the parallelogram law is the **triangle rule.** This rule allows one to obtain the resultant by drawing just the two vectors in tip-to-tail fashion and then forming the resultant by connecting the tail of the first vector to the tip of the second vector. It does not matter which vector is drawn first since vector addition has the **commutative property.** This property means that two vectors can be added together, in any order. That is:

$$R = A + B = B + A.$$

This property can be shown graphically by drawing the vector **A,** then drawing the vector **B** beginning from the tip of vector **A,** as illustrated in figure 11.3. The resultant, **R,** is identical to the resultant obtained by drawing **B** first and then adding **A.**

Vector addition also has the **associative property.** This implies that three or more vectors can be added together in any order. That is:

$$R = A + B + C = B + C + A = C + A + B \text{ etc.}$$

This is shown graphically in figure 11.4 and is called the **polygon rule,** since the resultant is obtained by joining the tail of the first vector to the tip of the last vector of the polygon formed from joining all the vectors in a tip-to-tail fashion. Note that it is possible that the resultant can be a zero vector in which case the tip of the last vector in the sum will be joined to the tail of the first vector. As an exercise, draw the other three polygons of the three vectors in figure 11.4 (i.e., **A + C + B, B + A + C,** and **C + B + A**). All six resultants will have the same length (when drawn to the same scale), the same angle, and point in the same direction.

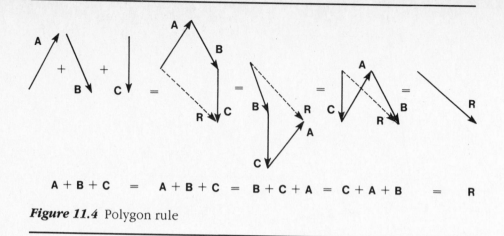

$$A + B + C \quad = \quad A + B + C \ = \ B + C + A \ = \ C + A + B \quad = \quad R$$

Figure 11.4 Polygon rule

ANGULAR KINEMATICS

Radian Measure

Angular kinematics includes quantities similar to those of linear kinematics: angular distance, angular speed, angular displacement, angular velocity, and angular acceleration. One obvious difference is the units of measure. Whereas linear measures use metres, angular quantities are measured in radians (abbreviated rad). The SI system also permits the use of degree measurements (abbreviated deg) and revolutions (abbreviated r) but in many cases these units are not as convenient as radians.

The radian is a special unit which actually has no physical units. The number of radians in any angle is defined as the ratio of arc length to radius. Therefore, a **radian** is defined as the angle formed by an arc length of one radius. This angle is shown in figure 11.5. The equation which describes this relationship follows:

$$\theta = s \, / \, r \qquad \text{[radians or no units]}$$

where θ, called theta, represents the angle, s represents the arc length, and r represents the radius. Notice that since arc length and radius are both measured in metres, the units of θ cancel out. It is normal practice to include these units when specifying angles even though they are unitless; e.g., write 1.06 rad or 1.06 radians.

It happens that the number of radians in a semicircle is a very special number, called pi (π). Since there are 180 degrees in a semicircle the number of degrees in a radian may be defined as

$$\pi \text{ radians} = 180 \text{ degrees}$$

therefore

$$1 \text{ radian} = 180 \, / \, \pi \simeq 57.3 \text{ degrees.}$$

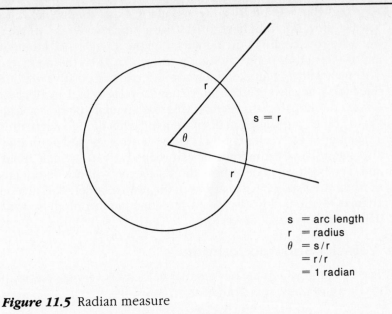

s = arc length
r = radius
θ = s/r
  = r/r
  = 1 radian

Figure 11.5 Radian measure

The symbol $\simeq$, which means "approximately equal to," is used because π is a transcendental number which cannot be completely described by a finite number of digits (one of its special properties).

Relationship between Linear and Angular Measures

The equation which defines a radian may also be used to relate the linear movement of a point travelling a circular path to the angular movement of the body or vice versa. By rearranging the equation, such that the arc length, which represents the linear dimension, is on one side, we have

$$s = r\,\theta \qquad \text{[m]}$$

where s represents the arc length or linear distance in metres, r represents the circle's radius in metres, and θ is the angular distance in radians. Note that the angular distance must be in radians for the equation to be valid.

For example, to compute the circumference of a circle (s_c) substitute the value for the number of radians in a complete circle (i.e., 2π) for θ and the circle's radius for r to obtain the well-known equation

$$s_c = 2\,\pi\,r. \qquad \text{[m]}$$

Note that the units of measure on both sides of an equation must be the same; yet in the above equation it would appear that the right-hand side has units of radian metres. However, as was pointed out previously, the radian actually is a ratio with no physical units and may be omitted as a dimension. Note also that it is acceptable to include the number π in an answer; thus, a 45 deg angle could be written as $\pi/4$ rad.

Selected Principles of Biomechanics

It is common practice that angular measurements like linear measurements follow the right-hand rule. That is, angular directions are determined by curling the fingers of the right hand in the direction of the angular measure and if the thumb points along a positive axis then the measure is positive. This means that a counterclockwise direction is positive while a clockwise direction is negative. Furthermore, angular velocity and acceleration, like their linear counterparts, are vectors, whereas angular speed is a scalar quantity. On the other hand, angular displacement, even though it has direction, is not a member of the vector family because it does not add according to the parallelogram law. For instance, if you rotate positive 90 deg about the X-axis and then positive 90 deg about the Y-axis you will not be oriented the same as when you make these rotations in the reverse order. This demonstrates that angular rotations do not possess the commutative property which is a fundamental property of all vectors.

Angular Velocity and Acceleration

The equation which defines angular velocity is very similar to the equation for linear velocity. It is defined as

$$\omega = \theta / t \qquad [\text{rad/s}]$$

where ω, called omega, is the angular velocity, θ is the angular displacement in radians, and t is the time interval in seconds. Similarly, the definition for angular acceleration is

$$\alpha = \omega / t \qquad [\text{rad/s}^2]$$

where α, called alpha, is the angular acceleration, ω is the angular velocity in radians per second, and t is the time interval in seconds.

KINETICS

Universal Law of Gravitation

The **universal law of gravitation** defines the force of attraction that exists between objects. In biomechanics, only the force of attraction with the earth is of relevance since other gravitational forces are too small to affect the motion of a human or of human-propelled projectiles.

This law also defines the force known as weight. **Weight** is the force caused by the pull of gravity, usually the earth's. Since weight is a force, it is measured in units of newtons (which was defined earlier in the section on force), and its direction is straight down toward the centre of the earth. Mathematically, the weight of an object or person on earth is defined as

$$W = m\,g \qquad [\text{N}]$$

where W is weight in newtons, m is mass in kilograms, and g is acceleration due to earth's gravitational attraction in m/s². The value g, as in g-forces, varies slightly depending upon altitude and latitude (the earth not being perfectly spherical or of uniform density). For all practical purposes, however, it may be considered a constant equal to 9.8 m/s². Its exact value for any given location on earth would have to be determined experimentally.

When solving biomechanical problems it is important to recognize the difference between weight and mass and to be able to convert from one to the other. To convert from mass to weight, multiply the mass in kilograms by 9.8 m/s² to obtain weight in newtons and to convert weight in newtons to mass in kilograms divide by 9.8 m/s². Note that the term "weigh" may refer to measurement of either mass or weight. For example, a person can be said to weigh 50 kilograms or 490 newtons, but a person *cannot* have a weight of 50 kilograms.

Newton's First Law: Law of Inertia

This law, which forms the basis of the branch of mechanics called statics, can be stated in a number of ways. It was originally written in Latin by Newton and literally translated it states that "Every body continues in its state of rest, or of uniform motion in a straight line, unless it is compelled to change that state by forces impressed upon it."

Another way of stating the law might be: An object that is at rest or moving at constant speed in a straight line, called uniform motion, will remain so until acted upon by unbalanced external forces. This is to say that an object that is moving will tend to stay moving with unchanged speed along the same straight line and that an object that is at rest will tend to remain at rest.

Resultant Force

The term "unbalanced external forces" can be simplified by the concept of a resultant force. A **resultant force** is the vector sum of all of the external forces acting on the object. Thus, the first law can be stated more concisely as: If the resultant force acting on an object is zero then the object will remain at rest or in uniform motion. Consequently, if we know all the external forces acting on the object and that these vectors add up to zero, then we know that the object's state of motion will not change. That is, it will remain motionless or it will keep moving in a straight line at constant speed.

The converse of the first law is also valid; that is, if an object is motionless or in constant linear motion then the resultant force acting on the object is zero. For example, if a heavy car is stationary we know that the road must be strong enough to support the car; otherwise, gravity would pull the car down. The force exerted by the ground which pushes up on the car must be equal to the weight of the car or else the car would sink into the roadbed. If we then try to push the car and it does not move, then there must be an external force resisting our push. This resisting force is provided by the friction between the ground and the car tires. By putting the car in neutral and taking off the brake, our push may then be strong enough to start the car moving. In this case, the frictional force is not large enough to "balance" our push and, thus, the car must start to move. How quickly and in which direction the car will move is the subject of Newton's second law.

Another area where the first law can be applied is to projectile motion. For example, if you observe the hammer throw from an overhead view, the hammer will, upon release, leave the curve along the line tangent to the point of release. (The **tangent** of a curve is a straight line which touches the curve at one point and is at right angles to the radius of the curve at that point.) It will continue along this line until it strikes the ground or another object.

The reason is that there are no external forces acting on the hammer in the horizontal plane. The hammer will curve toward the ground if we view the hammer from a sagittal plane (side view) due to the influence of gravity. However, since there are no horizontal external forces during the hammer's flight, air resistance having negligible influence, the hammer must travel a straight-line path and will move at constant speed along this path.

Newton's Second Law: Law of Acceleration

The second law of motion is more descriptive than the first law because it not only defines when an object will change its state of motion or of rest but also how fast and in what direction it will move. A translated version of the second law is: "Change of motion is proportional to the motive force impressed; and is in the same direction as the line of the impressed force." This is to say that whenever a non-zero resultant force acts on an object the object will change its state of motion or of rest in response and that the response will be proportional to the force and in the same direction as the force. Change of motion refers to the object (1) changing its direction of motion, as, for example, turning or moving along a curved path, (2) changing its speed, or (3) changing both direction and speed. These changes of motion are collectively called **accelerations.**

The converse of this law is also valid. That is, whenever an object accelerates then there must be a non-zero resultant force acting on the object proportional to the acceleration and in the same direction as the acceleration.

This law may be stated mathematically as

$$\mathbf{F} = m\,\mathbf{a} \qquad [\text{N}]$$

where **F** represents the resultant force acting on an object which has mass m and acceleration **a.** The boldface indicates that both force and acceleration are vector quantities. Note that this equality is only true when a consistent system of units of measure is used. The International System of Units (SI) is a consistent system which specifies that forces be measured in newtons, mass in kilograms, and accelerations in metres per second squared. As mentioned previously, newton is therefore defined as the force required to accelerate a mass of one kilogram at the rate of one metre per second squared.

This equation can be used to determine the resultant force acting on an object if the object's acceleration is known. This is an area of mechanics called **inverse** or **indirect dynamics** and is of particular interest to biomechanists since it is often difficult or impossible to measure all the forces acting on an athlete, especially in a competitive environment. It is, however, usually possible to record an athlete's motion, through cinematography or television, and then mathematically determine the velocity and acceleration.

For instance, to determine the resultant force acting on a sculler the forces of each oar, the seat, and the footboards would have to be measured. This is not an easy task considering the equipment would have to be onshore since the sculler does not want to carry deadweight down the course. On the other hand, the acceleration of the sculler and boat can be calculated from a film of the race and the masses of the boat and body parts measured or estimated.

Direct dynamics deals with how an object will move knowing the forces acting on it. This is an area of primary interest to bioengineers who design artificial limbs or want to predict how an object will move under the actions of known forces or motors. It is also becoming of greater interest to physical educators, kinesiologists, and therapists who want to predict the movements of athletes or to instruct patients in new patterns of muscle contraction.

Moment of Force and Torque

To create angular motion in an object or person a force must be applied to the object, such that the force's line of action does not pass through the object's centre (of gravity). Consequently, this kind of force is called an **eccentric force** or an **eccentric thrust** because its direction is off-centre. The tendency of a force to create angular motion is called its **moment of force.** It is given this name because it is the product of the magnitude of the force and the moment of the force about an axis.

The concept of moment of force is one of the most important in biomechanics because it measures the ability of a muscle or muscle group to cause rotation. Moment of force may be defined in the following way:

$$M = r\,F \qquad [\text{N} \cdot \text{m}]$$

where M represents moment of force, r represents the moment of the force from an axis, and F represents the magnitude of the force including its direction (+ or −). The common unit of measure for moments of force is the newton metre, abbreviated N·m. Consequently, the moment r should be measured in metres and the force F in newtons.

In physics, the term **moment,** as in moment of force or moment of inertia, refers to the perpendicular distance from a particular point to an axis. Thus, the term **moment about an axis** or, equivalently, moment arm refers to the perpendicular distance from the line of a force to an axis. Moment, since it is similar to a radius (being the distance from an axis or centre), is usually represented by the small letter r.

Other names for moment of force, which are often encountered in the biomechanics literature, are **torque** and **joint torque.** These terms, however, are more appropriately applied to moments of force about longitudinal axes, such as internal and external rotations of body parts (e.g., supination or pronation of the forearm and trunk twisting), or the moment of force created by motors and engines. Although there is some ambiguity, moment of force is often shortened to moment. The context should identify whether the term refers to a moment of force or a moment arm length.

Another way of defining moment of force relates back to Newton's laws. According to the second law, to change the linear motion of an object or a person an external force must be applied. A similar requirement is also true before changes can be made to the angular motion or the spin of an object or person. This relationship, which is a form of Newton's second law, may be written

$$M = I\,\alpha \qquad [\text{N·m}]$$

where M represents the magnitude of the resultant moment of force acting on the object in newton metres, I represents the moment of inertia of the object in kilogram metres squared, and α represents the angular acceleration of the object in radians per second squared. The concept of moment of inertia is similar to that of mass but is for angular motion. A more precise description will be presented later.

Recall that a resultant force is the sum of all the external forces acting on an object. Similarly, a resultant moment of force is the sum of all the external moments of force acting on an object. Furthermore, just as forces have direction so do moments of force. The direction of a moment follows the right-hand rule, described previously. Thus, a counterclockwise moment is defined defined as being positive and a clockwise moment is defined as being negative. Moments of force, like forces, also add according to the parallelogram law and, therefore, are members of the family of vectors. However, this is not important to know unless you are dealing in spatial (3-D) motion since in planar motion all moments share the same axis and, therefore, may be added algebraically (the common axis being an axis perpendicular to the plane of the motion).

Moment of Inertia

Moment of inertia refers to the reluctance or resistance of an object to change in its angular motion. It is the angular equivalent to mass but has a number of distinct differences from mass. The moment of inertia of a body, particularly a human body, is very difficult to determine computationally or empirically. Unlike mass, the moment of inertia of a body cannot simply be measured by a weigh scale. More complicated instruments must be used and therefore the measurement of moments of inertia will have to wait for a more advanced course in biomechanics.

It is sufficient, at this point, to understand that the moment of inertia of an object increases as its mass increases. In addition, moment of inertia varies with how the mass within an object is distributed. The more concentrated the mass is around a point the lower will be the moment of inertia. Thus, it is easier to swing a short bat than a long bat, and a small diameter wheel is easier to rotate than a large diameter wheel. Also, it is easier to spin a ball, where all of the material within the ball is reasonably close to the centre of the ball, than it is to spin a bat, where the mass at either end of the bat is relatively far from the centre of the bat.

Moment of inertia also varies with the axis of rotation, in contrast to mass which resists linear motion equally in any direction. As the mass of an object moves farther away from an axis of rotation the moment of inertia of the object will increase as the square of the displacement, or moment, from that axis. Consequently, the moment of inertia of the arm about its long axis is much smaller than its moment of inertia about a mediolateral axis or anteroposterior axis. Furthermore, the moment of inertia of an object about an axis that passes through its centre of gravity is smaller than any other parallel axis. This relationship may be defined as follows: for a point mass of m kilograms, the moment of inertia of this mass about an axis r metres away would be

$$I = m\ r^2. \qquad [kg \cdot m^2]$$

Thus, if a 10 kg mass is moved from 1 m to 2 m from an axis its equivalent moment of inertia will increase from 10 kg·m² to 40 kg·m²—a four-fold increase!

Newton's Third Law: Law of Reaction

Newton's third law, translated, states that "For every action [force] there is always an opposed equal reaction [force]; or, the mutual actions of two bodies on each other are always equal and directed to opposite parts." In other words, for a force to exist there must also exist a reaction force which is equal in magnitude, acts along the same line of action, but has opposite direction. Therefore, there can be no action force without a simultaneous reaction force. For example, to begin walking one must first push backwards against the ground. Usually, the ground is capable of providing a sufficient reaction force, called a ground reaction force. But, if it is covered with highly polished ice, then a push will not result in a movement of the body as a whole (i.e., movement of the centre of gravity). Instead the foot that is pushing will slide along the surface and other parts of the body will move the same amount in the opposite direction resulting in no net movement of the body.

A corollary of this law is that the sum of all internal forces within a body is zero. For example, when a muscle contracts producing a force at one end it will also produce a reaction force at the other end which when added, vectorially, to the action force will produce a zero resultant. The only way to produce a non-zero resultant force on the body from within the body is to be able to react against something in the environment (i.e., something external to the body). If this is not possible then it will not be possible for the body to propel itself. Examples of reaction forces that are used to propel or accelerate the human body include frictional forces, viscous or fluid forces, and centrifugal forces. All of these forces exist in response to some action force.

Centripetal and Centrifugal Forces

A **centripetal force** is the force that is required to keep a body moving on a curved path. Its direction is always toward the centre of curvature of the path, which in the case of circular motion is toward the centre of the circle. Its associated reaction force is called a **centrifugal force.**

A good example of centripetal and centrifugal forces occurs with high jumpers who run curved approaches. Running a curved approach will require the jumper to provide a force that is directed toward the centre of the curve. This force, called a centripetal force (centre-seeking), will create as its reaction a centrifugal force (centre-fleeing) according to the third law.

The centrifugal force will be directed opposite to the centre of the curve and be parallel to the surface of the run-up. This force will attempt to rotate the jumper mediolaterally toward the outside of the curve while the jumper is running the curve. But, since it is a reaction force, it will immediately disappear once the jumper has left the ground. Therefore, if the jumper takes off along a line parallel to the bar then he or she will not be able to clear the bar. An oblique trajectory is necessary for successful clearance.

The speed with which an athlete can run a curve is dependent upon how large a centripetal force the athlete can produce. This is the reason for banking indoor tracks where the bends are usually tight. The tighter the bend the greater must be the centripetal force. Since the centripetal force is mainly a frictional force and therefore limited in magnitude, the athlete must slow down while negotiating the bend. By banking the track surface, the direction of the athlete's ground reaction force is more centripetally directed, enabling the runner to make a greater change in his or her linear motion. However, these forces will require the runner to lean toward the centre of the curve to prevent the ground reaction force—centrifugal force—from creating a rotation about the anteroposterior axis of the runner.

Another example of centripetal and centrifugal forces is the forces exerted during the hammer throw. In this skill, the thrower spins a hammer (actually a 16-pound shot at the end of a wire) approximately three-and-a-half times and then releases it. Because the hammer is always rotating, a centripetal force must always be present to keep the hammer moving along the curved path. The stronger and more skilled the thrower, the greater will be the centripetal force that can be created. The centrifugal force is the force that the thrower feels in his/her hands and must be strong enough to overcome lest the hammer be released prematurely (the very reason for having high fences around the hammer throw area). This is the reason that hammer throwers wear gloves and have strong grip strength.

Frictional Forces

All frictional forces are reaction forces since they only exist when an active force is present. **Frictional forces** occur when two surfaces that are in contact attempt to move across one another. They are always directed parallel to the surfaces in contact and limited in magnitude depending upon the nature of both surfaces, the magnitude of the force pushing them together (called the normal force), and whether the two surfaces are already in motion or stationary. A **normal force** is the component of a force that is perpendicular (at right angles) to a surface or an axis.

There are two laws of dry friction (fluid friction will not be considered): one for when the surfaces are not moving (**static friction**), and one for when the surfaces are moving (**kinetic friction**). The equations which describe these relationships are

$$F_s = \mu_s F_n \qquad [N]$$

$$F_k = \mu_k F_n \qquad [N]$$

where F_s and F_k represent the static and kinetic frictional forces, respectively; μ_s and μ_k represent the coefficients of static and kinetic friction, respectively; and F_n represents the normal force. These equations imply that frictional forces increase as the normal force increases or as the coefficient of friction increases or both. Both coefficients of friction depend upon the nature of the two surfaces and can only be determined empirically (through experiments). Experiments have shown that static coefficients are about 25 percent larger than kinetic coefficients; therefore, it always requires more force to get an object moving than to keep an object moving.

As an example, consider pushing a 50 kg box across the floor. The coefficients of static and kinetic friction might be 0.30 and 0.25, respectively. The normal force will be equal to the weight of the box which is (W = m g = 50 × 9.8 =) 490 N. Therefore, the magnitudes of static and kinetic friction would be 147 N and 122.5 N, respectively.

When the person starts to push, the frictional force and motive force will increase together and as long as the motive force is less than 147 N the box will not move since the vector sum of these two forces is zero. As the person continues to push, the motive force will eventually exceed 147 N. At this instant the box will immediately accelerate at a rate equal to the motive force minus the maximum kinetic frictional force of 122.5 N. As long as the person provides a force greater than 122.5 N the box will keep accelerating.

If the motive force drops to exactly 122.5 N the box will keep moving at constant linear speed (Newton's first law). If the force drops below 122.5 N the box will begin to decelerate and will eventually stop, in which case the person would have to again supply a force greater than 147 N. However, if before the box stops the person pushes with a force exceeding 122.5 N the box will accelerate again. It is therefore important to keep the box moving at all times to minimize the amount of force that needs to be exerted.

Continuity of Human Movements

Efficient human movements should always be made with the minimum amount of discontinuity and jerkiness. Jerky movements require greater expenditures of physiological energy (oxygen cost or ATP) than will smooth continuous movements. This is especially true when movements are performed in or on fluid media, such as swimming or rowing, or when air resistance is large, as in cycling.

Discontinuities of movement occur mainly during landings or impacts with the environment or other objects. These cause the body or parts of the body to experience relatively large accelerations and consequently large forces. These forces must then be absorbed by the body in some way. The best way of absorbing these forces is to utilize the muscle's ability to contract eccentrically. That is, a muscle actively contracts while it is being stretched or lengthened.

For example, during the first half of the stance phase of running, ankle plantar flexors, knee extensors, and hip extensors of the landing leg are all performing eccentric contractions to absorb the impact forces exerted by the ground. The bones and ligaments are also capable of absorbing impact forces; however, excessively large forces or repetitive impacts over a long period can result in damaging these structures by causing stress fractures in bones or ruptures to ligaments. Muscles, on the other hand, can accept repeated impact forces and recover more quickly than bones or ligaments.

It is therefore desirable, whenever possible, to reduce the number and magnitude of discontinuities and minimize jerkiness in movements. This can be done in a number of ways. In skills such as swimming, rowing, or kayaking, changes in acceleration (i.e., jerk) are reduced by applying forces against the water in longer, smoother strokes rather than quicker, more forceful strokes.

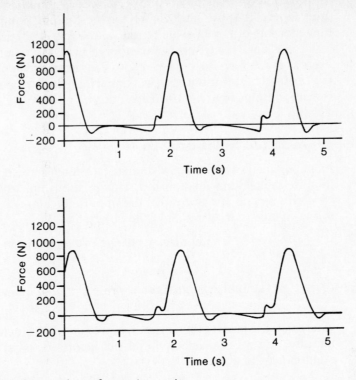

Figure 11.6 Propulsive forces in rowing

This is not to say that the stroke rates are reduced but only that each stroke is performed with a more steady pull or push. Similarly, it is more efficient to run a race at constant or nearly constant speed although the amount of energy saved in this way is not as great as can be saved in aquatic-type events.

Figure 11.6 illustrates two methods of force generation in rowing. The top tracing shows a greater peak force than the bottom tracing. However, due to the viscous nature of water, the stroke forces in the top tracing will require in the long run a greater level of exertion and result in fatigue setting in sooner than for the stroke forces shown in the bottom tracing. The bottom tracing will produce smaller rates of acceleration yet will give the same amount of thrust to the boat (since the areas under the two tracings are equal) but since there will be less resistance (drag) from the water, it will require less physiologic exertion from the rower.

To reduce the impact forces in events such as triple or long jumping, hurdling, or running, athletes should land with their leg slightly bent so that the leg can collapse allowing the leg muscles to contract eccentrically. To land with a straight leg from the "hop" phase of triple jumping, for example, is to guarantee a severe heel contusion (bruise). Another feature of most landings, especially those immediately before running jumps, is to contract the hip extensors or knee flexors to reduce the foot's forward velocity. This will result in a smaller frictional impact force since the ground does not have to exert as much force to stop the foot's forward movement (Newton's second law). This is best illustrated in walking where the forward velocity of the foot is nearly zero prior to heel-strike yet during midswing it is moving relatively quickly.

Impulse-Momentum Relationship

An important tool for analyzing human movements uses a principle called the impulse-momentum relationship. This relationship, which is derived from Newton's second law, states that the impulse of a force on an object is equal to the change in momentum of the object. That is,

$$\text{impulse} = \text{change in momentum}$$

or

$$\text{impulse} = \text{final momentum} - \text{initial momentum}$$
$$= m\, v_f - m\, v_i \qquad [\text{kg} \cdot \text{m/s or N} \cdot \text{s}]$$

where m is the mass of the object, v_f represents the velocity of object after the impulse, and v_i is the velocity of object before the impulse. Alternately, the relation may be written

$$\text{final momentum} = \text{initial momentum} + \text{impulse}$$
$$m\, v_f = m\, v_i + \text{impulse}. \qquad [\text{kg} \cdot \text{m/s or N} \cdot \text{s}]$$

The amount of impulse of a force may be defined as the magnitude of the average force times the duration of the force. But, since it is usually difficult to obtain the average force, impulse may also be defined as the area under a force-time tracing (force history). These tracings may be obtained by using force measuring devices (dynamometers), such as force platforms or force transducers, and appropriate recording devices, such as chart recorders, storage oscilloscopes, or computers equipped with analogue-to-digital (A/D) converters. Figure 11.7 is a picture of a Kistler force platform that is connected to a minicomputer equipped with A/D converters for measuring the ground reaction force in three dimensions and its point of application.

Figure 11.8 is an illustration of a typical vertical force history of a runner after running across a force platform. The dotted line represents the runner's body-weight line. Notice that the magnitude of the vertical force peaks at approximately three times the runner's body weight. This impulse is large enough to propel the runner upward into the next stride even though the runner's initial momentum was downward due to gravity.

Figure 11.7 A Kistler force platform

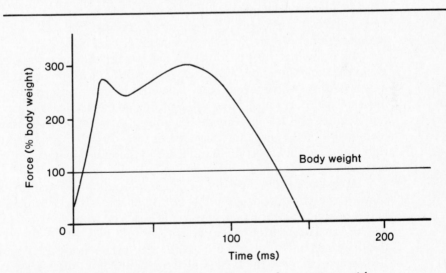

Figure 11.8 Vertical ground reaction forces of a running stride

This relationship may also be used to compute the velocity of a person after a thrust. For example, if a sprinter or swimmer is starting from a set of blocks that are instrumented to measure and record the forces produced at the feet, it will be possible to compute the velocity of the athlete after pushing off from the blocks. Using the previous equation and assuming that the athlete's initial velocity is zero (i.e., no rolling starts) we can find the final velocity by dividing both sides of the equation by the mass of the athlete. Thus,

$$v_f = \text{impulse} / m. \qquad \text{[m/s]}$$

This equation may also be used to predict the takeoff velocity of people performing standing jumps, such as the block, vertical, or standing broad jump. Knowing this velocity it would then be possible to compute the height to which the jumper would rise.

Work and Power

Work

Mechanical work is done when a force causes an object or person to move through a displacement. The amount of work done by a force is defined as the product of the force times the displacement produced. That is,

$$U = F s \qquad \text{[J]}$$

where U represents the work done in joules by the force, F is the magnitude of the force in newtons in the direction of the displacement, and s represents the magnitude of the displacement in metres.

Notice that the unit of work is the joule (J) when newton metres would seem appropriate. This is to distinguish work units from the units of moments of force. Both quantities are dimensionally equivalent (in the base units kg· m^2/s^2) but represent physically quite different quantities. Always use the newton metre for the unit of moment of force and the joule for the unit of work or of energy—mechanical, electrical, or chemical.

Be aware that this equation only holds when the force and displacement are in the same direction. A force does no work unless the object it acts upon moves because of the force. Thus, isometric muscle contractions (where the muscle experiences no change in length) do no mechanical work even though they require physiologic (chemical) energy to maintain their levels of contraction. Normal (perpendicular) forces also do not work since they act at right angles to the direction of motion and therefore do not contribute to the motion.

An example of the use of this equation would be to quantify the amount of work done by dragging a 500 N box 30 m across a floor which has a coefficient of kinetic friction of 0.30 with the box. The work done to move the box will be equal to the frictional force of ($F_f = \mu_k F_n = 0.30 \times 500 =$) 150 N times the displacement 30 m or 4.5 kJ. Note that it does not matter how long the person takes to move the box—only how far and how much force is required. When time is an important consideration the quantity power, presented at the end of the chapter, is the more appropriate measure.

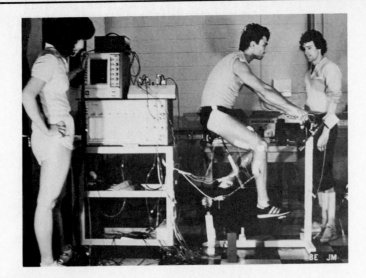

Figure 11.9 A bicycle ergometer for measuring work

Moments of force can also do work. The work done by a moment of force has the same units as that of work done by a force. The work done by a moment of force is the product of the magnitude of the moment of force times the angular displacement. That is,

$$U = M\theta \qquad [J]$$

where U is the work done, M is the magnitude of the moment of force in newton metres, and θ is the angular displacement in radians. The radian unit of measure in the above equation is essential but it is not carried with the joule dimension since it is a dimensionless unit of measure (refer back to the section on radian measure).

The measurement of human work is usually done by devices called ergometers, literally work meters, which are calibrated to provide a specific resistance force or moment of force while the subject being measured performs some activity. There are many types of ergometers with the most common being the bicycle ergometer, an example of which is shown in figure 11.9.

To compute the work done on a bicycle ergometer one must know the resistance and the number of revolutions performed. For example, if a person pedalled for 300 revolutions (there are 2π radians per revolution) at a resistance of 50.0 N·m the amount of work would be

$$U = M\theta = 50.0 \times 300 \times 2.00\pi = 30\ 000\ \pi\ J \simeq 94.2\ kJ.$$

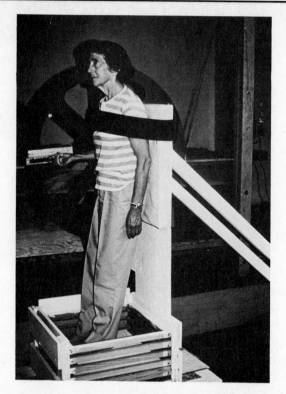

Figure 11.10 A dynamometer for measuring forearm power

If a person pedalled against a load of 100 N for 6.00 r (revolutions) on a bicycle with a wheel circumference of 1.00 m the amount of work would be

$$U = F s = F (r \theta) = 100 \times (1.00 \times 6.00 \times 2.00 \pi)$$
$$= 12\ 000\ \pi\ J$$
$$= 37.7\ kJ$$

Power

Power is probably the most important measure for differentiating among high-performance athletes since it is the measure of the rate of doing work. That is,

$$P = U / t \qquad [W]$$

where P is the power in watts, U is the work done in joules, and t is the time in seconds taken to do the work. Another way of determining the power of a force is by multiplying the magnitude of the force times the velocity of the point on which the force is acting. That is,

$$P = F v \qquad [W]$$

where F is in newtons and v is in metres per second. Similarly the power of a moment of force is

$$P = M \omega \qquad [W]$$

where P is the power in watts, M is the moment of force in newton metres, and ω is the angular velocity in radians per second of the object being turned.

Power can be measured by special dynamometers that measure or control the speed of a motion and the force exerted by the muscles against a force-measuring lever. An example of such a dynamometer is illustrated in figure 11.10. By knowing the rate of contraction and measuring the exerted force, the instantaneous power output at any joint angle and the peak power may be determined. For example, a force of 120 N at an angular speed of 3.00 rad/s (approximately 180 deg/s) represents a power of 360 W.

PART FOUR

Sociocultural and Psychological Foundations

CHAPTER 12

Sociocultural Context and Values in Sport

John C. Pooley

As an element of culture, sport tends to be treated less seriously when compared to music, the arts, and literature. This may be explained in both traditional and contemporary terms. Traditionally sport has two antecedents. One was the form used and refined by those higher classes in society who used it for leisure, a diversion from the more important things in life; the other was the use made of it by the lower classes as an antidote to unexciting lives made so by dull, repetitive work in foundries, factories, and farms. Today, although sport is now more talked about, watched, or read about, it continues to command a lower status than other cultural forms. This may be because, with some exceptions, sport is unenduring, although film records are now more often kept. It has not yet become an intellectual or philosophical concern of thinkers, writers, and scholars who could require, by their attention, that it be considered carefully and enjoyed more lastingly—even cherished as other forms are. Compared with the other cultural forms, sport may be discussed, even argued about, but not treated seriously. Few have recognized it as drama or examined the rituals present. Its lack of importance is emphasized in one sense by its relegation to the last pages of the daily paper and the last minutes of the news. With notable exceptions, its report and record are left to the less qualified journalists and writers. Its noteworthiness is measured in scores and statistics, spiced with reports of violence and unfair tactics, rather than quality of movement and measured skill. The study of physical skill, however manifested in academic settings, is still accorded less importance than other subjects. Sport's

long-standing connection with physical education, with its paramount symbolism of sweat and stink, retard its serious treatment. Social scientists in universities have generally ignored sport as an institution to be investigated or interpreted. It is still not as well understood as other institutions such as the family, education, religion, and the military.

Although sport is still struggling to find an important place in the culture, an increasing number of individuals consider sport to be very important to them and it is commanding an increasing amount of time and space in the media. At times such as the occasion of an Olympic Games, a very substantial proportion of populations observe and are absorbed by sport. This interest is likely to increase dramatically and intensify with the inclusion of video recordings of sporting events and performances in home video libraries. This advent will allow individuals to collect, enjoy, and be influenced by sport in much the same way as they would be by literature and music. Still, sport's history is only now being recorded and explained, its political significance analyzed, and its social and psychological importance investigated.

SOCIOCULTURAL STUDIES: THEIR GENESIS AND DEVELOPMENT

Until the 1950s, physical education, the forerunner of other health- and recreation-related studies, gradually became more accepted as an area of study in North American universities. It was heavily reliant upon the natural sciences such as anatomy and physiology to give it both substance and status. It was generally agreed that a healthy body resulted from one's involvement in physical activity. At that time, the most appropriate (if not the only) health professionals available—medical doctors—were appointed as directors or chairs of newly constituted physical education major programs in North American universities. Their presence resulted in the formation of curricula which stressed biology, chemistry, anatomy, and physiology from science faculties, and exercise physiology and kinesiology taught in departments of physical education. Even though a history of physical education course was usually included and foundations or principles courses subsequently introduced, the heavy emphasis on physical science (both basic and applied) complemented the emphasis on pedagogy, for most programs were designed to prepare physical education teachers for public schools.[1]

Since curricula in universities are slow to change, it is not surprising that newer subject areas like motor learning and sport psychology were slow to be accepted. These and other (at that time) less traditional subjects, however, were eventually introduced, particularly in the late 1950s and early 1960s. Applied natural and social sciences were joined by parent sciences like psychology and sociology, while the single history of physical education course had a "basic" history course as its forerunner. Later, philosophy and comparative physical education and sport courses joined sociology of sport or sociocultural sport and physical education courses, giving a more balanced and diverse program.

Sociocultural studies in sport and physical activity were introduced much later than natural science related courses like exercise physiology and kinesiology in physical education and recreation degree programs in North American universities. This occurred internationally also; for example, disparate socialist and capitalist cultures have generally highlighted physical science courses and have given much less or token attention to sociocultural studies—a bias which still prevails. Countries like the Soviet Union and the United Kingdom are examples. In spite of this, the importance of **sociocultural studies,** here defined as the study of human social behaviour in sport and physical activity settings/contexts, is now accepted. Specific titles of courses with a social-cultural emphasis which may be included in physical education and recreation major curricula are Sociology of Sport; Psychology of Sport; Psychology of Coaching; Sociopsychological Studies in Physical Education and Sport; Comparative Physical Education and Sport; History of Sport and Recreation; Philosophy of Sport and Physical Education; Sociology of Leisure; and Leisure Studies.

SOCIOLOGY OF SPORT

If sociology is the study of human social behaviour using the scientific method, sport sociology is the study of social behaviour in sport settings. Sociologists and sport sociologists may expand their range of analysis to include intercultural comparisons. Consequently, intercultural studies applied to sport (and expanded here to physical activity settings generally) imply an investigation of concepts such as competition and socialization in more than one society and more than one culture.

Accepting the uniqueness of individuals, sociologists seek to find social explanations for behaviours by examining groups, not individuals (whether in sport, religion, family, or education settings). For example, violence practiced in contact sport would be analyzed to determine underlying causes. These might include pressure on athletes to win games or administrators and coaches urging players to use physical and psychological abuse on opponents to nullify skill. The emphasis, however, is upon seeking answers by examining (questioning, interviewing, observing, testing) many cases rather than one or two cases (individuals or teams). People are social animals and one way to explain their interactions with others is to examine social settings. Although something may be learned about violence in sport by examining one case, usually much more can be learned by studying many cases. Usually a pattern will emerge to explain the causes of violence, from which the sociologist might state with confidence that under certain circumstances violence can be predicted. With further replication, perhaps under varying circumstances (professional and amateur, university and community, and for different sports), a theory might be offered which subsequently can be tested over time and refined if necessary. It is in this systematic, or scientific, study of sport groups that sport sociologists spend their time.

Sociology is a descriptive rather than a normative discipline.[2] That is, a sociologist describes what is, rather than what ought to be. Usually, sociologists—including sport sociologists—generate knowledge which is used by others. In the world of sport those using this knowledge include coaches, administrators, university and college teachers working in professional preparation institutes, parents, media personnel, and athletes. In a growing number of cases, however, sport sociologists have chosen to wear "two hats"; that is, they have found answers to problems and have added suggestions for what ought to be done. Whether they ought to fulfill both tasks is a controversial issue. Some social scientists argue that it is impossible to remain impartial (to maintain scientific rigour) if one is saying what ought to be as well as what is. Those who apply the knowledge they have gained from their research, as well as others, argue that the knowledge is applied by others to situations incorrectly or not at all and that they, the researchers, are in a better position to say what ought to be. This issue is unresolved. However, there is a danger that the results of studies can be biased in favour of what the researcher, wearing the second hat, believes ought to be. Researchers, influenced by expectation, may interpret the collected data in a way that would support their view of what ought to be.

SOCIOCULTURAL STUDIES IN CANADA

Sociocultural studies became a feature of university programs in physical education and sport sciences in Canada in the late 1960s. Graduate programs had appeared five to ten years earlier in American institutions; in fact, most of those who began to offer courses in the sociology of sport and sociocultural studies had, almost without exception, been graduates of American universities. The most common of these were several "Big Ten" universities, especially Illinois and Wisconsin, and the University of Massachusetts.

In Canada, several Ontario universities were prominent in offering courses leading to undergraduate and sometimes graduate degrees or had researchers active in the social science of sport. The most notable of these were Waterloo, Queen's, Windsor, and York. Several faculty at the University of Alberta were also active either in the teaching or researching of sport sociology. Finally, a number of universities widely dispersed in Canada have offered and continue to offer undergraduate and, in some instances, graduate programs which include sociocultural studies. A detailed account of the development of the sociology of sport as an academic discipline has been recorded by Loy, McPherson, and Kenyon (1977).[3]

DEFINITIONS OF MAJOR CONCEPTS

The major concepts which interest sociocultural scholars in sport and physical activity settings are play, games, physical activity, and sport. Contexts which provide the basis for study include ethnicity, race, society, culture, gender, religion, occupation, group, and education. Moreover, the sociocultural scholar seeks to understand the reasons for group and individual behaviour, whether conforming or deviant.

Play, Physical Activity, and Sport

Play is a relatively easy term to define; it is activity which is free, spontaneous, and has no measurable outcome. Play is engaged in merely because it is fun. When one is involved in a **game,** one has taken sides and plays against another person, team, or an object. An activity remains a game when the result is unimportant. This implies that one can engage in a game vigorously with great spirit but that the outcome is inconsequential or to be forgotten hours or even minutes after its conclusion. Play and games need not be physical activities.

Physical activity is a generic term including all human movement; **sport** is a term with many meanings, depending on its use. However, sport is physical activity but all physical activity is not sport. To explain further, sport has a narrower identity or meaning and usually implies a formal setting with rules, officials, and an established structure. Thus, a national or provincial sport governing body provides the basis for a physical activity to be called a sport.

For example, if a group of people, regardless of numbers, age, or sex, spend an hour on an ice surface passing a puck or even playing a pick-up game of hockey, they are engaged in *physical activity.* If, on the other hand, a group of players meets regularly to play hockey against another group, according to specific rules to which both groups have earlier agreed, and if officials are present to enforce those rules, the players are engaged in the *sport* of ice hockey. If the structure is even more formalized with the teams being part of a league, and if the league is sanctioned by a provincial association (or sport governing body), which itself is part of a collective body like Saskatchewan Sport or Sport Ontario, the sport has become more **institutionalized.** This means that it has become more formal, more complex structurally, and bound by more regulations.

To summarize, two or three children on a street shooting pucks or baskets are engaged in physical activity. The same children playing ice hockey in a rink or basketball in a gym with officials in attendance and scores being recorded are engaged in sport. It may be helpful to refer to chapter 2 and review more fully the concepts of play and sport.

Society, Culture, and Sociology

The term **society** is given to an association of persons united by a common set of objectives, principles, or interests. It may be applied in a narrow sense to link together a relatively small group of people who share an interest in a leisure activity or occupation, or it may link millions in a precise geographic location. For example, the Epimian Society is made up of members sharing a special interest in wine, whereas Canadians, most of whom reside in Canada, are members of a Canadian society. Both are social communities which endure as long as the values and principles which bonded them initially also endure. Nonetheless, principles, interests, and values change. They are dynamic; disintegration of a society will occur when the group is unable to agree on the changes.

Culture is the term applied to patterns of learned behaviour that distinguish a particular social group from other groups. These patterns of learned behaviour represent interests that may be material or nonmaterial. It is, therefore, appropriate to refer to two or more cultures within the same geographical or political boundary. For example, Inuit culture is in many ways different from the dominant culture which persists in the southern portion of Canada; both groups form part of a "Canadian mosaic" and are likely to call themselves Canadians. However, as in the United States, a large number of cultures based on ties such as ethnicity or religion may also prevail, each with its specific values, customs, or beliefs which provide identity and allegiance. In complex societies, people may be part of two or more cultures.

Sociology is the study of groups (a group being two or more) to identify persistent patterns of behaviour which prevail and departures from the pattern, to better understand the group being studied. Common rather than individual factors are sought, as are enduring explanations of the phenomenon under study.

Values, Norms, and Deviants

Values are opinions about desirable behaviours or actions. As might be expected, there are disagreements about values on both individual and societal levels. That is, the choice and the emphasis given to values will differ between individuals and societies. For example, one person may consider achievement to be important, another may consider this unimportant. Or, one may consider achievement as a value to be very important, while another considers it only slightly important. Similarly, different societies and cultures have selected (or more appropriately, practice) different values and have different hierarchies or rank orders for values. It is the societal choice and emphasis given to values which concerns sociologists.

It is important to remember that values do not evolve overnight but become established over time; they *develop* slowly as a product of economic, social, and historical conditions. They *change* just as slowly since an opinion about what is important can only be shaped after much reflection and by trial and error. Values influence our behaviour; in the formative years and beyond, we accept and practice a set of values. In general, we practice values which suit us (make us feel comfortable) in the society in which we find ourselves. We therefore conform to the society's values or **norms** (ways of doing things). If we depart radically from the value system prevalent in our society, we are **deviants** in it. Values are learned through social relationships which occur at home, in school, and in communities in which we live. These social relationships may be with parents, siblings (brothers and sisters), extended family members (aunts, uncles, grandparents), peers (school and playmates), or significant others (teachers, church leaders, coaches).

GOALS AND METHODS

Sport sociologists apply scientific principles and methods to their study of human behaviour in sport and physical activity settings. They study patterns of behaviour, devise theories regarding causes, and state, prove, or disprove hypotheses. For example, a coach might want to know which type of training schedule will result in the highest attendance by athletes at practices; a recreation director may need to know whether to offer single-sex or coed aerobic classes or both and how many of each. These questions can be answered systematically and quite accurately, provided care is taken to follow the rules of scientific investigation. There is nothing haphazard about behaviour; rather, it is relatively stable and predictable under given circumstances. For example, a volleyball or ice hockey team can be expected to behave in the same way in certain situations; the more similar these situations, the more they can be expected to behave in the same way. Training sessions which have a set pattern of activities and a corresponding set of expectations will result in similar responses from the squad. Similarly, game situations would bring similar responses. Only when something unusual occurs, outside the range of experiences of that squad, could a different response occur. Even then, for a squad which has been together on many occasions over several seasons and which has been prepared carefully for most exigencies, the response might be controlled and expected. We think of such teams or groups as predictable; if the response was unusual we would be surprised or shocked—it would be unexpected and therefore would seldom occur. Moreover, another team in the same sport, made up of individuals of the same age, sex, and social background with a similar training regime and millieu, is likely to respond in the same or a similar way to a given situation. The greater the similarity between the teams, the greater the similarity of their response to the situation.

Sociologists, and social scientists generally, rely on this high degree of predictability. In a variety of research endeavours, the sociologist finds answers to questions asked by coaches, recreation leaders, physical education teachers, and even government departments. How then is research conducted and what are the principles to which one must adhere? Before responding to these questions, it should be stated that whole books have been written on sociological research, even on each aspect of the research process. A recent useful monograph is that by David Whitson entitled "Research Methodology in Sport Sociology," published by the Canadian Association for Health, Physical Education, and Recreation in 1977.[4]

Research is based on theories or a series of propositions about social sciences. For example, if children fail in their sport experience they are likely to be unhappy. If persistently unhappy, they will likely discontinue their involvement. A sport sociologist may therefore wish to determine how failure occurs, how it is perceived, and how often it can occur before withdrawal from the activity. It may be that failure is the result of uneven or stressful competitive settings controlled by, on the one hand, a league structure and, on the other, a coach who selects players whose skill does not match the competitive situation. Depending on the age of the children, there may be too much stress on competition, irrespective of the skill of the whole team. Other factors related to coaching behaviour and the expectations of the players may help to explain withdrawal. The researcher reviews the theories available, matches one to the specific problem, and deduces a relationship between two or more concepts. It might be that an overemphasis on winning in sport by a coach leads to withdrawal, or that consistent team losses, especially when results are publicized, may result in players withdrawing from that team. These are hypotheses which can be tested; they are, in fact, predictions from particular situations.

Often, as in this case, there is no established theory, merely pieces of research which have been conducted which have shown an association between an overemphasis on winning and "dropping out." This means that a theory relating to withdrawal in sport is being developed. When a series of studies has shown a consistent association between concepts, a theory is evolving. If, when established theories are applied, the results are not consistent with the relationship predicted, a theory may be modified or changed. Science, whether natural or social, continues to evolve in this way.

As previously stated, hypotheses show relationships between two or more concepts (terms): for example, "sport" and "social mobility" or "sex difference" and "the intramural program." The direction of the hypothesis is based on previous research findings or an established theory. The researcher thus determines what data (or facts) are needed and how these data are to be collected.

Methods of Collecting Data

There are several methods of collecting data; each will be identified with a brief explanation. The **survey** using a questionnaire (short-answer form) is the most common method employed to collect data since a relatively large number of cases (individuals) can be questioned at the same time. Questionnaires can be administered over a short time period by interviewing over a telephone or face-to-face using the same questions for each respondent. Occasionally lengthy interviews are used, simply because more in-depth information is required. When conducting a survey, only a **sample** needs to be questioned. If this sample is created by choosing individuals within the whole group by using random numbers (therefore all individuals within the group have an equal chance of being selected), general assumptions can be made about the whole population from which the sample is taken. This is called **extrapolating.** Consequently, it is usually not necessary to sample (take into consideration) every person in the population if the whole population is large. If all the population members are surveyed, the investigation is termed a **census.** This method is used if the population is small.

Data can also be collected by **observation** using either **field observations** when, for example, observing the playing behaviours of children during street hockey games, or as a **participant observer** when the researcher actually joins in the activity, as in being a member of a training squad in field hockey. It is assumed, of course, that the researcher has a high enough skill level to join in without feeling or looking foolish.

A third method used by social scientists is making a **secondary analysis** of existing data (data already collected). This may occur in instances where the researcher is unhappy with the initial analysis or wishes to compare his or her own data with that previously collected. Secondary data analysis, however, usually occurs when a researcher makes use of data collected on a larger, perhaps national, scale. Large amounts of data are collected by government or provincial agencies, not all of which are used.

There are additional methods of conducting sociological or other research. Data may be reviewed from a variety of other research papers or books stored in libraries or after a literature search in information retrieval centres such as the one at the Coaching Association of Canada offices in Ottawa. Behaviours may be observed in a laboratory in which subjects are assigned tasks or given problems to solve in small groups. (This is the usual method of psychologists or motor learning specialists.) A **case study** approach may be used where a single individual (for example director of Sport Canada) or team (Montreal Canadiens) is asked a series of questions. More than one of the above methods may be used from which conclusions can be drawn. The case study method is generally regarded as weak in terms of extrapolating from the findings but it has to be used occasionally because of limited access to cases.

In applying one or more of these methods, the most common type of research is **cross-sectional;** representative sections of a population are sampled at the same time. The alternative is to undertake a **longitudinal** study where individual cases are systematically studied over a period of time, sometimes years.

SOCIAL THEORIES

Sport sociologists tend to adopt one of two different models which they use to explain the place of sport in society. One is the **structural-functional model,** the most dominant theory applied by Canadians such as McPherson and Kenyon and Americans Luschen and Loy. This theory relates sport to existing and established social roles and structural positions in society. Sport forms adapt to societal needs set in a modern industrial society. This implies a bureaucratically administered social order in a largely urban setting. Sport functions as an activity or series of activities which integrate people into the established mainstream of values and norms. That is, through one's involvement in sport as athlete, coach, official, administrator, or fan, one is socialized into accepting the set of values which dominates in society at that time. This learning is termed by some as a process of **enculturation.**[5] Moreover, it is understood that the values or norms are generally enduring. They change little and only very slowly over time. Sport and other forms of physical activity, such as physical education classes in schools or programs organized by YM/YWCAs or church groups, serve to form stable personalities and release tension and aggression in a controlled and therefore acceptable way.

The second model is called the **conflict** or **conflict-coercion model** which views sport as a means to change established practices in society. Change and conflict are viewed as basic features of society. For example, in instances where athletes may demand more power in the decision-making process or where fans react outside the normal bounds of acceptability, some sport sociologists view these behaviours as acceptable, unavoidable, and necessary. One way of differentiating between the two theories is that functionalists view these latter behaviours as mischievous or deviant, whereas those adopting a conflict model stance would consider them fundamental aspects of social life. Canadians Gruneau, Kidd, Cantelon, and Beamish would probably fit the general mould of those adopting the conflict model. Underlying the stances taken by these and other sport sociologists is a Marxist view of society which states that modern capitalist society is based upon class domination and motivated by economic conditions. The contrasting state has the masses in control with the presumed opportunity for individuality and change as an accepted mode of behaviour.

Social scientists, including sport sociologists, may grasp both theories from time to time. Typically the thinking might be that sport fulfills a functional need readily explained and understood, and generally acceptable in status quo maintenance. At the same time, issues such as athletes' challenge to the existing power base and fan violence can be used and legitimized on the ground that radical steps are a necessary way to bring about change to an equal distribution of resources.

SPORT REFLECTING SOCIETAL VALUES

As one might expect, the values in sport are, in general, a reflection of the values in society. This is logical. However, to say that values emphasized in sport shape the values in society seems much less clear. To some extent they may do so; to a large extent they are likely to have little or no impact since the larger society is more powerful and therefore more influential than any single one of the institutions within it.

We have already deduced that values evolve over time, are societally or culturally focused, and will vary according to setting. What then are the values which dominate Canadian society? Which of these are emphasized in sport settings? Is there evidence to suggest that values emphasized in sport affect values in the broader society?

Values in the capitalist society of Canada are dramatized in sport and the arts; therefore, sport and the arts reinforce or contribute to the values which prevail. It is reasonable, as presented by Kidd (1982), to believe that hockey represents the passion and the struggle of life in the Canadian winter.[6] Styles of playing the same sport, which mirror the values of different cultures, partly evolve in this way. That is, the Canadian style of ice hockey—which emphasizes physical strength and aggression, individual rather than team focus and acclaim, and physical courage—is different from Swedish or Soviet hockey. We are not discussing skill but the mode of play.

When discussing Canadian society and Canadian values it is important to understand that there are many cultural groups within Canadian society; these are divided between traditional and contemporary (or modern) cultural groups. Traditional cultural groups are those with a long history, the best known of which are the Indian and Inuit (Eskimo). Probably the most outstanding example of a more contemporary cultural group is that of the French Canadians (made up of subgroups such as Québecois and Acadians) which is distinguishable from the larger group of English-speaking Canadians in terms of norms, values, and mores as well as language. These differences have led to a more formal recognition of this group in Canadian society through acts of government.

Within the so-called English-speaking group (anglophones) are subgroups who have immigrated from many parts of Europe, the United Kingdom, South and Central America, the Caribbean, and Asia. Apart from those who bring with them the French language (immigrants from France and Haiti are examples), and who therefore join the francophone group, most align themselves with anglophones since this is the most dominant group in terms of language and influence. First generation immigrants are likely to continue speaking the language of their birth (German, Polish, Slovak, Italian, for example) but subsequent generations increasingly speak English as a consequence of influences in school, through the media (especially television), and from peer interaction.

This process, called **assimilation** into the larger or **core** society, may take more than one or two generations to complete. Nonetheless, separate cultural groups may still continue to maintain specific elements of their culture for several generations and in some instances, especially where a number of cultural groups favour the same activity or life-style, may influence the core society to accept, among other things, their behaviours or values.

If, for example, particular play, game, or sport forms are emphasized in these subcultures, the values which dominate within such settings are likely to play an important part in the establishment of values within the group as a whole, not just when practicing the activity. This is because the physical activity may, in fact, highlight the ethnicity. Soccer has served that purpose for Italians and Greeks, though it will have less impact the more the sport is accepted by the society as a whole—which is now occurring. Game forms germane to traditional societies, for example a number of unique Arctic Games "sports," will serve a similar purpose.

Factors such as the size of the subculture, the degree to which it merges with the larger core society, its subsequent degree of assimilation (how far it is absorbed into the core society), and both the type and form of specific sports which become merged with the core society will determine whether values are unique or not. Still, it is more likely that eventually the values of the dominant core society will influence the subcultural values practiced. One example is soccer. Since the core society is rapidly accepting this sport (measured in increasing numbers of second and third generation Canadians playing it), and since the ethnic identity of clubs is being slowly diffused, core society values are likely to be transmitted through the sport to the subculture. This will not occur in settings where tight ethnic enclaves inhibit acceptance of core society members; in other words, where, for example, a Greek soccer club prevents or discourages a core society member from joining it.

It can be seen that Canadian culture (identified for the sake of discussion as a core society culture) has been, is, and will be influenced to varying degrees by other traditional and contemporary subcultures within it. Play, game, and sport forms help to shape the values of the culture but are themselves practiced under the influence of the cultural (whether core or subcultural) values which pervade a host of social settings (home, work, church, leisure environments, and so on). As already suggested, Canadian values are affected by these forces and physical activity forms are shaped by the values which prevail more than they shape these values.

The discussion so far has used "core" society to refer to what may generally be termed English-speaking Canada, even though some groups will be inclined to use other languages by preference, especially in selected ethnic settings. However, this is only partially appropriate in a country which declares itself bilingual; French-speaking Canada represents a hefty minority. Figures for primarily French-speaking Canadians vary between 17 percent and 25 percent, even though French-speaking Canada mainly tends to be geographically confined to the province of Quebec and northern New Brunswick. Since, at present, only a small percentage of anglophones speak French, the unique cultural values found in Quebec and New Brunswick can only influence the rest of Canada when the following conditions are met. First, French language becomes more widespread; second, the larger core society willingly acknowledges that different but equal values exist in French-speaking areas; and third, that lines of communication are arranged between the two. The Canada Games, begun in 1969, which bring together young athletes every two years from each of the ten provinces and two territories, may aid in such communication. Other interprovincial competitions of many sorts and at different age levels also provide communication possibilities, although the amount of communication depends upon the structure provided and the efforts made by competition administrators, team managers, and coaches, rather than the athletes themselves. Athletes are naturally in an adversary role; if very little social interaction is planned between the teams and they are segregated totally or partially on the basis of accommodation and eating arrangements, sport settings might contribute more to intracultural or intrasocietal conflict than cooperation.

APPLYING SOCIAL THEORIES TO SPORT IN CANADA

As earlier defined, the functionalistic perspective can be applied to understanding the role of sport in Canadian society. This means that in considering the part played by sport in contributing to social order in Canada, many would agree that sport reinforces an already established hierarchy of roles and statuses which exist for members of the society. Individuals earn or are designated differential statuses in society; increased education and eventual occupational roles result in an individual's achievement of a high status within a group of friends, the larger community in which the individual is located, and in the society as a whole. Some individuals enjoy a high social status because of family position; they are born into a higher-status family and inherit its reputation. However, an individual's level of education and occupation largely dictate the position each holds in society.

Furthermore, this arrangement (or model) of societal members presumes that not everyone will be able or permitted to enjoy a high status. That is, scarce resources allow only a section of society to enjoy high status. This is known as the functional view of society.

To understand the role of sport in reinforcing the prevailing functionalism, sport's structure must be examined. This requires a consideration of sport programs in the school and community. Physical education classes are also important settings for studying the dynamics of this perspective.

With the foregoing in mind, it may be argued that, with little opportunity to do otherwise, individuals in Canadian sport and recreation settings fit into the established order of things. This begins at a young age when Canadians are directed to follow already set training regimes, organized and ordered by authority figures like the sport administrator, coach, or manager. There is little room for individual interpretation of game or sport forms. Aspiring athletes, whether elite in their age group or not, soon learn to accept the established order of "doing things" or withdraw from the activity altogether. From a broader perspective this means that inequality of opportunity exists, in terms of participation, use of existing facilities or equipment, and access to scarce resources such as skilled leaders. Furthermore, the central social value which permeates sport—achievement—dominates the way physical activity is organized and practiced, so that youth sport settings which are often established to provide equal chances for all who show interest usually become hierarchical in nature. Very quickly, more opportunities are provided for the skilled performer than the poor or average performer. For example, this has occurred in soccer, football, gymnastics, swimming, ice hockey, and basketball. It has occurred for boys as well as girls and it has happened and is continuing to happen in interschool sport as well as in community-based programs. Even in some elementary and secondary school physical education settings, equal opportunities are not provided for all. That is, the existing social value of achievement, carried over from the examined subjects in school and permeating sport generally, prevails to the point where some programs are highly competitive. Consequently, it is difficult or impossible for the average or poor performer to continue participating with the same opportunities as the more skillful performers.

This reinforces the notion that sport (as organized physical activity), games, and even more casual forms of interactions in physical activity (any kind of activity organized beyond the free, spontaneous actions in play) serve the function of perpetuating existing inequalities already in place in society. This is the rationale for arguing that sport fulfills a functional perspective.

The opposite theoretical stance, that of a conflict perspective (outlined earlier), can be argued less convincingly when applied to sport in Canada. In one sense, those experiencing inequality (e.g., less-skilled athletes when compared with their skilled counterparts; athletes compared to coaches; and female compared to male athletes) are many and varied. Certain identifiable groups in sport settings are exploited. There is little opportunity for mobility through sport, and the status quo in terms of order and control cannot and is not being changed. The conflict theorist therefore would argue that change is either impossible or scarcely possible—that being in conflict, so to speak, with the existing hierarchy does not work. This theorist would also argue that those attempting to change the status quo would be unsuccessful and in many cases would be ignored or outlawed. In reality, this means that innovative coaches, individual-minded athletes, and progressive sport bodies interacting in conservative environments must expect resistance to new ideas, especially if they are radical enough to require a change in control or a sharing of power.

In recent years, however, there is some evidence to suggest that some changes are being implemented in sport. For example, a growing number of sport governing bodies in Canada have now taken a more moderate stance with respect to imposing highly competitive sport models on children. This has occurred because knowledgeable, concerned experts responsible for technical programs have been successful in persuading sport administrators that highly structured competition imposed too early in a young athlete's life (under age ten or twelve, for example) not only "turns off" more potential athletes than it "turns on," but actually inhibits skill development. Young athletes drop out because the activity is less fun than they expected or no fun at all; consequently, they find other things to do. The quest to win as the driving force for participation stresses physical size as opposed to fitness and generally rewards product over process, which means that skill and its development (so essential in the early stages of learning a sport) are rewarded and encouraged less than victory, however achieved.

There is also some evidence to suggest that athletes are at least listened to. This is true both for professional athletes now earning proportionately higher salaries than ever before and for amateur athletes in some enlightened environments, who are being invited to share in choosing the type of training programs offered and in the selection of teams, for example. The certification program offered by the Coaching Association of Canada, certain sport governing bodies in Canada (particularly their technical arms), and the Canadian Council for Children and Youth have contributed to a more open policy for

Sociocultural Context and Values in Sport

sport, where the athlete's welfare and interest are considered more important than their ability to produce results. Nevertheless, victory-hungry parents continue to make ugly scenes on the sidelines and the pressure to win on coaches and players alike continues to dominate home and community interactions in the sport domain. Similarly, school and university coaches continue to be hired for their ability to achieve quick results rather than to facilitate players' ultimate satisfaction from playing to the best of their ability in an atmosphere of honest endeavour and good fellowship with teammates and the opposition.

In summary, the dominant perspective in Canadian and North American sport and physical activity is that it functions to reinforce existing social stability. Functionalism stresses equilibrium, not change, and it is this stance which is currently in effect. Sport modes are conservative. Where change does occur it almost always occurs slowly and with considerable resistance against the prime movers.

COMPARISON WITH OTHER SOCIETIES AND CULTURES

An important subarea of the sociocultural study of sport and physical activity is a comparison with other societies and cultures. Comparisons can be made between continents, countries, provinces or states, communities, or even schools or teams within a community.

Again, reference is made to traditional subcultures within Canada. These include the Inuit and Indian communities, often, though not only, found in the north, as well as contemporary enclaves of more recent origin such as Italian or Greek communities found in both urban and rural environments. Each group has its own values which may be the same as, or different from, those of the larger society. The more individuals' lives are circumscribed by social interactions largely confined to such a community, the more likely values are to be transmitted in a narrower context. This concept would hold for sport. Similarly, as indicated earlier, no study of Canadian sport and physical activity can be complete without acknowledging what Boileau, Landry, and Trempe (1976)[7] call the profound differences in the two principal ethnic groups in Canada. A second extended review of existing literature pertaining to ethnic sport in Canada is by Redmond (1980).[8] One of his tasks was to illustrate some of the ways in which sport contributes to ethnic diversity. This is shown by the fact that the form any given sport takes in one culture may be different from the form in another.

For example, the worldwide sport of soccer is played differently by Europeans and South Americans; the style of play is different, as is the use of physical aggression and verbal interchanges. South American soccer emphasizes refined techniques and short interpassing, while Europeans use a longer passing style and powerful tackling. It says much for the ability of officials when few games break down in anger or are beset by serious incidents, given such a contrast in approaches.

A sport may also be used or treated differently in the same broad culture group. Again using the example of soccer, the widespread growth of the sport in the United States and Canada, though popularized mainly by expatriate Europeans, has been modified for the North American "market."

Two examples will illustrate this point. Since tie games are much less acceptable in a culture which emphasizes the need for an outright winner, overtimes or "shoot-outs" (several players from each team try to score goals on an individual basis within prescribed limits) are often used. Games are locally divided into quarters (rather than halves which is the usual worldwide practice) and some coaching is permitted during play. Both strategies allow a greater role for the coach; neither of these are seen in other countries but have become part of soccer in North America to match the value attached to coaching. Of course, these approaches, or styles, are in a continuous state of flux, each contributing to the subcultural values in the sport as a whole.

Similar parallels could be drawn between the North American and Japanese styles of playing baseball, the former emphasizing individuality, emotional reaction, and an absence of allegiance to one club. The opposite occurs in Japan where teamwork, controlled behaviour, and loyalty are practiced, reflecting prevailing values in the overall culture.[9]

The more two countries play together, at any level from full international to youth teams at club level, the more likely it is that values will merge. Each will learn from the other, especially if competition is also accompanied by joint coaching courses and officiating clinics.

This now tends to occur in most sports where international competition occurs. A good example is the series of international ice hockey competitions held between socialist countries in Eastern Europe and Canadian and United States teams representing the capitalist West. There still remain unique differences in coaching styles and match play, for example, but players and coaches have undoubtedly learned from each other during the lengthening period of interaction.

Intrasocietal differences can be seen when comparing sport in Canada and the United States. The powerful United States continues to exert a major influence on its northern neighbor. This occurs specifically through media coverage of the major team sports in the United States on Canadian television and because many Canadian coaches and some players have been trained in the United States. It also occurs since many of the professional athletes in two of the high-exposure team sports in Canada, Canadian football and baseball, are Americans. A similar pattern exists in universities with a fair proportion of Americans on Canadian university basketball teams. While ice hockey players from Canada still dominate United States teams in the National Hockey League and university leagues, thereby redressing the balance somewhat, this influence is expected to change as more Americans improve enough to join the university and professional teams.

Clumpner and Smith (1983)[10] drew attention to the "conspicuous differences" between high school interscholastic programs in the same sport in Canada and the United States. The strength of national values is highlighted by this study in view of the adjacent geographical area selected: the province of Alberta and the state of Washington. This should not be surprising since Chandler (1981)[11] found intranational differences in emphasis and focus of physical education and games programs in Canadian private schools. Similarily, Fiander (1981)[12] found marked differences in opportunities for and involvement in intramural and interscholastic sports within the same Canadian province, as a function of size and location (urban or rural). Earlier, Macintosh and King (1976)[13] also found variations of the proportion of students involved in interscholastic sport in Ontario.

Intersocietal differences in sport and physical activity are not confined to type of activity. Nor are they restricted to elite sport comparisons. Patterns of emphasis are established in school physical education programs. For example, Vertinsky and Cuthbert (1984)[14] compared teaching preferences of physical educators in Canada and Britain. They concluded that Canadian physical educators placed emphasis upon fitness and the development of skills for future life-styles, while British teachers attached more importance to fun and the promotion of team spirit as major physical education goals.

We can therefore acknowledge a variety of intercultural differences in patterns of sport and physical activity. As Sutton-Smith and Roberts (1970)[15] concluded from their study of game preferences across many cultures, dimensions such as physical skill, strategy, and chance are associated with different types of cultures, with all three dimensions being relevant only to modern industrial societies.

Consequently, cross-cultural and cross-societal studies are important in understanding more about our own national variations, their antecedents, and current foci. Comparative studies allow us to see our own emphases in clearer perspective and we are therefore in a much better position to assess whether suggested changes would enhance or detract from the development of sport and physical activity in Canada. Moreover, they indicate patterns supported cross-nationally which lend evidence to our own sport delivery systems.

SUMMARY

In this, the first of two chapters devoted to sociocultural studies with a Canadian perspective, an overview of sport as an aspect of culture is followed by a brief discussion of the way sociocultural studies were introduced to North American universities generally, and Canadian universities in particular. Goals and methods of sport sociologists are outlined. An introductory treatment of the two theories generally used to help explain sport and physical activity in society, namely the functional and conflict perspectives, is presented. These theories are applied to Canada. The chapter concludes with some comparisons being made between cultures and societies and a rationale for such studies.

NOTES

1. Reet Howell, "The Socio-Cultural Area in the Study of Physical Education," *Gymnasion* 12(2) (Summer 1975):16–19.

2. William F. Kenkel and Ellen Voland, *Society in Action* (San Francisco: Caufield Press, 1975), 10.

3. John W. Loy, Barry D. McPherson, and Gerald S. Kenyon, *The Sociology of Sport as an Academic Specialty: An Episodal Essay on the Development and Emergence of a Hybrid Subfield in North America* (Ottawa: CAHPER, 1977).

4. David J. Whitson, *Research Methodology in Sport Sociology* (Ottawa: CAHPER, 1977).

5. Walter E. Schafer, "Sport, Socialization and the School: Toward Maturity or Enculturation" (Paper presented at the Third International Symposium on the Sociology of Sport, Waterloo, Ontario, 1971).

6. Bruce Kidd, "Sport, Dependency and the Canadian State," in *Sport, Culture and the Modern State,* ed. Hart Cantelon and Richard Gruneau (Toronto: University of Toronto Press, 1982), 284.

7. Roger Boileau, Fernand Landry, and Yves Trempe, "Les Canadiens Francais et les Grands Jeux Internationaux," in *Canadian Sport: Sociological Perspectives,* Richard Gruneau and John G. Albinson (Don Mills, Ontario: Addison-Wesley, 1976), 141–69.

8. Gerald Redmond, *Sport and Ethnic Groups in Canada* (Ottawa: CAHPER, 1980).

9. James Boersema, "Baseball: Oriental Style," *Soldiers* 34, (June 1979): 28–31. See also Eldon E. Snyder and Elmer A. Spreitzer, *Social Aspects of Sport* (Englewood Cliffs, NJ: Prentice-Hall, 1983), especially pp. 53–56.

10. Roy Clumpner and Gary J. Smith, "Interscholastic Football: Comparisons in Program Administration Between Canada and the United States" (Proceedings of the FISU Conference Universiade '83, University of Alberta, Edmonton, Alberta, 1983), 708–18.

11. Timothy Chandler, "Physical Education and Games in Private Schools: A Comparative Analysis" (M.Sc. thesis, Dalhousie University, Halifax, Nova Scotia, 1981).

12. Paul R. Fiander, "The Role of Extracurricular Activities in Public Senior High Schools in Nova Scotia as Perceived by the Principal" (M.Ed. thesis, The Atlantic Institute of Education, Halifax, Nova Scotia, 1981).

13. Don Macintosh and A. J. C. King, "The Role of interschool Sports Program in Ontario Secondary Schools: A Provincial Analysis," Ontario: Ministry of Education, 1976.

14. P. Vertinsky and J. Cuthbert, "Profiles of Physical Education Strategies: A Cross-national Comparison of English and Canadian Teachers," in *International Review of Sport Sociology,* 1984.

15. Brian Sutton-Smith and John Roberts, "The Cross-cultural Psychological Study of Games," in *The Cross-cultural Analysis of Sport and Games,* ed. Gunther Luschen (Champaign, IL: Stipes, 1970).

CHAPTER 13

Socialization Into, Via, and Out of Physical Activity and Sport

John C. Pooley

At the moment of birth, we have everything to learn about ourselves, our family, and society in general. We learn through our sensory systems by seeing, hearing, touching, and so on. We also learn from people with whom we come into contact; our parents first, then siblings, members of our extended family, our peers, our teachers, and religious leaders. We also learn from the media, especially television. The host of experiences with which we are bombarded influences our behaviour depending upon our values and their relation to the values dominant in the millieu around us.

All those with whom we are in contact are models to be observed and copied. This is true of our parents as well as our best friend; it holds for the sport or folk hero we admire and the television character we enjoy. Through them and our imitation of their characteristics, we learn ways of doing things and thereby values, prejudices, and norms. What we learn (that is, what we internalize and repeat), as well as what we discard, is mediated by a series of rewards and punishments. This way of learning about the world around us both formally, by instruction, and informally, by observation and imitation, is called **socialization.** The process of socialization is most vigorous during our preadult years for at that time we are moulding and stabilizing a personality, although it may be modified subsequently.

Socialization also occurs through our involvement in physical activity, whether playing alone, in spontaneous simple games with peers, or in more formal settings in which motor skills are practiced in schools of the community, often in the presence of adults. We are both socialized *by* these experiences, through our interactions with fellow players or those subordinate to the activity such as coaches, officials, and administrators, and *into* the activity in the first place. That is, we find it attractive enough to want to learn a motor skill (or improve the skills we have) or join a group of others practicing the same skill. In some cases, the practice of physical activity becomes unappealing, either because our interests change or because the environment is not what we expected. Consequently, we withdraw from it.

THE PROCESS OF SOCIALIZATION: ITS RELATION TO SPORT AND PHYSICAL ACTIVITY

We have learned that values are generally acceptable ideals that form the basis for actions and that these are learned in a wide variety of situations, of which the sport setting is one. It follows that the more time young people spend in sport, the greater chance that the values learned will have an impact strong enough to affect an individual's behaviour in situations other than in sport. For example, for a young swimmer or figure skater who, for several years from age seven, spends two to four hours each weekday training, values such as hard work and personal discipline might well be applied to their school work or home behaviours more than by peers who have not had the same or similar experience. This is by no means automatic, but it is logical that the many hours of experience which some young Canadians have in sport will have more than a fleeting impact upon them. Furthermore, in instances where the extent and intensity of the experience is equal to or greater than other experiences in the home, school, or community, values learned or emphasized in sport will more likely persist.

Socialization is used as a means, therefore, to prepare the young to be desirable members of society as prescribed by the value set (the range of values which can readily be identified in the society such as achievement, commitment to hard work, and delayed rewards). There is an assumption that an entire population ought to accept these and other values as desirable, but this is not so. It is too idealistic, for within the Canadian core society (that is, the prevailing major cultural group of anglophones) there is some disagreement about the actual values which ought to dominate as well as the emphasis placed on each of them. This is related to people's religious and political convictions; for example, New Democratic Party (NDP) affiliates might have very different opinions about the degree of emphasis on competition, compared with Liberal and Conservative party members. Moreover, we have acknowledged in the previous chapter that Canadian society is made up of a number of different traditional and cultural groups. This is called **cultural pluralism,** a term also applied to the United States society. Consequently, although a broad set of values can be identified, one must not expect unanimity either in type or importance given to each.

Often, without conscious thought being given to the process, sport and physical activity experiences are used to socialize young people. Adults in the capacity of sport leaders, specifically as coaches, physical education teachers, managers, administrators, and officials, inculcate in the young the values which they practice or believe are desirable. They do this without necessarily understanding what these values are (they may not be able to articulate or understand which values they are practicing) or that the form the values take in their lives (level of consciousness and action) may be unsuitable or undesirable for a young boy or girl. For example, the hard work imposed on a group of swimmers or gymnasts for extended periods, or a strong competitive emphasis (which some coaches may not recognize), may often be unreasonable for a child of ten. Often these values (which is what they are) are handed down from adult to child with unexpected consequences. The most effective teaching may be unintended and subliminal.[1]

The socialization process is, therefore, a process of interaction between the socializee (person being socialized) and the socializer (person influencing the socializee). Generally, the socializer is either older or has a more dominant personality than the socializee, hence the influence will be in the direction stated. An example would be a coach as the socializer and an athlete as socializee. In some instances, however, where perhaps a young inexperienced coach is interacting in a training session with an experienced mature athlete, roles may be reversed with the flow of influence being from athlete to coach. This occurs infrequently. Furthermore, much socialization occurs in groups (within teams for example), with the more senior athletes influencing the juniors or "rookies."

Inappropriately socialized leaders in the sport domain will presumably consistently socialize athletes inappropriately. This may happen in instances where coaches are allowed to practice without attending any coaching course and thereby not receiving information about relevant values and emphases appropriate for young people.

Socialization Into, Via, and Out of Physical Activity and Sport   **289**

It must also be acknowledged that within the cultural mosaic of Canada, sport leaders representing different ethnic groups may emphasize different values—a situation which is fraught with possibilities for tension and division as well as unification and cohesion. For example, a coach who is a British immigrant may appear to be more interested in his or her athletes playing fair than playing to win, which might appear odd to some other immigrants or long-standing members of the core society. As Redmond (1980) said in one of his concluding remarks in a monograph on ethnic sport in Canada, "It is important to recognize the status of sport as a significant cultural factor when the ethnicity of a multicultural society is studied; a factor which reflects both its advantages and disadvantages, as well as its opportunities and problems."[2] Later he pointed out that sport can be unifying or divisive; it can bind diverse cultural groups together or drive them apart.[3]

What has been discussed is the application of an **interactionist perspective** to our understanding of socialization. Interaction is the pattern of contact, communication, or influence between individuals.[4] In this theoretical stance is embodied a social-learning orientation made popular by Bandura and Walters (1963).[5] Social learning takes place by the imitation of **significant others** found in one or more of the social systems identified.

Much of the learning of sport roles occurs during childhood and adolescence. However, before considering which values might be emphasized under the umbrella of socialization via sport, we must first consider how, when, and where socialization into sport and physical activity occurs.

SOCIALIZATION INTO PHYSICAL ACTIVITY AND SPORT

In a variety of ways, young children are socialized into physical activities—for example, by being encouraged to play with balls and other implements, and to run, jump, and throw by observing older brothers and sisters or neighbourhood peers. To varying degrees, parents encourage their offspring to become active in play by introducing simple physical activities, and by purchasing sporting equipment on festive occasions and birthdays. Even from a very young age, however, there is a tendency for adults to be sexually selective; boys are given sporting equipment and girls receive traditional female artifacts like dolls.[6] Girls are encouraged to skip and dance, boys to play hockey or basketball. Boys of European families might be given soccer balls. Young children's first introduction into lead-up activities associated with established sports also reflects locally popular youth sport programs. For example, if there are rinks and pools available and sport clubs centred upon hockey, figure skating, and swimming, children will be encouraged to try these sports in a modified way. Since some sports are selective on the basis of social class as well as sex, an observer should expect to see children of middle-class parents encouraged to swim, figure skate, and jog (as a prelude to running). This is because in Canada and elsewhere in Western culture, sport is not democratized.[7] Although some sports like football, ice hockey, basketball, field hockey, and soccer are played by children from families with various social-class backgrounds, other sports such as swimming, figure skating, jogging, sailing, and skiing (downhill and cross-country) attract children (and adults) from middle-class backgrounds.

Implicit in the discussion so far is an assumption that children are encouraged to participate in physical activities and sport as contestant, performer, or athlete. This has been termed **primary involvement** by Kenyon (1969).[8] However, there are numerous other roles in sport in which the young involve themselves; these are initially roles of consumer (as observer, listener, reader, or discussant), and eventually roles of coach (or teacher), administrator, and official, however modest and informal these roles may be. The latter are termed **secondary roles** in sport.[9] Although the young are often avid consumers of sport, provided they are also primarily involved, few appear to be socialized into coaching, administrative, and officiating roles, although it might be argued that they quite easily could be. Either informally, in home and community involvements (sand lots and parks), or more formally through physical education classes and in sport clubs, young people from an early age could be introduced to these "other" roles. They rarely are, although it is likely the young people and the sports represented would be richer if longer apprenticeships were served in these secondary roles.

Perhaps the first researcher to examine the degree and mode of involvement in sport roles in cross-national perspective was Kenyon (1968).[10] Collecting data from secondary school students from Canada, Australia, England, and the United States, he found more similarities than differences in the way young people are socialized into and through sport across national boundaries. He also found that there was a close relationship between primary and secondary involvement. For example, young people heavily involved in sport as athletes are also avid consumers of sport. There is, however, little evidence to determine the degree to which young people are socialized into the sport roles of teacher (or coach) and official. An exception is a study completed by Pooley (1979)[11] of physical education students from several countries, including Canada, who demonstrated that during their youth, they had some teaching and officiating experiences, usually arranged through the school system. Nevertheless, it must be emphasized that this was a select group of young people, presumably highly motivated to become involved in such roles, given their choice of physical education as a major at college or university.

As indicated earlier, the application of social learning theory to our understanding of socialization seems logical and reasonable. Associated with one's choice to become involved in sport is the notion of role theory where the individual is a social actor ready to try out and eventually accept roles relating to sport.[12] In so doing, a child imitates significant others as they act out roles in sport, principally and initially as athlete, and eventually, though apparently only in the minority, as coach, administrator, and official. Naturally, there are a range of behaviours associated with each role, some normative, some deviant. Consequently, the subsequent role performance of each athlete will depend upon the behaviour of role models. These may be at close quarters (for example, parents, siblings, peers, and coaches) or more distant models such as university or professional athletes observed firsthand or viewed on television. Through this process, which is complex and many-faceted, aspiring athletes (or role performers) are drawn into practicing sports. Through reinforcement and repetition of their behaviours they become athletes themselves.

The complexity of being socialized into play, games, and sport has been carefully outlined by Loy and Ingham (1973).[13] It is important to note that there are significant cultural, subcultural, and situational variations present and that role incumbents bring a range of personal attributes with them as they become involved in sport. As Kenyon and McPherson put it, they possess knowledge, skills, and dispositions which characterize the role in question.[14]

Following early influences from home environments, the school, first through physical education classes and then through intramural and interschool opportunities, is a powerful setting for socializing youth into sport and physical activities. This is closely followed by community agencies such as sport clubs, though the existence of community-based playgrounds and some freely accessible indoor facilities sometimes contributes to an involvement without adult intervention. This latter type of opportunity would appear to be less available to the young. Complex societies provide fewer opportunities for free and spontaneous play on the assumption that adult sport leaders are better for the young, and facilities cost money for which only adults can pay the rent—a state of affairs heavily criticized by Devereaux (1976).[15] He has argued strongly against diminished opportunities for child-centred play, games, and sport.

Typically in Canada, young people are socialized into sport which is characterized by increasing formalization and institutionalization. For example, Podilchak (1983)[16] has shown how the development of youth soccer in Canada (using Calgary, Alberta as a case study) has occurred in the past fifteen years. He identified four levels of organization control: community house league; city competition; provincial play-offs; and national sport governing body interprovincial competition. These span six two-year levels from ages seven to eighteen. Such a hierarchy of competition can be expected in cultures or nations which reward achievement. A less structured series of opportunities linked to competitions, or no competition at all, may be expected in cultures or nations valuing participation. Or, to put this another way, several levels of opportunity and a diminished emphasis on achievement are to be expected in cultures which are oriented to participation or where the *process* of involvement in sport rather than the *product* is more highly valued. For example, the existence of several teams in each age category in many high schools in Australia and New Zealand suggests an emphasis on participation, whereas American and Canadian high schools, which feature one team in each age category or one team in a given sport in the entire school, would seem to emphasize achievement. Furthermore, traditional societies such as the Inuit in Canada or the Aboriginals in Australia emphasize participation rather than achievement in sport, reflecting the cultural value of cooperation rather than competition.[17]

Few researchers appear to have concentrated their research on socialization into sport roles. Those who have collected data in this area have asked questions of either already established elite performers such as Olympic aspirants,[18] college players,[19] or young male ice hockey players in Canada.[20] Evidence suggests individuals are socialized at a young age (probably about age eight or nine); are successful from an early stage; try a variety of sports before concentrating on one; and are given positive reinforcement by significant others—especially fathers, peers, and coaches. Socialization is also mediated by a series of other variables such as social class, sex, birth order, and geographic location, one or more of which may account for the time, type, and intensity of socialization into sport.[21] Secondary involvement, especially in the role of sport consumer, appears to occur at the same age as primary involvement; varies between the sexes with boys more involved than girls; and is greatly influenced by the mass media.[22] The process appears to follow a similar pattern in other countries such as Finland and Britain, as reported by Andrews (1979),[23] and in Australia and South Africa, as shown by Pooley (1979).[24] Finally, the type of school (state or private) may have an impact upon the range of sport involvement, as well as upon the type of sport played. For example, in his study of Canadian private schools for boys, Chandler (1981)[25] reported that traditional British sports such as rugby, soccer, rowing, and even cricket were offered to all, and there appeared to be less specialization than in Canadian state schools.

In summary, children are encouraged to become involved in physical activity from a very young age. In doing so, they become part of one or more sport and physical education social systems. These social systems are the family, school, peer group, and local sport organizations, all of which form a network to influence young people to become involved as participants or consumers of sport and physical activity. In explaining this process, the interactionist perspective has been used. This encompasses a variety of insights and propositions about individuals, groups, and social relationships.[26] The application of role theory accounts for the learning of sport roles by exposing the role aspirant to a variety of reinforcements provided by significant others.[27]

SOCIALIZATION VIA PHYSICAL ACTIVITY AND SPORT

Having been socialized into physical activity or sport, a second dimension of the socialization process is activated, namely socialization via, or as the result of, experience in play, games, and sport.[28] The young are exposed to the values which prevail in various settings, and mediated by personal characteristics they bring with them, learn about and practice these values. This is partly dependent upon the characteristics of the activity (formal or informal, team or individual activity, adult- or peer-directed)[29] and the cultural context in which the activity is practiced.

Play, games, and sports each offer different opportunities for socialization.[30] For example, play has an important role in early childhood socialization in family environments, or in simple dyads when two children either as siblings, cousins, or neighbourhood friends play together. Somewhat larger peer groups become the focus of activities as games are played by preadolescents and thereby the setting is more complex and the process more formalized. Subsequently, during adolescence, sport provides opportunities for values to be learned, usually more directly from adults either in educational institutions in physical education classes, intramurals, or interschool competitons, or in the community through formalized youth sports programs organized by adults.

These stages are influenced by local factors so that the impact of each type of activity may vary for each child. For example, some children may be forced into a larger group from a very young age, and introduced to more structured games. Alternatively, the opposite may happen. Still others may be enrolled in a series of formal sport clubs when quite young and then directed by adults toward early competition, perhaps before age nine or ten. The kind and type of values learned are mediated by the values in the culture when the child matures and the presence of adults, coupled with the type of values they espouse. Since each sport has its own subcultural values which may be different in some respects from the values in other sports, what children learn may vary from sport to sport.

After early experiences playing alone and then in dyads and small groups, many children in Canada have an abbreviated experience in games where, left to themselves, they would learn to be leaders and followers, or organizers and creators of new games. In such circumstances they would learn to be capable of modifying activities to suit available conditions with respect to equipment, facilities, and numbers present on any one occasion. Although such circumstances exist (sometimes throughout physical education classes in schools), during adolescence and later, many children are denied opportunities to learn from such experiences because they are organized into formal sport groups from a young age in swimming or gymnastics, or in teams as in ice hockey, basketball, and soccer. From ages seven to ten, they are taken by parents to sport clubs to the extent that for many children physical activity becomes adult-directed at a time when children might benefit from being left alone to learn skills and values referred to earlier. In short, they miss playing games which *they* direct. Often, their sport experiences become increasingly more structured and oriented toward achievement, with fun and enjoyment less important than winning.

The system of youth sport is, to varying degrees, exclusive on the basis of ability; better players are encouraged, poorer players are discouraged. This practice tends to favour early-maturing children, since they are bigger and stronger and may be better coordinated than their peers of the same chronological age.[31]

The importance of success, soon established in many sport clubs as a central value to which youngsters must strive, may be functional or dysfunctional in terms of the values learned by being involved in such programs. Whereas achievement is a worthy value because it usually requires other positive values such as discipline, hard work, selflessness, and dedication (thereby emphasizing sport's functional potential), it also may lead to dysfunction when winning becomes so paramount that poor sportsmanship, cheating, and arrogance are displayed and internalized. It must also be understood that such "noble" values as hard work and dedication can, if taken to extremes, lead to early withdrawal from the sport. For example, one of the purposes of learning a motor skill is to provide lasting pleasure so that the skill can be practiced into adulthood and become part of the individual's life-style.

In an environment which stresses too much commitment and too many hours of training, with its possible consequent withdrawal from the sport at an early age, the anticipated lasting benefit from learning the skill in the first place will have been lost. It is well known that too much emphasis on the need to win, and the time-consuming and arduous training required to ensure it, may be expected to lead to early withdrawal from the activity, especially for those who are unsuccessful—that is, are not "winners."[32] Since only a few are winners and the majority are losers, the current model for youth sport in Canada and the United States (as well as other countries) is not necessarily the most desirable since the principal aim, and in practice sometimes the only one, is to produce a winner.

A HIGHLY COMPETITIVE MODEL FOR YOUTH SPORTS

Portions of this section are taken from research done by Pooley (1986).[33] We may assume that many believe the present competitive structure which prevails in some countries (that is, a highly selective process based upon innate skill, intensive pressure coaching from a young age, an emphasis upon achievement manifested in interindividual or intergroup competition, and a high rate of attrition) is desirable. Unquestionably, this model prevails in North America.

Results are that (1) average or moderate performers are discriminated against; since their performance is given negative reinforcement, skilled leadership is denied them and facilities become unavailable; (2) too much early pressure in training or competition for the skilled leads to "burnout" and subsequent withdrawal or early dropout; and (3) skill development is inhibited, since the pressure to win takes precedence over the development of techniques and subsequent skill in a logical progression.[34]

Each of these outcomes of the highly competitive sport model could be explored more fully if space permitted, although a good deal of empirical research still needs to be done. It is probable that the relationship of stress to competitive settings has aroused the most interest, with research by Scanlan and Passar (1978), Watson (1977), and Hendry and Thorpe (1977) as examples.[35] There is, however, an increasing concern about youthful competition, typified by Leonard Koppett (1981),[36] a sports reporter of the New York Times who said,

> over-organized games have at least *four* harmful effects on children:
> 1. They make competitive results too important too early . . .
> 2. They segregate children by athletic ability, socially as well as in the make-up of teams, at an age when such classification is undesirable and unfair . . .

3. They rob the children involved of the opportunity to learn to do things themselves . . .
4. They entice some children into physical actions that are bad for growing bodies . . .

As Koppett concludes, "Organized competitive sports for the young turn off more than they turn on."

ALTERNATIVES TO THE HIGHLY COMPETITIVE MODEL

There would appear to be valid alternatives to the prevailing North American model of highly competitive youth sport. These take into account theories of skill acquisition, socialization, and growth and development; empirical studies relating to cross-national settings; the importance of culture-specific sport; and pragmatic considerations. Only a few examples will be cited here.

In the Federal Republic of Germany, interschool competition has been stimulated by the *Jugend trainert fur Olympia* (Youth Training for Olympics), begun in 1969, and the *Bundesjugend-Spiele* (Federal Youth Games) which are held twice each year. Both are broadly based programs where "specialization with emphasis on achievement in sport contests is uncommon." It is left to the elaborate system of sport clubs to develop competitive sport.[37]

Elsewhere, researchers in Australia found that when analyzing juniors in an adult-rules cricket game, players whose batting technique was less developed were found to (1) bat less often, (2) bat less time in each inning, (3) occupy lower-order positions, (4) have less of the strike (face fewer balls), and (5) score fewer runs.[38] The authors recommended modifications "in order to provide equitable involvement." The other techniques of bowling and fielding were treated in the same way; again, implications were that modifications were recommended. A trial modified game was played, following which comparisons were made with the adult game. Results showed that the "team score in the modified game was higher by 50 runs than the average team score in a normal game" and "the team generally had almost double the catching and throwing opportunities in the modified game, while fielding opportunities varied only marginally."[39]

The authors concluded that not only did the modified game generate more opportunities for each player to practice the techniques of bowling and fielding, but run-scoring opportunities were greater. As shown in this study, "the introduction of modified rules clearly created the opportunity for more players to be involved in all aspects of the game."[40] In 1984, encouraged by the positive responses to the modified game, the Australian Cricket Board instituted Kanga Cricket as a game suitable for children aged eight through twelve.[41] Similarly, an earlier study by Gibson (1977)[42] of boys aged ten to thirteen years who participated in Junior Australian Rules Football showed that one-third of the players did not get an opportunity to develop their skills during adult-style games and that the games were dominated by only 10 percent of players in each skill area. He also found there was no system or pattern in the play and that packs continually formed around the ball, with physical size determining participation. The author concluded that this led to deteriorating skill levels and a decrease in players' level of interest (supported by motivation scores collected during the season) and ultimately to attrition. The author put forth two models for the development of under-ten and under-fourteen football.[43]

These studies are very important since they provide empirical evidence for the efficacy of modified conditions in major team sports. The methodology needs to be replicated with different age groups and different sports in different countries. If possible, a longitudinal study ought to be initiated to compare the consequences of modified approaches in team games with the "adult approach" under a variety of disparate conditions.

Australians have recognized the importance of the modified games approach to sport for children. A report prepared for the Division of Recreation in Tasmania and the Tasmanian State Schools Sports Council by Gillian Winter in 1980 centres upon modified approaches to sport for Australian children. The report also presents a series of guidelines to assist organizations concerned with the process of modifying major games. It should be noted that modified approaches are also being incorporated in the sport of netball,[44] and for a number of years "Little Athletics" (meaning track and field in North American language) and modified rugby have been widely practiced. A study undertaken by Martens et al. (1984)[45] in the United States sought to determine the effect of having an adult pitch to nine- and ten-year-olds in baseball. Results of this nontraditional approach showed that players were more active both offensively and defensively. They concluded that this modified approach was more advantageous to the individual's skill development.

Finally, a strategy to reduce competitiveness in sports for youth in Canada, with special reference to soccer, was advocated in 1978.[46] It met with considerable interest and sympathy by those who administered youth soccer. Increasing support for mini soccer occurred and there was a de-escalation of interprovincial play for the younger age groups.

LESSONS TO BE LEARNED FROM THOSE CONTINUING TO PRACTICE SPORT

It may be worth considering why people age forty-five and above continue to take part in regular physical activity when most of their peers dropped out much earlier.[47] It is likely that those in exercise programs such as running, swimming, cycling, skating, and skiing have responded to the health-related publicity which is widely used. However, those continuing to be involved much later in life in culturally traditional competitive sports such as soccer, basketball, tennis, and field hockey probably do so because their main motivation at a younger age was intrinsic rather than extrinsic. Although interested in becoming fit or retaining a level of fitness, many are motivated by the feel of the ball, the pass well made, the sweetness of the stroke, or the power in the shot rather than whether they won or lost the game.

Many who direct youth sport, either as coaches or administrators, are products of a highly competitive youth system and know of no other from which to draw when leading the present generation. Therefore, the cycle is likely to continue unless more evidence is made available to point out the shortcomings in the competitive model and until much greater care is taken when selecting future leaders.

The future does look more promising, however, as some sport administrators and coaches are beginning to apply principles of growth and development to models of sport development. In Canada, for example, the sport governing bodies of basketball and volleyball are now setting in motion plans for appropriate sport experiences according to age and ability. Each model de-emphasizes early competition, extrinsic rewards, and the "adult" form of the sport. By contrast, these sports are emphasizing the development of fundamental skills in an atmosphere of fun, incorporating peer officiating, early success, small-sided teams, and good sportsmanship.[48]

THE CAPACITY OF SPORT TO MIRROR POSITIVE OR NEGATIVE VALUES IN SOCIETY

Great faith is lodged in the ability of games and sports environments to establish desirable conduct in the young which will be expressed in other areas of their lives and become entrenched enough to be carried into adulthood. Physical education classes have long been considered a powerful medium for the teaching of moral standards, while youth sport programs have been regarded as rich in potential for the transmission of positive values from one generation to the next. In fact, sport became a feature of institutional life in schools and universities and within youth club or church club settings because of its potential to enrich human life by defining and perpetuating qualities such as fair play, honesty, losing graciously, and winning without arrogance. There is some agreement that these qualities can be developed in the sport environment.[49] Certainly, developing moral and social values is frequently cited as a worthy objective of interscholastic and intramural programs internationally.[50] As Duthie (1983) said, "those of us who live in a technological society rely on games heavily for they teach us how to behave and how to respond. We not only reward those seen to be highly successful . . . but admire and value the ways in which these individuals achieve their goals."[51]

Examples from "successful" sport programs can be used to demonstrate sport's potential. Some athletes speak of the tremendous respect they have for their coach for teaching them to play with courage and conviction (positive attributes in our society) and to play honestly and enthusiastically. Although victory is sweet, to have performed to the best of one's capabilities is a value felt to have its origins in sport settings. To play fairly, a characteristic which enobles any sporting endeavour, is often taught in school physical education classes, and some coaches emphasize this behaviour.

The Canadian Council on Children and Youth has recently endorsed fair play codes which, though designed to remind all connected with youth sport that young people are not to be exploited for personal gain, also reemphasize the potential sport has for inculcating desirable values in society.[52] Similarly, the National Association for Sport and Physical Education in the United States drew up a Bill of Rights for Young Athletes[53] which reminded controlling bodies of sport's potential as well as their responsibilities. There are also those who feel that competitive sport is pure[54] or has an idyllic image even at the professional level and suggest we do "not queston [its] positive value to society and the nation."[55] Rather, they argue, it is the entrepreneurs in sport who tarnish that image. However, sport can only enhance positive values if those values are prevalent in society and if the agents in positions of power (coaches, physical education teachers, and parents) emphasize them.

There seems to be at least one contemporary setting where a generalized code of sportsmanship, including an acceptance of fair play, is the norm. Such a stance, at least declared and probably found, is in the conservative confines of private schools. For example, a code issued by the Ontario Headmaster's

Association (representing private schools in Canada) includes a series of eight statements designed to provide a framework for competition. Two of these are as follows: "No advantages are to be sought over others, except the advantage of superior skills," and "To win is always desirable, but to win at any cost utterly defeats the purpose of the game."

Although sport settings have the potential to foster society's positive values, violence and cheating (negative elements) have become widespread because these elements are common in society.[56] For example, domestic violence and cheating on one's spouse are not rare; community vandalism and cheating in business are well established; and deviance at the highest political levels and international terrorism are frequent. Since sport is more shaped by than shapes society,[57] strong counterforces within sport must evolve if the trend is to be reversed. In spite of an acceptable code of ethics which may be stressed in professional preparation courses[58] or youth sport coaching programs (settings where some future leaders are trained, for example), the values of the "real world" of school, university, and community are much more dominant and offset "ideal" standards. In fact, when considering aggressive sport acts leading to violence and cheating as one of a number of negative values in sport settings, one might question whether educational institutions and youth sport organizations live up to their responsibility to contribute to the development of well-balanced members of society or whether they simply contribute to the problem.

In sport, the coach is the most important socializing agent.[59] Other athletes, usually more experienced and more talented, are also role models.[60] Physical education teachers, either in their own right or when acting as coach, are also important, since their contact with athletes, especially during the formative years, is likely to be significant.[61] It is they who must share the blame for sport's ills. A reasonable conclusion is that negative values in sport are often condoned or encouraged by coaches at youth and school level and by physical educators. Presumably many parents are either unaware of the development of bad habits on ice, field, or court surfaces or do not care. The caricature of the ice hockey parent in Canada suggests that some encourage negative behaviour from their offspring.

VIOLENCE AND CHEATING

Violence and cheating have become more than rare occurrences. They are seen at professional and lower levels, especially in high-profile or national sports in specific countries; examples are football in the United States,[62] ice hockey in Canada,[63] and soccer in Europe (particularly Britain)[64] where violence is especially prevalent on and off the field of play.

Cheating is amply demonstrated and drug abuse is common in a number of professional and Olympic sports. Moreover, cheating generally seems to have become more subtle and therefore somehow insidious. For example, in soccer, a defender "standing on the ball" to gain advantage when a free kick has been awarded is a subtle rather than a blatant form of cheating. In theory, in any situation in which a moral decision has to be made, there is only one right act which it is one's duty to do. This phrase would probably be greeted with derision in most sport settings and consequently, it cannot be presumed that most youth leagues and youth teams practice good sportsmanship and fair play. Violent acts like spearing in hockey, kicking at an opponent in soccer, butting in football, and pitching at a batter in softball or baseball are relatively common practices. Furthermore, the better performers and team captains (role models for other players) are not necessarily more honest or do not necessarily demonstrate more integrity than other players;[65] coaches with the best win-loss record are prone to teaching by intimidation and sharp practice; and many become successful by breaking rules. For example, in a study undertaken in 1976 at a Canadian university[66] to determine the views of highly competitive athletes about cheating, it was found that 72 percent of a university basketball team's players voted *for* cheating. These players said their coach encouraged rule breaking (86 percent). By contrast, a men's recreation league team's percentage was 70 percent against cheating, but 60 percent said their coach encouraged rule breaking.

Eitzen (1981) boldly stated that the "structure of sport . . . actually promotes deviance,"[67] while Heinila (1980) broadly perceives the demise of fair play. As he said, ". . . fair play is losing its meaning in regulating the behavior of sportsmen and sportsleaders and is becoming a form of idealism divorced from reality and ripe to be dumped in the waste basket of sport."[68]

It would seem that the International Committee for Sport and Physical Education's concern for the maintenance of fair play as a central foundation of all sport has gone unheeded. In 1969 its Declaration of Sport stressed that if fair play disappeared from sport, "competitions would become occasions to cheat, lie and be brutal; they would no longer create but destroy human relationships and sport would lose its main justification."[69]

Lack of fair play in university sport was revealed in a recent study by Jones and Pooley (1986), who investigated the degree to which cheating in university sport was culture specific. They interviewed a small sample of Canadian and British athletes to determine how cheating was defined; whether there were differences between countries in cheating behaviour; and whether cheating was practiced in specific situations. Results showed that cheating was widely practiced; that the definition of "knowingly breaking the rules" was the same for both groups; and that cheating by Britons is more subtle and by Canadians more blatant. Both considered the others cheated more.[70]

However, rule infraction seems unrestricted by type and level of sport. In his exposé of ice hockey from the perspective of young players, Vaz (1982) pointed out that rule infraction is institutionalized at all levels of play, meaning not only that it is widely practiced but also morally approved.[71] A key finding in his research is that those who wish to excel are "obliged to violate rules and to engage in certain forms of violence. Failure to do so obviously jeopardizes their chances of success."[72] A normative ice hockey subculture exists which institutionalizes combatlike values of aggressiveness and toughness which constitute the foundation for a developing subculture of violent action and rule infraction.[73]

Socialization Into, Via, and Out of Physical Activity and Sport

From a series of modest empirical studies of young people's views about cheating, completed over several years by senior undergraduate students[74] under the direction of John Pooley, the following general findings are warranted.

1. Irrespective of the sport, some athletes will cheat to win. The range is 10 percent to 80 percent.
2. Males are willing to cheat more frequently than females.
3. As age increases, so does the propensity to cheat to win.
4. Selective cheating occurs as a function of each sport; that is, some forms of cheating become institutionalized.

Whether there exist many sports which keep winning in perspective with fair play is doubtful. Even in a relatively new sport like rhythmic (sportive) gymnastics, the weighting of ribbon sticks and the placing of adhesive on the ends of ropes, both contrary to the rules, have been practiced. Consequently, young athletes are bombarded with instances of cheating; these appear to become more pronounced as the higher levels of competition are reached. Furthermore, unethical behaviour is not only seen to be practiced by fellow athletes and coaches but also officials. In sports where the judging of style occurs (for example, in figure skating, gymnastics, and diving), an increasing number of allegations have been made about officials who score on the basis of the athletes' origin rather than purely on merit. Naturally, most young athletes are fully aware of these practices. Often coaches urge their athletes to cheat; some athletes need little encouragement to do so; administrators exploit; and officials are afraid to make a crucial call against a home team.

Alternatively, the practice of physical activity and sport can improve the quality of life of those primarily involved by enhancing self-esteem, providing year-round enjoyment, and contributing to the development of worthy citizens who demonstrate high standards of integrity and altrusim. Simiarily, those in secondary roles in sport such as coaches, officials, and administrators are, in many cases, enriched by the sport millieu to become satisfied and happy citizens of their communities. Such people contribute to the development of athletes by their sensitivity, dedication, and industry, often spanning many years.

SOCIALIZATION OUT OF PHYSICAL ACTIVITY AND SPORT

In a review of the literature relevant to those who withdraw from sport, Loy et al. (1978) acknowledge that voluntary or involuntary retirement can occur at any age. However, they emphasize that "if the withdrawal is involuntary, it is perceived as failure by the individual and the reaction can be traumatic, especially for a child whose peers continue to be involved and whose parents expect him or her to participate in sport."[75]

Orlick (1973) found in a study of Canadian eight- and nine-year-old children that many nonparticipants and dropouts indicated they "never" or "never again" would join a sport team. He indicates "A system which makes 'being good' [skillful] a prerequisite to playing does not appear to foster mass participation."[76]

In another study, sixty dropouts aged seven to nineteen years who were boys and girls who had participated in cross-country skiing, hockey, baseball, swimming, and soccer were surveyed. Of these, 67 percent indicated they had dropped out because of the emphasis on competition (specifically, 50 percent because of the seriousness of the program, lack of enjoyment, and emphasis on winning and being the best, and 17 percent because the coach left people out, criticized too much, and pushed too hard) and 31 percent because of a conflict of interest.[77] The researcher noted:

> . . . that at the elementary school age level none of the children said they dropped out due to conflict of interest reasons. . . .All children indicated that they dropped out for reasons revolving around the competitive emphasis of the program. . . .Lack of exposure in the form of playing time— 40%. . . .Lack of exposure to successful or rewarding experiences— 60%. . . .The programs, by their present structure and emphasis and the agents of these programs (i.e., the coaches) often appear to work together in a kind of conspiracy to eliminate children, particularly if they are of lesser skill levels.[78]

Two case studies taken directly from Orlick and Botterill's text, *Every Kid Can Win*,[79] graphically illustrate why children drop out. They are interviews with very young players who had negative experiences in soccer.

> Case 1: Eight-year-old soccer dropout. (Started at eight, dropped out at eight, about three-fourths of the way through the season.)
> Q Are you going to go out (for soccer again)?
> A I was planning on it, but I don't think I will.
> Q Why not?
> A It's not that much fun anymore.
> Q Did you play for the whole season?
> A For the last three games I didn't play, but the other games I did.

Q Why did you decide to stop?

A 'Cos whenever we had a game I was usually an extra so I didn't get to play very much.

Q So what did you do during the games?

A Just stand around and let the mosquitoes eat me.

Case 2: Seven-year-old soccer dropout. (Started soccer at seven, dropped out at seven—within a few weeks after starting.)

Q How did you like it last year when you went out for soccer?

A I didn't like it very much 'cos they never let me play. They just let the good guys play . . . the little guys just have to stand around . . . and watch.

Q Are you going to go out again?

A If they let me play I would.

Q Were there a lot of kids who didn't play?

A Yup, most of the team didn't get to play . . . just some guys did . . . just the big guys. Everybody else just stands around.

Q Did you stay for the whole season?

A I stayed a couple of weeks . . . then I quit because I never got to be what I wanted to.[80]

These interviews suggest that such experiences could contribute to low self-esteem. High-level achievement in sports is generally rewarded; the majority of performers will suffer from the comparison. That is, children who come into contact with a new sport and are told they are "no good" are likely to have a low opinion of themselves. Therefore, unless strategies are used to lessen the attention given to elite performers, fewer children will progress from middle childhood into adolescence and beyond participating in high-exposure team sports.

Results of another Canadian study showed that approximately one-third of boys aged ten to fifteen dropped out of soccer because of the emphasis on competition. Almost half had a conflict of interest. Ten percent withdrew principally because of poor communication[81] (they missed practices or games because they were unaware of changes in the schedule).

A more recent Canadian study is unusual because it used only females; it is comprehensive because it compared those continuing to compete with those who had withdrawn from the sport. Brown (1983) found that withdrawal from swimming was related to the athletes' perception of the absence of both diversity and conspicuousness of opportunities for the sport; the lack of social support from significant others; the degree to which swimming had become less important to the individual's sense of self-identity; the extent to which negative outcomes were associated with involvement in sport; and the diminishing degree of commitment to the role of competitive swimming.[82]

Carlisle (1978) suggested many factors which account for dropping out. Among these are being scared by competition, pressure of homework, seasonal dropouts when children join better sports, and too much effort required.[83] She suggests that improving the attitude of coaches, making the activity more fun, and promoting team effort will promote a feeling of success and thereby counter the tendency to withdraw from a sport. At least one soccer coach in Australia (Hansen, 1978) believes attrition is the major problem. As he says, ". . . it [soccer] has become a sport for little boys and little girls."[84]

Therefore, although young people are socialized out of sport because of an overemphasis on competition (and consequently, the more talented athletes are favoured, with negative consequences for the average or poor performer), research shows that many leave a sport for other reasons. They leave for alternative experiences either in other sports or other leisure pursuits, a fact which may be considered natural and part of the process of developing a varied life-style.[85]

Although some children would enjoy continuing to participate in a particular sport or sport in general, they may find they are socialized out of sport for one reason or another. Many withdraw without being forced out and therefore their self-esteem is not marred. They find other fields to conquer and other experiences to enjoy. Finally, some will return at a later date, possibly in adulthood, to enjoy taking part perhaps in other sports for other reasons not experienced when they were young. Thus, some are resocialized into sport and physical activity when adults; that is, they unlearn previously internalized norms in sport and learn new ones in their place.

SUMMARY

This chapter has used an interactionist perspective to understand the process of socialization as it applies to young people's involvement in sport and physical activity. Some elements of role theory also have been used to emphasize the part played by others with whom the socializee interacts. Socialization is used to explain how and under what circumstances the young are encouraged to take part in sport and physical activity. When this occurs, as well as the differences between informal play settings, more formal game settings, and often extremely formal and institutionalized sport settings, are contrasted. Different modes of involvement are also explained, although primary involvement as athletes is emphasized. The roles of adults, especially as parents and coaches and to a lesser extent as officials and administrators, are explained.

Subsequently, the effect of multivarious experiences in sport and physical activity is discussed. These settings vary greatly on their impact on role incumbents; the point is made that sport is inherently neither good nor bad. In general, the impact of the sport reflects the emphasis placed on each experience by adults acting out their roles in the many settings in which the young are exposed.

The duration of young people's primary involvement in sport as athlete or casual participant is considered in the light of their reasons for withdrawal. The conclusion is drawn that the impact ranges from damage to their self-esteem to a normal modification in life-style based upon changing interest. The latter presumably would have no deleterious effect, being part of an evolving process.

One final point is that although the discussions have concentrated on North American research with, where possible, a Canadian application, some international research has been included. In particular, the application of Australian studies (given the similarity between that country and Canada) has been especially emphasized.

NOTES

1. N. J. Demerath, III and Gerald Marwell, *Sociology: Perspectives and Applications* (New York: Harper and Row, 1976), 92.

2. Gerald Redmond, *Sport and Ethnic Groups in Canada* (Ottawa: CAPHER, 1980), 76.

3. Ibid., 78.

4. Demerath and Marwell, *Sociology: Perspectives and Applications,* 138.

5. A. Bandura and R. Walters, *Social Learning and Personality Development* (New York: Holt, Rinehart and Winston, 1963).

6. Carolyn W. Sherif and Gillian D. Rattray, "Psycho-social Development and Activity in Middle Childhood (5–12 years)," in *Child in Sport and Physical Activity,* ed. J. G. Albinson and G. M. Andrew (Baltimore: University Park Press, 1976), 100.

7. Richard S. Gruneau, "Class or Mass: Notes on the Democratization of Canadian Amateur Sport," in *Canadian Sport: Sociological Perspectives,* Richard S. Gruneau and John G. Albinson, (Don Mills, Ontario: Addison-Wesley, 1976), 108–41.

8. G. S. Kenyon, "Sport Development: A Conceptual Go and Some Consequences Thereof," in *Aspects of Contemporary Sport Sociology,* ed. G. S. Kenyon (Chicago: The Athletic Institute, 1969), 77–84.

9. Ibid.

10. Gerald S. Kenyon, *Values Held for Physical Activity by Selected Urban Secondary School Students in Canada, Australia, England and the United States* (Madison: University of Wisconsin, 1968).

11. John C. Pooley, "Prior Involvement in Sport and Physical Activity by Physical Education Majors: A Cross-National Study of Students from the United States, England, Canada, Australia and South Africa" (Paper presented at the ICHPER Congress, Kiel, West Germany, July 1979).

12. Gerald S. Kenyon and Barry D. McPherson, "Becoming Involved in Physical Activity and Sport: A Process of Socialization," in *Physical Activity: Human Growth and Development,* ed. G. Lawrence Rarick (New York: Academic Press, 1973), 303–32.

13. John W. Loy and Alan G. Ingham, "Play, Games and Sport in the Psychosocial Development of Children and Youth," in *Physical Activity: Human Growth and Development,* ed. G. Lawrence Rarick (New York: Academic Press, 1973), 257–302.

14. Kenyon and McPherson, "Becoming Involved in Physical Activity," 306.

15. E. C. Devereaux, "Backyard versus Little League Baseball: The Impoverishment of Children's Games," in *Social Problems in Athletics,* ed. D. Landers (Urbana: IL: University of Illinois Press, 1976).

16. Walter Podilchak, "Organizational Analysis of Youth Sports" (Unpublished paper, University of Calgary, 1983).

17. R. Gerald Glassford, "The Life and the Games of the Traditional Canadian Eskimo," in *Handbook of Social Science of Sport,* ed. Gunther R. F. Luschen and George H. Sage (Champaign, IL: Stipes Publisher, 1981), 78–92.

18. Gerald S. Kenyon, (Unpublished study, University of Wisconsin, 1968).

19. Barry D. McPherson, (Unpublished study, University of Wisconsin, 1968).

20. Michael D. Smith, "Social Learning of Violence in Minor Hockey," in *Psychological Perspectives in Youth Sports,* ed. F. L. Smoll and R. E. Smith (Washington: Hemisphere Publications, 1978), 91–106; and Edmund W. Vaz, *The Professionalism of Young Hockey Players* (Lincoln: The University of Nebraska Press, 1982).

21. Barry D. McPherson, L. N. Guppy, and J. P. McKay, "The Social Structure of the Game and Sport Millieu", in *Child in Sport and Physical Activity,* ed. J. G. Albinson and G. M. Andrew (Baltimore: University Park Press, 1976), 161–200.

22. Ibid.

23. John Andrews, *Essays on Physical Education and Sport* (Cheltenham, England: Stanley Thornes, 1979), 148–52.

24. Pooley, "Prior Involvement in Sport and Physical Activity."

25. Timothy Chandler, "Physical Education and Games in Private Schools: A Comparative Analysis" (M. Sc. thesis, Dalhousie University, Halifax, Nova Scotia, 1981).

26. Demerath and Marwell, *Sociology: Perspectives and Applications,* 71.

27. Kenyon and McPherson, "Becoming Involved in Physical Activity," 306.

28. McPherson, Guppy, and McKay, "The Social Structure of the Game," 172.

29. Walter Podilchak, "Boys Perceptions of Peer and Adult Organized Games" (M. Sc. thesis, Dalhousie University, Halifax, Nova Scotia, 1980).

30. Loy and Ingham, "Play, Games and Sport."

31. Sherif and Rattray, "Psycho-social Development," 99.

32. D. Gould et al. "Reasons for Attrition in Competitive Youth Swimming," *Journal of Sport Behavior* 5 (1982): 155–65; John C. Pooley, "Drop-outs from Sport: A Case Study of Boys' Age Group Soccer" (Paper presented at the American Alliance for Health, Physical Education, Recreation and Dance National Conference, Boston, Mass., 1981); and E. W. Vaz, *The Professionalization of Young Hockey Players* (Lincoln: University of Nebraska Press, 1982).

33. John C. Pooley, "A Level Above Competition: An Inclusive Model for Youth Sport," in *Sport for Children and Youths,* ed. D. Feltz and D. Gould (Champaign, IL: Human Kinetics Press, 1986), 187–94.

34. Gould et al., "Reasons for Attrition;" D. Gould, T. S. Horn, and J. Spreeman, "Sources of Stress in Junior Elite Wrestlers," *Journal of Sport Psychology* 5 (1983): 159–71; T. K. Scanlan and W. Passar, "Factors Related to Competitive Stress Among Male Youth Sport Participants," *Medicine and Science in Sports* 19(2) (1978): 103–8.

35. L. Hendry and E. Thorpe, "Pupils' Choice, Extracurricular Activities: A Critique of Hierarchical Authority?" *International Review of Sport Sociology* 12(4) (1977): 39–49; Scanlan and Passar, "Factors Related to Competitive Stress;" G. G. Watson, "Games, Socialization and Parental Values: Social Class Differences in Parental Evaluation of Little-League Baseball," *International Review of Sport Sociology* 12(1) (1977): 17–48.

36. L. Koppett, *Sports Illusion, Sports Reality* (Boston: Houghton Mifflin, 1981).

37. E. Rehbein, "Physical Education in Schools in the Federal Republic of Germany" (Paper presented at the Fourth International Symposium for Comparative Physical Education and Sport, Malente (near Kiel), 1984).

38. J. Evans and K. Davis, "An Analysis for the Involvement of Players in Junior Cricket," *Sports Coach* 4(3) (1980): 26–31.

39. Ibid., 28.

40. Ibid., 31. See also David Shilbury, "An Analysis for the Involvement of Players in Junior Cricket Under Existing Modified Rules" (Graduate diploma research, West Australian College of Advanced Education, Perth, W.A., 1983).

41. Peter Spence, *Australian Cricket Board Junior Policy* (Jolimont, Victoria: The Australian Cricket Board, 1984).

42. B. Gibson, "Participation in Junior Australian Rules Football," *Sports Coach* 1(3) (1977): 15–25.

43. Ibid.

44. J. Brown, "Netball is Catching," *Sports Coach* 4(1) (1980): 48–52.

45. Rainer Martens, Francine Rivkin, and Linda A. Bump, "A Field Study of Traditional and Non-Traditional Children's Baseball," *Research Quarterly for Exercise and Sport* 55(4) (1984): 351–55.

46. J. C. Pooley, "An Alternative Model to Reduce Competitiveness in Sports for Youth: The Case of Soccer" (Paper presented at the AGM of the Canadian Soccer Association, St. John's, Newfoundland, 1978).

47. R. A. Harootyan, "The Participation of Older People in Sports," in *Social Approaches to Sport,* ed. R. M. Parkin (1982), 122–47.

48. See the developmental models for basketball and volleyball by writing to the respective association at 333 River Road, Ottawa, Ontario, K1L 8H9, Canada.

49. Walter Schafer, "Sport, Socialization and the School" (Paper presented at the Third International Symposium on the Sociology of Sport, Waterloo, Canada, 1971). Interestingly, values like fair play and sportsmanship are believed to grow "out of gambling" from the British nineteenth century sporting tradition. See Andrew Strenk, "What Price Victory—The World of International Sports and Politics," *The Annals of the American Academy of Political and Social Science* 445 (September 1979): 137.

50. See Bruce Bennett, Maxwell Howell, and Uriel Simri, *Comparative Physical Education and Sport,* 2d ed. (Philadelphia: Lea and Febiger, 1983).

51. James H. Duthie, "Minor Sport: A Major Social Institution," *Action,* Canadian Council on Children and Youth, 3(1) (Spring 1983): 4.

52. National Task Force on Childrens' Play, *Fair Play Codes for Children in Sport* (Ottawa: Canadian Council on Children and Youth, 1979). See also the *Code of Sportsmanship* published by the Ontario (Private) Headmaster's Association.

53. Jerry Thomas et al., *Youth Sports Guide for Coaches and Parents* (Washington: AAHPER, 1977).

54. Max Rafferty, "Interscholastic Athletics: The Gathering Storm," in *The Athletic Revolution*, ed. Jack Scott (New York: The Free Press, 1971), 13–22.

55. Arthur Johnson, "Congress and Professional Sports: 1951–1978," *The Annals of the American Academy of Political and Social Science* 445 (September 1979): 109.

56. Michael Smith, "Towards an Explanation of Hockey Violence: A Reference Other Approach," *Canadian Journal of Sociology* 4 (Ma 1979): 105–24; Michael Smith, "Violence in Today's Sports," *Scholastic Coach* 1 (1st June 1980): 16–20, 25; and Gunther Luschen, "Cheating in Sport" (Paper presented at the symposium "Sport and Deviancy," State University of New York at Brockport, 9 December 1971).

57. Rex Thompson, "Sport and Ideology in Contemporary Society," *International Review of Sport Sociology* 2(13) (1978): 81–93, which analyzes the relationship between the value structure of sport and dominant ideological values. See also Gerald Kenyon, "Sport and Society: At Odds or in Concert?" in *Athletics in America*, ed. Arnold Flath (Corvallis, Oregon: Oregon State University Press, 1972).

58. Institutionally, it would appear that ethical, moral, and behavioural standards are, with some exceptions, ignored in the United States and Australia. See Carol Pooley, "Professional Standards in Physical Education: A Cross-National Comparison," *Comparative Physical Education and Sport* VII, No. 1 (1985): 22–39.

59. See George Sage, "An Occupational Analysis of the College Coach," in *Sport and Social Order*, ed. Donald Ball and John Loy (Reading, MA: Addison-Wesley Pub. Co., 1975), 391–455; George Sage, "Sociology of Physical Education/Coaches: The Personal Attributes Controversy," *Research Quarterly for Exercise and Sport* 51 (1st March 1980): 110–21; and Victor Mancini and Michelle Agnew, "An Analysis of Teaching and Coaching Behaviours," in *Sport Psychology: An Analysis of Athlete Behaviour*. ed. William Straub (New York: Movement Publications, 1978), 277–84.

60. Guido Nocker and Michael Klein, "Top-level Athletes and Idols," *International Review of Sport Sociology* 1(5) (1980): 5–17.

61. Wayne Westcott, "Effects of Teacher Modeling on Children's Peer Encouragement Behaviour," *Research Quarterly for Exercise and Sport* 51(3) (1980): 585–87.

62. John Underwood, "An Unfolding Tragedy," *Sports Illustrated* 49(7) (August 1978): 68–82.

63. Michael D. Smith, "Hockey Violence: A Test of the Violent Subculture Hypothesis," *Social Problems* 27(2) (December 1979): 235–47.

64. John C. Pooley, *The Sport Fan: A Social-Psychology of Misbehaviour* (Ottawa: CAHPER, 1979).

65. V. Narancic, "The Dynamic Training and Integrity of Sportsmen," *International Journal of Sport Psychology* 9(3) (1978): 227–30 for a perceptive essay on athlete's responsibilities.

66. Fred Promoli, "Cheating in Sport: A Comparison of Two Basketball Teams" (Unpublished paper, Dalhousie University, 1976), 15.

67. D. S. Eitzen, "Sport and Deviance," in *Handbook of Social Science of Sport,* ed. G. R. F. Luschen and G. H. Sage (Champaign, IL: Stipes Pub. Co., 1981), 400.

68. K. Heinila, "Ethics in Sport" (Paper given at the World Scientific Congress, Tbilisi, 1980), 3.

69. Ibid.

70. J. G. Jones and J. C. Pooley, "Cheating in Sport: A Comparison of Attitudes Towards Cheating of Canadian and British Rugby Players," in *Comparative Physical Education and Sport,* vol. 3, ed. M. L. Krotee and E. M. Jaeger, (Champaign, IL: Human Kinetics Press, 1986), 335–45.

71. E. W. Vaz, "The Professionalization of Young Hockey Players (Lincoln: The University of Nebraska Press, 1982), 8.

72. Ibid., 9.

73. Ibid., 39.

74. These were George Matthews, Chris Pottie, Eric Haughn, and Brenda Ogilvie, Dalhousie University, 1978.

75. John W. Loy, Barry D. McPherson, and Gerald Kenyon, *Sport and Social Systems* (Don Mill, Ontario: Addison-Wesley Pub. Co., 1978), 235.

76. T. D. Orlick, "Children's Sport—A Revolution Is Coming," *CAHPER* 39(3) (Jan.–Feb. 1973): 11–14.

77. T. D. Orlick, "The Athletic Drop-Out: A High Price for Inefficiency," *CAHPER* 41(2) (Nov.–Dec. 1974): 21, 24–27.

78. Ibid., 25.

79. T. Orlick and C. Botterill, *Every Kid Can Win* (Chicago, Il.: Nelson-Hall, 1975).

80. Ibid., 21–23.

81. John C. Pooley, "Drop-Outs from Sport: A Case Study of Boys Age Group Soccer" (Paper presented at the AAHPERD National Conference, Boston, April 1981).

82. B. Brown, "Factors Influencing the Process of Withdrawal by Female Adolescents from the Role of the Competitive Age Group Swimmer" (Unpublished doctoral dissertation, University of Waterloo, 1983). Cited in Barry D. McPherson, "Sport Participation Across the Life Cycle: A Review of the Literature and Suggestions for Future Research," *Sociology of Sport Journal* 1 (1984): 217.

83. Ursula Carlisle, "The Drop Out Rate," *The International Swimmer* (August 1978): 13.

84. Howard Hansen, "Responsibility for the Drop Out Rate," *The International Swimmer* (November 1978): 19.

85. McPherson, "Sport Participation Across the Life Cycle," 217.

CHAPTER 14

Psychological Concepts of Physical Activity and Sport: An Overview

David Anderson

Few areas of sport and physical activity have elicited more interest and study in recent decades by teachers and coaches, sport scientists, journalists, and observers than those psychological concepts and theories that relate to **PERS** studies, in particular those which affect teaching and performance. This chapter will introduce some of the broader issues and approaches in the psychology of sport and physical activity, thus, it is hoped, leading students to further examination and understanding of this important area.

AREAS OF STUDY

It is generally accepted that human activity is causal and that the causes can be discovered and explained, for the most part, through scientific research and/or analysis. The science of **psychology** is the description, explanation, and interpretation of human behaviour; more specifically, it is the study of the responses of organisms to stimulation.[1] The primary focus is the study of the psychological process underlying responses of organisms to stimulation. Therefore, physical activity and sport psychologists are involved in using the theories, concepts, instruments, and techniques of the field of psychology as they pertain to human movement. This area of inquiry is usually approached

in an interdisciplinary context which requires not only a comprehensive knowledge of the psychological process but also a complete understanding and appreciation of what Vanderzwaag calls "the physical activity or sport experience."

Two aspects have served to mislead, and perhaps confuse, beginning students in **PERS** studies with regard to this synthesized focus. First is the significant overlap between the two fields of **PERS** studies and psychology. This is so evident that several subclassifications or subdisciplines of study have now evolved, as will be noted later. The second concern that a **PERS** practitioner should have derives from the use of the language of psychology. It is as specific as the language of ice hockey or basketball. Just as "pick on the weak side" and "forechecking" are very specific terms for the basketball or ice hockey player respectively, so too are the terms "motivation," "feedback," and "stimulus" to the psychologist. As any physical activity, recreation, or sports specialist well knows, all sports terms and ideas are interconnected; similarly interconnected are terms used in psychology. These terms and concepts must be understood within the proper context if the student is to obtain a practical grasp of the processes as they pertain to the sport experience. Too often physical activity and sport instructors and coaches apply what they believe are psychological concepts with limited knowledge of the purpose or of the consequences of the application, therefore creating an unhappy or negative result such as using adult motivational techniques on children.[2]

It should be noted that although there is some disagreement as to where or how the content should be grouped for study because of the overlapping nature of concepts, the subject matter itself is not in question. This chapter will classify these perspectives or approaches to the psychology of physical activity, recreation, and sport in the following manner: growth and development, motor skill learning, sport psychology, personality development, and social-psychological concepts. It will conclude with some observations concerning the psychology of leisure and recreation.

GROWTH AND DEVELOPMENT

Growth and development are essential characteristics of all living things. They reflect the orderly transition from conception to maturity of living beings who are often shaped by genetic endowment and environmental forces.[3] The terms growth and development, although often used interchangeably, are not synonymous. **Growth** is a quantitative change in the body structure which is measurable by increases in height, weight, or size of bodily proportions. **Development,** conversely, is most often a qualitative term referring to one's biological cell and tissue makeup as changes in characteristics or complexity of the organism occur—as, for example, the continuing changes in one's nervous or hormonal systems through early childhood. Development is concerned not only with quantitative structural changes (growth) but also with the integration of these changes with other functions of the body. It includes the variety of sociopsychological and biological attributes acquired by a child as he or she grows up. Development occurs in an orderly and coherent pattern which results in new characteristics and abilities of the individual. In order to reach their greatest effectiveness, instructors of physical activity and sport must relate their teaching methods to these growth patterns. The normal human sequence of motor development is predictable and of particular significance to practitioners of **PERS.**

Further consideration should be given by **PERS** practitioners to a full range of concepts, theories, and established ideas that are part and parcel of the growth and development of an individual. One such principle is that of the process of **maturation,** which is governed by inherent genetic determinants and refers to an ongoing process of physiological and anatomical change relatively independent of environmental conditions. If the environment is abnormal in any way, the maturation process will be affected.[4] Some of the changes are regulated by a *biologically determined time schedule* (for example, those which occur during adolescence—the onset of puberty) and are very consequential to the readiness of the individual to learn physical skills. Singer describes **readiness** as that time when maximum sensory, physical, motivational, and psychological capacities are present for a learning experience.[5] To illustrate this readiness, one could observe infants through to early childhood and should perceive that in using hands and fingers, rolling over, crawling, pulling up to a standing position, standing, and walking, children follow a regular sequence and that these motor skills occur in the same order in most infants. Not all children go through the sequence at the same rate, but the order in which they move from one stage to the next is generally the same in all infants and in all cultures. Therefore, motor development appears to be directed by the preparedness of the maturational process, and within wide limits, the environment in which the child is reared seems to have little influence. Another way to portray readiness is to consider the development of more complex motor patterns which are so necessary in learning sports skills. Once again it is noted by Singer:

> Physical readiness to learn tasks includes both neurological and muscular maturation. . . .Research shows that motor skills cannot be developed until a child's neuromuscular system is sufficiently ready. The ability to coordinate motor patterns into a highly skilled act (depends on) learning . . . maturation is what makes learning possible. A child will learn a motor task most effectively when prerequisite maturation has occurred. Until such time practice has very little effect upon the success of acquiring skilled motor performance.[6]

Although this natural sequence of development is a continuing process, extending over the individual's life span, there are stages in development that are broadly identified as infancy, childhood (early and late), adolescence, and adulthood. Psychologists refer to these developmental stages in a relatively precise manner that implies (1) behaviour at a given stage is organized around a dominant theme, (2) behaviour at one stage is qualitatively different from that which appears in earlier or later stages, and (3) as previously stated in the discussion on readiness, children go through the same stages in the same order.[7] There seems little doubt that interference by environmental factors—such as restricting the physical surroundings in infancy—can retard motor development. However, this does not seem to have a lasting effect if severity is not too great, as increased stimulation appears to overcome this delay. There is substantial evidence that other areas of human development such as language, intelligence, and personality may be permanently affected by early infant or childhood experiences. These findings do have direct bearing on the methods of instruction and the kinds of programs and content which should be utilized by recreationalists, physical educators, and sport coaches.

It cannot be stressed too strongly that a specialist in **PERS** studies must acquire a thorough grounding in the concepts and ideas of what is generally called "growth and development" of humankind. The scope of this knowledge is extensive and ranges from Piaget's theories describing the stages of cognitive or intellectual growth, to personality and social development concepts, to identification theories, to Erik Erikson's psychological stages in a lifelong process of learning, to list but a few areas of study.

Finally, it should be noted that research has found that people often choose their sport or physical activity by the physical characteristics they have inherited. Teachers, coaches, and recreationalists must realize this possibility as it will tend to determine a participant's choices and place limitations on the abilities of their students and players.

MOTOR LEARNING AND DEVELOPMENT

This field of study is directly concerned with the conditions which can facilitate the acquisition and/or improvement of motor skills.[8] The extent of the inquiry can span the physical skills of infancy and childhood which seem to develop naturally with limited guidance, to the refinement by accomplished

performing athletes of sports skills which are related to the external quality of instruction. In the discussion that follows, the chief concern will be with the prescriptions involved with motor skills learning and development that pertain to late childhood, adolescence, and to a degree, adulthood. It is within these stages that either through institutionalization or through formal and informal social structures and professional physical activity that recreational and sports instructors exert the greatest impact and influence upon an individual's motor learning process. However, in being selective one does not wish to give the impression that motor development during the maturation stages of infancy and early childhood are not crucial and extensive. Quite to the contrary, infancy is a time of rapid physical growth and learning that can be seriously affected by environmental factors such as diet, motor usage, and physical restrictions. Early childhood, on the other hand, is a period of development characterized by the refinement of existing motor patterns, the building of new patterns upon those present, and by exploring and adapting patterns which can resolve new movement experiences.[9]

An important consideration when studying human behaviour is the necessity of differentiating between the concepts of learning and performance. **Learning** is defined as a relatively permanent change of behaviour that occurs as a result of experiences. Although physical growth is often a prerequisite for motor learning, physical growth alone is not sufficient to guarantee learning and therefore must be accompanied by experiences. On the other hand, **performance** is the actual behaviour shown by the individual and is often a temporary and/or situational act. Consequently, performance only infers that learning has taken place and since the learning process cannot be readily observed, this inference is tenuous. It should then be made clear that not all performance reflects true learning. For example, a novice golfer may inadvertently draw or fade a golf ball before he has been taught the necessary movement patterns to attempt the act consciously, or a person may shoot and sink a basketball before learning how to shoot.

The ability to discuss motor learning theory is greatly restricted by the limitations of a section within a single chapter. However, it is generally accepted that two traditional schools of thought have provided the basic concepts currently applied to motor learning. The first of these different approaches toward the study of psychology is **behaviourism** or **stimulus-response (S-R) psychology** as proposed by American psychologists John B. Watson and B. F. Skinner who submitted that psychology should examine ". . . the stimulus-responses that elicit behavioral responses, the rewards and punishments that maintain these responses, and the modifications of behavior obtained by changing the patterns of reward and punishments."[10] Stimulus-response psychology is not concerned with the consciousness of man or his introspection—these are considered private and individualized and therefore are not scientifically measurable. For behaviourists, measurable behaviour should be the sole subject matter in psychology. This mechanistic approach to the study of human behaviour and learning, per se, has limited appeal with today's psychologists; nevertheless, modern developments in the psychological process, specifically in motor learning, have evolved from the early work of the behaviourists. The second approach toward understanding human behaviour, the cognitive approach, was developed partly in reaction to the narrowness of the stimulus-response view. To conceive of human actions purely in terms of stimulus input and response output was seen as simplistic and negated too many areas of human functioning. **Cognitive psychology** studies ". . . the mental processes of perception, memory and information processing by which the individual acquires knowledge, solves problems and plans for the future."[11] This approach attempts to address the mental process in an objective and scientific manner.

One cannot leave this brief reference to psychological approaches without indicating at least two additional descriptions of what psychology is and how it should be examined. The first of these is the **psychoanalytic approach** of Sigmund Freud who suggested that much of our behaviour stems from processes that are unconscious; by this he meant that the thoughts, wishes, and fears of a person influence behaviour. Further, he stated that these motives or causes within all of us are *innate instincts* and therefore reason may not explain much of human behaviour. Second, more recently there have evolved from the thoughts of existential philosophy the concerns of **humanistic psychology** which, like the cognitive school, emphasizes the study of the mental process rather than behaviour. However, the humanistic psychologist concerns himself more with the inner life and experience of the individual in contrast to the cognitive psychologist's concern with perception, codifying, categorizing, and representing information in memory. The humanist's interests are in an individual's self-concept and the methods of self-actualization.[12] It suffices to say that most psychologists take an eclectic viewpoint and use different concepts for different phenomena.

The most accepted concept of motor learning to the practicing physical activity or sport specialist seems to revolve around the processes of sensing, perception, and cognition. The senses of the body receive information and/ or energy and relay this stimulation through the nervous system to the cortex of the brain. This information then serves as the basis for perception which is a cognitive process of identification and interpretation. As suggested by Singer, ". . . the perceptions of kinesthetics, proprioceptive, auditory, visual and cutaneous sensitivities are probably the most significant" to specialists in **PERS.**[13] For additional knowledge in this area one can refer to the theoretical frameworks of Whiting (1969), Christina and Shaver (1972), Gentile (1972), or Robb (1972), who are among many scholars who have developed analytical models of perceptual-motor learning and performance. Simply put, the information processing of motor skills learning has four operational phases: (1) **input,** which is the sensory information or stimulation that arrives at the conscious brain; (2) **perception** or **decision making,** which is giving meaning to the stimulation and organizing an appropriate response; (3) **output,** which is the execution of the response, and (4) **feedback,** which is the acknowledged result of the response.[14]

Motor Learning Constructs

Let us now consider some additional constructs within the process of motor learning and development which will have bearing on the methods of instruction. These are transfer of learning, modelling and shaping, and whole-part method of instruction. **Transfer of learning** occurs when in the performance of a task, the action is affected by some previous learning and/or practice. This influence can have a positive effect, a negative effect, or no noticeable effect at all upon the learning or performance of a new skill or task. There has been in recent years a debate concerning the degree of significance between *general transfer,* which suggests that peripheral knowledge and skills can be and are transferred, and *specific* or *identical transfer,* which proposes that only closely related or identical tasks have significant transferability. Recent observational research seems to substantiate both theories as relatively accurate so the debate, for the most part, can be put aside and focus can be directed upon the identificaton of transfer of learning principles. The following are some of these principles as listed by Singer.

1. The performer should practice the skill in the same form, speed, etc., and under the same or similar environmental conditions that approximate real situations;
2. The more similarity between the elements of the skills, the greater the amount of positive transfer;
3. When negative transfer occurs, the two learning situations contain similar stimuli but require different responses;
4. Transfer is affected by the amount of practice on the prior skill, motivation and method of practice;
5. If transfer is to be optimized, the learner must be aware of what skill or portion of skill is to be transferred.[15]

Modelling occurs when a person observes the behaviour of another, then performs some or all of that behaviour. This form of imitation is an effective means of changing behaviour in the learner. The procedure can involve a visual demonstration of a skill or portion of a skill by the instructor or competent performer, or the use of cinematographic techniques such as films, videotapes, or biomechanical graphics. Although visual demonstration is the bread and butter of modelling motor skills, especially at beginning and intermediate learning stages, the development of exacting and refined methods of cinematographic modelling for the elite or advanced performer has progressed rapidly in the past two decades. Cinematographic description, analysis, and prediction of human movement patterns in sports have now reached the level of a science. Hence, it is important to note that modelling of a task must be done correctly or not at all. The idea of **shaping** is closely associated with the concept of modelling in that it is the procedure which reinforces a closer and closer approximation of a desired result. This method of instruction exemplifies the proposition that "practice makes permanent" a particular task or skill an individual is trying to learn and then perform. An instructor's or coach's objective is to try to help the learner make permanent the very best movement response possible. If an instructor combines modelling with shaping and reinforces each imitation of the skill that gets closer to the desired performance, positive motor learning is likely to result.

The problem arises for a physical activity or sports instructor as to which tasks or skills should be taught by the part method of teaching and which could be more appropriately taught by the whole method. The **part method** basically breaks down a skill or motor pattern into constituent parts. Then each part is taught and hopefully mastered in a building-block process which leads to the ultimate development and performance of the whole motor pattern. The **whole method** requires that the complete motor pattern be taught and learned in one phase. Many examples supporting the use of the part method of teaching can be found in the skills of such sports as basketball, football, ice hockey, and in other sports where complex "open" motor patterns are required. **Open skills** refer to those skills that are influenced, in their performance, by such environmental conditions as an opposing player, the climate, or the game situations. Likewise there are numerous examples that can demonstrate the necessity for using the whole method of instruction within those sports which are dominated by "closed" motor patterns (e.g., gymnastics, swimming, and diving). **Closed skills** refer to those skills which are repetitious and complete in nature (such as swimming strokes, horizontal spins and twists, etc.) that are little affected by the environment because the latter is wholly or partly regulated in some way. Instructors can gain assistance in their decision as to the teaching method that would be appropriate for a given motor skill or pattern by undertaking a task analysis of the skill or movement pattern.

Task analysis identifies the important parts of the whole skill. . . .If the parts appear to be independent of each other, they can be practiced (or taught) separately. . . .If the parts are organized so that their synchronization is crucial to success, then the skill should be practiced (taught) as a whole.[16]

Further concepts of psychology that significantly affect motor learning and development are discussed in the next section of this chapter. Although the sport psychology section is mostly concerned with psychological aspects of performance, it has been established that proper learning is a necessary requisite to the execution of a task. Consequently, topic areas in that section such as practice, training and drilling methods, motivation, and feedback do have immediate bearing on motor skill learning and development. There are many theorists and practitioners of **PERS** who maintain that the unique essence or core of the discipline and many of its professions lies in the knowledges and instructional methods encompassing motor learning and development. Thus, additional space and time must be allotted to this area of study in physical activity and sport psychology.

SPORT PSYCHOLOGY

There is a tendency by those scholars who propose that sport studies or sport science should be the main focus of study of the discipline to use the phrase "sport psychology" as a broad or all-inclusive term which would include the subcategories that are mentioned in this chapter. Although one has considerable sympathy with this approach, it is our intention to adopt a narrower scope and to use the term **sport psychology** as depicting those psychological concepts which pertain to the preparation of athletes for sport performance. There seems little doubt that there is a growing involvement by many societies in the improvement of sport performance and the increased recognition of the importance of psychological or mental preparation of athletes.

The historical beginnings of this recently developed subdiscipline (sport psychology) stems from the 1928 publication by Coleman Griffiths of his textbook *Psychology and Athletics,* which sets forth some of the better-known psychological concepts of the period as they related to sports competition. This significant but little recognized first step was followed by John Lawther's *Psychology of Coaching* in 1951. By the mid-1970s, the field was being well served by a number of competent research publications and texts. Although sport psychologists with practical experience were slow to emerge, the theoretical framework for this applied science was being established. In the last two decades, with the presence of several international and national symposia and congresses for sport psychology and the publication of several scholarly journals (the most noteworthy being the *International Journal of Sport Psychology*), communication of ideas and research within the field has been greatly enhanced.

A recent development in the field of sport psychology should be noted. Much of the effort of psychology in sport up to the 1970s concentrated on the relatively short-term, terminal aspects of behaviour in sport pre-performance.

However, led in North America by such sport psychologists as Canadian Richard Alderman, scholars now recognize a broader view of performance, which encompasses the total behaviour of the participant rather than just the discrete tasks of performance. Positive support is mounting for this approach as increasing behavioural problems are being identified in the areas of actual and post-performance, as well as those of pre-performance. This increasing focus on mental preparation procedures of sports performance is not only influenced by the thrust of the sport psychologist. These procedures have also gained ever-increasing support from coaches and athletes as it becomes more evident that the difference between average and excellent performance in sports competition is that of mental attitude. The importance of mental preparation becomes increasingly evident as the relative differences of the physical skills and abilities among elite athletes become less pronounced. How athletes think and feel is therefore crucial to their performance, and mental preparation can be learned and developed in the same way as physical skills. With this point in mind, some of the concepts of psychology which can assist a coach or athlete to maximize performance will be examined.

Motivation

In recent years much has been said about the term motivation and its place within athletic preparation. Further, a great deal of this information is derived from, or interpreted by, what can be called an amateurish understanding of the human motives, needs, and desires that constitute motivational behaviour. **Motivation** may be defined as the drive to achieve some goal—an inner urge toward purposeful activity.[17] Two basic functions are involved in the motivational process. The first and most commonly known is that of initiating or supporting arousal within the performer. This energizes the body's resources for vigorous and intense activity. The second is a function of direction, as it assists decisions of behaviour to specific ends. By this it is meant that an individual is motivated in some way in his choices of personal goals and direction. These two aspects are not independent of each other and generally human behaviour is the result of both functions. A further concept involved in the understanding of the term is the source of a person's motivation which is derived from the individual's drive (or arousal state) that results from some biological need, such as need for food, water, or avoidance of pain. This aroused condition motivates the person to remedy the need. Drives or motives are instigated by a need; therefore, **need** refers to the physiological state and **drive** (or motives) refers to the psychological consequences of a need. The distortion in the application of motivation techniques to the sports experience is legendary when so frequently the normal needs of, say, learning, participation, enjoyment, cooperation, and/or competition are supplanted by the drive to win. The drive to win a competition as a basis for motivating participants can have dangerous consequences when applied indiscriminately to early stages of physiological and psychological development which are found in childhood and adolescence. An additional concern of researchers has been to identify what a participant's **optimum level of arousal** should be in performance and, further, to correlate the various levels of arousal to types of sports and specific positions and roles within sport. It should be noted that this optimum level of arousal differs not only within each athlete but differs from one sport to another and—even more perplexing—from one game situation to another. Finally, motivational theories and techniques should never be attempted haphazardly or frivolously but should be applied in a controlled, purposeful, and directive manner in the preparation for performance or learning.

Practice

It should be remembered that the next series of terms relating to sports performance has as great a relevance to the educational procedures of motor learning as it does to the preparation of athletes. When one begins to discuss the significance of practice and training upon motor learning and therefore performance, the reasons for practice must be established. Basically, they are twofold: first to increase speed of performance, and second to increase accuracy. Advancement in skill performance is dependent on these two factors along with the intent of the individual to improve, as practice alone will not necessarily result in proficiency. This point is even more evident as the complexity of the motor patterns increases. One cannot learn or perform a sports skill by mere perception of it or by merely thinking about it; one must do it and then practice to increase competency. Learning to perform is an active process. Thus practice and training serve the purpose of directing the learning

and performance process through the various ability levels toward proficiency.[18] One of the most highly researched areas in the performance of motor skills is that of the relative values of massed practice and of distributive practice. **Distributive practice,** which is characterized by short, intense training periods interspersed with frequent rest periods, is generally recommended for most motor learning and performance. However, **massed practice** schedules, which are characterized by less intense but continuous drilling with infrequent rest periods, have demonstrated their importance in research and application, especially when certain gross motor patterns are involved and endurance or conditioning is a factor in performance. There seems to be no optimal practice schedule for all skills; therefore each series of performance tasks must be analyzed in relation to the athlete's abilities and the conditions under which the practice must take place. According to Singer, the essential purpose of **drilling**—frequent repetitions of the same task—is to move the performer to the **automatic phase** which is distinguished by the ability to perform a necessary response consistently, with minimum error and little conscious effort. Drilling a response to this stage reduces the need of cognitive control and consequently allows for a greater concentration by the performer on other factors in a game.

A survey of sport psychology would not be complete without some general analysis of the terms feedback, reinforcement, and mental imagery as they affect sports performance. As indicated earlier, practice in itself does not improve performance. An additional component needed, besides intent, is the presence of appropriate feedback. **Feedback** is described as the information arising out of the performer's responses.[19] This information can be **intrinsic** in that bodily senses, such as feel (proprioceptive), sight (visual), or hearing (auditory), can relay back to the performer's cognitive process any necessity for performance correction. Still another way in which feedback can be developed is by the **extrinsic** procedure or **augmented feedback.** In this process, instructors, coaches, fellow participants, or at times even spectators can, by verbal or cinematographic means, communicate behavioural changes as needed. The knowledge of result (feedback) is of such significance to an athlete that when it is absent performance levels decrease and when it is present performance levels improve. The immediacy of feedback is also of relevance in that the quicker the response information can be given to the performer, usually the better the adjusted performance will be. Also, the more specific the knowledge of results, the more effective will be the modification.

Psychologists use the term **reinforcement** in a relatively broad sense in that it is any condition that increases or maintains the strength of a response. A *positive reinforcer* may be any reward mechanism, even a few encouraging words or stickers on a football helmet to denote good play. Contrary to general knowledge and usage in the field of **PERS,** *negative reinforcement* may simply mean the removal of some condition or stimulus which tends to hinder performance. It does not necessarily refer to a negative, punitive, or detrimental action on the part of coaches, teachers, or others. The intention of both negative and positive reinforcement is to assist in increasing performance levels. Punitive acts of instruction within the sports experience have had little support by psychologists, or for that matter by society as a whole, as their purpose is quite unclear. Yet, such acts have survived and flourished. However, in one specific situation, what might be called a negative act has gained support from sport coaches. The situation referred to is the ability of a coach to establish the attention (eye-to-eye contact) of the athlete in a difficult setting. It is often stated and practiced that a **controlled negative act** (such as close proximity with a loud voice, a sharp noise, or a demonstrative movement—waggling of fingers, strong grip on shoulders, etc.) directed to the athlete(s) in question is attention getting. From this point proper communication, reinforcement, or feedback may begin. There seem to be few coaches in sport, particularly team sport, who by their experience do not support this singular use of a perceived negative or detrimental act for the sole purpose of getting the attention of athletes. The use of individual overt acts of punishment seems to have little place in sport. Nevertheless, it would appear that further thought and research must be given to the value or appropriateness of controlled, and possibly purposeful, covert acts that have had negative connotations.

The necessity of physical practice in the acquisition of a motor task, or more specifically a sports skill, has been discussed. It has also been substantiated that **mental imagery** or **mental practice,** which is the cognitive (mental) rehearsal of a motor task without any overt motor movements, will facilitate the learning and performance of a motor skill.[20] An example of mental practice would be the imagery used by a diver or gymnast, just before performance, as he or she mentally rehearses a dive or exercise. Proponents of mental practice do not suggest that such rehearsal supplants physical practice. They stress, rather, that this technique is available to augment physical practice during nonactive periods of training or just prior to performance. The review of research in this area by Richardson (1967) and again by Corbin (1972) summarizes the findings in this manner:

> There seems to be little doubt that mental practice (M.P.) can positively affect skilled motor performance, especially when practice conditions are "optimal." It is equally clear, however, that mental practice is not always an aid to performance and that factors such as practice type, the skill task and the nature of the performance ultimately reflect the extent of the behaviour change resulting from M.P.[21]

It is hoped that this brief look at some of the psychological principles and concepts affecting performance in sport is sufficient to indicate the need for all **PERS** practitioners to be more aware of the intricacies and the many variables involved in preparing their athletes.

PERSONALITY DEVELOPMENT IN SPORT

Personality according to Hollander is ". . . the sum total of an individual's characteristics which make him unique." He categorizes personality in three distinct levels:

1. *The psychological core* which includes one's attitudes and values, one's interests and motives and one's self-concept.
2. *Typical responses* which are learned modes of adjustment to one's environment, such as, one's reactions to frustration, humour and anxieties.
3. *Role-related behaviour* or one's understanding of the social setting in which one is placed.[22]

In pursuing the relationship between personality and sports, a question that has often been asked is whether there is an "athletic personality" and whether it differs from other, or nonathletic, personalities. If the search to answer the question proves to have a positive result, then the natural extension of the question would be, Does participation in physical activity and sports initiate or enhance personality change and/or development within an individual? Further, if the characteristics of an athletic personality could be determined with any certainty, the repercussions throughout the educational and sports worlds would be monumental. From this knowledge, predictions could be made, with some degree of accuracy, concerning performance in sports.

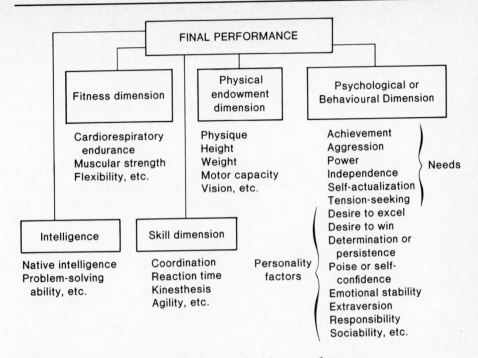

Figure 14.1 Underlying dimensions of athletic performance

SOURCE: Adapted from Alderman, 1974: 6.

The ability to predict who would be most likely to succeed as a competitive athlete at various levels of achievement—and who would not—could save countless millions of dollars spent annually throughout all sporting societies in their search for exceptional athletes. If the athletic personality could be identified, a sequential timetable might be created of when to foster the development of the behavioural dimensions indicated in figure 14.1.

From Alderman's graphic description of final performance traits in figure 14.1, five major categories are identified: intelligence, fitness, skill, physical endowment, and psychological or behavioural dimensions. It is possible that the first four categories listed can be evaluated fairly reliably. However, it is that final category, psychological dimensions, where valid measuring instruments and techniques fall short of scientific requirements. This long list of traits in the psychological dimensions category is in essence the athletic personality. Sport science, in one sense (four out of five major categories), is so close and yet so far from predicting the probability of success by athletes in performance. Some of the more popular psychological inventories used in attempting indirectly to measure the personalities of individuals who participate in physical activity and sports are the Cattell 16 Personality Factor Test, the Minnesota Multiphasic Personality Test (MMPT), the California Personality Test (CPT), the Edwards Personal Reference Schedule (EPPS), and the Athletic Motivational Inventory (AMI). There are several empirical questions of validity and reliability that have arisen concerning the last listed inventory (AMI), and it is recommended that the review and analysis by Rainer Martens in his book *Social Psychology and Physical Activity* (chapter 10) be read before its use. Other measurement techniques used to evaluate athletic personality are interviews, observations, ratings, and projective tests.[23] As mentioned previously, all of these techniques struggle, in the sense of scientific methodology, to obtain acceptable levels of validity.

The conclusion must then be made that sports personality research has yet to uncover any useful, specific relationships between personality and athletic performance and that research methods and tools must be improved upon. Singer does suggest, however, that some generalizations from existing research can be made.

1. Although it seems that particular activities attract certain personalities, it is not clear how the traits interact with each other to affect activity selection.
2. The influence of participation in athletic and physical education programs on personality is largely undetermined.
3. Athletes, as a group, typically have personalities that differ from those of nonathletes.
4. A unique personality profile of the average athlete or the superior athlete has yet to be drawn. However, the personaity traits found in superior athletes appear to be similar to those found in high-achieving people.[24]

Further, in a study of Ogilvie and Tutko of American superior female athletes, it was shown that there was ". . . a greater tendency toward introversion, greater autonomy needs, and a combination of qualities suggesting that they are more creative than their male counterparts. They show less need for sensitive and understanding involvement with others. Women competitors are more reserved and cool, more experimental, more independent than male (athletes)."[25]

SOCIAL-PSYCHOLOGICAL CONCEPTS

In recent years there has been an ever-increasing awareness of the social-psychological (psychosocial) implications of physical activity and sport upon a culture. The extent to which a nation has developed its collective and individual consciousness toward physical activity often reflects its growth in such areas as political philosophy, historical traditions, economics, national health policies, and cultural patterns. The breadth of **social psychology** is significant because as a behavioural science it is ". . . the scientific study of human behaviour as influenced by the present behaviour and products of human beings, individually and collectively, past, present and future."[26] It aims to explain the cause and effect of human behaviour upon **PERS** by the scientific processes of research, such as field and laboratory studies and experiments, while using the techniques of observation, subjective reports, sociometric methods, attitude assessments, surveys, and so on. Now add the focus of physical activity and in particular the explosion of "physical technology" in **PERS** instruction, methods, and knowledges and one can easily perceive a desperate need for a corresponding "social technology" or sociocultural understanding of the effects a society exerts upon the individual sportsperson and vice versa.

The concern of psychosocial study is with the process of social influence. This social influence occurs whenever an ". . . individual responds to the actual or implied presence of one or more other individuals . . . in the following three forms: 1) person-to-person interaction [psychology of **PERS**], 2) person-to-group interaction [social psychology of **PERS**], and 3) group-to-group interaction [sociology of **PERS**]."[27] The above categorization of social influence clearly indicates a unique area of study which is the domain of the social psychologist when it is contrasted to its founding disciplines of psychology and sociology. The subject matter of this individual-to-group interaction can range from such diverse study areas as the basic instructional methods of motor or sports skills learning (a physical education teacher teaching a skills class) to many constructs which are part and parcel of sport or elite sports (such as competition and cooperation, aggression and violence, team cohesion, leadership, and spectatorism) to the recreational and leisure concepts of socialization, volunteerism, participation, and individual fitness. It therefore must be obvious to the student of **PERS** studies that social-psychological principles, concepts, theories, and practices cross the boundaries of all the categories of the physical activity identification continuum as presented in chapter 2. Further, the student should be aware that several of the topic areas referred to in the sociocultural chapters (chapters 12 and 13) are often the cultural point for research within the framework of psychosocial study.

Further consideration of the social influence categories will suggest that a single thesis or question can be viewed from several perspectives. For instance, the question of aggression and violence in sport can be analyzed from the point of view of an individual's behaviour toward another person: in football, an offensive centre's reactions to a nose tackle, or in hockey, a player's response to a severe check. Likewise, violence can be considered in group behavioural relationships in such contexts as team-to-team, team-to-spectators, spectators-to-teams, or spectators-to-spectators. The last association may have seemed isolated or remote to many observers and social researchers of sport in earlier periods. However, the image of the death and destruction brought by English and Italian soccer fans in Belgium in 1985, as only one of many contemporary examples of the collective violence focused around sport, has sport sociologists searching for explanations of the causes and effects of such travesties. Additionally, the implications of violence and aggression in physical activity and sport can be viewed within psychosocial parameters as, for example, the influence of parents, siblings, peer group, team members, or coaches upon individual participants.

In conclusion, to paraphrase Bryant Cratty, physical activity and sports participation and viewing are seldom neutral experiences for those involved. Hence, careful consideration and examination of social-psychological issues in **PERS** ". . .may influence individuals who interact within sports situations so that negative outcomes are minimized, while the opportunities for achieving positive social outcomes are maximized."[28]

PSYCHOLOGY OF LEISURE AND RECREATION

Since much of this chapter concerns itself with issues and concepts which seem more appropriate in a scenario of sport and physical recreation, it seems necessary to refer briefly to a few general, but accepted, theories of the relation of leisure/recreational pastimes to the development of individual characteristics. First, the reader's attention is directed to the chapter on terms and definitions (chapter 2) and the subsequent discussion of play theories. It was indicated that the role of play at each stage of early life—infancy, childhood, and adolescence—has a significant effect upon the physical and psychological development of the person. In fact, it is rigorously supported by many educational and child psychologists that a young child learns more and develops human behavioural patterns better through play than through any other form of activity, and that domains of affective, cognitive, and psychomotor learning are directly related to the quality and quantity of leisure/play of children. If we associate with this viewpoint (1) the realization that personality development is for the most part a procedure cultivated during one's early, formative years, and (2) the observation that most play is participated in during unobligated or leisure time at all age levels, then the importance that leisure-time play has on the maturation of personality characteristics of the individual becomes clear. A suggested *psychologically oriented definition of leisure* would emphasize self-development and fulfillment through freely chosen, meaningful activities that make leisure (activity) particularly relevant and valuable to a person and/or society.[29]

History states clearly that as a culture moves toward a leisure society (see chapters 2 and 15)—and many contemporary cultures are close to this—it seems imperative that one must guard against the dangers of an inactive lifestyle. With this statement in mind, and with the knowledge that concepts and attitudes about recreation, sport, and leisure pursuits can be shaped and changed by many factors, leisure activities have gained general acceptance as benefits are identified and their positive effects on the individual are better understood and explained. An example of this shaping is illustrated by the studies of Murphy, Williams, et al., who have identified a wide range of behaviours which are influenced by recreational activities participated in during leisure time. These behaviours, along with examples of the activities that influence them, are socializing behaviours (club memberships, dancing, community affairs); associative behaviours (people loosely grouped through common interests, e.g., hobbies); competitive behaviours (sports, games, outdoor activities); risk-taking behaviours (mountain climbing, sport parachuting); exploratory behaviours (travel, hiking); vicarious experiences (reading, television, spectating); sensory stimulation (music or art appreciation); and physical expression (activities which involve physical expression without competition—yoga, fitness running, aerobics).[30]

Finally, there is an increasing interest in research by psychologists, sociologists, and leisurists alike as to the positive implications that leisure/recreational activities may have upon mentally handicapped persons as well as the relationship of these activities to the improvement of the quality of life for the aged.

The studies of Karl Menninger, who pioneered the interrelatedness of leisure pastimes and the mentally ill, found that well-adjusted clients involved themselves in twice as many hobbies as did the clients who were more seriously ill.[31] There has also been extensive program development with the mentally handicapped in the last decade which uses physical activities and games for improvement in the basic learning process of "life skills" (how to dress, personal health habits, etc.) with some positive results. However, one should not necessarily construe from this and other similar research findings or observations that good leisure habits automatically lead directly to improved learning and quality of life for the mentally ill or handicapped. The implications are more for the leisure or recreational therapist who now has an additional modality or instrument by which to increase a client's perceived control of his or her sociopsychological well-being and to diffuse the sense of helplessness which is a prevalent characteristic of most mentally ill persons.

In somewhat the same vein, serious attention is being given by leisure/recreation practitioners and psychosocial scientists to the benefits of good leisure activities for the aged. Aging is often accompanied by psychological, sociological, and physical **inactivity.** This inactivity is accepted not only by society but also by the elderly themselves. The belief that older persons desire to withdraw from social interaction, physical activity, and individual responsibility is a tragedy which imposes disastrous consequences not only on the individual but on society as a whole. This **theory of disengagement** should be buried along with many other myths and stereotypes of the aged. It should be realized that any human process, such as attitude toward aging, can be changed, modified, manipulated, and in certain circumstances even reversed. The following adapted statement, with emphases added, clearly identifies some general viewpoints which are a basis for optimism:

> Sociologists, political scientists, economists, psychologists, public health and physical activity specialists, and educators are coming to recognize "ageism" as a critical social problem. [They] . . . assert that "ageism" is one of the greatest of all social problems in that it will directly affect most of us regardless of race or sex. . . .As a society we desperately need to develop new understandings of the aging process, new perspectives on the problems of the elderly, and new policies for the future. . . .We must take account of the older person's need for self-respect, the continuing importance of meaningful involvement in the lives of others, and the potential for promoting the full use of existing physical and mental capacities

and abilities. . . .*Older people can and do learn.* Persons of all ages need to be provided with opportunities to learn new knowledges and new skills. *Older persons can and do change.* Among prevalent [sociopsychological] theories regarding aging, we concur with the **activity theory,** which holds that active individuals find life more satisfying than do those who withdraw from the mainstream of society. Recent clinical and research evidence generally supports the thesis that physical and mental deterioration can be slowed by continuing activity. . . .*There is considerable support for the theory that social withdrawal patterns of the elderly can be delayed and even reversed through physical and mental activities [leisure pastimes] of socializing games and exercise sessions.*[32]

SUMMARY

This chapter clarifies the interrelatedness of physical activity and sport and the discipline of psychology. It groups this body of knowledge into five subclassifications of study: growth and development, motor skills learning, sport psychology, personality development, and sociopsychological concepts. A brief discussion of some selected ideas and theories is given to illustrate the breadth of the subject area and to indicate the interconnection of all the areas of physical activity and sport psychology. Finally, some opinions are expressed on the emerging theories and viewpoints relating to leisure pastimes and their effects upon individual well-being.

NOTES

1. Robert N. Singer et al., *Physical Education: Foundations* (New York: Holt, Rinehart and Winston, 1976), 247.

2. Harold J. Vanderzwaag and Thomas J. Sheehan, *Introduction to Sport Studies from Classroom to Ballpark* (Dubuque, IA: Wm. C. Brown Company Publishers, 1978), 193–94.

3. Earle F. Zeigler et al., *Physical Education and Sport: An Introduction* (Philadelphia: Lea and Febiger Publishers, 1982), 117.

4. Singer et al., *Physical Education: Foundations,* 235.

5. Ibid.

6. Ibid.

7. Rita L. Atkinson, Richard C. Atkinson, and Ernest R. Hilgard, *Introduction to Psychology,* 8th ed. (New York: Harcourt, Brace, Jovanovich Publishers, 1983), 65.

8. Robert E. Gensemer, *Physical Education: Perspective, Inquiry, Applications* (New York: Saunders College Publishers, 1985), 234.

9. Zeigler et al., *Physical Education and Sport: An Introduction,* 126.

10. B. F. Skinner, "Selection by Consequences," *Science* 231 (1981): 501–4.

11. Atkinson, Atkinson, and Hilgard, *Introduction to Psychology,* 8th ed., 8–9.

12. Atkinson, Atkinson, and Hilgard, *Introduction to Psychology,* 8th ed., 10.

13. Singer et al., *Physical Education: Foundations,* 250.

14. Gensemer, *Physical Education: Perspective, Inquiry, Applications,* 136.

15. Singer et al., *Physical Education: Foundations,* 257.

16. Ibid., 256.

17. Ibid., 259.

18. George H. Sage, *Introduction to Motor Behaviour: A Neuropsychological Approach* (Reading, MA: Addison Wesley Company Publishers, 1977), 390–91.

19. Singer et al., *Physical Education: Foundations,* 255.

20. Sage, *Introduction to Motor Behaviour: A Neuropsychological Approach,* 405.

21. C. B. Corbin, "Mental Practice," in *Ergogenic Aids and Muscular Performance,* ed. W. P. Morgan (New York: Academic Press, 1972), 93–118.

22. Rainer Martens, *Social Psychology and Physical Activity* (New York: Harper and Row Publishers, 1975), 145 (attributed to E. D. Hollander).

23. Singer et al., *Physical Education: Foundations,* 261.

24. Ibid., 262.

25. Bruce C. Ogilvie and Thomas A. Tutko, "Sport: If You Want to Build Character, Try Something Else," *Psychology Today* 5 (1971): 61–63.

26. J. E. McGrath, *Social Psychology: A Brief Introduction* (New York: Holt, Rinehart and Winston Publishers, 1964), 1.

27. Martens, *Social Psychology and Physical Activity,* 5.

28. Bryant J. Cratty, *Social Psychology in Athletics* (Englewood Cliffs, NJ: Prentice-Hall, 1981), 3.

29. Donald C. Weiskopf, *Recreation and Leisure: Improving the Quality of Life,* 2d ed. (Boston: Allyn and Bacon, 1982), 68.

30. James Murphy et al., *Leisure Service Delivery System: A Modern Perspective* (Philadelphia: Lea and Febiger Publishers, 1973), 9–10.

31. Karl Menninger, *Love Against Hate* (New York: Harcourt, Brace and World Publishers, 1942), 185.

32. John E. Nixon and Ann E. Jewett, *Introduction to Physical Education* (New York: Saunders College Publishers, 1980), 326–27.

PART FIVE

Some Contemporary Trends within PERS in Canada

CHAPTER 15

The Present and the Future

David Anderson

When one ventures beyond the confines of institutions of higher learning and into the sometimes harsh world of the workplace, certain professional realities must be expected and confronted. These realities are often perceived differently from the idealistic environment of universities than they truly are. Although the text frequently refers to changes and trends which are occurring within the field of physical activity, recreation, and sport, it is hoped that this final chapter will, in capsule form, reemphasize for some readers, and identify for others, various experiences which might be anticipated as they enter and pursue their careers.

PHYSICAL EDUCATION TRENDS

Early Careers

It was evident in Canada during the educational explosion of the 1960s that teachers of physical education could anticipate not only reasonable chances of employment within the various school systems, but that their teaching curriculum would be, for the most part, within their chosen field. In other words, physical education majors could expect to teach basic physical activity classes, administer intramural programs, and be involved (if required) in interscholastic coaching. By the 1980s these expectations were drastically modified. With the advent of fewer students, financial restraints, expanded curricula, and a necessity to improve instruction and the coaching of interschool teams, school boards, superintendents, and principals began to realize a need for

greater flexibility in teaching assignments. Therefore, while requiring professional qualifications in teaching areas like physical education, administrators sought to increase the number of subjects in which any one teacher would instruct.

Physical education became a leading subject area for this diversification in teaching because of expanded programming in all its subareas. The result of this required teaching flexibility and expansion is the hiring of qualified physical education graduates, the reduction of their teaching load within the subject, and the requiring of increased instruction and supervision in other or similar educational fields. This implies that physical activity and sports specialists who wish a career in teaching should be establishing in their undergraduate studies a strong secondary teaching major or minor. In addition, they should seek qualification in one or more specialized areas of coaching. In short, full-time teaching positions in physical education are presently, and will be for the foreseeable future, a rare commodity. Physical education teachers must expect diversified assignments, especially at the initial stages of employment.

Late Careers

There comes a time for some, whether for physical reasons, family commitments of time, mental fatigue, or merely a personal desire for change, when a strong wish develops for a new career. Understandably, this is a common occurrence with physical educators. The trends of the past few decades seem to be holding true in that physical education teachers do have the option and ability, within school systems, to move to a secondary teaching area (e.g., English, geography, sciences, history). Additionally, there seems to be a belief, supported by administrators, that student counselling and administration are a natural outgrowth for the experiences and talents of physical educators. As an example, within the high school administrative structure in the school division of the city of Winnipeg, five out of the nine high school principals have had either extensive teaching experience in physical education and sport or a degree in some form of PERS studies.

Curriculum

Curriculum content and methods of teaching physical education continue to grow and develop at all educational levels, placing upon physical educators a continuing need for upgrading knowledge and techniques. Elementary curricula continue to foster and support new programs and methodology within physical activity courses such as "New Games" activities, expanded approaches to movement education, outdoor education, and rhythmics, to name but a few. Junior and senior high school programs will continue the trend of teaching sport and physical recreational activity skills with an ever-broadening choice of activities such as team handball, rhythmic gymnastics, rugby, numerous aquatic activities, cross-country and downhill skiing, outdoor recreation, and a host of other individual and group sports and games. However, this expanding activity list is negatively counterbalanced by the decline in class contact hours at the high school level for most Canadian students. This fact, also noted in chapter 6, leads one to consider seriously the limited professionalism exhibited by physical educators, as well as the public's perception of the value of physical activity and sport.

Professional Responsibilities

It is sincerely hoped that the present apathy exhibited by physical education specialists toward professional and curriculum concerns will disappear. The past record in Canada of physical education and sport specialists to commit themselves to the sociopolitical systems in education, in order to establish rigorous curriculum content and the corresponding instructional time to apply it, has been abysmal. In too many regions in Canada, physical education and sports programs are still considered a fringe subject in schools. A student in PERS studies should now know that this ought not to be the case at any educational level, and should aggressively pursue, through professional associations, measures to rectify this ill-conceived notion. The values derived from good physical education and sports programs within the education system are well documented throughout this text. Sadly, it is still necessary to substantiate the role of physical education and sport to many teaching colleagues, to administrators, and to the general public.

LEISURE SOCIETY AND THE RECREATION IMPERATIVE

Earlier in the text, it was mentioned that Canadian society, like most advanced Western cultures, is striving to achieve what might be called the leisure society. This life-style is often described by theorists as that point in a society's development when discretionary time, for the majority of its citizens, reaches approximately 30 to 35 percent of a standard time frame, such as a day, a week, or a month. In achieving this unobligated time it is necessary to understand that the productivity and financial rewards to the individual or to society continue to expand. However, the work time needed to accomplish this result becomes less. This process, therefore, creates greater discretionary time for leisure pursuits. It also must be realized that in most industrial societies, like Canada, where achievement is a meritorious characteristic, individuals desire and strive for the leisure society. For the most part, the means by which today's cultures will reach this objective is through technological advancement.

Historically, one should comprehend that some form of a leisure society has been attained by selected groups in past cultures, such as the ancient Egyptian, Greek, Roman, and certain South and Central American cultures. This development was usually achieved not only by the intellectual dominance of a particular ruling class, but by their aggression upon neighboring societies. In these cases, this permitted slavery to be the means of creating the leisure society for the ruling class of the dominant culture. These historical facts are mentioned because the outgrowth of these achievements was cultural, intellectual, and productivity stagnation which eventually led to disintegration of the society. Anthropologists and sociologists concur in the belief that a significant cause in the collapse of these cultures was their inability to deal with the increase in discretionary time in a meaningful and constructive manner.

Industrial nations are about to be confronted with the same problem of how to prepare for the imminent arrival of the leisure society. This question is often referred to as the *recreation imperative*. The responsibility for meaningful preparation will fall largely upon the shoulders of future recreationist, leisurist, physical activity, and cultural professionals. How to lay the foundations for this inevitable increase in discretionary time must be examined now and constructive and worthwhile solutions presented. This will be no easy task. PERS specialists know that Canada has a unique and sometimes conflicting delivery system for its leisure, recreational, physical activity, and cultural needs. It involves a multitude of public, private, and commercial agencies and associations. Who will do what, for which segment of the population, and how? This is the recreation imperative, and PERS professionals must be prepared with answers to the questions and the leadership to attain them.

LEGAL LIABILITY IN PERS

It is not the intention of these few paragraphs to describe or define the limits of legal liability as it pertains to many varied professionals in PERS. Suffice it to mention that as professionals we are responsible to the society in which we function for our actions, competencies, and the programs which we operate. Therefore, any negligent act is open to a civil suit against the individual and the agency for which one may work. The trend in the 1980s is for the Canadian society to hold professions more accountable for negligent behaviour than in the past. With the possible exception of the medical profession and its paraprofessionals, PERS vocations seem to be receiving an ever-increasing scrutiny by the public. This is a justifiable concern on the part of the public for at least three significant reasons. First, it is because many PERS programs and activities have elements of physical and psychological risk contained within them (for example, outdoor recreational activities of all kinds and aggressive competitive sports and games). Second, it is because programs often are instructed or supervised by unqualified individuals, such as many persons involved in amateur sports coaching and community recreation programs. Third, organization, instruction, and supervision often involve children and adolescents, who are most vulnerable to the excesses and omissions of their leaders. For these reasons, a burden is placed upon qualified professionals to be constantly diligent in their professional practices.

With the above in mind, some of the areas within PERS which seem most susceptible to legal action based upon negligence are as follows: (1) improper first-aid application or athletic injury care and prevention, (2) transporting participants in private vehicles, (3) improper ratio of participants to instructors or supervisors, (4) lack of emergency accident procedures, (5) unqualified instructors, (6) unsafe equipment, environment, or facilities, and (7) excessive physical and psychological demands upon individuals to perform. This list is by no means all-inclusive but represents some of the key areas which are often open to litigation based upon negligence on the part of the responsible individual and/or agency.

However, having implied less than a positive picture concerning legal liability to this point, let us briefly examine some of the protection one has against undue legal harassment and what can be done to minimize difficult situations. There are legal concepts which assist and protect practitioners from being overly defensive and cautious regarding their programs and their skills. Negligence is difficult to prove as proof requires that the actions of the practitioner must be beyond the bounds of behaviour which would normally be expected from any other *reasonable and prudent* person of similar qualifications and in similar circumstances. Also applicable is the legal view that any person participating voluntarily in leisure, recreational, or sport activities must accept some *assumption of risk* by choosing to be involved. Also relevant is the concept of *contributory negligence* which means that the injured party, or plaintiff, has in some manner been partially to blame for the accident.

Finally, stemming from the above-mentioned problem areas, the following list provides some procedures which could be followed in order to alleviate any feelings of insecurity or apprehension by either a professional or volunteer leader involved in physical activity and sport.

1. Maintain up-to-date first-aid and CPR certification. If involved in aquatics programs, an appropriate certification should be maintained.
2. Verify that the employing agency carries adequate liability insurance or acquire personal liability insurance.
3. Maintain current standards of prevention and care of athletic injuries.
4. Ensure that when some form other than public transportation is used, proper liability insurance is carried on all vehicles.

5. Keep up-to-date in the procedures to be followed in emergency situations—especially those involving outdoor recreation and contact sports.
6. Regularly ascertain the safety of all equipment and facilities to be used.
7. Ensure that the qualifications, knowledge, and skills to instruct specialized activities are present (for example, to instruct activities such as gymnastics, aquatics, camping, boating, and mountaineering).

In addition, one responsible for staffing must seek out qualified and experienced instructors, whether they be professionals, paraprofessionals, or volunteers. It may be necessary to develop in-service training programs for staff.

By developing consistency in the above-mentioned guidelines, and others which may be specific to certain situations, any accusation of negligence should be avoided.

INDIVIDUAL AND NATIONAL FITNESS

The growing desire of many Canadians over recent decades to improve the level of their personal physical fitness will not only reap positive benefits to individuals by improving their quality of life, but will, in the long run, be reflected in socioeconomic terms by reducing health and hospital costs and increasing productivity. Fueled by individual and collective will, by the views of the medical and PERS professions, by commercial product advertising, by our national advertising agency for fitness (Participaction), and countless other concerned associations and groups, it appears likely that the individual desire for fitness, in all parts of the nation, will be with us for years to come.

The repercussions of this "fitness craze" do, and will continue to, create concerns as to how the demand for programs will be satisfied and managed within the Canadian delivery system. The trend at this time is for the public and private recreation institutions and commercial agencies to bear the brunt of program delivery. Whether this solution is the appropriate one is debatable. However, it is a fact. It is also a fact that only those agencies (municipal recreation departments, YM/YWCAs, health spas, and some private sports clubs) do, and can, cater to a cross section of the population, particularly the adult segment.

This creates a significant problem with regard to leadership qualifications, as the burden of proper physiological and kinesthetic knowledge is placed upon the least-prepared (academically) profession in PERS studies, the recreationist. At present, the undergraduate and graduate preparation in recreation studies spends little time in developing bioscience comprehension. This will have to change quickly. Some private agencies are presently bearing the responsibility for the fitness training process, notably the certification of fitness and aerobic instructors by the YMCAs of Canada. They are to be commended for the role they are fulfilling. The leadership crisis in fitness programming is most notable in the commercial area of health spas. Because of the desire for increased profit margins and the resulting aggressive sales techniques employed, few PERS professionals can be found in the commercial fitness system. This is unacceptable and can only be resolved by public and professional demands for improvement and/or by government intervention in legislating minimum standards for fitness instructors and program operators. The necessity for resolving this problem of underqualified instructors in the commercial fitness agencies should not be underestimated, as they service by far the greatest number of Canadian adults in their quest for personal fitness, better health habits, and an improved quality of life.

As previously implied, the upshot of this fitness craving by Canadians is that recreationists will need a greater understanding of man's physiological and kinesthetic functions, or that physical educators and/or fitness specialists will become a necessary adjunct to the recreation delivery system in Canada to a greater extent than at present.

POSTSECONDARY EDUCATION IN PERS STUDIES: UNDER REVIEW

It is most likely that financial restraint within universities and colleges will continue for some time. One of the repercussions of this limitation is that university boards, administrators, and senates are closely examining the curricula of their respective institutions. Several disciplines and professional programs, especially newly formulated ones such as PERS studies, are under severe scrutiny as to whether they should be a part of the postsecondary educational process. This review procedure has occurred, or is now to be exercised, across the nation, from the University of British Columbia in the far west to the University of Winnipeg in the central region to Dalhousie University in the east. No university or college is likely to be immune. The relevance of this problem may not be immediately discernible to the undergraduate student in PERS studies. Nevertheless, if considered in the terms of his or her future educational requirements and the needs of future students, restriction of courses in the field would have a negative consequence.

This critical self-examination by postsecondary institutions is often perceived as a threatening and unnecessary questioning of well-established curricula and departments. There is some justification for viewing this process with concern, as already departments and programs in recreation, physical education, and sports have been lost from various universities. Possibly a more positive approach to this reevaluation is to view it as an opportunity to prove the discipline's (and its professions') maturity and significance.

From this latter position, the following academic and organizational suggestions may assist professionals in clarifying a disciplinary position for PERS studies within the setting of a university. The following statements emanate in part from concepts discussed in chapter 1.

1. That the discipline (PERS studies) establish itself as a major area of study within the social or human sciences, thus providing a major in the degree of arts or science, either in physical activity and sports studies or recreational studies. Another alternative would be to achieve independent faculty status which awards its own degree.
2. That the discipline continue to service physical education and education majors only through, or in conjunction with, faculties of education.
3. That the curriculum for a major in sport and physical activity studies should be, for the most part, a different sequence of courses and requirements than would be a major in recreational studies.

However, in considering the above points, the departments of sport and physical activity studies should realize that their curricula are discipline oriented, and physical education or education methodology courses (as indicated in the second statement) should exist in their offerings only through necessity or structural convenience. If possible, these should be taught in education faculties.

The objective of the above suggestions is to indicate clearly the difference between legitimate disciplinary studies—the single most important purpose of a university—and professional preparation course sequences and degrees. For example, historians, mathematicians, and biologists normally must first study their disciplinary knowledge and methodology, and only afterward instructional methods in their fields. PERS studies should be approached in a similar manner. Such an academic structure will gain the respect of, and equal status with, sister disciplines in the university or college environment.

WOMEN IN CANADIAN SPORT

To some extent Canadians must be thankful that when it became culturally appropriate for women to take their rightful, and belated, place among sports people, it was achieved without major acrimony and without excessive delays. This is said with some degree of certainty when one views the historical record of women's full and equal participation in Canadian sport as compared to the United States. Although there were European nations who perceived the inequity of opportunity and the misplaced stigmas associated with women's sport earlier than Canada, Canadians were not far behind these cultures in identifying and trying to correct the injustices. Canada has worked diligently since World War II toward creditable sports programs for women and girls without the need of federal or provincial equal opportunity legislation (e.g., Title IX [U.S.]) or the brief development in the 1970s of dual jurisdictional bodies (e.g., NCAA and AIAW [U.S.]). We must, however, recognize in retrospect that equal opportunity programs for women and girls in Canada did (and still do) experience some difficult moments. Certain educational and sports institutions were slow to comprehend that the issue was basically nondebatable. With understanding and progressive leadership from both the dominant male establishment and the emerging spokeswomen of sport, the foundations for women's sports programs were entrenched by the late 1950s and the early 1960s. In the 1970s and 1980s these programs have continued to expand in quantity and quality.

Nevertheless, to this day stumbling blocks are still evident for females in sport, not so much as the right to participate but in some cases how best this can be done. In the past few years there have been some difficulties when girls in their early teens have wished to continue to play within boys' programs in ice hockey, soccer, and football. This usually arises because of the lack of an equal program of quality or because there are too few girls who wish to participate in the sport at this age. This issue will most likely be resolved within regional jurisdictions with different solutions tailored to specific situations. However, the areas in which one still finds significant inequity of opportunity, or even a degree of discrimination, are in the fields of sports administration and the coaching of women's sports. There are two views of this problem. One is that the male-dominated administrative and coaching structures of women's sports is slow to change. The other is that there is still a lack of knowledge, skill, and experience on the part of women aspiring to move into these support areas of women's sport. Some who hold this latter view often rationalize that this may be a cultural reality in that many sportswomen find it difficult to make long-term commitments to their specific areas of sport. Social and cultural responsibilities, whether perceived or real, are in many cases greater for women than they are for men (e.g., childbearing and rearing). Yet in the area of coaching and administration, committed women were beginning to rise to the surface by the late 1970s and early 1980s throughout the Canadian sports scene. One of the most notable is Dr. Abigail Hoffman who is presently director of the National Fitness and Sport Directorate in Ottawa. The following is but a brief list of Canadian women who have recently (in the 1970s and 1980s) achieved distinction in administration or coaching: Kathy Shields (coaching/U.B.C.), Barbara Graham (coaching/ figure skating), Mariana Van de Merive (coaching/field hockey), Dr. Pat Lawson (administration and coaching/University of Saskatchewan), Irene MacDonald (coaching/diving), Elizabeth Hoffman (administration and coaching/field hockey), Marilyn Savage (coaching/gymnastics), Marilyn Promfort (administration/U.B.C.), Caroline Letheren (coaching/gymnastics), Joyce Fromson (administration/University of Manitoba), Dr. Elizabeth Ready (research/University of Manitoba), Dr. Joan Stevenson (research/Queen's University), Dr. Barb Schrodt (historian/U.B.C.), and certainly Elizabeth Chard, past president of the Canadian Interuniversity Athletic Union, to name just a few.

THE ENVIRONMENT: ITS USES

Either from the increase in participation figures or from the total monies spent by Canadians in the past few decades in their ever-expanding pursuit of the outdoors, recreationalists, naturalists, and environmental specialists can easily ascertain the growing need for nature-oriented outdoor recreational facilities and programs. This desire of Canadians to take a greater interest in, and be involved with, the natural environment is a trend of the present and probably of the future. As the effectiveness of technology expands and leisure time in-creases, greater attention is focused on the individual need for a more peaceful, "back to nature" life-style.

The pressure that is applied to existing facilities and especially to the natural environment is often more than it can bear. Adding to this stress is the continuing requirement of our many natural resources and of petrochemical and manufacturing industries to expand production for sound national eco-nomic growth. These conflicting interests compound the problems of envi-ronmental deterioration. It is not a pleasing project, nor for that matter a profitable one, to realize that one cannot fish, drink the water, swim, or camp beside many Canadian waterways because of sterility or pollution. Also, it is difficult to comprehend that our forests, wilderness, and their animal species are being destroyed faster than they can be replenished.

It is therefore imperative that, along with environmentalists, native groups, and special, small segments of the population, parks and recreation specialists be evermore diligent and passionate in demonstrating aggressive leadership. They must direct their energies to the establishment of national and provincial industrial policies that take into consideration the preservation of the Canadian outdoors. Outdoor recreation pursuits, which are often the leisure activities of the average Canadian, are in jeopardy of becoming the exclusive, costly pastimes of fewer and fewer of our people. This must not be allowed to happen, and all concerned with the natural environment within PERS must strive to help in the development of strategic plans for its protec-tion and use as well as to assist in the fostering of a national consciousness for support.

APPENDIX A

Outstanding Sports Achievements by Canadians

Since the nineteenth century, when international competitions were introduced for many sports, Canadians have been among the best in the world in a remarkably wide range of activities, both individual and team.

CANADIAN MEDAL WINNERS AT THE OLYMPIC GAMES

The modern Olympic Games, first held in 1896, have become the standard against which all other accomplishments are measured, and the winning of a medal in the Games—gold (G), silver (S), or bronze (B)—is a mark of outstanding achievement. The following list comprises the Canadian winners of these medals.

SUMMER OLYMPIC GAMES	EVENT	MEDAL
1900 George Orton	2500m steeplechase	G
George Orton	400m hurdles	B
1904 Etienne Desmarteau	56-lb weight throw	G
George Lyon	Golf	G
Galt Football Club	Soccer	G
Winnipeg Shamrocks	Lacrosse	G
Argonauts Club	Rowing (eights)	S
Mohawk Indians Club	Lacrosse	B
1906 Bill Sherring	Marathon	G
Donald Linden	1500m walk	S

SUMMER OLYMPIC GAMES	EVENT	MEDAL
1908 Robert Kerr	200m	G
All-Canada team	Lacrosse	G
Walter Ewing	Trap shooting	G
T. Garfield-MacDonald	Triple jump	S
George Beattie	Trap shooting	S
Trap shooting team	Team event	S
Robert Kerr	100m	B
Edward Archibald	Pole vault	B
Calvin Bricker	Long jump	B
Col Walsh	Hammer throw	B
Cycling team	400m pursuit (team)	B
N. B. Jackes, F. P. Toms	Rowing (pairs)	B
Rowing team	Rowing (eights)	B
Canadian Army gun team	Military rifle (team)	B
Aubert Côté	FS wrestling (bantamweight)	B
1912 George Goulding	10,000m walk	G
George Hodgson	400m freestyle	G
George Hodgson	1500m freestyle	G
Calvin Bricker	Broad jump	S
Duncan Gillis	Hammer throw	S
William Happeny	Pole vault	B
Frank Lukeman	Pentathlon	B
Everand Butler	Rowing (sculls)	B
1920 Earl Thomson	110m hurdles	G
Albert Schneider	Boxing (welterweight)	G
Chris Graham	Boxing (bantamweight)	S
Georges Prud'homme	Boxing (middleweight)	S
George Vernot	1500m freestyle	S
Chris Newton	Boxing (lightweight)	B
Moe Herscovitch	Boxing (middleweight)	B
George Vernot	400m freestyle	B
1924 Vancouver Rowing Club	Rowing (fours)	S
University of Toronto Rowing Club	Rowing (eights)	S
Shooting team	Trapshooting	S
Doug Lewis	Boxing (welterweight)	B
1928 Percy Williams	Men's 100m	G
Percy Williams	Men's 200m	G
Women's Relay	4 × 100m	G
Ethel Catherwood	Women's high jump	G
James Ball	Men's 400m	S
Fanny Rosenfeld	Women's 100m	S
Doug Stockton	FS wrestling (middleweight)	S
John Guest, Joseph Wright	Sculls	S
Men's Relay	4 × 400m	B
Ethel Smith	Women's 100m	B
Raymond Smillie	Boxing (welterweight)	B
Argonaut Rowing Club	Rowing (eights)	B
Men's Relay	Swimming 4 × 200m freestyle	B
Jim Trifunow	FS wrestling (bantamweight)	B
Maurice Letchford	FS wrestling (welterweight)	B

SUMMER OLYMPIC GAMES	EVENT	MEDAL
1932 Duncan McNaughton	Men's high jump	G
Horace Gwynne	Boxing (bantamweight)	G
Alex Wilson	Men's 800m	S
Hilda Strike	Women's 100m	S
Women's Relay	4 × 100m	S
Dan MacDonald	FS wrestling (welterweight)	S
Yachting team	8m (International class)	S
Alex Wilson	Men's 400m	B
Philip Edwards	Men's 800m	B
Philip Edwards	Men's 1500m	B
Men's Relay	4 × 400m	B
Eva Dawes	Women's high jump	B
Charles Pratt, Noel DeMille	Rowing (double sculls)	B
Hamilton Leanders	Rowing (eights)	B
Yachting team	6 metres R-class	B
1936 Francis Amyot	Canoeing (Canadian 1000m)	G
John Loaring	Men's 400m hurdles	S
Team	Basketball (men's)	S
Harvey Charters, Frank Saker	Canoeing (Canadian 10,000m)	S
Philip Edwards	Men's 800m	B
Elizabeth Taylor	Women's 80m	B
Women's Relay	4 × 100m	B
Harvey Charters, Frank Saker	Canoeing (Canadian 1000m)	B
Joseph Schleimer	FS wrestling (light middleweight)	B
1948 Douglas Bennett	Canoeing (Canadian 1000m)	S
Women's Relay	4 × 100m	B
Norman Lane	Canoeing (Canadian 10,000m)	B
1952 George Genereux	Trapshooting	G
Ken Lane, Don Hagwood	Canoeing (Canadian 10,000m)	S
Gerald Gratton	Weightlifting (middleweight)	S
1956 University of British Columbia	Rowing (fours)	G
Gerald Ouellette	Small-bore rifle, prone	G
University of British Columbia	Rowing (eights)	S
Irene MacDonald	Women's 3m springboard	B
Equestrian team	3-day team event	B
Gilmour Boa	Small-bore rifle, prone	B
1960 University of British Columbia	Rowing (eights)	S
1964 George Hungerford, Roger Jackson	Rowing (pairs)	G
William Crothers	Men's 800m	S
Douglas Rogers	Judo (80 kg)	S
Harry Jerome	Men's 100m	B

SUMMER OLYMPIC GAMES	EVENT	MEDAL
1968 Equestrian team	Grand Prix jumping	G
Ralph Hutton	Men's 400m freestyle	S
Elaine Tanner	Women's 100m backstroke	S
Elaine Tanner	Women's 200m backstroke	S
Women's Relay	4 × 100m freestyle	B
1972 Leslie Cliff	Women's 400m individual	S
Bruce Robertson	Men's 100m butterfly	S
Donna-Marie Gurr	Women's 200m backstroke	B
Men's Relay	4 × 100m	B
Yachting team	Team (Soling)	B
1976 Greg Joy	Men's high jump	S
John Wood	Canoeing (Canadian 500m)	S
Michel Vaillancourt	Equestrian (Grand Prix jumping)	S
Cheryl Gibson	Women's 400m individual	S
Men's Relay	4 × 100m medley	S
Nancy Garapick	Women's 100m backstroke	B
Nancy Garapick	Women's 200m backstroke	B
Shannon Smith	Women's 400m freestyle	B
Becky Smith	Women's 400m individual	B
Women's Relay	4 × 100m freestyle	B
Women's Relay	4 × 100m medley	B
1984 Larry Cain	Canoeing (men's 500m C-1)	G
Hugh Fisher, Alwyn Morris	Canoeing (men's 1000m K-2)	G
Sylvie Bernier	Women's 3m springboard	G
Lori Fung	Rhythmic gymnastics	G
Men's Rowing	Rowing (eights)	G
Linda Thom	Women's air pistol	G
Alex Baumann	Men's 200m individual medley	G
Alex Baumann	Men's 400m individual medley	G
Victor Davis	Men's 200m breaststroke	G
Anne Ottenbrite	Women's 200m breaststroke	G
Willie deWit	Boxing (91 kg)	S
Shawn O'Sullivan	Boxing (71 kg)	S
Alexandra Barre, Sue Holloway	Canoeing (women's 500m K-2)	S
Larry Cain	Canoeing (men's 1000m C-1)	S
Steve Bauer	Cycling (men's road race)	S
Curt Harnett	Cycling (men's 1000m [overall])	S
Betty Craig, Tricia Smith	Rowing (women's pairs)	S
Women's Rowing	Rowing (fours with cox)	S
Victor Davis	Men's 100m breaststroke	S
Anne Ottenbrite	Women's 100m breaststroke	S
Men's Relay	4 × 100m medley	S
Sharon Hanbrook, Kelly Kryczka	Synchronized swimming (duet)	S
Carolyn Waldo	Synchronized swimming (solo)	S

SUMMER OLYMPIC GAMES	EVENT	MEDAL
Women's Relay	4 × 100m	S
Women's Relay	4 × 400m	S
Jacques Demers	Weightlifting (75 kg)	S
Bob Molle	FS wrestling (100 kg)	S
Evert Bastet, Terry McLaughlin	Yachting (Flying Dutchman)	S
Dale Walters	Boxing (54 kg)	B
Women's team	Canoeing (500m K-4)	B
Hugh Fisher, Alwyn Morris	Canoeing (men's 500m K-2)	B
Mark Berger	Judo (+95 kg)	B
Men's Rowing	Rowing (fours)	B
Daniele Laumann, Silken Laumann	Rowing (men's sculls)	B
Robert Mills	Rowing (men's sculls)	B
Cam Henning	Men's 200m backstroke	B
Mike West	Men's 100m backstroke	B
Women's Relay	4 × 100m medley	B
Ben Johnson	Men's 100m	B
Men's Relay	4 × 100m	B
Lynn Williams	Women's 3000m	B
Chris Rinke	FS wrestling (82 kg)	B
Yachting team	Yachting (Soling)	B
Terry Neilson	Yachting (Finn)	B

WINTER OLYMPIC GAMES	EVENT	MEDAL
1920 Winnipeg Falcons	Ice hockey	G
1924 Toronto Granite Club	Ice hockey	G
1928 University of Toronto Grads	Ice hockey	G
1932 Team	Ice hockey	G
Alex Hurd	Speed skating (men's 1500m)	S
Montgomery Wilson	Figure skating (men's singles)	B
Alex Hurd	Speed skating (men's 500m)	B
William Logan	Speed skating (men's 1500m)	B
William Logan	Speed skating (men's 5000m)	B
Frank Stack	Speed skating (men's 10,000m)	B
1936 Team	Ice hockey	S
1948 Team	Ice hockey	G
Barbara Ann Scott	Figure skating (women's)	G
Suzanne Morrow, Wallace Diestelmeyer	Figure skating (pairs)	B
1952 Team	Ice hockey	G
Gordon Audley	Speed skating (men's 500m)	B
1956 Frances Dafoe, Norris Bowden	Figure skating (pairs)	S
Lucille Wheeler	Skiing (women's downhill)	B
Team	Ice hockey	B

WINTER OLYMPIC GAMES	EVENT	MEDAL
1960 Anne Heggtveit	Skiing (women's slalom)	G
Barbara Paul, Robert Wagner	Figure skating (pairs)	G
Team	Ice hockey	S
Donald Jackson	Figure skating (men's singles)	B
1964 Vic Emery team	Bobsleigh (four-man)	G
Debbi Wilkes, Guy Revell	Figure skating (pairs)	B
Petra Burka	Figure skating (women's)	B
1968 Nancy Greene	Skiing (women's giant slalom)	G
Nancy Greene	Skiing (women's slalom)	S
Team	Ice hockey	B
1972 Karen Magnussen	Figure skating (women's)	S
1976 Kathy Kreiner	Skiing (women's giant slalom)	G
Cathy Priestner	Speed skating (women's 500m)	S
Toller Cranston	Figure skating (men's)	B
1980 Gaetan Boucher	Speed skating (men's 1000m)	S
Steve Podborski	Skiing (men's downhill)	B
1984 Gaetan Boucher	Speed skating (men's 1000m)	G
Gaetan Boucher	Speed skating (men's 1500m)	G
Brian Orser	Figure skating (men's)	S
Gaetan Boucher	Speed skating (men's 500m)	B

CANADIAN GOLD MEDALLISTS AT THE COMMONWEALTH GAMES (BRITISH EMPIRE, BRITISH EMPIRE & COMMONWEALTH, BRITISH COMMONWEALTH GAMES)

YEAR	COMPETITOR	EVENT
1930	Percy Williams	Men's 100y
	Alexander Wilson	Men's 440y
	Men's Relay	4 × 100y
	Leonard Hutton	Men's long jump
	Gord Smallacombe	Triple jump
	Victor Pickard	Men's pole vault
	F. Munroe Bourne	Men's 100y freestyle
	Men's Relay	4 × 200y freestyle
	Jack Aubin	Men's 200y
	Alfred Phillips	Men's highboard
	Alfred Phillips	Men's springboard
	Pearl Stoneham	Women's highboard
	James Trifunov	Wrestling (52 kg)
	Clifford Chilicott	Wrestling (62 kg)
	Howard Thomas	Wrestling (68 kg)

YEAR	COMPETITOR	EVENT
	Reg Priestley	Wrestling (74 kg)
	Mike Chepwick	Wrestling (82 kg)
	L. McIntyre	Wrestling (90 kg)
	Earl McCready	Wrestling (100 kg)
	E. Bole, R. Richards	Rowing (double sculls)
1934	Harold Webster	Men's marathon
	Samuel Richardson	Men's long jump
	C. T. Sylvanus Apps	Men's pole vault
	Robert Dixon	Men's javelin
	Women's Relay	660y
	Robert McLeod	Cycling (10 miles scratch)
	George Burleigh	100y freestyle
	Men's Relay	4 × 200y freestyle
	Men's Relay	3 × 100y medley
	Phyllis Dewar	Women's 100y freestyle
	Phyllis Dewar	Women's 440y freestyle
	Women's Relay	3 × 100y medley
	Women's Relay	4 × 100y freestyle
	Judith Moss	Women's springboard
	Robert McNab	Wrestling (62 kg)
	Joseph Schleimer	Wrestling (74 kg)
1938	Men's Relay	4 × 110y
	Harold Brown	Men's long jump
	Eric Coy	Men's discus
	James Courtwright	Men's javelin
	George Sutherland	Men's hammer
	Robina Higgins	Women's javelin
	Thomas Osborne	Boxing (81 kg)
	Robert Pirie	Men's 110y freestyle
	Robert Pirie	Men's 440y freestyle
	Women's Relay	4 × 110y freestyle
	Terry Evans	Wrestling (82 kg)
1950	C. William Parnell	Men's mile
	Leo Roininen	Men's javelin
	Peter Salmon	Men's 110y freestyle
	George Athans	Men's springboard
	James Varaleau	Weightlifting (82.5 kg)
	G. Gratton	Weightlifting (75 kg)
	Henry Hudson	Wrestling (74 kg)
	Maurice Vachon	Wrestling (82 kg)
1954	Men's Relay	4 × 110y
	Rowing team	Rowing (eights)
	Micky Bergin	Boxing (60 kg)
	Wilfred Greaves	Boxing (67 kg)
	William Patrick	Men's highboard
	G. Gratton	Weightlifting (82.5 kg)
	Keevil Daly	Weightlifting (middle heavyweight)
	Doug Hepburn	Weightlifting (+90 kg)
	Fencing team	Men's sabre team event
1958	Rowing team	Rowing (eights)

YEAR	COMPETITOR	EVENT
1962	Bruce Kidd	Men's 6 miles
	Harold Mann	Boxing (67 kg)
	Richard Pound	Men's 110y freestyle
	Mary Stewart	Women's 110y butterfly
1966	Harry Jerome	Men's 110y
	Dave Steen	Men's shot put
	Abigail Hoffman	Women's 880y
	Gilmour Boa	Shooting (small bore)
	James Lee	Shooting (centre-fire pistol)
	Men's Relay	4 × 110y medley
	R. Jacks	100y butterfly
	Marion Lay	Women's 110y freestyle
	Elaine Tanner	Women's 110y butterfly
	Elaine Tanner	Women's 220y butterfly
	Elaine Tanner	Women's 440y individual medley
	Women's team	4 × 110y freestyle medley
	Pierre St. Jean	Weightlifting (75 kg)
	Richard Chamberot	Wrestling (90 kg)
1970	Dave Steen	Men's shot put
	Debbie Brill	Women's high jump
	James Paulson	Badminton (men's singles)
	Jocelyn Lovell	Cycling (10 miles scratch)
	William Kennedy	Men's 100m backstroke
	William Mahony	Men's 100m breaststroke
	A. Byron McDonald	Men's 100m butterfly
	Toomas Arusoo	Men's 200m butterfly
	George Smith	Men's 200m individual medley
	George Smith	Men's 400m individual medley
	Men's Relay	4 × 100m
	Angela Coughlan	Women's 100m freestyle
	Beverley Boys	Women's highboard
	Beverley Boys	Women's springboard
	Russ Prior	Weightlifting (110 kg)
	Edward Millard	Wrestling (100 kg)
1974	Yvonne Saunders	Women's 400m
	Glenda Reiser	Women's 1500m
	Jane Haist	Women's shot put
	Jane Haist	Women's discus
	John Primrose	Shooting (trap)
	Harry Willsie	Shooting (skeet)
	Jules Sobrian	Shooting (free pistol)
	William Hare	Shooting (rapid-fire pistol)
	Men's Relay	4 × 100m freestyle
	Men's Relay	4 × 100m medley
	Wendy Cook	Women's 100m backstroke
	Patti Stenhouse	Women's 100m butterfly
	Wendy Cook	Women's 200m backstroke
	Leslie Cliff	Women's 200m individual medley
	Leslie Cliff	Women's 400m individual medley
	Women's Relay	4 × 100m freestyle
	Women's Relay	4 × 100m medley
	Beverley Boys	Women's highboard
	Cindy Shatto	Women's springboard

YEAR	COMPETITOR	EVENT
1978	Russ Prior	Weightlifting (110 kg)
	Egon Beiler	Wrestling (62 kg)
	Terry Paice	Wrestling (90 kg)
	Claude Pilon	Wrestling (100 kg)
	Bruce Simpson	Men's pole vault
	Borys Chambul	Men's discus
	Phil Olsen	Men's javelin
	Claude Ferragne	Men's high jump
	Carmen Ionesco	Women's discus
	Diane Jones Konihowski	Women's pentathlon
	Kelly Perlette	Boxing (71 kg)
	Roger Fortin	Boxing (81 kg)
	Jocelyn Lovell	Cycling (10 miles scratch)
	Jocelyn Lovell, Gordon Singleton	Cycling (tandem sprint)
	Jocelyn Lovell	Time trial
	Women's team	Gymnastics (team event)
	Elfi Schlegel	Gymnastics (women's individual all-round)
	Men's team	Gymnastics (team event)
	Philip Delesalle	Gymnastics (men's individual all-round)
	John Primrose	Shooting (trap)
	Yvon Trempe	Shooting (free pistol)
	Jules Sobrian	Shooting (rapid-fire pistol)
	Desmond Vamplew	Shooting (full-bore rifle)
	Graham Smith	Men's 100m breaststroke
	Graham Smith	Men's 200m breaststroke
	Dan Thompson	Men's 100m butterfly
	George Nagy	Men's 200m butterfly
	Graham Smith	Men's 200m individual medley
	Graham Smith	Men's 400m individual medley
	Men's Relay	4 × 100m medley
	Men's Relay	4 × 100m freestyle
	Carol Klimpel	Women's 100m freestyle
	Cheryl Gibson	Women's 200m backstroke
	Wendy Quirk	Women's 100m butterfly
	Robin Corsiglia	Women's 100m butterfly
	Lisa Borsholt	Women's 200m breaststroke
	Women's Relay	4 × 100m freestyle
	Women's Relay	4 × 100m medley
	Linda Cuthbert	Women's highboard
	Janet Nutter	Women's springboard
	Michel Mercier	Weightlifting (60 kg)
	Russ Prior	Weightlifting (110 kg)
	Jean Marc Cardinal	Weightlifting (+110 kg)
	Ray Takahashi	Wrestling (52 kg)
	Egon Beiler	Wrestling (62 kg)
	Richard Deschatelets	Wrestling (82 kg)
	Stephen Danier	Wrestling (90 kg)
	Wyatt Wishart	Wrestling (100 kg)
	Robert Gibbons	Wrestling (+100 kg)

YEAR	COMPETITOR	EVENT
1982	Marc McKoy	Men's 110m hurdles
	Milt Ottey	Men's high jump
	Bruno Pauletto	Men's shot put
	Angela Taylor	Women's 100m
	Debbie Brill	Women's high jump
	Women's Relay	4 × 100m
	Clarie Backhouse, Joanne Falardeau	Badminton (women's doubles)
	Shawn O'Sullivan	Boxing (71 kg)
	Willie deWit	Boxing (91 kg)
	Tom Guinn	Shooting (free pistol)
	Jean F. Senegal	Shooting (air rifle)
	Fred Altmann, Brian Gabriel	Shooting (skeet team)
	Mike West	Men's 100m backstroke
	Cam Henning	Men's 200m backstroke
	Victor Davis	Men's 200m breaststroke
	Dan Thompson	Men's 100m butterfly
	Alex Baumann	Men's 200m individual medley
	Alex Baumann	Men's 400m individual medley
	Kathy Bald	Women's 100m breaststroke
	Anne Ottenbrite	Women's 200m breaststroke
	Women's Relay	4 × 100m medley
	Bob Robinson	Wrestling (62 kg)
	Chris Rinke	Wrestling (82 kg)
	Clark Davis	Wrestling (90 kg)
	Richard Deschatelets	Wrestling (100 kg)
	Wyatt Wishart	Wrestling (+100 kg)
1986	Ben Johnson	Men's 100m
	Angella Issajenko	Women's 200m
	Atlee Mahorn	Men's 200m
	Lynn Williams	Women's 3000m
	Graeme Fell	Men's steeplechase
	Mark McKoy	Men's 110m hurdles
	Men's Relay	4 × 100m
	Women's Relay	4 × 400m
	Ray Lazdins	Men's discus
	Milt Ottey	Men's high jump
	Scott Olson	Boxing (48 kg)
	Billy Downey	Boxing (57 kg)
	Asif Dar	Boxing (60 kg)
	Howard Grant	Boxing (63.5 kg)
	Dan Sherry	Boxing (71 kg)
	Lennox Lewis	Boxing (+91 kg)
	Debbie Fuller	Diving (3-metre)
	Debbie Fuller	Diving (10-metre)
	Kathryn Barr, Andrea Schreiner	Rowing (women's double sculls)
	Guy Lorion	Air rifle
	Sharon Bowes, Guy Lorion	Air rifle (team)
	Bill Baldwin, Alain Marion	Full-bore rifle (team)
	Claude Beaulieu, Tom Guinn	Free pistol (team)

YEAR	COMPETITOR	EVENT
	Michael Ashcroft, Gale Stewart	Small-bore rifle, prone (team)
	Mark Tewksbury	Men's 100m backstroke
	Sandy Goss	Men's 200m backstroke
	Victor Davis	Men's 100m breaststroke
	Allison Higson	Women's 100m breaststroke
	Allison Higson	Women's 200m breaststroke
	Donna McGinnis	Women's 200m butterfly
	Jane Kerr	Women's 100m freestyle
	Alex Baumann	Men's 200m individual medley
	Alex Baumann	Men's 400m individual medley
	Women's Relay	4 × 100m freestyle
	Men's Relay	4 × 100m medley
	Michelle Cameron, Carolyn Waldo	Synchronized swimming (duet)
	Sylvie Frechette	Synchronized swimming (solo)
	Denis Garon	Weightlifting (100 kg)
	Kevin Roy	Weightlifting (110 kg)
	Ron Moncur	Wrestling (48 kg)
	Chris Woodcroft	Wrestling (52 kg)
	Mitch Ostberg	Wrestling (57 kg)
	Paul Hughes	Wrestling (62 kg)
	Dave McKay	Wrestling (68 kg)
	Gary Holmes	Wrestling (74 kg)
	Chris Rinke	Wrestling (82 kg)
	Clark Davis	Wrestling (100 kg)
	Wayne Brightwell	Wrestling (+100 kg)

CANADIAN GOLD MEDALLISTS AT THE PAN AMERICAN GAMES

YEAR	COMPETITOR	EVENT
1955	H. Stewart	Women's 100m freestyle
	B. Whittall	Women's 400m freestyle
	L. Fisher	Women's 100m backstroke
	B. Whittall	Women's 100m butterfly
1959	Ernestine Russell	Gymnastics (women's all-round)
	Ernestine Russell	Gymnastics (women's vault)
	Ernestine Russell	Gymnastics (women's balance beam)
	Ernestine Russell	Gymnastics (women's uneven bars)
	G. R. Oullette	Shooting (small-bore rifle, prone)
	G. R. Oullette	Shooting (small-bore rifle, three positions)
	Shooting team	Small-bore rifle (prone)
	Equestrian team	Three-day event (team)
	Men's Relay	400m medley

YEAR	COMPETITOR	EVENT
1963	Don Bertoia	Men's 800m
	Alex Oakley	Men's 20 km walk
	Abby Hoffman	Women's 800m
	Nancy McCredie	Women's shot put
	Nancy McCredie	Women's discus
	William Weiler	Gymnastics (men's all-round)
	William Weiler	Gymnastics (men's vault)
	William Weiler	Gymnastics (men's floor)
	T. E. Dinsley	Men's springboard
	Yachting team	Dragon class
	Men's Rowing	Eights
1967	Harry Jerome	Men's 100m
	Andy Boychuk	Men's marathon
	Nancy McCredie	Women's shot put
	Brian Norris, Bon Bossey	Canoeing (10,000m C-2)
	Bill Cordner	Canoeing (1000m C-1)
	Arpad Simonyik	Canoeing (1000m K-1)
	Arpad Simonyik	Canoeing (500m K-1)
	Marcel Roy	Cycling (150 km road race)
	James Day	Equestrian (jump)
	Susan McDonnell	Gymnastics (women's uneven bars)
	Doug Rogers	Judo (super heavyweight)
	Michael Johnson	Judo (light heavyweight)
	Alf Mayer	Shooting (individual English match rifle)
	Ralph Hutton	Men's 200m backstroke
	Elaine Tanner	Women's 100m backstroke
	Elaine Tanner	Women's 200m backstroke
1971	Stephanie Berto	Women's 200m
	Abby Hoffman	Women's 800m
	Debbie Brill	Women's high jump
	Brenda Eisler	Women's long jump
	Debbie Van Kiekenbelt	Women's pentathlon
	Jocelyn Lovell	Cycling (men's 1000m individual time trial)
	Christilot Hanson	Equestrian (dressage)
	Equestrian team	Dressage
	Equestrian team	Three-day event
	Equestrian team	Jumping
	Donna-Marie Gurr	Women's 100m backstroke
	Donna-Marie Gurr	Women's 200m backstroke
	Sylvia Dockerill	Women's 100m breaststroke
	Jane Wright	Women's 200m breaststroke
	Leslie Cliff	Women's 200m individual medley
	Leslie Cliff	Women's 400m individual medley
	Women's Relay	400m medley
	Elizabeth Carruthers	Women's 3m springboard
	Nancy Robertson	Women's platform
	C. Chan	Weightlifting (flyweight)

YEAR	COMPETITOR	EVENT
1975	Joyce Yakubowich	Women's 400m
	Women's Relay	4 × 400m
	Diane Jones	Women's pentathlon
	Chris Clarke	Boxing (lightweight)
	Jocelyn Lovell	Cycling (men's 1000m time trial)
	Christilot Boylen	Equestrian (dressage)
	Brad Farrow	Judo (63 kg)
	Wayne Erdman	Judo (70 kg)
	Rainer Fisher	Judo (80 kg)
	Men's Rowing	Fours with cox
	Janet Nutter	Women's platform
	Russ Prior	Weightlifting (heavyweight)
	Egon Beiler	Wrestling (62 kg)
	Howard Stupp	Wrestling (62 kg–Greco-Roman)
1979	Diane Jones Konihowski	Women's pentathlon
	Scott Neilson	Men's hammer throw
	Bruce Simpson	Men's pole vault
	Gord Singleton	Cycling (sprint)
	Gord Singleton	Cycling (1 km–trial)
	Claude Langlois, Eon D'Ornellas	Cycling (400m–individual pursuit)
	Women's team	Gymnastics (team event)
	Monica Goermann	Gymnastics (women's all-round)
	Sherry Hawco	Gymnastics (women's balance beam)
	Monica Goermann	Gymnastics (women's uneven bars)
	Brad Farrow	Judo (65 kg)
	Louis Jani	Judo (80 kg)
	Bruce Ford, Pat Walker	Rowing (men's double sculls)
	Brian Dick, Tim Storm	Rowing (men's pairs without cox)
	Guy Lorion	Shooting (air rifle)
	Men's team	Shooting (team free pistol)
	Anne Gagnon	Women's 200m breaststroke
	Helen Vanderburg	Synchronized swimming (solo)
	Kelly Kryczka, Helen Vanderburg	Synchronized swimming (duet)
	Terry Hadlow	Weightlifting (middle heavyweight)
	Doug Yeats	Wrestling (Greco-Roman featherweight)
	Howard Stupp	Wrestling (Greco-Roman lightweight)
	Terry Nielson	Yachting (laser)
	Men's team	Softball
1983	Dave Steen	Men's decathlon
	Laslo Babits	Men's javelin
	Ranza Clark	Women's 1500m
	Charmaine Crooks	Women's 400m
	Men's team	Field hockey
	Mark Berger	Judo (men's +95 kg)
	Louis Jani	Judo (men's 86 kg)
	Philip Haggerty, Robert Mills	Rowing (men's double sculls)

Outstanding Sports Achievements by Canadians

YEAR	COMPETITOR	EVENT
	Rowing team	Men's fours without cox
	Kathy Bald	Women's 200m breaststroke
	Anne Ottenbrite	Women's 100m breaststroke
	Women's team	Synchronized swimming
	Jacques Demers	Weightlifting (74 kg)
	Garry Kallos	Wrestling (90 kg–sambo)
	Jeff Steubing	Wrestling (74 kg–Greco-Roman)
	Ray Takahashi	Wrestling (52 kg–freestyle)
	Men's team	Softball
	Women's team	Softball

CANADIAN GOLD MEDALLISTS AT THE WORLD UNIVERSITY GAMES

YEAR	COMPETITOR	EVENT
1965	Bill Crothers	Men's 1500m
1975	Bishop Dolegiewicz	Men's shot put
1977	Graham Smith	Men's 100m breaststroke
	Graham Smith	Men's 200m breaststroke
	Marion Stuart	Women's 100m breaststroke
	Anne Gagnon	Women's 200m breaststroke
1983	Guillaume Leblanc	Men's 20 km walk
	Dave Steen	Men's decathlon
	Philippe Chartrand	Gymnastics (men's high bar)
	Alex Baumann	Men's 400m individual medley
	Alex Baumann	Men's 200m individual medley
	Mike West	Men's 100m backstroke
	Jill Hetherington, Karen Davis	Tennis (women's doubles)
	Jill Hetherington, Bill Jenkins	Tennis (mixed doubles)
	Men's team	Basketball

APPENDIX B

International System of Units (SI)

Table B.1 shows some of the SI or metric units of measure. Table B.2 shows the prefixes and their abbreviations which may be used with metric units.

   The following is a list of rules that should be followed when reporting results in metric units.

1. No period should be used after the abbreviated versions of metric units. For example, 5.6 N (short for newtons), 3 kg (short for kilograms), or 0.1 s (short for seconds) are correct forms; but 10 m. and 20 sec. are incorrect forms.

2. A centered period ($\cdot$) may be used to separate units involving combined quantities, such as N$\cdot$s for newton seconds or kg$\cdot$m² for kilogram metres squared.

3. Do not capitalize a unit that was derived from a proper name when spelling out the unit even though the unit's abbreviation is a capital letter; examples of such units include the watt (W), the newton (N), hertz (Hz), the pascal (Pa), and the joule (J).

4. A slash (/) may be used to indicate an arithmetic division of units, such as m/s for metres per second or N/m² for newtons per square metre.

5. Do not mix abbreviations and nonabbreviated forms in an expression. For instance, the following are *incorrect* forms: newtons per m, kg.metres, and N.seconds.

6. The prefixes hecto, deca, deci, and centi should be avoided, excepting for the measurements of area, volume, and length, such as hectare, centilitre, and centimetre.

7. When pronouncing metric units that have a prefix, the accent should always be placed on the prefix, that is, kilo'-metre versus kilo-metre'.

8. When writing out numbers with greater than four digits on either side of the decimal point, use a space instead of a comma to separate digits into groups of three as, for example, 23 400 m or 0.001 63 m. This is because the comma is used in many countries as a decimal point. It is permissible to omit the blank in four digit numbers, such as 1000, 7988, etc.

Table B.1 International System of Units (SI)—Canadian Standards Association

QUANTITY	UNIT	SYMBOL	EXPRESSION
length	metre	m	
mass	kilogram	kg	
	tonne	t	1000 kg
time	second	s	
	minute	min	60 s
	hour	h	3600 s
plane angle	radian	rad	
	degree	°, deg	$(\pi/180)$ rad
	minute	'	1/60 degree
	second	''	1/3600 degree
	revolution	r	2π rad
frequency	hertz	Hz	1/s
force	newton	N	$kg \cdot m/s^2$
pressure, stress	pascal	Pa	N/m^2
energy, work	joule	J	$N \cdot m$
power	watt	W	J/s
area	square metre		m^2
volume	cubic metre		m^3
	litre	L	dm^3
linear velocity, speed	metre per second		m/s
linear acceleration	metre per second squared		m/s^2
angular velocity	radian per second		rad/s
angular acceleration	radian per second squared		rad/s^2
density	kilogram per cubic metre		kg/m^3
moment of force	newton metre		$N \cdot m$
temperature	degree Celsius	°C	
	kelvin	K	
linear momentum	kilogram metre per second		$kg \cdot m/s$ or $N \cdot s$
linear impulse	newton second		$N \cdot s$ or $kg \cdot m/s$
moment of inertia	kilogram metre squared		$kg \cdot m^2$

Table B.2 International System of Units Prefixes—Canadian Standards Association

MULTIPLYING FACTOR		PREFIX	SYMBOL
1 000 000 000 000	$= 10^{12}$	tera	T
1 000 000 000	$= 10^{9}$	giga	G
1 000 000	$= 10^{6}$	mega	M
1 000	$= 10^{3}$	kilo	k
100	$= 10^{2}$	hecto	h
10	$= 10^{1}$	deca	da
0.1	$= 10^{-1}$	deci	d
0.01	$= 10^{-2}$	centi	c
0.001	$= 10^{-3}$	milli	m
0.000 001	$= 10^{-6}$	micro	μ
0.000 000 001	$= 10^{-9}$	nano	n
0.000 000 000 001	$= 10^{-12}$	pico	p

Credits

Chapter 9, Figure 9.1, 9.6, 9.7

From J. H. Wilmore and David L. Costill, TRAINING FOR SPORTS AND ACTIVITY, 3d ed. Copyright © 1988 Wm. C. Brown Publishers, Dubuque, Iowa. All Rights Reserved. Reprinted by permission.

Figure 9.2 a & b, 9.3, 9.4

From Kent M. Van De Graaff, HUMAN ANATOMY. Copyright © 1984 Wm. C. Brown Publishers, Dubuque, Iowa. All Rights Reserved. Reprinted by permission.

Figure 9.12

From John W. Hole, Jr., HUMAN ANATOMY AND PHYSIOLOGY, 3d ed. Copyright © 1984 Wm. C. Brown Publishers, Dubuque, Iowa. All Rights Reserved. Reprinted by permission.

Figure 9.13

From Stuart Ira Fox, HUMAN PHYSIOLOGY. Copyright © 1984 Wm. C. Brown Publishers, Dubuque, Iowa. All Rights Reserved. Reprinted by permission.

Chapter 10, Figure 10.3

From J. H. Wilmore and David L. Costill, TRAINING FOR SPORT AND ACTIVITY, 3d ed. Copyright © 1988 Wm. C. Brown Publishers, Dubuque, Iowa. All Rights Reserved. Reprinted by permission.

Figure 10.4, 10.5, 10.9

From Stuart Ira Fox, HUMAN PHYSIOLOGY. Copyright © 1984 Wm. C. Brown Pub-

Figure 10.11

From Kent M. Van De Graaff, HUMAN ANATOMY. Copyright © 1984 Wm. C. Brown Publishers, Dubuque, Iowa. All Rights Reserved. Reprinted by permission.

Index

AAU of C. *See* Amateur Athletic Union of Canada (AAU of C)
Abduction, 170, 171, 173, 176
Absolute frame of reference, 162
Absorption, 220
Abstract challenge, 27
Academic Centre for Gifted Athletes (ACGA), 109
Acceleration, 243–44
    and angular velocity, 248
    law of, 250–51
ACGA. *See* Academic Centre for Gifted Athletes (ACGA)
Acids, amino and fatty, 222, 223
Actin, 196
Activity, and leisure, 16–17
Activity theory, 330
Act to Encourage Fitness and Amateur Sport, 103, 121, 134, 137
Adduction, 170, 171, 173, 176
Adenosine diphosphate (ADP), 198, 199
Adenosine triphosphate (ATP), 195, 197, 198, 199, 200, 201, 202, 203, 230, 256
ADP. *See* Adenosine diphosphate (ADP)
Aerobic processes, 199
Aesthetics, 51, 54, 55
Agencies
    multi-sport, 122–24
    private, 128
AIAW, 343
Alderman, Richard, 320, 325
Alpha efferent motoneuron, 205
Alpine Club of Canada, 132
Amateur Athletic Union of Canada (AAU of C), 122–23

Amateur sport and recreation, delivery system, 97–130
Amateur sport clubs, 116–20
Amateur sport delivery system, 115–25
AMI. *See* Athletic Motivational Inventory (AMI)
Amino acids, 223
Amphiarthroses, 192, 194
Amputations, 164
Anabolism, 230
Anaerobic processes, 199
Analysis
    secondary, 275
    temporal, 239
Anatomical foundations, 159–263
Anatomical frame of reference, 162
Anatomical position, 162
Anatomy
    applied, 166–77
    of bones, 189–92
    human, 161–85
    of synovial joints, 193
    terminology of, 162–66
Andrews, John, 293
Angle of pull, 178, 179
Angular kinematics, 246–48
Angular velocity, and acceleration, 248
Anterior, defined, 166
Anthropometry, 239
Appendicular skeleton, 190, 191
Applied anatomy, 166–77
Arguments, 54
Aristotle, 17
Arm
    force and load, 180
    moment, 178, 179

Arousal, optimum level of, 321
Arousal-seeking theory, of play, 23
Articular system, and skeletal system, 188–95
Articulation, 192–95
Art of PERS, 4
Art of sport, 51
Assimilation, 220, 278
Associative property, 245
Assumption of risk, 339
Athenian leisure, 17
Athlete Assistance Program, 142
Athletic Motivational Inventory (AMI), 326
Athletics, 29–30
Athletic studies, 8
ATP. *See* Adenosine triphosphate (ATP)
Atrophy, 164
Augmented feedback, 323
Australian Cricket Board, 296
Automatic phase, 322
Axes, 162–63
Axial skeleton, 190, 191
Axiology, 54, 55
Axis, moment about an, 254

Baka, Richard, 66
Balance theory, of play, 20
Ball and socket joint, 193, 194
Bandura, Albert, 290
Basic instruction program, 104
Basketball, 69–70
Beamish, 276
Beauty of Sport: A Cross-Disciplinary Inquiry, The,
    52
Beers, W. George, 66–67
Behaviourism, 316
Beliveau, Jean, 83
Bell, Marilyn, 80
Bending, lateral, 172
Berlyne, D. E., 23
Best Ever Program, 146–48, 155–56
Biceps brachii, 179, 183
Biceps femoris, 179, 183
Bicycle ergometer, 261
Bill of Rights for Young Athletes, 299
Biochemical pathways, 201
Biology of Physical Activity, The, 219
Biomechanical foundations, 159–263
Biomechanics, principles of, 235–63
Blackstock, C. R. "Blackie," 110
Blake, Hector "Toe," 83
Blood, and oxygen, 213, 214
Bluenose, 75–76
Body subject, 58
Boileau, Roger, 282
Boldfacing, and vectors, 241

Bone cells, types of, 189, 190
Bones
    anatomy of, 189–92
    and growth, 190–92
    and homeostatic mechanisms, 189
Botterill, C., 303
Boxing, 72
Boy in Blue, 68–69
Boys' Clubs of Canada, 128
Boy Scouts, 128
B.P.E. degree, 38
Bradycardia, 218
Brain, 203
Breathing, 209
Bright, Johnny, 81
British North America Act, 100
Brothers of the Wind, 75
Brown, B., 304
Bruner, Jerome S., 22, 23
Brusso, Noah, 72
Bundesjungend-Spiele, 296
Burns, Tommy, 72

CAC. *See* Coaching Association of Canada (CAC)
CAHA. *See* Canadian Amateur Hockey Association
    (CAHA)
CAHPER. *See* Canadian Association of Health,
    Physical Education, and Recreation
    (CAHPER)
Caillois, Roger, 24
Calcium, 225
    and bone growth, 190–92
California Personality Test (CPT), 326
Campagnolo, Iona, 143, 151
Canada Fitness Award, 141
Canada Food Rules Guide, 233
Canada Games, 140
Canadian Amateur Hockey Association (CAHA),
    122
Canadian Association of Health, Physical
    Education, and Recreation (CAHPER), 7,
    102, 110–11, 274
Canadian Colleges Athletic Association (CCAA),
    114
Canadian Council for Children and Youth, 281,
    299
Canadian Intercollegiate Athletic Union (CIAU),
    112, 113, 114
Canadian Interuniversity Athletic Union, 344
Canadian Medical Association, 134
Canadian mosaic, 272
Canadian National Exhibition, 69
Canadian Olympic Association (COA), 116, 123
Canadian Olympic Committee, 131

Canadians
and Commonwealth Games, 352–57
and Olympic Games, 347–52
and Pan American Games, 357–60
and sports heritage, 65–95
and World University Games, 360
Canadian Sports Advisory Council (CSAC), 123, 133, 134
Canadian Sports Pool Corporation (CSPC), 151
Canadian Standards Association, 362, 363
Canadian Track and Field Association (CTFA), 122
Canadian Women's Intercollegiate Athletic Union (CWIAU), 112
Canadiens, Montreal. *See* Montreal Canadiens
Cantelon, Hart, 276
Carbohydrates, 220
Carbon dioxide, 211, 212
Cardiac output, 218
Cardinal frame of reference, 162
Cardiovascular system, 215–19
Careers, 37–44, 335–37
Carlisle, Ursula, 304
Cartesian frame of reference, 238
Cartesianism, 57
Case study, 275
Catabolism, 230
Catharsis theory, of play, 22
Cattell 16 Personality Factor Test, 325
Caughnawaga Indians, 67
CCAA. *See* Canadian Colleges Athletic Association (CCAA)
CEGEP. *See* College d'Enseignement General et Professional (CEGEP)
Cells, bone, 189, 190
Census, 275
Centennial Fitness Awards, 103
Central nervous system (CNS), 203–7
Centre of gravity, 163–65
Centrifugal force, 254
Centripetal force, 254
Cerebellum, 207
Challenge, abstract, 27
Challenge to the Nation: Fitness and Amateur Sport in the Eighties, 152
Chandler, Timothy, 293, 294
Chard, Elizabeth, 344
Cheating, and violence, 300–303
Chicago's World Fair, 69
Chlorine, 230
Choice, free, 14
Christina, 317
Chronology of sport, 65
Chronometry, 239
CIAU. *See* Canadian Intercollegiate Athletic Union (CIAU)

Cinematography, infrared, 166
Circumduction, 176, 177
Clark, Sandy, 69
Classes, of levers, 179–84
Closed skills, 318
Club, amateur sport, 116–20
Clumpner, Roy, 294
CNS. *See* Central nervous system (CNS)
COA. *See* Canadian Olympic Association (COA)
Coaching, profession in Canada, 42–44
Coaching Association of Canada (CAC), 124, 139–40, 152, 275, 281
Coercion, 276
Cognitive psychology, 316
Coherence theory, 54
Collection methods, data, 275–76
College d'Enseignement General et Professional (CEGEP), 114
Commercially operated recreation centres, 128
Commonwealth Games, and Canadians, 352–57
Community colleges, 114–15
Commutative property, 245
Compensation theory, of play, 20
Competence motivation theory, of play, 23
Competition, 295–97
elite sports, 29
Competitor, 75
Compound disciplines, 5
Conacher, Lionel, 76–77
Condyloid joint, 194, 195
Conflict-coercion model, 276
Conflict model, 276
Connective tissue, 195
Contemporary trends, in PERS, 333–45
Continuity, of human movements, 256–58
Continuum theory, of physical activity, 31–33
Contractile unit, functional, 196–98
Contraction, sliding filament theory of, 197
Contributory negligence, 339
Controlled negative act, 323
Corbin, C. B., 324
Core society, 278, 279
Corporate sport, 28
Corpuscles, pacinian, 206
Cortex, motor, 203
Corticospinal tracts, 205
Cosmology, 54
Council of Women, 125
CP. *See* Creatine phosphate (CP)
CPT. *See* California Personality Test (CPT)
Cratty, Bryant, 328
Creatine phosphate (CP), 199
Credits, 365–66
Critical philosophy, 54
Cross Canada Sports Demonstration Tour, 140

Cross-sectional study, 276
CSAC. *See* Canadian Sports Advisory Council (CSAC)
CSPC. *See* Canadian Sports Pool Corporation (CSPC)
CTFA. *See* Canadian Track and Field Association (CTFA)
Cultural pluralism, 289
Culture, society, and sociology, 272
Curriculum, trends, 337
Cuthbert, J., 294
Cutler, Dave, 81
CWIAU. *See* Canadian Women's Intercollegiate Athletic Union (CWIAU)
Cycling, 78
Cyr, Louis, 67–68

Daily quality physical education, 102–3
Data, collection methods, 275–76
Decision making, 49, 317
Declaration of Sport, 301
Deep, defined, 166
Deformable solids, mechanics of, 235–36
de Grazia, Sebastian, 18
Delivery system
    amateur sport, 97–103, 115–25
    integrated sport and recreation, 8
    recreation, 97–103, 125–29
Demonstration Tours, 140
Department of National Health and Welfare, 134, 233
Depression, 173
Descartes, Rene, 238
Development
    and growth, 313–14
    and motor learning, 314–19
    personality, 324–26
Developmentalism theory, of play, 22
Devereaux, E. C., 292
Deviants, values, and norms, 273
Dewey, John, 58
Diaphragm, 212
Diarthroses, 192, 193, 194
Diastolic pressure, 217
Diefenbaker, John, 134
Diet, balanced, 223, 224, 232
Digestion, 220
Direct dynamics, 251
Directional nomenclature, 165–66
Discipline
    defined, 5–7
    and profession, 3–12
Discretionary time, 15
Disengagement, theory of, 329
Displacement, and distance, 240–41

Distal, defined, 166
Distance, and displacement, 240–41
Distance running, 73–74
Distributive practice, 322
Dorsal, defined, 166
Dorsiflexion, 167, 169
Drilling, 322
Drive, 321
Dryden, Ken, 83
Dualism, and monism, 56–58
Dumazedier, Joffre, 17
Duthie, James H., 299
Dynamics, 236
    inverse, indirect, and direct, 251
Dynamometer, 262

Earl Haig Secondary School, 109
Eccentric force, 251
Eccentric thrust, 251
ECG. *See* Electrocardiogram (ECG)
Edgerton, 219
Edington, 219
Edmonton Eskimos, 80–81
Edmonton Grads, 77
Education, physical. *See* Physical education
Education sport delivery system, 100–115
Edwards, Harry, 28
Edwards Personal Reference Schedule (EPPS), 326
Einstein, Albert, 237
Eisenhardt, Ian, 133
Eitzen, D. E., 28, 30, 301
Electrocardiogram (ECG), 218, 219
Electrolytes, 230
Elementary schools, 102–3
Elevation, 173
Elimination, 220
Elite sport, 29–30
Ellis, M. J., 21, 23
Employee recreation programs, 128
Enculturation, 276
Endochondral ossification, 189
Endomysium, 196
Energy
    excess or surplus, 22
    processes, 198–203
    sources of, 200–203
Environment, uses of, 344–45
Epimysium, 196
Epistemology, 54
EPPS. *See* Edwards Personal Reference Schedule (EPPS)
Ergometer, 261
Eskimos, Edmonton. *See* Edmonton Eskimos
Essentialistic goals, 49
Ethics, 54, 55

Euclidian geometry, 237
Eversion, 172
Every Kid Can Win, 303
Excess energy, 22
Exclusion, and sport, 27
Exercise in Education and Medicine, 74
Existence, 15
    and leisure, 17–18
Expiration, 212
Extension, 167, 168, 173
External, defined, 166
External respiration, 209
External rotation, 174
Extrapolation, 275
Extrinsic procedure, 323

Fats, 222
Fatty acids, 222
Federal Green Paper, 137
Federal–Provincial agreements, 135–36, 152–53
Federal–Provincial Ministers Conference, 153
Feedback, 317, 323
Field observation, 275
First-class levers, 180–81
First law of motion, 239, 249–50
Fitness
    individual and national, 340–41
    total, 61
Fitness and Amateur Sport Act, 103, 121, 134, 137
Fitness and Amateur Sport Directorate, 134,
    136–37
Fitness Institute, Toronto, 146
Flat bones, 189
Flexion, 167, 168, 173
Fluids, mechanics of, 235
Food. *See* Nutrition
Force
    centripetal and centrifugal, 254
    frictional, 255
    line of, 178, 179
    moment of, 251–53
    and Newton, 240
    normal, 255
    resultant, 249–50
Force arm, 180
Foundations
    anatomical, physiological, biomechanical,
        159–263
    historical and philosophical, 45–158
    sociocultural and psychological, 265–331
Foundations of Physical Education, 6
Four Masks, 75
Frames of reference, 162–63, 238
Free choice, 14
Freud, Sigmund, 316

Friction, static and kinetic, 255
Frictional forces, 255
Fromson, Joyce, 344
Frontal plane movements, 170–72
Fuels, body, 220–24
Fulton, Robert, 71
Functional contractile unit, 196–98
Funding, 148–49

Game Plan, 141–43
Games, 31
    and sociocultural activity, 271–72
Gas exchange, 211, 212
Gastrocnemius, 180, 181, 182
General transfer, 317
Gentile, 317
Geoffrion, Bernie, 83
Gerber, E. W., 55
Germany, Jim, 81
Gibson, B., 296
Girl Guides, 128
Girls' Clubs of Canada, 128
Gliding joint, 194, 195
Glucose, 220
Glycogen, 220
Glycolysis, 201
Goals
    essentialistic and progressivistic, 49
    and methods, 273–76
    personal, 49
Godbey, Geoffrey, 19
Golgi tendon organ (GTO), 206
Goos, Karl, 22
Governing bodies, sport, 120–22
Government, in sport and recreation, 131–58
Grads, Edmonton. *See* Edmonton Grads
Graduate studies, 39–40
Graham, Barbara, 344
Grants-in-aid program, 141
Gravitation, universal law of, 248–49
Gravity, centre of. *See* Centre of gravity
Greek philosophy, 17, 19, 56
Greene, Nancy, 81
Grey, Earl, 75
Grey Cup, 80, 81
Griffiths, Coleman, 319
Growth, and development, 313–14
Gruneau, Richard, 276
GTO. *See* Golgi tendon organ (GTO)

Halifax Yacht Club, 118
Hall, G. S., 22
Hanlan, Edward "Ned," 68–69
Hart, Marvin, 72
Harvey, Doug, 83

Index

Health and Welfare Canada, 134, 233
Heart, 216, 217, 218
Heart rate, 218
Heinila, K., 301
Hemoglobin, 212
Hendry, L., 295
Henry, Franklin M., 5
Heritage, Canada's sport, 65–95
High-Performance Athletic Assistance Program, 155
High-Performance Sport Centre Program, 146–48
High schools, 103–11
Hinge joint, 194, 195
Historical foundations, 45–158
History of sport, 65, 84–94
Hockey, 76–77
Hockey Canada, 139
Hoffman, Elizabeth, 344
Holistic concept, of leisure, 19
Hollander, 324
Homeostatic mechanisms, and bone, 189
Homo Ludens, 24
Horizontal abduction, 173, 176
Horizontal adduction, 173, 176
Horizontal extension, 173
Horizontal flexion, 173
Howe, Gordon, 81–82
Huizinga, Johan, 24
Human anatomy, 161–85
    terminology of, 162–66
Humanistic psychology, 316
Human kinetics, 8
Hummason, Ira, 69
Hutchinson, John, 25
Hutton, Samuel, 71
Hyperextension, 167
Hyperflexion, 167

Ice Bird, 75
Idealism, 56, 57
Identical transfer, 317
Identification, program, 32
Imagery, mental, 324
Impulse-momentum relationship, 258–60
Inactivity, 329
Indian World Lacrosse Championship, 67
Indirect dynamics, 251
Individual fitness, 340–41
Inertia
    law of, 239, 249–50
    moment of, 252–53
Inferior, defined, 166
Informal sport, 28
Infrared cinematography, 166
Ingestion, 220

Ingham, Alan G., 292
Innate instincts, 316
Input, 317
Insertion, 178
Inspiration, 212
Instincts, innate, 316
Instinct theory, of play, 22
Institutionalization, 272
Integrated sport and recreation delivery system, 8
Interactionist perspective, 290
Interdisciplinary approach, and careers, 37–38
Internal, defined, 166
Internal rotation, 174
International Committee for Sport and Physical
    Education, 301
International Journal of Sport Psychology, 319
International Olympic Committee (IOC), 116
International system of units (SI), 237–38, 361–63
    prefixes, 363
Interschool program, 105–8
Intramural program, 105
Intrinsic information, 323
Introduction to Physical Education, An, 51
*Introduction to the Philosophy of Physical
    Education and Sport, An*, 55
Inuit, 277, 282
Inverse dynamics, 251
Inversion, 172
Involvement, primary, 291
IOC. *See* International Olympic Committee (IOC)
Iron, 225
Irregular bones, 189

Jahn, Friedrich, 57
James, William, 58
Jauch, Ray, 81
Jelinek, Otto, 149, 151
Jerome, Harry, 82
Jewett, Ann E., 51
Johnson, Ben, 244
Johnson, Jack, 72
Joints, classification of, 192–95
Joint torque, 252
Jones, J. G., 301
Joy of Effort, 75
Jugend trainert fur Olympia, 296

Kaplan, Max, 19, 24
Kenyon, Gerald S., 7, 9, 276, 291, 292
Kidd, Bruce, 276, 277
Kinematics, 236
    angular, 246–48
    linear, 240–46, 247–48
Kinesiology, 8, 166–77
Kinetic friction, 255

Kinetics, 8, 237, 248–63
King, A. J. C., 294
Kistler force platform, 258, 259
Knee-jerk reflex, 205
Knowledge, 54
Know Ourselves: The Report on the Commission on Canadian Studies, To, 66
Knox, Walter, 72–73
Koppett, Leonard, 295, 296
Kraus, Richard, 18, 20
Kwong, Normie, 81

Lacrosse: The National Game of Canada, 66
Lafleur, Guy, 83
LaLonde, Newsy, 83
Lamb, Arthur S., 110
Landry, Fernand, 282
Lateral, defined, 166
Lateral bending, 172
Lateral rotation, 173, 174
Law, and liability in PERS, 338–40
Law of acceleration, 250–51
Law of inertia, 239, 249–50
Law of reaction, 253–55
Lawson, Pat, 344
Lawther, John, 319
Learning, 315
    motor, 314–19
    transfer of, 317–19
Left rotation, 173
Legal liability, in PERS, 338–40
Leisure, 14–20
    and activity, 16–17
    and holistic concept, 19
    and mind and existence, 17–18
    psychology of, 328–30
    and time, 15
Leisure in Your Life, 19
Leisure society, 337–38
Leisure studies, 8
Le systeme international d'unites. *See* International system of units (SI)
Letheren, Caroline, 344
Levers, of musculoskeletal system, 177–85
    classes of, 179–84
Liability, legal, 338–40
Ligaments, 195
Linear kinematics, 240–46, 247–48
Line of force, 178, 179
Line of pull, 178, 179
Ling, Per Henrik, 57
Lived body, 58
Load arm, 180
Logic, 54–55
Longboat, Tom, 73–74

Long bones, 189
Longitudinal study, 276
Loto Canada, 150
Lotteries, 150–51, 156
Lowe, Benjamin, 52
Loy, John W., 7, 10, 276, 292, 303
Lungs, 211, 212
Luschen, G. R. F., 276
Lyon, George, 74

MacDonald, Irene, 344
McDougall Commercial High School, 77
McGill University, 69, 74, 110
McIntosh, Bob, 69
Macintosh, Don, 294
McKenzie, R. Tait, 74–75, 110
McLeod, Bob, 69
McPherson, Barry D., 276, 292
Magnetic resonance imaging (MRI), 166
Manitoba, and leisure, 16
Maritimes Intercollegiate Athletic Union, 112
Martens, Ranier, 297, 326
Marxism, 276
Mason, Bernard, 23
Mass, space, and time, 238–40
Massed practice, 322
Mathieu, Andre, 51
Maturation, 313
Measure, radian, 246–47
Mechanical advantage, and speed advantage, 184–85
Mechanics
    of deformable solids, 235–36
    of fluids, 235
    Newtonian, 237–40
    of rigid bodies, 235–37
Medial, defined, 166
Medial rotation, 173, 174
Medulla oblongata, 204
Men of Zorra, 69
Mental imagery, 324
Mental practice, 324
Merleau-Ponty, 58
Metabolism, energy, 200
Metaphysics, 53, 54
Metcalfe, A., 116
Methods
    of data collection, 275–76
    and goals, 273–76
    part and whole, 318
    of philosophical inquiry, 52–55
Miles, Rollie, 81
Mind, and leisure, 17–18
Minerals, and nutrition, 224–33
Minnesota Multiphasic Personality Test (MMPT), 326

Mitchell, Elmer, 23
Mitochondria, 202
Mixed sport and recreation delivery system, 8
MMPT. *See* Minnesota Multiphasic Personality Test
    (MMPT)
Modelling, 318
Models, 9–11, 276, 295–97
Moment about an axis, 251
Moment arm, 178, 179
Moment of force, and torque, 251–53
Moment of inertia, 252–53
Momentum, impulse-. *See* Impulse-momentum
    relationship
Monism, and dualism, 56–58
Montreal Canadiens, 82–83
Montreal Curling Club, 116
Montreal Football Club, 116
Montreal Golf Club, 116
Montreal Lacrosse Club, 67, 116
Montreal Olympic Club, 116
Montreal Snow Shoe Club, 116
Moon, Warren, 81
Moral values, 50
Morenz, Howie, 83
Morgan, W. J., 55
Motion
    first law of, 239, 249–50
    second law of, 243, 250–51
    third law of, 253–55
Motivation, 320–21
    and play, 23
Motor control pathways, 204
Motor cortex, 203
Motor learning, and development, 314–19
Motor neuron, 205
Motor team, 187–207
    support systems to, 209–33
Motor unit, 205
Movement nomenclature, 166–77
Movements
    continuity of, 256–58
    frontal plane, 170–72
    sagittal plane, 167–70
    transverse plane, 173–76
    triaxial, 176–77
MRI. *See* Magnetic resonance imaging (MRI)
Multi-sport agencies, 122–24
Municipal recreation, 125–28
Munro, Billy, 69
Munro, John, 138
Murphy, James F., 19
Muscle spindles, 206, 207
Muscular system, 195–203
Musculoskeletal system, levers of, 177–85
Myofibrils, 177, 196

Myofilaments, 196
Myoglobin, 213
Myosin, 196

NAIA. *See* National Association of Intercollegiate
    Athletics (NAIA)
Naismith, James, 69–70, 77
National Advisory Council on Fitness and Amateur
    Sport, 134
National Association for Sport and Physical
    Education, 299
National Association of Intercollegiate Athletics
    (NAIA), 112
National Coaching Association of Canada, 44
National Coaching Certification Program, 44,
    139–40, 154
National Collegiate Athletic Association (NCAA),
    343
National Conference on Fitness and Health, 102
National fitness, 340–41
National Fitness and Sport Directorate, 344
National Hockey League, 81, 82, 83
National Lacrosse Association, 67, 120
National Physical Fitness Act, 131, 133
National Sport and Recreation Centre, 121, 124,
    139
National Sport Organization (NSO), 122
National Sport Technical Services Organization,
    152
NCAA. *See* National Collegiate Athletic Association
    (NCAA)
NDP. *See* New Democratic Party (NDP)
Need, 321
Negative reinforcement, 323
Negligence, 339
Nervous system, 203–7
Neumeyer, Esther, 25
Neumeyer, Martin H., 25
Neurons, 205
New Democratic Party (NDP), 289
*New Perspectives for Elementary School Physical
    Education Programs in Canada*, 102
Newton, Isaac, 239, 249
Newton (N), unit of force, 240
Newtonian frame of reference, 162
Newtonian mechanics, concepts of, 237–40
New York Times, 295
Nineteenth century, and canadian sport, 66–72
Nixon, John E., 51
Nomenclature
    directional, 165–66
    movement, 166–77
Normal force, 255
Norms, values, and deviants, 273
North York Board of Education, 108

NSO. *See* National Sport Organization (NSO)
Nutrition, and human performance, 219–33

Objectives, personal, 48–49
Observation, 275
Ogilvie, Bruce C., 326
Olympic Games, 29, 51, 70, 73, 79, 131
    and Canadians, 347–52
Olympic Shield, 75
Onondaga Indians, 73
Onslaught, 75
Ontario Headmaster's Association, 299–300
Ontario-Quebec Intercollegiate Athletic
    Association, 112
Ontology, 54
Open skills, 318
Organized sport, 28
Origin, 178, 238
Orlick, T. D., 303
Ossification, 189
Osteoblasts, 189
Osteoclasts, 189
Osteocytes, 189
Osterhoudt, R. G., 55
Ottawa–St. Lawrence Intercollegiate Athletic
    Association, 112
Output, 317
Oxygen, 199, 200, 211, 212, 213, 214
Oxymyoglobin, 213, 214

Pacinian corpuscle, 206
Page, Percy, 77
Pan American Games, and Canadians, 357–60
Parallelogram law, 241, 244–46
Parker, Jackie, 80, 81
Participant observer, 275
Participation. *See* Sport Participation Canada
    (Participation)
Part method, 318
*Partners in Pursuit of Excellence: A National
    Policy on Amateur Sport*, 152
Passar, W., 295
Pathways
    biochemical, 201
    motor control, 204
Peden, Bill "Torchy," 78
Perception, 317
Performance, 315, 325
    and nutrition, 219–33
Perimysium, 196
Period time, and physical education, 25
Peripheral nervous system (PNS), 203–7
PERS. *See* Physical education, recreation, and
    sport (PERS)
Personality, development, 324–26

Personal objectives, 48–49
Philosophical concepts, 47–76
Philosophical foundations, 45–158
Philosophy, social-political, 55
Phosphorus, 230
Phosphorylation, 199
Physical activity
    continuum theory of, 31–33
    and socialization, 287–310
    and sociocultural activity, 271–72
Physical education, 25–26, 59–62
    daily quality, 102–3
    trends, 335–37
Physical Education: Foundations, 9
Physical education, recreation, and sport (PERS)
    art and science of, 4
    contemporary trends, 333–45
    discipline and profession, 3–12
    and human anatomy, 161
    introduction, 1–44
    and legal liability, 338–40
    philosophical concepts, 47–63
    and postsecondary education, 341–42
    psychological concepts, 311–31
    terminology, 13–36
Physical recreation, 8
Physiological foundations, 159–263
Physiology, and motor team, 187–207
Piaget, Jean, 23
Pietri, 73
Pivot joint, 194, 195
Planes of reference, 162–63
Planning, and policy, 151–52, 156
Plantar, defined, 166
Plantar flexion, 167, 169
Plante, Jacques, 83
Platonism, 57
Play, 20–24
    and sociocultural activity, 271–72
    theories of, 20, 21–24
    and work, 20
Playground Association of America, 125
Pluralism, cultural, 289
PNS. *See* Peripheral nervous system (PNS)
Podilchak, Walter, 292
Policy, and planning, 151–52, 156
Politics, 54, 55
Polygon rule, 245, 246
Pooley, John C., 291, 293, 295, 301, 302
Positive reinforcement, 323
Posterior, defined, 166
Potassium, 230
Power, and work, 260–63
Practice, 321–24
    distributive and massed, 322
    mental, 324

Pragmatic theory, 54
Pragmatism, 61
Prefixes, international system of units, 363
Pressure gradients, 212
Price, George, 71
Primary involvement, 291
Prince of Wales, 67
Prince Philip, 134
Private agencies, 128
Profession
    coaching in Canada, 42–44
    defined, 5–7
    and discipline, 3–12
Program identification, 32
Progressivism, 61
Progressivist goals, 49
Promfort, Marilyn, 344
Pronation, 173, 175, 176
Proposed Sports Policy for Canadians, 138
Proprioception, 206–7
Pro-Rec. *See* Provincial Recreation Program
    (Pro-Rec)
Proteins, 223
Protraction, 170
Provincial, Federal-, agreements. *See* Federal-
    Provincial agreements
Provincial governments, sport and recreation,
    153–56
Provincial Recreation Program (Pro-Rec), 132
Provincial sports federations, 124
Proximal, defined, 166
Psychoanalytic approach, 316
Psychological foundations, 265–331
Psychology
    cognitive, 316
    defined, 311
    humanistic, 316
    of leisure and recreation, 328–30
    overview, 311–31
    social, 326
    and social concepts, 326–28
    sport, 319–24
    stimulus-response, 316
Psychology and Athletics, 319
Psychology of Coaching, 319
Public school system, 100
Pull, angle of and line of, 178, 179
Pyramidal tracts, 204

Quadriceps femoris, 184
Quantity, scalar, 240
Queen's University, 102, 344

R. *See* Resultant (R)
Radian measure, 246–47

Raine, Al, 81
Reaction, law of, 253–55
Reaction board method, 165
Readiness, 313
Ready, Elizabeth, 344
Reality, 54
Recapitulation theory, of play, 22
Recreation, 8, 24–25
    employee programs, 128
    government in, 131–58
    and leisure society, 337–38
    municipal, 125–28
    psychology of, 328–30
Recreational sport, 28
Recreation associations, 129
Recreation centres, commercially operated, 128
Recreation delivery system, 125–29
Recreation imperative, 338
Recreation theory, of play, 20
Redmond, Gerald, 66, 116, 282, 290
Reference, frames of. *See* Frames of reference
Reflexes, 205
Regan, Gerald, 152
Reinforcement, 323
Relative frame of reference, 162
Relaxation theory, of play, 20
Report of the Task Force on Sport for Canadians,
    121
"Research Methodology in Sport Sociology," 274
Respiratory system, 209–15
Resultant (R), 244
Resultant force, 249–50
Retraction, 170
Richard, Maurice, 83
Richardson, 324
Right-hand rule, 238
Right rotation, 173
Rigid bodies, mechanics of, 235–37
Risk, 339
Rivens, Richard S., 6
Robb, 317
Roberts, John, 294
Roles, secondary, 291
Roman culture, 19
Rosenfeld, Fanny "Bobby," 78–79
Ross, Elijah, 71
Rotation, 173, 174
Rowing, 71–72, 257
Royal Canadian Air Force, 133
Royal Canadian Mounted Police, 116
Rubenstein, Louis, 71
Russell, Bertrand, 19
Ryerson, Egerton, 100

Saddle joint, 194, 195
Sage, George H., 28, 30
Sagittal plane movements, 167–70
Saint John Four, 71–72
Sample, 275
Sarcomere, 197
Sask Sport, 124
Savage, Marilyn, 344
Scalar quantity, 240
Scanlan, T. K., 295
Schmitz, 31
Schrodt, Barbara, 66, 344
Science of PERS, 4
Scott, Barbara Ann, 83–84
Secondary analysis, 275
Secondary roles, 291
Second-class levers, 180, 181–82
Second law of motion, 243, 250–51
Secretion, 220
Self-expression theory, of play, 23
Sensory neuron, 205
Shaping, 318
Shaver, 317
Sheehan, T. J., 7
Shields, Kathy, 344
Short bones, 189
Shrubb, Alfie, 73
SI. See International system of units (SI)
SIG. See Special interest group (SIG)
Significant others, 290
Simon Fraser University, 8
Singer, Robert N., 6, 7, 9, 28, 314
SIRC. See Sport Information Resource Centre
    (SIRC)
Six Nations Reserve, 73, 74
Skeletal muscle, organization of, 196
Skeletal system, and articular system, 188–95
Skeleton, axial and appendicular, 190, 191
Skills, closed and open, 318
Skinner, B. F., 316
Sliding filament theory of contraction, 197
Smith, Gary J., 294
Socialization
    and physical activity and sport, 287–310
    process, 288–90
Social-political philosophy, 55
Social-psychological concepts, 326–28
Social psychology, 326
Social Psychology and Physical Activity, 326
Social theories, 276–77, 280–82
Society
    core, 278, 279
    culture, and sociology, 272
    and leisure, 337–38
    and sport, 299–300

Sociocultural context, and values in sport, 267–85
Sociocultural foundations, 265–331
Sociocultural studies, genesis and development,
    269, 271
Sociology, culture, and society, 272
Sociology of American Sport, 28
Sociology of sport, 270
Sodium, 230
Soleus, 179
Solids, deformable, 235–36
Solubility, and vitamins, 224–25, 226–27
Space, mass, and time, 238–40
Spatial imaging systems, 166
Special interest group (SIG), 110
Special schools, 108–10
Specific transfer, 317
Speculative philosophy, 54
Speed, and velocity, 242–43
Speed advantage, and mechanical advantage,
    184–85
Speisz, Adolf, 57
Spinal cord, 203
Spindles, muscle. See Muscle spindles
Spiritual satisfaction, 57
Sport, 26–29
    amateur, 97–130
    art of, 51
    Canada's heritage, 65–95
    and Canadians at Olympic Games, 347–52
    elite, 29–30
    governing bodies, 120–22
    government in, 131–58
    historical highlights, 84–94
    multi-, agencies, 122–24
    and personality development, 324–26
    and socialization, 287–310
    and society, 299–300
    and sociocultural context, 267–85
    sociology of, 270
    women in, 343–44
Sport Action, 140
Sport and recreation delivery system, defining,
    97–100
"Sport and the Body: A Philosophical
    Symposium," 55
Sport B.C., 124
Sport Canada, 121, 152
Sport Canada: Recreation Canada, 139–43
Sport Canadiana, 66
Sport clubs, amateur, 116–20
Sport delivery system, amateur, 115–25
Sport Information Resource Centre (SIRC), 140,
    152
Sport Medicine Council, 152
Sport Nova Scotia, 124

Sport Participation Canada (Participation), 103, 140

Sport psychology, 319–24

Sport science, 7

Sports Federation of Canada, 123

Sports federations, provincial, 124

Sport studies, 7, 8, 9–11

Sprinter, 75

S-R psychology. *See* Stimulus-response (S-R) psychology

Stanley Cup, 82, 83

Static friction, 255

Statics, 236

Stereoroentgenography, 166

Stereo X ray, 166

Stevenson, Joan, 344

Stimulus-response (S-R) psychology, 316

Strathcona, Lord, 102

Strathcona Trust Fund, 102, 131

Streit, Marlene Stewart, 84

Strength, defined, 178

Stroke volume, 218

Structural-functional model, 276

Studies, undergraduate and graduate, 39–40

Study of sport, 9–11

Subsistence, 15

Summer Olympic Games, 347–51

Superficial, defined, 166

Superior, defined, 166

Supination, 173, 175, 176

Surplus energy, 22

Sutherland, Ed, 69

Sutton-Smith, Brian, 294

Syllabus of Physical Exercises for Public Elementary Schools, 102

Symons, T. H. B., 66

Synarthroses, 192, 194

Synovial joints, anatomy and types, 193–95

Systolic pressure, 217

Tachycardia, 218

Tangent, 250

Task Force on Sport for Canadians, 135, 137–38

Tasmanian State Schools Sports Council, 297

Taylor, Fred "Cyclone," 75

Technical Planning and Evaluation Section, 152

Temporal analysis, 239

Tendons, 177, 195

Terminology
    anatomical, 162–66
    directional, 165–66
    PERS, 13–36
    sociocultural studies, 271–73

Theology, 54

Theory, social, 276–77, 280–82

Theory of disengagement, 329

Theory of the Leisure Class, The, 18

Third-class levers, 180, 182–84

Third law of motion, 253–55

Thorpe, E., 295

Thrust, eccentric, 251

Time
    discretionary, unobligated, leisure, 15
    space, mass, 238–40

Tissue, connective, 195

Toronto Tennis Club, 118

Torque
    joint, 252
    and moment of force, 251–53

Total fitness, 61

Toward a National Policy on Amateur Sport, 137, 151

Toward a Philosophy of Sport, 53

Transfer of learning, 317–19

Transverse plane movements, 173–76

Trempe, Yves, 282

Trends, contemporary, 333–45

Triangle rule, 245

Triaxial movements, 176–77

Trilogy of man, 56

Trudeau, Pierre, 143

Truth, 54

Tug-of-war, 69

Tutko, Thomas A., 326

Undergraduate studies, 39–40

Universal law of gravitation, 248–49

Universities, 112–14, 115

University of Alberta, 8

University of British Columbia, 342, 344

University of Kansas, 70

University of Manitoba, 344

University of Ottawa, 8

University of Saskatchewan, 344

University of Waterloo, 8

University of Winnipeg, 8, 342

Unobligated time, 15

Valgus, 172

Validity, 54

Values, 54
    moral, 50
    norms, and deviants, 273
    and sociocultural context, 267–85

Van de Merive, Mariana, 344

Vanderzwaag, Harold J., 7, 10, 20, 30, 31, 52

Varus, 172

Vascular system, 216

Vaz, E. W., 301

Veblen, Thorstein, 18

Vectors, 241, 244–46
Velocity
    angular, 248
    and speed, 242–43
Vertinsky, P., 294
Vezina, Georges, 83
Victoria, Queen, 67
Victoria Cricket Club, 118
Victoria Rowing Club, 118
Vigor, and sport, 28
Violence, and cheating, 300–303
Vitamins, and nutrition, 224–33

Walters, R., 290
Water, and nutrition, 224–33
Water compartments, 231
Watson, G. G., 295
Watson, John B., 316
Weight, 248
Weightlifting, 67–68
Weiskopf, Donald C., 22
Weiss, Paul, 57
Whited, Clark, 7
Whiting, 317
Whitson, David J., 274

Whole method, 318
Wilkinson, Tom, 81
Williams, Percy, 79–80
Winter, Gillian, 297
Winter Olympic Games, 351–52
Women, in Canadian sport, 343–44
Wood, Thomas D., 62
Work, 33
    and play, 20
    and power, 260–63
World University Games, and Canadians, 360

X ray, stereo, 166

YMCA. *See* Young Men's Christian Association
    (YMCA)
Young Men's Christian Association (YMCA), 69,
    118, 128, 276, 340–41
Young Women's Christian Association (YWCA),
    128, 276, 340–41
Youth Training Act, 131
YWCA. *See* Young Women's Christian Association
    (YWCA)

Zeigler, Earle F., 7, 50, 55
Zorra Township, 69